THE BIRTH OF
AN OPERA

THE BIRTH OF AN OPERA

FIFTEEN MASTERPIECES

from

POPPEA TO WOZZECK

Michael Rose

W · W · Norton & Company New York London

For information about permission to reproduce selections from this book,
write to Permissions, W. W. Norton & Company, Inc.,
500 Fifth Avenue, New York, NY 10110

For information about special discounts for bulk purchases, please contact
W. W. Norton Special Sales at specialsales@wwnorton.com or 800-233-4830

Manufacturing by RR Donnelley, Harrisonburg
Book design by Margaret M. Wagner
Production manager: Julia Druskin

Library of Congress Cataloging-in-Publication Data

Rose, Michael.
The birth of an opera : fifteen masterpieces from Poppea
to Wozzeck / Michael Rose. — 1st ed.
p. cm.
Includes bibliographical references and index.
ISBN 978-0-393-06043-0 (hardcover)
1. Operas—Analysis, appreciation. I. Title.
MT95.R67 2013
782.109—dc23

2012039470

W. W. Norton & Company, Inc.
500 Fifth Avenue, New York, N.Y. 10110
www.wwnorton.com

W. W. Norton & Company Ltd.
Castle House, 75/76 Wells Street, London W1T 3QT

1 2 3 4 5 6 7 8 9 0

In memory of

HANNS HAMMELMANN
fons et origo,

in gratitude
to the many friends, colleagues and
members of my long-suffering family
who have in one way or another
contributed to this book
over more than fifty years,

and with love and thanks

to Beth

Contents

List of Illustrations

Preface

So, ANOTHER BOOK ABOUT OPERA? With operatic
activities of all kinds cropping up in new and unexpected places, and
screens big and small making international performances available to
a wider and wider public, surely the shops and Web sites are already
flooded with books on every aspect of this apparently inexhaustible
subject. What is different about this one that might invite your jaded
attention?

First, what it is not. It is not another history of opera, and although
the works it deals with are arranged in chronological order, there is no
attempt to link them in a consecutive historical narrative. It does not
offer overall views of composers or librettists, or appraisals of singers and
other performing celebrities, or critical studies of operatic productions. It
makes no claim to musicological originality, indulges in no complicated
musical analysis, contains no musical examples and uses the barest possible minimum of technical terms. And there is no detailed description
of the contents of each opera (though brief plot summaries are available
in an appendix for those whose memories need jogging).

In fact, it is only incidentally about the operas themselves. It is about
how they were written, and to some extent I suppose why, and in the end
its content is human. By bringing together as comprehensive a collection
as possible of contemporary documents—letters, memoirs and personal
accounts left by composers, librettists, performers, managers and anyone else involved—and linking them with an informed commentary, it
aims to re-create as nearly as possible the circumstances in which fifteen
individual masterpieces have been put together. It is, if you like, a lateral
approach, but one that may perhaps offer a different perspective to lovers
of opera by capturing the tangle of personalities, and the often bizarre
interactions of chance, genius, practical necessity and dogged determina-

tion that have again and again combined to create end products of such compelling power.

Perhaps I should say a word about the title of the book. It is taken from a series of radio programmes, written by the late Hanns Hammelmann and myself and broadcast on the BBC's Third Programme at irregular intervals between 1955 and 1971. The original idea (and title) were Hanns's; he was working with Ewald Osers on the translation of the correspondence between Richard Strauss and Hugo von Hofmannsthal, and had devised a script from the letters about *Der Rosenkavalier*—the text to be spoken by actors, with copious musical illustrations. Not being a musician himself, he enlisted my help and, after the programme had been successfully aired, its producer, Christopher Sykes, suggested that Hanns and I should write another one together. We did—and the resulting series of twenty-two joint broadcasts was only brought to an end by Christopher's retirement from the BBC and Hanns's death at the early age of fifty-six.

Hanns was a man of enormous charm and formidable intelligence, and the measure of intellectual rigour that he provided was crucial in curbing my rather more discursive enthusiasms. After his death I wrote another three programmes which were produced by Hallam Tennyson, and the series petered out. But the discussions and arguments that Hanns and I had fought out together during that long and stimulating collaboration defined an approach to opera that has fascinated me ever since, and the idea of reshaping and expanding the scripts in some literary form has always been at the back of my mind. I tried one or two in the Covent Garden house magazine and the Glyndebourne programme book, but there the matter rested—and might have gone on doing so had I not found a publisher patient and persevering enough to allow me the time I needed to rethink and reassess this diverse accumulation of material and to restructure it in readable form.

By that time the original title had become so much a part of my thinking that it seemed perverse not to use it again—it indicates very precisely, after all, what each chapter of the book is about. But a lot has happened in the fifty-odd years since those first scripts were written: I am fifty years older, for a start. This may or may not be a good thing, but in either case it would be surprising if my ideas had not developed during that time. Besides, the idiom of the written word follows very different rules from its spoken counterpart and, although I am aware that here and there an occasional phrase still bears the stamp of Hanns's style, the responsibility for the present text is mine, and the chapters that follow have only a limited connection with their ancestors of fifty years ago.

The original idea and the original intention of course remain, and naturally most of the original documents, but I have revisited the sources, refreshed the translations and rescued valuable details that had been excluded from the radio scripts by the harsh realities of BBC transmission timing; new material has come to light, more reliable versions of early documents have become available, and the march of musicology has thrown up a quantity of intelligent and thought-provoking commentary on all aspects of opera and its chequered history. The removal of the musical illustrations created problems of structure and necessitated a certain amount of musical description—some of it no doubt subjective, though I have tried to allow my own comments to be led as far as possible by the sources I quote. In any case, for a reading rather than a listening public, I felt the need for more historical background, particularly in the seventeenth and eighteenth centuries, whose operatic conventions may be less familiar. On the other hand, I wanted to retain something of the dramatic element that had been a feature of the original programmes, and I therefore decided to stick to the 'script' format, introducing all quoted material with the speaker's name. It is a technique that is obviously at its most effective where groups of letters already form a dialogue, but it has the broader advantage of eliminating the endless repetitions of 'he said', 'he replied', 'he next wrote', etc., which can soon become tedious, and for that reason, and for the sake of consistency, I have retained its use over the whole book.

The material available varied widely from opera to opera, and each chapter has needed different treatment. Clearly there is no problem when a more or less continuous exchange of letters exists between composer and librettist, as with Strauss and Hofmannsthal, for instance, or Verdi and Boito—or indeed Mozart and Varesco, with Mozart's father as intermediary. Berlioz and Wagner, who wrote their own librettos, had no specific interlocutor, but Wagner was never short of a word or two on the subject of his emotional and intellectual preoccupations, and Berlioz's gifts as an author and letter-writer were second to none, so the chapters on *Tristan* and *Les Troyens* also fell into place without much trouble. In most cases, however, the sources were various and mixed, and immutable blocks of ready-made material can be difficult to integrate into a coherent sequence—I was often glad of my childhood skill at jigsaw puzzles. To keep the narrative flowing I have occasionally transposed a sentence or two in a letter or document to provide a better link, but only when this involves no significant change in meaning or emphasis, and I have sometimes brought together separate passages on the same subject in a single 'speech', though with a separate reference to each individual source.

I know that there will always be different opinions about the precise historical value that can be placed on contemporary documentation. Old men 'remember with advantages', and memoirs and recollections, even from—perhaps *particularly* from—the individuals most closely involved, can always be suspect. Da Ponte is only the most notable example of a number who are guilty in this respect. Though letters may seem a safer bet, there is still the danger that the writer may have a personal agenda which twists facts or opinions to his own advantage. There are no more saints in the opera business than in any other sphere of human activity.

Yet such documents still have one overriding value: they are the only direct link that we have with events that are otherwise beyond our reach. In the end, all history that is not drawn from official record or archeological research is dependent on what has been written by observers who can no longer be questioned, and the fact that such material may be subject to human fallibility does not alter the fact that it is irreplaceable and therefore uniquely precious. But it does mean that documents of the kind I have used here have to be treated with tact and a degree of scepticism. Simple mistakes of detail, like dates or names, are mostly genuine faults of memory and are not important; they can almost always be corrected from archival sources. Palpable attempts to amend remembered facts are another matter. Librettists, who have felt themselves left out when an opera has brought fame and glory to its composer, are understandably prone to this form of revisionism, and they are obviously well equipped to carry it out. Their flights of fancy can be fun, but they are not helpful in building a balanced picture of what actually happened; I have tried to be fair in deciding how much to print and what to leave out, and when there is a borderline case that I found impossible to resist, I have provided a suitable warning.

One further word of warning might perhaps be worth adding. Opera is a performing art and has always been a prey to the ego of the individual performer; after long periods in which world-famous singers and virtuoso conductors have been the centres of attention, it is now the turn of the star producer. Most, if not all, of the operas in this book have been treated in recent years to 'modern' interpretations, sometimes stylish, sometimes stimulating, but often pretentious and inept. The best of them can reveal parallels with contemporary life which, even if not entirely consistent with the words, are thought-provoking and powerful as drama. But the tendency to produce the libretto—or rather the perceived meaning of the libretto—at the expense of the music can easily upset the delicate balance between music and text and produce results far from anything that the composer and librettist themselves had in mind, and it is what the composer and librettist had in mind that I have had in my mind while writing this book.

For reasons of space I have had to limit myself to one opera per composer—with the single exception of Mozart: the remarkable correspondence on *Idomeneo* cried out for inclusion and yet I felt it impossible to exclude Da Ponte from the book. And there will inevitably be readers who are disappointed not to find some favourite or significant opera included. But for good or ill the method I have chosen to use is entirely dependent on the contemporary material available, and it is a fact that in two periods—the early eighteenth and the early nineteenth centuries—there is little of interest in the way of letters between composers and their collaborators. This is a natural result of the existence, in both periods, of a broadly accepted operatic formula which made extended discussion unnecessary and encouraged a rapidity of turnover that in fact rendered it impossible. So, although the absence of Handel, Vivaldi, Bellini, Donizetti and early Verdi may be regrettable, the blame lies paradoxically with the very fertility and prodigality of what were surely two of the greatest eras of opera production. To those readers, on the other hand, who would have liked the book to continue further into the twentieth century, I can only say that I agree. But where contemporary documents are concerned, considerations of language (Janáček, Prokofiev, Shostakovich) and copyright (Stravinsky, Britten, Adams) have thrown up formidable barriers both linguistic and financial, and I would rather not do the twentieth century at all than do it at an inferior level.

For anyone undertaking a book as wide-ranging as this, the debt to specialists in various sectors of the field is bound to be huge, above all for the historical background in which each opera is set. I could certainly not have written the chapter on *Poppea* without reference to the magnificent scholarship of Tim Carter and Ellen Rosand, or on *Alceste* without that of Patricia Howard. And there are many writers on later operas to whose works I am equally grateful, even though I may not have used them as a source of direct quotation: Winton Dean, for example, on *Fidelio* and *Carmen*, Daniel Heartz on Mozart's operas, Philip Gossett on Rossini's, Julian Budden on Verdi's, David Cairns on Berlioz, Marcel Dietschy on Debussy. And the chapter on *Eugene Onegin* would have been impossible without the generous help of John Warrack, who not only identified the Russian sources of my quotations from Tchaikovsky and Taneyev, but also provided me with updated and authentic translations, and put me right on a host of points which a non-Russian speaker might easily have missed.

Except in the few cases where I was unable to see a reliable copy of the original language source, all the translations from Italian and French are my own. The translations from German are more varied in origin. In the case of *Ariadne auf Naxos*, to use any version other than Hanns and Ewald's would have been *lèse-majesté*, and I must also recognize Hanns's influence in the *Tristan* chapter; he always said that the Wagner prose works were untranslatable (and certainly the literal translations which Ashton Ellis so loyally churned out more than a hundred years ago are virtually unreadable), so I hope that I shall be forgiven if I have not always been strictly literal in my effort to make Wagner's ideas comprehensible to English readers. For the letters on *Idomeneo* between Mozart and his father, I have retained the old Emily Anderson translation in which I first knew them—though with the lightest of editorial touches here and there. For the rest, translations are my own unless otherwise indicated. I must confess, however, to a certain inconsistency in the treatment of proper names: as a general rule, I have used the names of operatic characters as they appear in the libretto, but in a few cases, particularly with classical subjects, it has seemed to me pedantic not to use familiar English translations—so Nero, not Nerone; Admetus, not Admète; Dido, not Didon; Aeneas, not Énée. (But Otello remains Otello, to distinguish him from Shakespeare's character).

As the dedication of this book implies, a vast number of people have made suggestions and contributions at all stages along its snail-like gestation. Over so extended a period it is hard to know where to start. I must begin, though, by recording my long-standing debt of gratitude to Gwen Hemsley and Susan James, both of whom unstintingly gave me the support that I needed as I struggled with the scripts and music for the original

Birth of an Opera programmes, and also to Elspeth Hammelmann, whose hospitality was one of the happiest aspects of my early work with Hanns, and Bezi Hammelmann, who later added to hospitality the admirable qualities of an accurate and speedy typist. Over the years help and advice of one kind or another have come from Robbie Landon, Bill Weaver, Richard Macnutt, David Cairns, Michael Kennedy, David Lloyd-Jones, Tom Hemsley, Timothy McFarland, John Amis, Robert Ponsonby, and many others. I am grateful to Dr Christian Strauss for permitting me to reprint material that was included in the original *Ariadne* script through the kind offices of the late Dr Willi Schuh; to M. Denis Herlin for providing me with valuable Debussy material which I had been unable to find in this country; and, memorably, to the late Baronessa Fassini-Camossi, whose enthusiastic operation, at the age of eighty-seven, of the musical box on which Puccini first heard the Chinese themes in *Turandot* was a particular pleasure of the work on that opera.

I could not have tackled the illustrations without the help of Richard Macnutt, who provided not only advice but pictures of Beethoven and Berlioz from his own collection, and I am also grateful to Michael Dandrea, who kindly provided a photograph of his excellent early copy of the Houdon bust of Gluck; Gunther Braam also offered much advice and help. To Angelo Hornak, I owe a special debt of gratitude for his generous help with the photography. Sources for other pictures will be found in the acknowledgements list below.

I have had many opportunities to be grateful to the staff at the British Library in London for their expertise in searching out obscure material that I was unable to disinter from the recesses of the catalogue, and also at the Barber Music Library in Birmingham (where Vicky, in particular, went out of her way to be helpful). At Norton I must offer my belated thanks to Maribeth Anderson Payne who, in far-off New York, must often have felt like giving me up in despair but somehow never did; and to Ariella Foss who, when the typescript was at last delivered, struggled valiantly with the complications of my sometimes idiosyncratic source references. Fred Wiemer's acute and well-informed editorial comments have made a valuable contribution to the final text. In London my sincere gratitude goes to Victoria Keown-Boyd for the quiet efficiency with which she relieved me of the onerous task of tracking down details of copyright, and my special thanks to Carol Russell for many friendly welcomes and invigorating cups of coffee. Nearer to home I must record my gratitude to Tiziano Riolfo, whose technical wizardry has more than once rescued this book from the (sometimes near-fatal) effects of my incompetence on the computer.

But in the end my deepest thanks go to three people who have been particularly associated with the writing of this book: my friend Jonathan Keates, who has read and given me the benefit of his advice on every single chapter as I completed it, and been unflagging in his encouragement; my publisher, editor and adviser, Alan Cameron, without whose patience, enthusiasm and practical support the book would never have been finished, let alone published; and my wife Beth, who introduced me to Alan in the first place, and without whose support it would quite simply never have been begun.

Michael Rose

THE BIRTH OF
AN OPERA

Claudio Monteverdi in his last years

L'incoronazione di Poppea

IN 1637, AT THE TEATRO SAN CASSIANO in Venice, the first opera house in the world opened its doors to the public.

Claudio Monteverdi was seventy that year—a considerable age for those days. He had been *maestro di cappella* at Saint Mark's for nearly twenty-five years, his reputation as a composer was huge and his output protean: sacred music ranging from the polyphonic style of his predecessors to the grandiose originality of the famous Vespers; seven books of madrigals (an eighth was still to be published) which stretched the form into something hardly recognizable as a madrigal at all; and two operas, written for the ducal court of Mantua, whose fame had spread through the whole of Italy. His duties at Saint Mark's had reduced his output for the theatre, but the sudden success of public opera in Venice rekindled his interest; with a burst of septuagenarian vigour that prompts comparison with the Verdi of *Otello* and *Falstaff* 250 years later, he produced three last operas—ending his career, at the age of seventy-five, with *L'incoronazione di Poppea*.

In 1637 opera was still something new in the Most Serene Republic. The brainchild of a group of well-born Florentine intellectuals, it had made its first tentative appearance a little over forty years earlier in a very different world—the world of aristocratic entertainment cultivated by the ducal courts of Renaissance Italy. Of course there had always been music in Italian courtly society. Songs, choruses and dances played a big role in the masquerades and theatrical entertainments that were staple fare at court festivities. Polyphony—that complex interweaving of individual voices mainly associated with the motets and masses of the church— spilled over into the secular field to produce the sixteenth-century madrigal, while the *intermedi*, the brief entertainments which had originally separated the acts of the pastorals and classical plays of Renaissance theatre, gradually assumed a spectacular life of their own and brought together many ingredients that later gave opera its musical substance. But the function of music at this stage was always to complement, or decorate, or at most to comment on the action of the spoken drama. What was missing was the musical continuity, the means of expressing the drama itself in musical terms, which alone makes the idea of opera possible.

It is typical of the classical preoccupations of the Renaissance that the crucial step was the by-product of an attempt to reinvent the music of the ancient Greeks—a difficult enterprise because, although descriptions existed in classical sources, no actual examples of the ancient music had yet come to light. The investigations into this recondite subject were undertaken by a study group (the so-called *camerata*) in the palace of Count Giovanni de' Bardi, an organizer of festivities for the Medici court, and were led by Vincenzo Galilei, the father of the astronomer. Galilei had no time for the artificialities of contemporary music; the elaborate textures of polyphony did little to satisfy the humanist need for individual expression, and in his *Dialogue on the Subject of Ancient and Modern Music* he poured scorn on 'the present way of composing and singing several airs in consonance at the same time'.

Galilei   For all the height of excellence of the practical music of the moderns, there is not heard or seen today the slightest sign of its . . . producing the virtuous, infinitely beneficial and comforting effects that ancient music produced. . . . For its sole aim is to delight the ear, while that of ancient music is to induce in another the same passion that one feels oneself. No person of judgment can understand the expression of sense and meaning through words set in this absurd manner, but only through one . . . very different from it.
[*Galilei: 81, 89*]

And so it was Galilei who first tried singing in what came to be called the *stile rappresentativo*, 'a difficult and some thought ridiculous undertaking,' wrote Bardi's son Pietro, 'in which he was helped and encouraged by my father'.   [*Solerti: 144*]

The essence of the *stile rappresentativo*, the theatrical or declamatory style, was that it set a single vocal line exactly to the natural rhythms and sense of the spoken word, and in so doing allowed a freedom and flexibility of expression that had never been attempted in music before. Giulio Caccini, the first musician to follow Galilei's lead, defined it as 'a certain noble *sprezzatura* [perhaps 'studied disdain'] of song, . . . a kind of music by which people might almost speak in harmony', and the airs and solo madrigals he produced in this style were widely admired. But his position came under threat in the 1580s with the arrival in Florence of Jacopo Peri, an accomplished artist ten years younger than Caccini (and endowed with attractive red-golden hair), who soon won equally golden opinions with performances in the new manner.   [*Id:* 57]

Pietro de' Bardi   . . . it was Jacopo Peri, in competition with Giulio, who revealed the true possibilities of the *stile rappresentativo* and, by remedying a certain roughness and excessive antiquity that could be felt in the music of Galilei, sweetened the style and with Giulio made it capable of moving the passions with rare effect. . . . [Of the two] Giulio had greater elegance of invention . . . Peri had more science; making use of a few chords and adopting the most meticulous precision in all respects, he discovered a way of imitating normal speech by which he achieved great fame.   [*Id:* 145–6]

With an idealised picture of Greek theatre constantly in mind, the step from using one singer to interpret the sentiments of a poem to using several to act out a simple story must have been a fairly obvious one. But by the time a suitable opportunity arrived, Bardi had left Florence for Rome, taking Caccini with him, and the patronage of Medicean music had passed to the wealthy merchant banker Jacopo Corsi, whose role in the development of opera was recorded by a younger colleague of Peri's.

Marco da Gagliano   After endless discussions about the way in which the classical authors presented their tragedies, how they introduced the chorus, whether they used song, if so what kind of song, and similar questions, [the poet] Ottavio Rinuccini set himself to write the story of *Dafne*, and Signor Jacopo Corsi of honoured memory . . . composed arias for part of it. Delighted by the result, he determined to see what effect they would make on the stage. Together with Signor Ottavio he discussed the idea with Jacopo Peri . . . [who,] on hearing of their plan, and liking the arias already written, set about composing the music for the rest.   [*Id:* 80]

Peri   Seeing that it was a question of dramatic poetry, and that it was therefore necessary to imitate in song the person speaking (and surely no one ever actually spoke in song), I decided that the ancient Greeks

and Romans . . . would have used a form of melody which, while sur-
passing that of ordinary speech, fell so far below the melody of song
itself that it assumed a form midway between the two. . . . So I rejected
every kind of song heard up to now, and devoted myself entirely to
seeking the imitative style that was needed for poems like these. . . .

I realized, too, that when we speak some words are intoned in such
a way that they can be adopted as a basis for harmony, and that we
make use of many more which are not so intoned before we come
back to another that offers the possibility of change to a new harmony.
So I took careful note of the accents and inflections that we use when
we are sad, or happy, or in similar states, and moved the bass [which
determines the harmony] in time to these, sometimes quicker, sometimes slower, in accordance with these emotions, and I held it firm,
regardless of dissonance or consonance until, after passing rapidly
through a succession of notes, the performer arrived at a word which,
in ordinary speech, would open the way to a new harmony.

And although I would not venture to claim that this was the form
of song used in the theatre of the Greeks and Romans, I nevertheless
came to believe that it is the only way in which the elements that
our music has to offer can be adapted to our speech. And so, after
expressing my opinion to the gentlemen [of the *camerata*] I demonstrated to them this new way of singing. . . .   [*Id:* 45–7]

Whether or not they really imagined it to be anything like the ancient
music about which there had been so much discussion, what Peri's audience heard on that occasion was the first attempt at the musical style
which later became known as 'recitative'—that is, the free, unmeasured
setting of vocal music by which, in one form or another, the narrative
thread was to be sustained in virtually every opera for the next three
hundred years.

Though very little of the music of *Dafne* has survived, the impression
it made was evidently encouraging.

Marco da Gagliano . . . The pleasure and astonishment which this
new spectacle produced in the minds of the listeners is impossible to
describe—enough to say that, on the many occasions that it has been
repeated, it has excited the same admiration and delight.

Realizing from this experiment how capable song could be of

expressing every sort of emotion, and observing that it not only did not (as many might perhaps have thought) lead to boredom but to incredible pleasure, Sig Rinuccini developed the idea still further and composed *L'Euridice*. . . .   [*Id: 80–1*]

Euridice was performed on 6 October 1600, as a part of the festivities celebrating the marriage of Maria de' Medici to Henri IV of France. By this time, however, Caccini was back in Florence and, his influence as a teacher being considerable, he was able to insist that any of his pupils who participated should only sing music that he had written for them himself. As a result, the first performance of *Euridice* was musically a mixed bag, and it was not until the publication of Peri's unadulterated score later in the same year that the world's first surviving opera appeared in definitive form.

In any case, the piece did not have the same success as *Dafne* and, apart from a single performance of Caccini's rival *Euridice* a couple of years later, the Florentine nobility seem to have temporarily lost interest in the new experiment. Among the guests at the royal wedding, however, was Vincenzo Gonzaga, Duke of Mantua, whose court was one of the most enterprising centres of musical activity in northern Italy; it had a vigorous theatrical tradition; and it was not long before the leaders of Mantuan intellectual circles decided to take up the Florentine idea. The subject chosen was *Orfeo*: the libretto was entrusted to the Duke's secretary, Alessandro Striggio, and the music to his *maestro di cappella*, Claudio Monteverdi.

By the end of 1606, Monteverdi had been in the service of Vincenzo Gonzaga for sixteen years and his musical director for five. He was younger than either Caccini or Peri, and he was also a much more adventurous composer—in fact, his latest book of madrigals had come under such severe critical attack from the disputatious theorist Giovanni Maria Artusi that in the preface to its successor he felt bound to make it known 'that I do not just write my music in a haphazard manner', and promise to defend his principles in a publication to be entitled *Seconda Pratica*—'The Second Practice, or the Perfection of Modern Music'.

Monteverdi   Some, who believe that there is no other practice than that taught by Zarlino [Artusi's teacher] will be amazed by this, but they may be assured that, where consonance and dissonance are concerned, there is another point of view quite different from the one that is generally accepted, which justifies the modern way of composing to the satisfaction of both reason and the senses . . . [*Paoli: 391–2*]

. . . Artusi's criticisms having been made 'according to the principles of the *prima pratica*', wrote Monteverdi indignantly thirty years later, 'that is, according to the ordinary rules, . . . and not in accordance with any true understanding of melody'.   [*Id: 321*]

And it was of course the proper function of melody that was now the chief issue. The great achievement of Florentine opera had been to create a language that made the development of sung drama a practical possibility, but deference to the supremacy of the text had limited its purely musical content. In *Euridice* the few short strophic songs offered little relief, and the much discussed *parlar cantando*, the single vocal line that carried the bulk of the text, did not always meet with approval: there had been disparaging comparisons to 'the monks' chanting of the Passion'. On the other hand the elegant lyricism of Caccini's vocal writing lacked the dramatic tension that Peri's had undoubtedly generated. What was still needed was the touch of genius that would give the new style a broader range of musical expression without losing its dramatic intensity, and expand the Florentine invention into something that really worked in the theatre. In Monteverdi's *Orfeo* the basic techniques remained the same, and certainly the first act, with its choruses of nymphs and shepherds, offered little that could not have found a place in the *intermedi* of courtly tradition—but with the entry of the messenger in the second act, the narration of Euridice's death and Orpheus's heart-broken reaction to it, Monteverdi at last revealed what could be done with the new invention, and achieved for the first time in history the fusion of drama, text and music that was always to be the heart of opera.

Nevertheless the audience for whom Monteverdi was writing was still accustomed to the theatrical world of the *intermedi* and the conventions of sixteenth-century theatre. And though, after two *Euridice*s in Florence, an *Orfeo* in Mantua may hardly seem an original choice, there was much good sense in presenting potentially sceptical listeners with a protagonist who was already in the habit of expressing himself in song. The crucial scene at the centre of the opera, in which Orpheus appeals to Charon to ferry him across the Styx, allowed Monteverdi to provide his star artist

with a display of vocal ornamentation that would delight the more con-
servative members of his audience while at the same time providing an
essential turning point in the drama. But although this masterly welding
of new and traditional elements into a coherent dramatic structure makes
Monteverdi's first opera a unique achievement, as far as the development
of opera is concerned, *Orfeo* is still the product of a courtly society and
retains many elements of the formal tradition that preceded it.

So long as Monteverdi's employment at the Mantuan court continued, it was a tradition that could not be avoided; when another opera
was required by the Gonzagas for an important dynastic celebration, the
subject—Ariadne's love for, and desertion by, Theseus—remained firmly
rooted in the same soil, its poetic treatment safely pastoral in manner.
What the music was like, we do not know because, with one exception,
the entire score of *L'Arianna* has been lost. The one exception, however,
Arianna's great lament, was enough to carry the fame of the opera all over
Italy, and from the confident manner in which this long and passionate
scene blends melody, declamation and the harmonic freedom of the *seconda prattica*, it is clear that the loss of the rest of the score is one of the
tragedies of operatic history.

The composition of *Arianna* and its spectacular production, though
highly successful, left Monteverdi in an exhausted and emotional state.
He retired to his home town of Cremona.

Monteverdi   I have to say that, unless I take some rest from working so
hard at music for the theatre, my life will certainly be a short one,
because as a result of the intensive labours to which I have recently
been subjected I have developed a pain in my head, and an itching
round my waist so violent and agonising that neither the cauteriza-
tion that I have had applied, nor the purges I have taken by mouth,
nor blood-letting or other powerful remedies, have so far been able to
put it right—or at least only in part—, and my father attributes the
pain in my head to continuous study, and the itching to the Mantuan
air which doesn't suit me, and is afraid that the air alone could before
long be the death of me. . . .   [*Id:* 33]

'It was owing to lack of time', he later wrote, 'that I came near to killing myself over *L'Arianna*', and he was only with difficulty persuaded by
the constant nagging of the Gonzagas to return to his duties.   [*Id:* 241]

During the next three years his main preoccupation was church music—most notably the volume containing the Vespers of 1610, which he dedicated and presented personally to Pope Paul V in Rome. This magnificent gesture may well have been an indication of his growing dissatisfaction with life in Mantua, and if he was actively looking for a new post, the matter was soon taken out of his hands. Early in 1611, Vincenzo Gonzaga died and was succeeded by his son Francesco; after only five months the new Duke, for no very clear reason, dismissed Monteverdi from his service, and for the first time in over twenty years the composer found himself without a job. But Monteverdi's reputation was by now universally recognised. His recent output of sacred music suggested a major church appointment; the Vespers, which had been printed in Venice, were conceived (perhaps deliberately?) in a style that would appeal to the procurators at Saint Mark's, and when the incumbent director of music there died, the Venetian authorities acted quickly to secure Monteverdi's services. By the beginning of October 1613 he was installed as *maestro di cappella* in the city where he was to spend the remaining thirty years of his life.

The new position brought Monteverdi a degree of authority and independence that he had never experienced before. His opinion was sought and generally deferred to on all matters concerning the music at Saint Mark's, and as the years passed, his influence extended to cover all musical matters in Venice.

Monteverdi   In the choir no singer is accepted . . . nor organist, nor deputy *maestro* . . . before [the members of the Signoria] take the opinion of the *maestro di cappella*, nor do they want any other report on matters concerning the singers than that of the *maestro di cappella*; nor is there any gentleman who does not esteem and honour me, and when I appear to direct a musical performance, whether in church or in chamber, I swear to Your Lordship that whole city flocks to hear it. . . .   [*Id: 149-50*]

But the one disappointing aspect of music in Venice was the lack of any opportunity for opera, and for this reason Monteverdi was reluctant to sever entirely the link with Mantua; for some eleven years from 1616 he maintained a fitful exchange of letters with Striggio concerning a succession of theatrical pieces for the Gonzaga court—of which, however, only three can properly be described as operas, and only one reached performance. The rest were contributions to *intermedi* or other courtly entertainments, and it is clear that Monteverdi was becoming impatient with the artificialities of this type of theatre. Presented with the libretto for a 'maritime fable' entitled *Le nozze di Tetide*, he wrote petulantly:

Monteverdi   I see that [many of] the characters are Winds—*amoretti*, *zeffiretti* and *sirene*—so that there will have to be a large number of sopranos, and what is more that the winds have to sing—the *Zeffiri* and the *Boreali*, that is. But how, dear Sir, am I to imitate the speech of the winds if winds don't speak? And how can I use winds to move the passions? Arianna moved people because she was a woman, Orfeo because he was a man—not a wind. Music by itself, without words, can imitate the blowing of the wind, or the bleating of sheep, or the neighing of horses or whatever you like, but it cannot imitate the speech of winds because there is no such thing. . . .

As a whole, I don't feel . . . that the story moves me in the least, and besides I find it difficult to understand. Nor do I feel that it leads me naturally to a conclusion that moves me; *L'Arianna* led me to a genuine lament, *Orfeo* to a genuine prayer, but where this leads me I have no idea. So what is it that Your Lordship would wish the music to do? . . .   [*Id*: 87]

For the one opera of this period that did get finished, the music has not survived. But difficulties with the librettist, the Mantuan court secretary Ercole Marigliani, dragged out the composition of *Andromeda* for nearly two years, and at the beginning of 1620, presented with a sudden expression of ducal impatience, Monteverdi wrote to Striggio with characteristic exasperation:

Monteverdi   . . . but to get it done so quickly now I shall only be able to make a poor job of it, and in the same way it will, I'm afraid, be badly sung and badly played because of the extremely short time available, and I am astonished that Sig. Marigliani is willing to become involved in such a dubious undertaking. There wouldn't even have been time if it had begun to be learned and rehearsed before Christmas—so now what does Your Lordship want me to do, when we still lack more than four hundred of the lines that are to be set to music? . . . These are not things that can be done in a rush like this; you know that with

L'Arianna, even after it had been finished and learned by heart, it still needed five months of intensive rehearsal. . . .   [*Id: 125*]

Monteverdi hated being hurried and, as he points out in the same letter, 'my work for the church has to some extent distanced me from the style of music required for the theatre'. But it also seems reasonable to question whether he was beginning to find the constraints of the traditional theatre inhibiting. The madrigals he was writing at this time (not to mention the Venetian operas that were still to come) suggest a growing fund of human and emotional understanding that needed a more direct dramatic outlet, and in 1624 he took a bold new step in the direction of dramatic realism.

Monteverdi   I have observed that the principal passions, or affections, of the mind are three in number, that is: anger, moderation and mildness or entreaty—as indeed the best philosophers declare, as the very nature of our voices, high, low, and medium, suggests, and as the art of music clearly acknowledges in the three terms *concitato* [agitated], *molle* [soft], and *temperato* [moderate]. But in all the compositions of past composers, though there are many examples of the *molle* and *temperato* manner, I have been unable to find any of the *concitato* style . . . and since I am aware that contrasts of mood can greatly move our minds—an end to which all good music should aspire— . . . I set myself . . . the task of rediscovering it. . . .   [*Id: 416–17*]

The practical result of this rather specious theorising was a curious little theatrical experiment, the *Combattimento di Tancredi e Clorinda*, in which a narrative text, from Tasso, is sung in deliberately rigid declamation to the accompaniment of realistic effects of battle and warfare, which give way intermittently to brief passages of dialogue between the combatants, and finally to the death of Clorinda. By this the audience of Venetian nobility at the Palazzo Mocenigo 'were moved almost to tears', but the piece as a whole, though an impressive demonstration of the *concitato genere*, is not entirely successful; its importance lies rather in what it attempts and in the effect that a new approach to realism had on Monteverdi's treatment of operatic characters and situations. And in this respect he had high hopes of his final project for the Mantuan court, *La finta pazza Licori* [*The feigned madness of Licori*], a comedy whose chief interest lay in the abrupt changes of mood of the supposedly mad heroine. The subject seemed to offer him the possibility of musical variety and, in the military scenes, good opportunities for sound effects in the *concitato genere,* and he spent several months with the librettist, Giulio Strozzi, trying to pull it into the workable dramatic shape that had now become indispensable to him.

Monteverdi   The plot doesn't seem to me bad . . . [but] certainly the role of Licori, because of its constant variety of moods, must not fall into the hands of a woman who is not able to play now a man, now a woman, with lifelike gestures and different emotions. . . .   [*Id:* 244]
   . . . She has excellent speeches in two or three places, but in two others it I think they could be better. . . . But . . . I shall not fail . . . to confer with Sig Strozzi, and, as I usually do, see that he elaborates [his text] with still more new and diverse scenes, as I shall explain to him as I think fit, and see if he can enrich it with more novel situations and added characters, so . . . that whenever [the *finta pazza*] appears she always introduces some fresh mood and change in the music, as well as in the acting. There is one place where   the mad girl is sleeping, and I would like [Aminta] to speak in a gentle voice, not with a voice that might wake her up, because the fact of his having to sing softly will give me the opportunity to introduce new music different in effect to what has gone before. . . .   [*Id:* 247–8]

Above all, what Monteverdi needed was a singing actress 'able to act the good soldier, now hesitant, now daring, and make herself absolute mistress of all the appropriate gestures, without fear or restraint' (a type of artist who would be indispensable when it came to creating the character of Poppea). Meanwhile, perhaps the subject of *La finta pazza Licori* was simply too artificial; in the end, the score was left unfinished and once again whatever music had been written was lost. In any case, it seems that the Mantuan connection was at last running out—and perhaps the patience of the Mantuan authorities as well, for Monteverdi could be infuriatingly dilatory; the Ferrarese composer Antonio Goretti, who acted briefly as his assistant at about this time, left a candid impression of working methods that do not suggest any great sense of urgency.   [*Id:* 264]

Goretti   We never go out of the house, and I alone go (with some difficulty) to Mass. Signor Claudio composes only in the morning and the

evening; after the midday meal he doesn't want to do anything at all.
I urge him on, and relieve him of such labour as I can—which means
that, after we have discussed and arranged it all together, I take the
work out of his hands, but I find it so intricate and confusing that
I give Your Lordship my word that it costs me more effort than if I
were to compose it all myself, and that if it were up to him to write it,
it would take time—a lot of time—and if I had not been constantly
at his elbow he would not have done the half of what he has done.
It is true that the labour is long and heavy, but still, he is a man who
likes to discuss things at length, in company, and for this reason I
keep to a rule for working hours, in order to reduce the opportunities
[for chat]—so that, all in all, I should like to point out that my job is
no small one. . . .   [*Fabbri, 1985: 274*]

Monteverdi had been lucky to find in Strozzi a helpful and compli-
ant librettist—'a worthy subject', Monteverdi rather patronisingly called
him, who 'has been kind enough to carry out my ideas with good will,
a consideration which has made it a great deal easier for me to set [his
text] to music'—and the relationship did produce one more theatrical
work, the opera *Proserpina rapita,* given again at the Palazzo Mocenigo.
Only one fragment of the music remains, a three-part canzonetta, *Come
dolce hoggi l'auretta,* which was eventually published in the ninth book of
madrigals after Monteverdi's death. But with that—owing partly to the
exigent demands of the authorities at Saint Mark's, partly to the political
upheavals that resulted in the sack of Mantua in 1630 and the plague that
decimated Venice for a year after it, partly perhaps to the composer's own
advancing age—Monteverdi's theatrical activity came to a standstill for
the next twelve years.

There was no apparent reason why it should start again. Venice had
so far shown little interest in the new form of musical drama; *Proserpina rapita* had been limited to a single performance, in private, and had
no successors. But the position of Venice in relation to the rest of Italy
had always been unique: as a republic with an elected ruler and a well-
regulated patrician constitution, it lacked the incentive to celebrate dynastic prestige, which claimed so much of the energy of the ducal courts of
the Renaissance. There was no court theatre, and theatrical activity took
place mainly in the carnival season, whose uninhibited celebrations and
masquerades had become famous all over Europe. So the true theatrical

tradition in Venice was essentially a popular one, depending upon visiting troupes of actors whose performances, often improvised, had their roots in the still-flourishing traditions of the *commedia dell'arte*.

Late in 1636, however, a group of performers of rather different character arrived in the city. The composer Francesco Manelli and his wife, a singer, had travelled from Rome to take part in an operatic performance in Padua earlier in the year; joined by the composer and librettist Benedetto Ferrari, the same troupe were invited to Venice to give a performance in the Teatro S. Cassiano, an old playhouse now being reopened as a musical theatre 'devoted for the most part to the entertainment of the esteemed public', and on 6 March 1637 the new building was inaugurated with *L'Andromeda*—libretto by Ferrari, music by Manelli, the title role sung by Manelli's wife. Though the boxes in the theatre were hired mainly by the patrician classes, tickets for the pit were on sale to all, and it can fairly be said that, for the first time in history, opera as an entertainment for 'the esteemed public' had arrived.   [*Mangini: 37*]

The success of *L'Andromeda* encouraged Ferrari and Manelli to try their hand again in the following year—and then, quite suddenly, opera in Venice took off. Rival theatres, keen to get in on the act, opened rapidly, the Teatro SS. Giovanni e Paolo in 1639, S. Moisè in 1640, the Novissimo in 1641; librettists and composers proliferated, and during the next four years no less than twenty operas reached the stage. Quite what Monteverdi thought of this new phenomenon, we don't know; it is not mentioned in his letters, though as the Grand Old Man of Venetian music and the effective supervisor of all musical activity in the city, he could not have failed to be involved. All the same, he hesitated to commit himself as a composer, and the owners of the Teatro S. Moisè no doubt regarded it as something of a coup when they were able to announce a revival of *L'Arianna* to inaugurate their new theatre. But in spite of substantial revision, Monteverdi's most famous opera now looked old-fashioned, and in any case he was by this time completing an entirely new work, *Il ritorno d'Ulisse in patria*, to be given later in the same season at the Teatro SS. Giovanni e Paolo—though a dedicatory letter by the librettist, Giacomo Badoaro, suggests that a calculated dose of flattery may have been needed to persuade Monteverdi to take the plunge.

Badoaro   From the Author to the most Illustrious and most Reverend Sig. Claudio Monte Verde, Grand Master of Music: It was not with the intention of competing with those talented intellects, who in recent years have presented their compositions in the theatres of Venice [that I dedicated myself to the composition of *Il ritorno d'Ulisse in patria*], but rather to stimulate the creative imagination of Your Lordship, and make it known to this city that, where warmth of human emotion is concerned, there is all the difference between a painting of the sun and the sun itself.   [*Rosand*: 408–9]

In spite of the influence of popular tradition, early Venetian opera still clung to subjects taken from classical or pastoral sources, and although the text of *Il ritorno d'Ulisse* invests its characters and relationships with human qualities far removed from the courtly formalities of *Orfeo*, and its unfailingly consistent musical setting provides dramatic intensity at an altogether different level, the libretto of Monteverdi's first opera for the Venetian public never quite gave him the opportunities for lyrical expression that he was now looking for. Whether or not the next one, *Le nozze d'Enea in Lavinia* (*The Marriage of Aeneas and Lavinia*), proved more fruitful, we do not know, because once again the music has entirely disappeared. But in the libretto for the third of his Venetian operas Monteverdi at last had a subject which provided him with a genuinely human, perhaps all-too-human, set of situations and characters.

Giovanni Busenello, the librettist of *L'incoronazione di Poppea*, was, like Badoaro, a member of the influential Accademia degli Incogniti—a society of Venetian intellectuals famous for the libertine and cynical tendency of its philosophy. Busenello understood better than Badoaro the crucial differences that separated an operatic libretto from a straight play. As Giulio Strozzi had observed with resignation, 'it is necessary for the poet to put aside his poetic warblings and episodes, which are but digressions, in order to make room for the divisions of the musical *Signori*', and in the preface to a later libretto Busenello, too, admitted his capitulation to the needs of music.

Busenello   I would have written with greater prodigality, and devoted my energies to finding a rather more elevated style, if the brevity and the conventions required by the [musical] stage had allowed me the freedom to do so. It is one thing to write an Ode, or a Sonnet, where rapture may inform the ideas, ecstasy inspire the intellect in delivering a sweet shock to the ears, and a sensual tremor of the heart accompany the invention of a conclusion that is both flattering and witty. It is quite another to compose a drama, where the characters have specific limits and use common speech, and where, if the tone becomes too exalted, it loses the right quality of appropriateness. . . .   [*Id: 413*]

It was an attitude well suited to the subject on which Busenello now embarked. He was thirty years younger than Monteverdi, and it seems likely that the choice was his—in any case, it was a strikingly original one: for the first time an opera libretto broke away from the mythological sources that had provided its subject matter since its Florentine origins, and treated instead a subject drawn, at least in its essentials, from recorded history. True, there is a brief (and very appropriate) prologue in which Fortune, Virtue and Love vie for ascendancy; true also that Cupid and Venus make one or two subtly integrated reappearances to urge their cause at critical moments in the drama; but in the main action no allegorical or mythological figure plays any part, and Busenello provides a framework in which the names, settings, and historical facts are classical, while the emotions, relationships and attitudes are entirely of Monteverdi's own time.

The main historical basis of his story came from Tacitus, whose portrayal of Poppea in Book XIII of *The Annals of Imperial Rome* is not a flattering one.

Tacitus   Poppea had every asset except goodness. From her mother, the loveliest woman of her day, she inherited distinction and beauty. Her wealth, too, was equal to her birth. She was clever and pleasant to talk to. She seemed respectable. But her life was depraved. Her public appearances were few; she would half-veil her face at them, to stimulate curiosity (or because it suited her). To her, married or bachelor bedfellows were alike. She was indifferent to her reputation—yet insensible to men's love, and herself unloving. Advantage dictated the bestowal of her favours.

. . . She was seduced by Marcus Salvius Otho, an extravagant youth who was regarded as peculiarly close to Nero, and their liaison was quickly converted into marriage. . . . Otho praised her charms and graces to the emperor. This was either a lover's indiscretion or a deliberate stimulus prompted by the idea that joint possession of Poppea would be a bond reinforcing Otho's own powers. . . . [In any case] delay was brief. Poppea obtained access to Nero, and established her ascendancy. First she used flirtatious wiles, pretending to be unable to resist her passion for Nero's looks. Then, as the emperor fell in love with her, she became haughty, and if he kept her for more than two nights she insisted that she was married and could not give up her marriage. . . . [In the end] Otho lost his intimacy with the emperor, and was soon excluded from Nero's receptions and company.   [*Tacitus*: 306–7]

Poppea may have been a bad lot, but she was flesh and blood. Sex and ambition were not exactly unknown in the corridors of power in seventeenth-century Italy, and the lurid story of the emperor's passion, and its consummation regardless of all obstacles, provided Monteverdi with material that he could certainly relate to the time in which he lived and the behaviour of its ruling classes. The libretto, which is the best that Monteverdi ever set, has often been condemned as immoral and even repugnant, but this is to apply false standards to a period very different from our own. In the late Renaissance, when memories of the licentious and murderous behaviour of Italian rulers were still relatively fresh in the public mind, Nero was hardly yet the undiluted monster which the nineteenth century made him out to be. In their need for strong and stable government, Monteverdi's contemporaries were more prepared to make allowances for eccentricity, tyranny and even brutality as the price of security. A popular work, *Gli infelici fini di molti huomini illustri* (*The Unhappy End of Many Illustrious Men*), published in Venice not long after Monteverdi's arrival in the city, depicts a character not unlike the young Henry VIII—a wilful and potentially dangerous young despot of charismatic charm and considerable intelligence, before power had completely ruined him.

Luigi Contarino   When Nero entered upon his imperial office, he aroused great hopes; he suppressed, or reduced, the intolerable burden of taxation; he gave five *scudi* to each and every citizen; he laid down an annual salary for impoverished Senators, and arranged for the soldiers of the Praetorian guard to have wheat every month without payment. When he was called upon to sign a death warrant, he said he regretted that he knew how to write; he refused the title of father of his country, and organised festivals in honour of Jupiter which lasted a full year, during which time he did not want anyone, no matter how deserving, to be condemned to death. . . . He was proficient in sculpture, painting, singing, playing the lyre and riding. He instituted a proper code of payments for lawyers, and saw to it that Senators had no financial advantages other than those received by the general public. In the end he went to Greece, where he competed with honour in the chariot races, and it was only when he returned to Rome, flushed with his success in the games, that he gradually became morose and criminal in his behaviour . . .   [*Contarino: 74*]

The political principles with which Busenello equips Nero sound all too familiar. 'The law is for the people, and I can abolish old laws and impose new ones as I choose. . . . Reason is for those who obey, not for those who command. . . . Force rules in peace . . . as the sword in war . . . and has no need to justify itself'. And when Seneca argues, 'He who is in the wrong always looks for excuses', Nero's reply is predictable: 'Right is the man who can do what he wants'. His commands to his inferiors can be startling in their violence, and the *concitato genere* is put to good use. But from the start this headstrong and impressionable young man is an easy target for Poppea, and the relationship between the two protagonists is treated with devastating realism. The very first scene between the lovers takes place as they end a night spent in one anothers' arms; words and music are steeped in physical passion, and when Nero speaks of his intention of renouncing his wife and marrying Poppea, she feeds his desire by every means at her disposal and has no difficulty in achieving her end. At their next meeting she aims in a new direction; turning up the erotic language—'How sweet, my lord, how soft did you find last night the kisses of these lips? . . . the apples of these breasts?'—she uses the predictable effect to reinforce her calumniation of the one man who still stands between her and her ambition, the emperor's tutor Seneca. And once again she is wholly successful: Nero impetuously orders Seneca's death, then turns to Poppea and bids her smile: 'today you will see what Love can do'. No opera, not even *Don Giovanni* or *Tristan*, is more consistently concerned with sex, and Nero is trapped in a web of sensuality.

Busenello, of course, had no compunction, now or later, in manipulating historical material to suit his dramatic purpose, and he claimed classical authority for his actions.

Busenello   According to sound doctrine, poets are given the licence to change not only fables but even history. . . . There is no need here to remind men of understanding how the best poets have always presented matters in their own way—in any case the [relevant] books are readily available, and erudition is no stranger in this world. . . .

It is necessary, to some extent, to please current taste, always

remembering the praise that Tacitus and Seneca gave to those who
deliberately attuned their intelligence to the tastes of their day. . . .
[*Rosand: 412*]

And in the preface to *L'incoronazione di Poppea* he took Tacitus at his word.

Busenello   Nero, in love with Otho's wife Poppea, sent Otho to Lusita-
nia on the pretext of an embassy in order that he could enjoy the pleasures of her love—this according to Cornelius Tacitus. But here the
facts are differently represented. Otho, in despair at finding himself
deprived of Poppea, gives way to frenzy and lamentation. Octavia,
Nero's wife, orders him to kill Poppea. Otho promises to do it, but
lacks the courage to take the life of his beloved Poppea; he changes
into the clothes of Drusilla, who had been in love with him, and thus
disguised enters into Poppea's garden. But Love disturbs him, and
prevents the death. Nero repudiates Octavia, disregarding the advice
of Seneca, and takes Poppea as his wife. Seneca dies, and Octavia is
driven out of Rome.   [*Curtis: xxii*]

What is more, recognising the transformation that was now taking
place from court spectacle to bourgeois entertainment, he wove into the
historical core of his drama the popular elements that Venetian audiences demanded. Two years earlier Badoaro, a more conventional librettist than Busenello, had introduced the comic figure of Irus into the
Homeric world of *Il ritorno d'Ulisse*, and his successor, the unknown
librettist of *Le nozze d'Enea in Lavinia*, had somewhat hesitantly followed his lead . . .

Anon.   . . . because I know the humour of many spectators who prefer
jokes like this to more serious matters; we can see this from the
way in which they were marvellously entertained by Irus—a type
of character that I would certainly not have introduced into a full
tragedy. . . .   [*Rosand: 411*]

But neither of them came anywhere near the imaginative elaboration to
which Busenello subjected the history of *Poppea* as it appears in the final
text of the opera.

What we do not know is how much this text owed to Monteverdi's intervention. There is no recognised operatic masterpiece about whose origins we have as little concrete evidence as we have for *L'incoronazione di Poppea*. The decline of Italian music publishing in the seventeenth century meant that none of the early Venetian operatic scores found their way into print, and in the absence of any autograph the only contemporary sources for the music of *Poppea* are two manuscript copies dating from shortly after Monteverdi's death, one in Venice and one in Naples (probably related to a revival of the opera there in 1651), neither of which can be assumed to represent Monteverdi's final intentions. Librettos generally fared better because they were needed by audiences, but even here there is no text, published or otherwise, that can be linked with the first performance. There are various manuscript librettos of uncertain date, and two printed versions, one associated with the Neapolitan revival of 1651, the other included in Busenello's complete works five years later. But comparison of these with the musical scores is not altogether easy—particularly since the most authoritative, Busenello's own publication, is a revised literary version rather than the text which Monteverdi himself would have used.

All the same, detailed comparison of the musical text with the printed librettos leaves no room for doubt that Monteverdi made cuts, additions and adjustments as and where he wanted them. Not that there was anything new in this—Badoaro had evidently had the same experience with *Il ritorno d'Ulisse*.

Badoaro   Now that I have seen the opera performed ten times. . . . I can affirm—and do so with enthusiasm—that my *Ulisse* is even more beholden to Your Lordship than the original Ulysses to the ever gracious Minerva. . . . We all admire with the greatest astonishment the richness of ideas—but not without some consternation, for I no longer know whether to recognise this work as my own. . . . [*Id:* 409]

Clearly anyone who now undertook to produce a text for Monteverdi would have known what he was taking on; Strozzi must surely have retailed his struggles with the libretto of *La finta pazza Licori* to his colleagues at the Accademia degli Incogniti, and the idiosyncratic working methods described by Goretti were no doubt well known to potential librettists. But it was the librettist of *Le nozze d'Enea in Lavinia* who really defined what it was that Monteverdi was looking for.

Anon.   Changes of emotion . . . greatly please our Signor Monteverdi,
since he has the opportunity to demonstrate the wonders of his art
in a varied range of emotional situations. . . . Music, besides needing lightness [in the text], also seeks clarity because, in combination
with its divisions and counterpoints, metaphors and other figures
of speech tend to obscure the meaning; for which reason I have
avoided far-fetched ideas and conceits and concentrated instead on
the emotions [*affetti*] as Signor Monteverdi desired, and to please
him I have also altered or omitted many of the things that I had
originally written . . .

So now you, *signori miei*, while tolerating the imperfections of my
poetry, may happily enjoy the sweetness of Monteverdi's music. . . .
for there is no spirit so unfeeling that he cannot turn and move it as
his talent dictates, adapting the musical notes to the words and the
passions in such a way that the singer must laugh, weep, grow angry
and show pity, or do whatever else the notes command, while the
listener, affected by a like impulse, is carried away by the variety and
strength of these same feelings.   [*Fabbri, 1985: 334*]

Whoever was ultimately responsible, the text for *Poppea* that Monteverdi eventually set to music is charged with emotional variety, and with
the opportunities for dramatic contrast which that provides: from the
unbridled lust of Nero to the philosophical acceptance of Seneca, the
high tragedy of Ottavia to the ruthless ambition of Poppea, the hopeless
passion of Ottone to the touching fidelity of Drusilla, the homely wisdom
of Arnalta to the drunken camaraderie of Lucano and the sharp wit of
the page, Monteverdi was confronted with a tissue of human contradic-
tions which he attacked with a gusto that is positively Shakespearian (in
fact he was barely three years younger than his great English contemporary). Right from the start, when Ottone returns to the home where
his wife and Nero are making love, and his desperate soliloquy is interrupted by two soldiers grumbling about the emperor over whose amorous
dalliance they are standing guard, there is an immediacy of expression
that has the ring of true music drama. The give and take of the dialogue
brings a sense of reality and prompts an alternation between recitative
and lyricism that is wholly natural: as Nero leaves Poppea's bed, Monteverdi strengthens the text with teasing little repetitions: *Signor, deh non
partire*—'Alas my lord, do not go', and the fourfold repetition of the kit-

tenish *Tornerai?*—'But you'll come back?'; when Nero speaks of putting away Ottavia, Poppea takes up his words in a quick series of breathless interjections: *In sin che . . . In sin che . . . non rimane . . . non rimane*—'until she . . . until she . . . has been . . . has been . . .'—'repudiated by me,' concludes Nero with a sudden burst of joy that is purely lyrical.

This new blend of recitative and near aria is a far cry from anything the Florentines had envisaged. But since *Il ritorno d'Ulisse* at least, Monteverdi's instinctive need for lyrical expansion had been finding the constraints of the earlier *stile rappresentativo* increasingly irksome—a feeling that was shared by his new Venetian audiences—and in fact it is the popular element in *Poppea* that provided him with most of the opportunities for tunefulness which so characterise this opera, and which give contrast and variety to the serious matter of the drama. The contrasts are not always kind: there is bitter irony in the abrupt transition from Seneca's death, with its agonised chromatic chorus of bystanders, to the innocent little song for the page boy (a Cherubino before his time), whose timid flirtation with the chambermaid at the same time echoes and gives some gentler gloss to the sexual encounter of his superiors; the soft and loving tones of the lullaby with which Arnalta, usually so fierce and caustic in her loyalty, sings Poppea to sleep in the garden, may provide us indirectly with a sort of lateral sympathy for Poppea herself, but the triumphant anticipation with which she later exults in her coming elevation as confidant to the new empress gains a cruel dramatic implication by following hard upon Ottavia's heartbroken farewell to Rome.

Aptly enough Ottavia, the *disprezzata regina*, is the one character whose music retains something of the earlier style of recitative; her great lament, though it has none of the formality of Arianna's and is far shorter, has a grandeur that could only belong to a tragic heroine, and it was this role that was taken by the one known star singer at the first performance of *Poppea*, the twenty-three-year-old Roman soprano Anna Renzi. Renzi had been brought to Venice in the train of another of the composer-entrepreneurs with whom the city was now filling . . .

Strozzi   . . . Signor Francesco Sacrati, who has marvellously . . . put together a magnificent chorus of the most exquisite swans of Italy, and all the way from the Tiber, in the extreme cold of a horrible season, has brought to the Adriatic a most enchanting siren, who sweetly seduces the heart, and delights the eyes and ears of the listeners. It is to the diligent efforts of Sig Sacrati that the city of Venice has to be grateful for the favour of the brilliantly accomplished Signora Anna.

[*Rosand: 414*]

Renzi, 'as talented in acting as she is excellent in music . . . and modest in all her behaviour', was widely admired in Venice, but of the many singers currently available in the city the only others who have been identified as possibly taking part are the soprano Anna di Valerio, who probably sang Poppea, and the castrato Stefano Costa, who may have sung Nero. The composition of the orchestra that accompanied them is equally unknown. Certainly the splendours of the court orchestra in Mantua were beyond the means of the company at the Teatro SS Giovanni e Paolo; in *Poppea* the *ritornelli*—that is, the 'little returns' of instrumental music that punctuate the various scenes of the opera—are written in three or four parts for unspecified strings, and though the character of the string writing often looks tempting, there is in fact no documentary justification for the trumpets and other instruments that are so often (and, it has to be said, so effectively) added in modern performances. The continuo instruments, which accompanied the solo voices, probably included the two harpsichords that were standard practice in seventeenth-century Venetian opera, as well as a varied group of lutes. But apart from this as little is known about the musical performance of *Poppea* as is known about the creation of the text.

About the staging, too, we can only speculate. In 1645 the English diarist John Evelyn visited Venice and left a famous description of the glories of Venetian opera.

John Evelyn   This night, having with my Lord Bruce taken our places before, we went to the Opera, which are Comedies and other plays represented in Recitative Music by the most excellent Musitians vocal and Instrumental, together with a variety of Seeanes painted and contrived with no lesse art of Perspective, and Machines, for flying in the aire, and other wonderfull motions. So taken together it is doubtlesse one of the most magnificent and expensfull diversions the Wit of Men can invent. . . . The Seanes changed 13 times. . . . This held us by the eyes and Eares til two in the Morning. . . .   [*Evelyn, II: 449–50*]

Evelyn's description gives an early indication of the way in which Venetian opera was to develop, to its eventual detriment, during the years after Monteverdi's death, and certainly spectacle had always been an important aspect of Venetian theatre. In the case of *Poppea* the only publication actually issued at the time of the first performance, a scenario which includes brief indications of the staging for each scene, describes the appearance in the prologue of Fortune, Virtue and Love '*nell'aria*'—which presumably implies some form of mechanical flying apparatus: and the intermittent appearances of Venus, Love and the Cupids were no doubt facilitated by similar theatrical devices. But, this apart, the scenario does not tell us much beyond what is already obvious from the text—that, until the last scene, *Poppea* offers little opportunity for spectacular stage effects.

And this is after all the most arresting single fact about *Poppea*: it is an opera about people, about extravagant, sometimes unattractive people, but about people none the less. It is the first opera in which the subject matter comes alive in the modern sense; the characters act consistently to arrive at a clearly defined conclusion, and the poet and composer use this material to create a musical drama in which human ambition, human instincts and human frailty are allowed to run their natural course to an end that accepts, for good or ill, the overwhelming power of love. Love? Sex? Satisfied ambition? The question is immaterial. *L'incoronazione di Poppea* is not a work in which moral judgments are made: whichever it is, Busenello and Monteverdi provided the resolution of the drama in a final duet that is touching and unforgettable in its simplicity.

That, at least, was the view of the final scene, and particularly of the final duet, which was very naturally accepted for the first three hundred years of the opera's existence. But it is not a view that has been adopted by twentieth-century scholarship.

In the absence of published scores, it was only in manuscript copies that the music for the early Venetian operas was preserved—if indeed it was preserved at all. Between the years 1637 and 1650 some fifty operas are known to have been performed in Venice, by as many as a dozen composers, but only twelve have survived: two by Monteverdi, nine by Cavalli and one by Sacrati. In the case of *Poppea* neither of the extant manuscripts even mentions the name of the composer. But the binding of the Venetian copy originally had his name, or part of it, stamped on the spine (subsequently overlaid by the alternative title *Il Nerone*), and in any case the attribution to Monteverdi was established on stylistic grounds— and indeed by reason of the sheer quality of the music.

But manuscripts like these were treated with less reverence than they would be today; they were passed from hand to hand for successive performances, roles were adapted to the voices of different singers, and music was cut or substituted to suit new audiences. The Venetian copy of *Poppea* is in the hand of the wife of Monteverdi's protégé Francesco Cavalli, and bears evidence of some editorial intervention by Cavalli himself; the opening sinfonia of the opera is in fact more or less the same as the opening sinfonia of Cavalli's *Doriclea* of 1645, and internal evidence strongly suggests that the role of Ottone was at some stage transposed and in part rewritten (presumably to accommodate a different singer). Elsewhere there are indications of other revisions of detail. But when these interventions took place, and whether any of them had Monteverdi's sanction, is difficult to establish with certainty; he was an old man in 1642, ill and tired but greatly respected and admired, and there may well have been willing hands in Venice to help him put the finishing touches to his last masterpiece. What is certain is that, at least until the last scene, the bulk of the drama is quintessential Monteverdi.

For the last scene the original scenario sets the stage as follows:

Scenario   The scene changes to Nero's palace. Nero, Poppea, Consuls, Tribunes, Love, Venus in Heaven, and Chorus of Cupids.

Nero formally attends the coronation of Poppea who, in the name of the People and the Senate of Rome, is crowned with the imperial diadem by the Consuls and Tribunes. At the same time Love descends from Heaven with Venus, Graces and Cupids, and similarly crowns Poppea goddess of beauty on earth. And so ends the opera.

[*Curtis:* 230]

And so, also, ends the libretto—both in Busenello's published version and in the Neapolitan publication of 1651. But not the musical manuscripts. The Neapolitan copy follows Busenello fairly closely, with two substantial choruses for Love and the Cupids, but the Venetian manuscript cuts out the Cupid choruses entirely. And the ravishing final duet for Poppea and Nero, with which both copies end, does not appear in Busenello's libretto at all. The words, in fact, can be traced back to the revised version of an opera by Benedetto Ferrari, of which only the libretto has survived. But the music?

Because of its formal and ceremonial subject matter the final scene of

Poppea was always likely to differ in style and atmosphere from the personal, individual idiom of the rest of the opera, and now twentieth-century scholarship has found more and more internal evidence that another hand than Monteverdi's was involved in its composition. There is nothing particularly unusual in this; a libretto of Strozzi's, performed in the same year and in the same theatre as *Poppea*, had music by three different composers, and in the busy musical world of Venetian opera there were plenty of potential collaborators: Cavalli, Monteverdi's pupil and assistant at Saint Mark's and the most gifted of his successors; Ferrari, for whom Monteverdi was 'the oracle of music—*questo bel Monte sempre verde*'; Sacrati, the man who had brought Anna Renzi from Rome and written a brilliantly successful opera for her in 1641. Expert opinion, much exercised in recent years, has now settled on Sacrati as the most likely candidate, and the evidence is convincing—though whether it quite justifies, in the most carefully researched score of the opera, the heading of the final scene 'Finale, composed by Francesco Sacrati', is perhaps another matter. Apart from anything else, if this is indeed the version of the opera that was heard at the first performance in 1643, it begs the question of how much Monteverdi himself may have been involved in what Sacrati did.

Nevertheless it does seem possible, even probable, that the music for *Pur ti miro*, that most moving of all Monteverdi's love scenes, may not be by Monteverdi at all. How much that matters is a question of personal feeling. If the music is not by Monteverdi, it is certainly by someone who knew and understood his style: the striking similarities to the little canzonetta from *Proserpina rapita* can hardly be coincidence. In any case, whether it is Monteverdi or a homage to Monteverdi, it provides a conclusion that is clearly based on the human message of the opera—a candid acceptance of the joys of sensuality that surely resonates more naturally with audiences of today than any number of choruses of Cupids or triumphs of Love. Admirers of Monteverdi may regret seeing the composer deprived of this last and most beautiful of his love duets, but in the circumstances of its composition, as in the morals of its plot, *L'incoronazione di Poppea* leaves no room for sentimentality.

Christoph Willibald Gluck, about 1775

Alceste

*When I undertook to write the music for Alceste I deter-
mined to abolish entirely all the abuses which have been introduced by the
ignorant vanity of singers or the excessive complaisance of composers, and
which have so long disfigured Italian opera and turned the most splendid and
most beautiful of spectacles into the most ridiculous and tiresome. I decided
to restrict the music to its proper function, that of expressing the true meaning
of the poetry and underlining the situations of the plot, without interrupting
or weakening the action with useless and superfluous ornamentation, and I
believed that it should achieve this in the same way as colour and a nicely
judged contrast of light and shade bring life to a well-ordered drawing, by
animating the figures without distorting their contours. . . .'* [Gluck, 1769]

THE PREFACE TO THE SCORE of *Alceste*, published in
1769 over the signature of Cristoforo Gluck, is one of the most celebrated
documents in the history of music, and the reform it introduced punctu-
ates, like a great question mark, the course of eighteenth-century opera.
By the middle of the century, however, there were already a good many
observers who were beginning to feel that the reform of Italian opera was
an urgent necessity.

The framework of *opera seria*, the existing model for any serious
opera in Italian, had been formulated by the Arcadian poet Pietro Tra-
passi, better known by his hellenised name of Metastasio. Metastasio's
influence was enormous, and his twenty-six librettos were set by virtually
every composer of opera until the end of the century—some of them as
many as eighty or ninety times. The plots, which sternly avoided comedy

and maintained a high moral tone, presented classical figures in intricate conflicts between love and duty, where conscience and nobility of character invariably won the day. The characters appeared in a sequence of carefully ordered scenes, each with a recitative designed to move the plot forward, followed by an aria that summed up the current emotional state of the character concerned; there were no ensembles except for an occasional duet and a perfunctory closing chorus, and the happy ending, or *lieto fine*, was more or less obligatory. It was a well-ordered approach, in tune with the best principles of the Enlightenment, and Metastasio was an elegant poet. But a succession of static arias allowed little opportunity for the development of action—particularly since they were almost always of the *da capo* variety, where the first part of the aria had to be repeated all over again with embellishments. So most composers gave little thought to the drama as a whole; they simply provided their soloists with singable material, and the sometimes astonishing displays of vocal acrobatics exhibited by the star singers, especially the castratos who were now at the height of their fame, took precedence over any pretence at dramatic credibility. Small wonder that audiences in Italy became bored, and that the opera house became a social meeting place where the chatter in the boxes was only occasionally interrupted in favour of a popular singer or a favourite aria.

This was the market for which Gluck's first operas were written— eight of them in Italy itself, and a further eight during his subsequent travels to London and round the courts of Europe. Though few survive complete, it is clear that these early works made little attempt to break with Metastasian convention; they had energy and perhaps a rather more 'modern' cut to the melody, but in general they followed the prevailing taste for clarity and formal elegance that had by this time replaced the contrapuntal richness of the baroque. Certainly they reveal no ambition for any serious operatic reform.

And yet there was always something different about Christoph Willibald Gluck. To begin with, he wasn't Italian. A forester's son, born in what is now northern Bavaria and brought up in Bohemia, he appears to have received little or no conventional musical training, and retained throughout his life the blunt, outspoken character of his peasant origin. 'A composer of marvellous fire, but mad', Metastasio called him in a letter to the great castrato Farinelli in 1751, and the judgment became more acerbic five years later when Metastasio remarked on 'the verve and noisy extravagance that have served him well in more than one theatre in

Europe'—adding acidly, 'according to observers with whose sufferings I can only sympathise'. By this time, though, Gluck, like Metastasio, had made his home in Vienna, and perhaps closer acquaintance had begun to sour the relationship between the two men; when Gluck's setting of Metastasio's *Antigono* was produced in Rome, the poet allowed himself what was, given the reputation of Roman audiences, a distinctly back-handed compliment. [*Metastasio: 681–2, 1152–3*]

Metastasio   I am most curious to find out how the music of our Gluck is received in Rome. His writing has a peculiar energy and, considering the taste which they tell me currently prevails in Rome, I should not be surprised if it pleased the public there.   [*Id: 1099*]

To distinguished visitors, however, like the English scholar Charles Burney, Metastasio's public image was nothing if not benign.

Burney   There are painted on his countenance all the genius, goodness, propriety, benevolence and rectitude, which constantly characterise his writings. I could not keep my eyes off his face, it was so pleasing and worthy of contemplation. His conversation was of a piece with his appearance: polite, easy, and lively. . . . Several jokes escaped him in the course of our conversation, and he was equally cheerful, polite, and attentive, the whole time. . . . We prevailed upon him to be much more communicative about music than we expected; for in general he avoids entering deep into any particular subject . . . [*Burney: 102, 104*]

It would certainly be hard to find a greater contrast to this paragon than the literary opportunist who arrived in Vienna in 1761 and was before long to transform Gluck's musical career.

Ranieri de' Calzabigi, an Italian of decent family born in the same year as Gluck, had drifted from Livorno to Naples and finally to Paris, where he was one of the multitude of adventurers who found the metropolis of the *ancien régime* a fertile ground for their many-sided gifts. Shrewd, and not above the more questionable type of financial operation, he was at one point engaged in the establishment of a lottery so shady that he came under the scrutiny of the Parisian police, in whose records he appears as 'a tall man, lean, dark, *fort rangé* and rather secretive'. One of his partners in the lottery scheme, which eventually seems to have led to his expulsion from Paris, was the notorious writer and libertine Giacomo Casanova, who left a rather unattractive description of their first meeting, at a time when Calzabigi was prevented from appearing in public by an unpleasant form of skin disease that obliged him to scratch himself continually . . .

Casanova   . . . but did not prevent him from eating with an excellent appetite, nor from writing or conversing, nor indeed from discharging all the bodily functions of a man in excellent health. . . . [He was] a shrewd calculator, well versed in financial affairs, familiar with the commerce of all nations, learned in history, a great lover of women, a wit and a poet . . .   [*Casanova*: 25]

Calzabigi's early work as a poet had attracted the praise of Metastasio, and he later seized the chance of attaching himself to the great man's reputation by editing a collection of Metastasio's works. But in spite of the fulsome tone of much of the long *Dissertazione* that he attached to the edition, it is clear that the polemical ideas to which he had been exposed in Paris had already raised doubts in his mind about the artificialities of the Metastasian formula. France was the one European country that had resisted the spread of Italian opera; the tradition of *tragédie-lyrique*, established by Jean-Baptiste Lully and his librettist Philippe Quinault and developed in the eighteenth century by Jean-Philippe Rameau, had from the start remained closer to the classical theatre, with added elements of the *ballet de cour* and much emphasis on spectacle. But what most distinguished it from its Italian counterpart was the naturalistic word setting; the development of the Italian aria had no parallel in France, where rhythms were flexible, the vocal line declamatory, and the distinction between *airs* and recitatives blurred. Years later, long after his collaboration with Gluck had ended, Calzabigi remembered:

Calzabigi   Twenty-five years ago I formed the opinion that the only music suitable for dramatic poetry, and above all for dialogue and for those arias that we call 'action arias', was that which, being animated and full of energy, came closest to natural declamation; also, that declamation itself was nothing more than an imperfect form of music, and that one could notate it as it is, if we only had at our disposal a large enough number of signs with which to indicate the many differences in pitch, the many inflections, the degrees of vehemence or gentleness—the infinity, so to speak, of varied nuances that we put into our voices as we speak. The music for any verses, therefore, being according to my idea simply a more skilful, more studied form of declamation, still further enriched by the harmony of the accompaniments, I felt that here lay the whole secret of composing music for a drama—that the more compact, energetic, passionate, touching, harmonious the poetry was, the more the music which sought to express it by following its true declamation would be the true music for this poetry, the music *par excellence* . . .

Filled with these ideas, I arrived in Vienna in 1761. . . .

[*Calzabigi, 1784: 133–5*]

By 1761, Gluck was already a familiar figure in Vienna. Though not prepossessing in appearance (Burney found him 'much pitted with small pox, and very coarse in figure and look'), he was described by Dittersdorf as 'always jovial in carrying out his duties . . . , well-read and with a knowledge of the wider world', and he forged valuable links with aristocratic patrons, eventually becoming music teacher to the Emperor's daughter, Marie Antoinette. More important, he attracted the attention of the newly appointed director of the Viennese theatres, Count Giacomo Durazzo, a reformer whose ideas about opera were strongly anti-Metastasian, and for a while he found himself providing music for a succession of French *opéra-comique* texts—a surprising (though in the event highly successful) undertaking for a composer who had so far devoted himself entirely to tragedy. But Durazzo soon turned his attention to ballet and its possibilities as a serious art form; with the collaboration of the ballet-master Gasparo Angiolini he devised a dramatic ballet on the subject of *Don Juan* with music by Gluck—'[who] has grasped perfectly the terrible content of the action', wrote Angiolini in his preface to the score, 'and striven to express the passions that are set in motion and the horror which pervades the final disaster . . .'. [*Prod'homme, 1948: 109*]

It was a first step in the new direction and, predictably, Calzabigi already had a finger in the pie. Though he was officially employed as secretary to the Imperial Chancellor, Count Kaunitz, he had made common cause with Durazzo and his circle. He now edited Angiolini's preface, perhaps contributed to the scenario of the ballet, then, never one to miss an opportunity, obtained permission to read Durazzo his dramatic poem of *Orfeo*.

Calzabigi [After I had read him my *Orfeo*] Count Durazzo . . . engaged me to give it in the theatre. I agreed, on condition that the music should be written in the way that I imagined it. He sent me to M. Gluck who, he assured me, would fall in with my ideas. M. Gluck was not then considered (wrongly no doubt) to be among our greatest masters. . . . No one [then] understood declamatory music, as I call it, and for M. Gluck, who did not pronounce our language well, it would have been impossible to declaim even a few lines accurately. I read him my *Orfeo*, and repeated several passages a number of times, pointing out the nuances that I put into my declamation, and indicating the suspensions, the slowing down and speeding up, the different tones of voice, sometimes heavy with meaning, sometimes weak, passing almost unnoticed, that I wanted him to make use of in his composition. I begged him, at the same time, to banish decorative passage work, cadenzas, ritornellos, all that is gothic, barbarous and extravagant in our music, and M. Gluck went along with my ideas.

But declamation slips away into thin air and often it cannot be recalled. . . . [And so] I tried to find signs that would at least mark its most salient characteristics. I invented several, placing them between the lines all through the text of *Orfeo*, and it was on such a manuscript, accompanied by written notes in the places where the signs provided insufficient guidance, that M. Gluck composed his music.

[*Calzabigi, 1784: 135–6*]

Orfeo has usually been regarded as the starting point of the Calzabigi-Gluck reform: for the first time in an Italian opera, *secco* recitative—that is, recitative accompanied only by the harpsichord and a continuo bass line—was abolished and the singers were accompanied by the orchestra throughout; there were no opportunities for exaggerated vocal display, and the plain, grief-stricken cries of Orfeo at the start of the opera were shocking to an audience who expected the star singer to introduce himself with a formal recitative and aria. Yet for all its importance *Orfeo* stands aside from the mainstream of *opera seria*. It remains essentially a pastoral drama on the French model—the solemn choral opening even modelled specifically on the tomb scene in Rameau's *Castor et Pollux*—and it owes its lasting success to the fresh charm of its arias and choruses (including, of course, the one tune of Gluck's that everybody knows) and the enchantment of its beautifully orchestrated ballet music.

Calzabigi needed to go further to prove his point. But in the event, after *Orfeo*, Gluck seems temporarily to have forgotten about reform.

Only a few months later he was back in Italy with yet another setting of Metastasio; in Vienna a new and highly successful *opéra-comique* was followed by more ballets and works for court festivities, and it was not until sometime in 1766 that he returned to the rigours of a second collaboration with Calzabigi.

Alceste is high tragedy in the sense so dear to the theatre of the seventeenth and eighteenth centuries and, it has to be said, it would not be easy to find a plot more consistently gloomy or devoid of stage action. Here is how Calzabigi himself summarised the argument:

Calzabigi   Admetus, King of Pherae in Thessaly and husband of Alcestis, is on the point of losing his life; Apollo, who has been received by Admetus when exiled from heaven, persuades the Fates to spare him, on condition that he finds someone to die in his place. Alcestis agrees to the exchange and dies, but Hercules, Admetus's friend, who arrives in Pherae at this point, rescues Alcestis from the powers of Death and restores her to her husband.

Such is the plan of the celebrated tragedy by Euripides entitled *Alcestis*, but in place of Hercules I have introduced Apollo who, as the recipient of Admetus's charity, works this miracle out of gratitude.
[*Prod'homme, 1948: 162*]

The principles on which Gluck based his setting of this subject were laid out in detail in the preface to the published score. Exactly who wrote the preface to *Alceste* has never been entirely clear: both librettist and composer later claimed authorship, but, although the signature at the end is Gluck's, the contents suggest the intellectual theorist rather than the musician. Nevertheless the relentless dramatic intensity with which Gluck set Calzabigi's libretto to music is unlike anything that had happened in opera before.

The seriousness of his approach is clear from the first note of his score. One of the weak points of *Orfeo* had always been the conventional sinfonia, tacked onto the beginning of the opera in deference to the Emperor on whose name day it was performed. But now 'I felt that the overture should prepare the spectators for the nature of the subject that is to be enacted', he wrote in the preface, 'and prefigure, so to speak, its argument'—and certainly there is no mistaking the import of the striding trombone arpeggio that opens the *Alceste* overture, or the sombre restlessness of the *andante* which follows. When the orchestra breaks off for the herald's fanfare and announcement of Admetus's approaching death, the tragic mood is already unmistakeably established. As in *Orfeo*, the opening scene is built around a great choral lament, though here what is required of the protagonist is not the abandonment of a lover to personal grief, but the dignity of a queen before her people. After a touchingly simple recitative (*secco* recitative, which rather surprisingly makes an occasional reappearance in this score) Alceste begins what appears to be a formal aria. But *Io non chiedo, eterni dei* obeys none of the rules, changes tempo and mood according to the sense of the words, does not make the required *da capo* repetition, and at its climax allows no dramatic exit but returns abruptly to the mourning chorus of her hearers.

Gluck   I did not want to arrest an actor in the passionate heat of dialogue simply to wait for some tiresome *ritornello* [or orchestral introduction], nor detain him in the middle of a word on a vowel favourable to his voice, nor make a display of his vocal agility in some long drawn-out passage, nor require him to wait while the orchestra gives him time to get his breath back for a cadenza. I did not feel bound to pass quickly over the middle section of an aria, where the words may well be the most impassioned and important of all, in order to be able to repeat regularly four times over the words of the first part, and so end the aria where perhaps the sense doesn't end, merely to allow the singer an opportunity to display the capricious variety of ways in which he can vary [the same music]. In short, I have striven to abolish all the abuses against which reason and good sense have long protested in vain.   [*Gluck, 1769*]

Radical though it may appear, the authors of the *Alceste* preface in fact owed many of their ideas to current thinking, and in particular to that most influential of documents on operatic reform, the *Saggio sopra l'opera in musica* by Count Francesco Algarotti. For Algarotti, as for Gluck, the restoration of a proper balance between lyrical expansion and the onward movement of the action was the root of the operatic problem; whatever the aria might contribute, it was recitative, in some form or other, that carried the development of the action and formed, as it always had, the backbone of the opera.

Algarotti   Many now living can remember certain passages of simple recitative that could move the feelings of an audience in a way that no aria of our own day is capable of equalling. . . . [But] composers nowadays pay almost no attention to the recitatives, as if, by their very nature, they were unable to give pleasure to anybody. . . . And equally the singers pay no attention to the way they are sung; they make no attempt to invest them with that power of expression that sculptures the words in the mind and in the heart . . . [but] devote all their studies to the singing, or rather the warbling and embellishing, of the arias. . . . Because they have never understood the correct methods of singing, they apply the same musical graces to every type of melodic line, and with their cadenzas, their trills, and their improvisations they ornament, complicate and disfigure everything. . . .   [*Algarotti, 1755: 14, 19*]

It was just this expressive power of former days that Gluck was determined to recapture. He may not, in fact, have abolished the ubiquitous *da capo* aria entirely—there are still arias in *Alceste* that could be so described. But in his hands the form was reduced to a reasonable use of the age-old musical need for recapitulation, leaving little opportunity for the vocal acrobatics of which he was so scornful. And always the meaning of the text came first.

Gluck   I believed that my greatest efforts must be directed towards the search for a noble simplicity, and I have avoided making exhibitions of virtuosity at the expense of clearness. Nor did I think mere displays of novelty were of any value if they were not suggested naturally by the situation and its musical expression, and there is no rule which I would not gladly have set aside in order to achieve the effect that I wanted. . . .   [*Gluck, 1769*]

Burney   He studies a poem a long time before he thinks of setting it. He considers well the relation which each part bears to the whole; the general cast of each character, and aspires more to satisfying the mind, than flattering the ear. . . . Music, in his hands, is a most copious, nervous, elegant, and expressive language. It seldom happens that a single air of his operas can be taken out of its niche, and sung singly, with much effect; the whole is a chain, of which a detached single link is but of small importance.   [*Burney: 91*]

Indeed some of them can hardly be identified as arias. The hesitant, nervous words in which Alceste tells the gods of her terrible decision to sacrifice herself blend imperceptibly out of the recitative that precedes them; they are plainly marked 'aria' in the score, but no eighteenth-century audience would have recognised them as such, and nor indeed do we. The whole of this scene is designed to support the meaning of the text, evoking the terrors of the underworld in the tentative gestures of the strings, the plaintive voice of the oboe, the haunting cry of the night bird in a little repeated figure on the clarinets. Orchestration like this makes it clear that Gluck's often-quoted remark to the journalist Olivier de Corancez, 'before I begin, my greatest concern is to forget I am a musician', should be taken with a pinch of salt.

Gluck   I felt that the orchestra ought to be introduced in accordance with the interest and intensity of the words, and not leave a sharp contrast in the dialogue between aria and recitative, so that the meaning of a passage should not be unreasonably broken up nor the force and warmth of the action wantonly dissipated.   [*Gluck, 1769*]

This relentless fidelity to the nuances of the text can tax the powers of even the most intrepid singer. The crucial scene, in which Admetus cross-questions his wife and at last discovers her intention, opens with his surprise at the tears with which she greets their reunion. But he is allowed only eighteen bars (not even marked 'aria') before Alceste intervenes and launches 219 bars of dialogue in recitative, with only the merest hint of occasional lyrical expansion, before giving way to the passionate outburst of Admetus's *No, crudel, non posso vivere*. It is an ideally effective vehicle for an exchange of such tormented cross-purposes.

But Admetus's predicament is profoundly equivocal; the conflicting loyalties of a king to his people, a husband to his wife, and a father to his children, make it virtually impossible for him to act with moral conviction, and for all his protestations of grief he doesn't always project as the positive counterpart demanded by the single-minded passion of Alceste. Though there is no denying the agonised intensity of *Misero! E che faro!*, by the beginning of the third act his continuing lamentations actually slacken the tension, and in the end it is to Alceste herself that the opera belongs—from the first, sombre invocation to the gods in which she offers to die in Admetus's place, to her appeal for permission to revisit her family before she finally submits to death, her confrontation with Admetus, her touching farewell to her children, and her six last stifled words. . . .

Algarotti   That old charge, made by critics against operatic perfor-mances, that the characters go to their death singing, arises only because the required harmony between the words and the music is lacking. If there were no vocal twittering when the passions are being expressed, and the music were written as it should be, then it would seem no more improbable that a person should die singing than recit-ing poetry.   [*Algarotti, 1763: 25*]

With such demands on the dramatic powers of the performers, it was clear that *Alceste* was going to need artists of a different calibre to the usual stars of *opera seria*, and as soon as the composition of the opera was completed, Calzabigi wrote to the Imperial Chancellor (by now *Prince Kaunitz*) who had assumed control of the Viennese theatres after the resignation of Count Durazzo.

Calzabigi   Whenever H[er] I[mperial] M[ajesty] and Y[our] H[ighness] give the order that *Alceste* be put on the stage, it is of paramount importance to choose suitable executants. Alceste and Admetus can-not be represented by just any singers, partly because of the nature of this new species of drama, which bases everything on the eye of the spectator and consequently on the action, but also because the music associated with it depends more upon expression than anything the Italians are nowadays pleased to call 'song'.   [*Hammelman: 609*]

More sure of himself now than twelve years ago, when he had writ-ten his preface to Metastasio's works, he pitches into his august colleague with marked lack of reverence.

Calzabigi   Only the dramas of the Abbé Metastasio, whose length—by reason of the large number of verses and musical arabesques—is such that they cannot, from the outset, hope to hold the attention of the spectator, enjoy the privilege of being 'saddles for all horses'. There it matters not whether a character in the drama is sung by a Farinelli, Caffarelli, Guadagni or Toschi . . . since the audience neither expects nor demands from the singers more than a couple of arias and a duet (and that without expecting to hear the words), having from the start abandoned any idea of taking an interest in the action. . . .

Matters are entirely different in the new plan of musical drama which has been, if not invented, at least first put into practice by me in *Orfeo*, and then in *Alceste*. . . . All is nature here, all is passion; there are no sententious reflections, no philosophy or politics, no paragons of virtue. . . . The plots are simple, not romanticized; a few verses are enough to inform the spectators of the progress of the action, which is never complicated or duplicated in servile, uncalled for obedience [to the demands of performers] but reduced to the dimensions of Greek tragedy. . . . In this plan, as your Highness will perceive, the music has no other function than to express what arises from the words, which are therefore neither smothered by notes nor used to lengthen the spectacle unduly—because it is ridiculous to hear the word 'amore' (for instance) prolonged in a hundred notes when nature has restricted it to three.

If this new plan . . . should meet with the approval of the public, and of the exalted taste of H[er] I[mperial] M[ajesty] . . . it is essential to adhere to it properly and not to confound it with that of Signor Metastasio, because ornaments for blondes do not suit brunettes. In the Abbé's dramas let the [the prima donnas] warble and scream their heads off in an aria about a murmuring brook so that you can't hear a word—it is no matter; in *Orfeo* . . . and *Alceste* we need actresses who will sing what the composer has written and not take it upon themselves to add their own ideas. . . .

Putting *Alceste* into the mouths of warblers like these would mean ruining both music and poetry and failing to achieve the proper aim, which is precisely to bring [poetry and music] together. [Given the proper singers] *Alceste* can succeed as a new, majestic and fascinating spectacle worthy of this court and a connoisseur like Your Highness. . . . Done in any other way it would better to leave unheard this child of my poor genius and Signor Gluck's sublime gifts, rather than let it be born a cripple. . . .   [*Id*]

Though Gluck's score was completed at latest by February 1767, and Calzabigi's letter to Kaunitz is dated 6 March, *Alceste* still had to wait a further nine months for its first performance. The closure of the Viennese theatres following the death of the young Archduchess Maria Josepha in October may have contributed to a last-minute delay in production, but it was the implementation of Gluck's and Calzabigi's novel dramatic ideas that really held things up, dragging out rehearsals and causing problems that were not easily or quickly overcome. In any case, the usual artists for *opera seria* in Vienna were not available: 'there are no singers here for serious opera', observed Leopold Mozart, who went to a performance with his son; 'even Gluck's tragic opera, *Alceste*, was performed entirely by *opera buffa* singers'. And in fact both Antonia Bernasconi, who played Alceste, and Filippo Laschi, who took the role of the High Priest, had made their names in Italian comedy—though Laschi seems to have lowered his normal tenor voice to baritone for the solemnities of the Temple of Apollo.   [*Anderson: 83*]

For Gluck, who had already disposed of the obligatory castrato by simply not writing a castrato role, the absence of customary warblers was a positive advantage. Laschi was as well known for his acting as for his singing, and of Giuseppe Tibaldi, the Admetus, Calzabigi later wrote: 'when Tibaldi played the role of Admetus for the first time he proved to be a really excellent actor, because he has a heart, and understands what he is saying . . . [He commanded] attention, interest, and tears'.
                                                                    [*Ricci: 628–9*]

With artists like this, Gluck could work with all the vigour and enthusiasm for which he was already famous. 'A very dragon, of whom all are in fear', Burney called him . . .   [*Burney: 89*]

Burney   . . . a great disciplinarian, and as formidable as Handel used to
   be, when at the head of a band. . . . During dinner we . . . talked more
   than we eat, [and he] recounted to me the difficulties he had met with
   in disciplining the band, both of vocal and instrumental performers,
   at the rehearsals of *Orfeo*, which was the first of his operas that was
   truly dramatic. . . . But he assured me, that he never found his troops
   mutinous, though he on no account suffered them to leave any part
   of their business till it was well done, and frequently obliged them to
   repeat some of his manoeuvres twenty or thirty times. . . . [*Id: 117, 99*]

With *Alceste* it seems to have been the chorus who gave him most trouble. For they, too, were required to act, to become the people of Thessaly—animated in the crowd scenes with Alceste and Admetus, overcome by awe in the Temple, or, harder still, breaking up into individuals in the extraordinary ensemble at the end of Act 1, where a succession of frightened Thessalian citizens find hurried excuses for not taking Admetus's place. Gluck found it difficult to assemble enough singers for the chorus and in the end had to enlist the help of the cathedral choir, who had little experience of the stage. The celebrated French ballet-master Jean-Georges Noverre, who had replaced Angiolini as choreographer to the Viennese theatres, found the composer in despair at rehearsal.

Noverre   It was demanding the impossible—how was he to make these statues move? Gluck was beside himself with anger and impatience: he threw his wig on the ground, he sang, he gesticulated—all useless! Statues have ears that hear nothing, eyes that see nothing, and I arrived to find this man so full of fire and genius reduced to a pitiable state of fury and vexation. He looked at me without speaking, then, breaking the silence, he said with a number of vigorous expressions which I don't print: 'Save me, my friend, from the agony I am in! For God's sake, make these automatons *move*. Here's what they are supposed to be doing: show them yourself, and I will be your interpreter'.

After spending two solid hours and using every possible means of expression with no result, I told Gluck that there was no way he could use these machines, that they would ruin everything, and I advised him to give up all idea of his choruses. 'But I need them,' he cried, 'I need them! I can't do without them!' His distress inspired me with an idea: I suggested that he should split up the singers and distribute them in the wings so that the audience wouldn't be able to see them, and I promised to replace them with the elite of my *corps de ballet*, whom I would show how to make all the gestures needed to express the music, and how to perform everything in such a way that the audience would believe that the actors they saw were the actors who were singing. Gluck came near to suffocating me in the excess of his joy . . .   [*Noverre: 161*]

The first performance of *Alceste* took place at the reopening of the Burgtheater on 26 December 1767. Though one contemporary diarist recorded that 'it was . . . found by the public to be pathetic and lugubrious', it was on the whole a success; Calzabigi claimed that, between the first season and its revival in 1770, the original Viennese production ran 'very successfully' for sixty performances, and some at least seem to have been gripped by the impact of the work . . .   [*Howard: 81; Ricci: 635*]

Burney   . . . which, say those who have seen it represented, was so truly theatrical and interesting, that they could not keep their eyes a moment off the stage, during the whole performance, having their attention so irritated; and their consternation so raised, that they were kept in perpetual anxiety, between hope and fear for the event, till the last scene of the drama. . . .   [*Burney:* 93]

It was not to be expected, however, that Metastasio's supporters would like it.

Burney   Party runs as high among poets, musicians, and their adherents, at Vienna as elsewhere. Metastasio and Hasse may be said to be at the head of one of the principal sects, and Calzabigi and Gluck of another. The first, regarding all innovations as quackery, adhere to the ancient form of the musical drama, in which the poet and musician claim equal attention from an audience; the bard in the recitatives and narrative parts; and the composer in the airs, duos and choruses. The second party depend more on theatrical effects, propriety of character, simplicity of diction and of musical execution, than on what they style flowery descriptions, superfluous similes, sententious and cold morality on one side, with tiresome symphonies and long divisions on the other.   [*Id:* 81–2]

Metastasio himself appears to have remained characteristically circumspect. He begged the writer of an ode in his honour to delete two strofes that made reference to Gluck . . .

Metastasio   . . . [because] the author of *Alceste* might think that the unfavourable opinions expressed of his drama are mine, and take offence at them, for which I should be extremely sorry—the more so because I do not believe it proper to have victory attributed to me in any presumed contest, the author having evidently taken the greatest care in his *Alceste* . . . [to follow] a course of action diametrically opposed to mine, which precludes all comparison.   [*Fucilla:* 588]

Nor was Gluck himself satisfied with the outcome. In the dedicatory letter attached to his next opera, *Paride ed Elena*, he expressed his disappointment at the reception of the recently published full score.

Gluck   The sole reason that persuaded me to issue my music for *Alceste*
in print was the hope of finding successors who would follow the new
path and, spurred on by the support of an enlightened public, would
dare to banish the abuses which have crept into Italian opera and bring
it as near to perfection as possible. I regret that I have so far attempted
this in vain. Those pedants and arbiters of taste, who abound in vast
numbers and represent the greatest barrier to progress in all the arts,
have declared their opposition to a method which, if it should gain a
footing, would at a stroke destroy all their pretensions as critics and
all their hopes as creators themselves . . . and so voices were raised in
unison against this barbarous and eccentric music. . . .   [*Gluck, 1770*]

Though both Gluck and Calzabigi made vigorous efforts to promote
their new concept of drama in opera, they realised that they had failed
to make the break-through for which they had hoped; *Paride ed Elena*
was the last of their joint 'reform' operas, and Gluck, his financial situation anyhow weakened as the result of an unwise involvement in the
management of the Viennese theatres, decided to direct his efforts elsewhere. Much in *Alceste* and *Paride ed Elena* had been derived from the
example of French opera, and in France itself the death of Rameau had
left a vacuum that had not yet been filled. So Gluck's eyes were already
turning towards Paris when, by chance, his attention was drawn to an
operatic adaptation of Racine's tragedy *Iphigénie en Aulide* by an attaché
at the French embassy in Vienna, François Louis du Roullet. The setting
he made of du Roullet's libretto must have been completed, at least in
his head, by September 1772, when he sang it to Burney 'nearly from the
beginning to the end, with as much readiness as if he had a fair score
before him'; in any case by this time du Roullet had already prepared
the ground in Paris with an anonymous letter to the *Mercure de France*,
announcing that 'the famous M. Glouch . . . has made a French opera
which he would like to see presented on the Parisian stage'. [*Burney: 91*]

Du Roullet   After having composed more than forty Italian operas,
which have had the greatest success in all the theatres where that
language is used, this great man has become convinced, as the result
of a thoughtful study of ancient and modern authors and profound
reflection on his art, that in their theatrical compositions the Italians
have strayed from the true path, and that the French form is the true
form of the musical drama . . .

[After recent experiences in Italy] M. Glouch . . . was persuaded that the Italian language, being more suited by its frequent repetition of vowels to what the Italians call *passages* [vocal ornamentation], had not the clarity or energy of French, and that the advantage which we have been accustomed to accord to the former was even destructive of the true style of musical drama, in which all such ornamentation is out of place, or at least weakens the expression. As a result of these observations, M. Glouch became indignant with the rash assertions of those of our famous writers who have dared to calumniate the French language by maintaining that it is not susceptible to great musical composition. In this matter nobody can be a more competent judge than M. Glouch; he has an excellent knowledge of both languages and, though he speaks French with difficulty, he understands it perfectly; he has made a particular study of it, knows all its subtleties and above all rules that govern its versification, which he observes most scrupulously.   [*Roullet: 169*]

'Everything in this composition seems to me to be in our tradition,' du Roullet writes enthusiastically, 'nothing in it foreign to French ears'—and he urges the directors of the Opéra to act quickly to secure Gluck's latest masterpiece for performance in Paris.

For Gluck this shameless piece of self-promotion had the advantage that, when no immediate reaction from the directors of the Opéra was forthcoming, he could keep the ball rolling by publishing a reply to it over his own name. Protesting that the author had been 'carried away' by feelings of friendship, and that 'I am very far from flattering myself that I deserve the eulogies that he has bestowed on me', he proceeds to dump the now redundant Calzabigi with a suitable display of gratitude, and announce his new aims in operatic reform.

Gluck   I would be even more deserving of reproach if I allowed myself to be credited with the invention of the new form of Italian opera whose success has vindicated the attempt; it is to M. de Calzabigi that the chief merit belongs, and if my music has achieved some measure of acclaim I am bound to acknowledge my debt to him, because it is he who set me on the path to developing the resources of my art. . . . Whatever talent a composer may possess, he will never produce more than mediocre music if the poet does not excite in him that enthusiasm without which all artistic creation is feeble and listless. . . . Being born in Germany, such studies as I have been able to make of the Italian and French languages do not, I believe, entitle me to analyse the subtle distinctions which might indicate a preference for one or the other, and I think all foreigners should abstain from judging between them. But what I do feel able to say, is that the language which suits me best will always be the one in which the poet furnishes me with the greatest variety of opportunities to express the passions, and it is this quality that I believed I had found in the words of the opera *Iphigénie* . . . I confess that I would be happy to produce *Iphigénie* in Paris because, by the effect that it would make, and with the help of the famous M. Rousseau of Geneva whom I intend to consult, we might perhaps, by seeking a type of melody that is noble, affecting and natural, allied to a declamation that exactly follows the prosody of each language and the character of each people, be able together to establish a means of achieving the end that I have in mind—which is to produce a music that is fit for all nations, and do away with the ridiculous distinction between national musical styles.   [*Gluck, 1773: 182–4*]

'A music fit for all nations'—it was a far broader ambition than the simple reform of Italian *opera seria*, and the bid for acceptance on the French operatic stage that Gluck now launched marked a decisive step towards its achievement. 'The enterprise is certainly a bold one', he wrote to Padre Martini in Bologna, 'and there will be many obstacles, because it will meet the opposition of national prejudice, against which reason is useless'.   [*Nohl: 20*]

Undaunted nevertheless, he arrived in Paris in November 1773, and threw himself with flamboyant energy into the preparation of *Iphigénie en Aulide*. His outspoken character and individual way of expressing himself at once attracted attention—according to Salieri he spoke French and Italian, even German, 'only with difficulty', and Count D'Escherny observed in his memoirs . . .

D'Escherny   . . . he spoke three or four languages without knowing any of them properly; he mangled them all equally, which gave his conversation a hint of the unconventional and the unpolished which charmed and attracted more than studied speech.   [*Howard: 122*]

It took more than charm, however, to excuse his behaviour at rehearsals, and Mme Gluck felt obliged to ask a painter friend, Johann Christian von Mannlich, to go with her 'to help me restrain my husband within with the limits demanded by French manners, and moderate the hostility that the orchestra and above all the women singers show him'.

Mannlich   He ran like a man possessed, from one end of the orchestra to the other; sometimes it was the violins who were getting it wrong, sometimes the basses, or the horns, or the violas. He would stop them short and sing them the passage, giving it the expression he wanted, but a moment later stop them again, shouting at the top of his voice, 'What the hell's the good of that!'. I could often see the moment coming when all the violins and other instruments would be sent flying at his head. . . .   [*Mannlich: 165*]

In the end, Mannlich was successful in persuading the artists that 'M. Gluck, as a foreigner, did not always realise the strength of his language when carried away by enthusiasm,' and the following April, supported by the influential patronage of his old pupil Marie Antoi-nette (now the *dauphine*), *Iphigénie en Aulide* achieved a sensational, if controversial, success. Barely three and a half months later Gluck followed it with a French version of *Orfeo,* and between them the two operas firmly established his position in Paris, earning the praise of even that most rigid opponent of French opera, the famous M. Rous-seau of Geneva.

But *Orphée et Eurydice* had the advantage of being cast in a form already familiar to French operatic tradition, just as *Iphigénie* had been, from its inception, a deliberate attempt to meet that tradition halfway. It was a different matter to adapt for the French market a work originally aimed specifically at the reform of Italian *opera seria*, and when Gluck got back to Vienna at the close of his first Paris season and embarked upon the revision of *Alceste*, he faced a challenge of a very different kind.

The text du Roullet provided him with was not so much a translation as a total remodelling of Calzabigi's libretto; he cut and transposed scenes, modified the plot, and catered for French taste by providing a greater vari-ety of mood and action, to lighten the all-pervading intensity of utterance that audiences of the original version had found so difficult. There were losses, and gains. The removal of the ensemble of prevaricating citizens at the end of Act I made it possible to close the act with Alceste's great invo-cation to the gods; it was a less original curtain but a more theatrically effective one—even if du Roullet's translation meant losing the awful solemnity of *Ombre, larve* in the Italian version and replacing it with the chattering semiquavers of *Divinités du Styx*. In Act II the suppression of the powerful scene in which Alceste begged the spirits of the underworld for time to bid her family farewell allowed the act to open with the ballets and festive choruses celebrating the recovery of Admetus. The abolition of the role of the confidant Ismene (a stock eighteenth-century conceit) tightened the action, though the demotion of the children to mute roles meant the loss of their two brief but touching interventions in their mother's grief; there were new arias for Alceste and Admetus, and at the beginning of Act III the introduction of a new scene in which Alceste confronts the infernal deities enabled Gluck to recover most of the music lost by the removal of the underworld scene in the previous act.

From Vienna, Gluck kept in close touch by letter with du Roullet, suggesting alterations, and cajoling and encouraging his collaborator in his new-found metier.

Gluck   When will you get over your scruples about *Alceste*? . . . To begin with you are writing for the lyric theatre, not a tragedy for actors, and that entirely changes the way you go about it. Though they are excellent masters of tragedy, neither Racine nor Voltaire has ever known how to write an opera, in fact no one else has ever identified what is needed as well as you. So it is sometimes necessary to ignore the old rules, and make new rules of one's own to produce great effects. These old Greeks were men with a nose and a pair of eyes, like the rest of us. We don't always have to submit to their rules like servile sheep. . . .   [*Gluck, 1914*: 8]

It was only over the end of the opera that disagreement really troubled the otherwise easy collaboration between the two men. Du Roullet apparently wanted to retain the original conclusion, ending the opera with the divine intervention of Apollo and a perfunctory final chorus, though probably with some elaboration to suit French classical pretensions.

Gluck   I don't find your dénouement at the end of the third act a happy one. It would be fine for an opera by Chabanon or Marmontel . . . , but for a masterpiece like *Alceste* it simply won't do. What the devil do you think the Muses are doing here with Apollo? They only make appropriate companions on Mount Parnassus, here they detract too much from the impact of the dénouement. I've had an idea, in a sudden flash, for a [new] ending that I think it is infinitely better, and which will set the seal on the beauty of your work.   [*Id:* 4]

In Gluck's solution, after Apollo has announced that the Fates have been persuaded to revoke their terrible decree, the scene changes and the reunited couple return from the grove of death to greet the mourning populace and open the way to a fully jubilant conclusion. But five months later the composer was still uncertain: 'I shall only be able to say which of the two endings I shall choose when I have finished the accompaniments of all three acts and can judge how the whole thing links up and blends together.'   [*Id:* 7]

Gluck   With your dénouement, the opera is turned upside down. . . . It begins with pomp and grandeur, your chorus is always in action, and during the first two acts the piece develops largely through them, for they do not wish to lose so perfect a king and queen. But when we come to the third act this chorus, which was so concerned about the preservation of its rulers, is seen no more. There's no further mention of them. And I say that the opera cannot end until these poor people have been consoled. It's no good your telling me that Apollo will bring them back again; that just looks like an *hors d'oeuvre*, dragged in by the skin of its teeth. Besides, Apollo would have to play the magician . . . to effect their return . . . In my dénouement, everything is prepared naturally, there's no need for miracles, and the piece finishes with the same pomp and grandeur as it had begun.   [*Id:* 8–9]

For Gluck, all this amounted to the virtual recomposition of his score. Though he kept the salient elements of his original material, he everywhere reworked his ideas, added new ones and enriched the orchestration. The whole emphasis of the opera was changed: some of the relentless intensity was lost, perhaps to the advantage of the overall effect on the stage; the classical austerity gained humanity, and certainly the drama became more workable as a piece of theatre. But the underlying power of the tragedy remained, and the extent to which Gluck became emotionally involved in its transformation was at an altogether different level from anything that had happened with *Orphée*.

Gluck   I become almost mad myself when I go through it all. The nerves
are strained for too long at a time, and the attention is gripped without respite from the first word to the last. This opera is a cask of late
bottled wine, whose flavour has concentrated at it centre; it is truly
magnificent, but too full-bodied to drink in any quantity. I pity the
poet and musician who try to create another of the same kind! . . . It
is a month now since it let me get any sleep, and my wife is in despair.
I seem to have a hive of bees constantly buzzing in my head. Believe
me, operas of this sort are lethal—I am beginning to appreciate the
shrewdness of Quinault and Calzabigi, filling their works with subsidiary characters and giving the spectator a chance to relax . . . An
opera like this is no entertainment, but a very serious occupation for
whoever sees it . . .   [*Id*: 5]

The illness that kept Gluck in Vienna throughout the summer of 1775
was, if not caused, at least exacerbated by the stress of rebuilding his
score, but by 1 January 1776 he was at last able to send the first two acts
of the opera to Paris. At the end of the month he wrote to an old friend,
the Abbé Arnaud:

Gluck   As for *Alceste*, I can tell you that the whole opera is better pro-
portioned than in the Italian version, and if I am able to get from
the chorus and soloists the expression and the action that I have in
mind, you will have a tremendous work, after which it is unlikely that
anyone will want to endure another. I confess, however, that I am not
satisfied with the dénouement . . . M. [du Roullet] says with good
reason that the action ends with the death of Alceste. But Euripides,
who I believe also knew the rules of the theatre, brings in Hercules
after her death to give her back to Admetus, and in this way avoids
strangling the drama with its own rules. For the grief of the people
at her death to make its effect, it must be in some location different
from that in which the catastrophe occurred, for the music will only
be effective if it is heard in the proper surroundings. . . .

We shall settle this point when I get to Paris, which I shall hasten
to do as soon as the season permits.   [*Id*: *11–12*]

Meanwhile he was beginning to think about the performance of
the opera. The artists now available to him were very different from the
opera buffa singers he had used in Vienna eight years earlier, and often

had exaggerated opinions of their own worth. Gluck's impatience with pretension was notorious. When the eminent soprano Sophie Arnould, rehearsing Iphigénie, had complained that in her role the music was all declamation and that she wanted to sing great arias, 'to sing great arias', replied Gluck, 'you have to know how to sing'. In the opening scene of *Orphée* the celebrated tenor Joseph Le Gros, making his first attempt at Orfeo's heart-broken cries of grief, produced a passionate outburst from the composer: [*Mannlich: 165*]

Gluck   Monsieur! It is inconceivable! All the time when you ought to be singing you shout, and now, when on one single occasion I ask you to cry, you can't bring yourself to do it. Don't give a thought, here, either to the music or to what the chorus is singing, but cry out at the moment I have indicated with as much pain as if someone was cutting off your leg—and, if you can, give this pain something from deep within you, something spiritual—a cry from the heart. . . .   [*Id: 255*]

And the treatment worked. After the performance it was observed that '[Le Gros] sang . . . with such warmth, taste, and even soul, it is difficult to recognise him . . . , his metamorphosis is to be regarded as one of the major miracles wrought by Gluck's magic art'.   [*Howard: 124*]

Le Gros was now the inevitable choice for Admetus, but the casting of Alceste was more controversial. Arnould was by this time nearing the end of her career; after her success as Iphigénie she had disappointed Gluck as Eurydice in *Orphée*, and in the revival of the opera her place had been taken by the singer of Cupid in the original production, Rosalie Levasseur—universally known as Mlle Rosalie. At twenty-six Levasseur was young to take on a role as challenging as Alceste, but 'schooled and moulded by the Chevalier Gluck himself', wrote the *Espion Anglois*, 'she has achieved a degree of perfection of which one wouldn't have believed her capable, [and] is today one of the best actresses on the stage'.
[*Prod'homme, 1948: 258*]

Even so, Gluck was vigilant.

Gluck.   Please tell Mlle Rosalie to take care to learn her part in outline only, because she cannot possibly understand the nuances, and the manner of delivery, without me; otherwise it would be infinitely more difficult, both for her and for me, to correct bad habits acquired in my absence. . . .   [*Gluck, 1914: 10*]

And then there was the High Priest.

Gluck   You might suggest to M. Berton [the manager of the Opéra] that
if M. Larrivée would like to undertake the role of the High Priest,
he would be certain to please the public as much or more than he
did as Agamemnon, because his recitative is the most striking piece
in the whole opera, and cannot fail once I have communicated my
intentions to him . . . The chorus must be given their parts [at once],
because they are always in action and must know their music by
heart, as if it were the Pater Noster.   [*Id: 10*]

Gluck was clearly counting on making a big effect with the Temple
Scene in Act I, and he was right: it was to go down to history as one of the
great dramatic *coups de théâtre* of eighteenth-century opera.

But it was for the orchestra above all that Gluck's personal supervision
was essential—all the more so because his instructions in the score and
parts were often imprecise. Having sent the singers their vocal parts while
he was still in Vienna, he told du Roullet, 'I shall be able to start rehearsals
at once when I arrive, and in two weeks will be able to instruct everyone
in their roles'. He wrote to the poet, Friedrich Klopstock: [*Id: 6*]

Gluck   As far as the vocal line is concerned, it is easy for anyone with
feeling—you only need to follow the instincts of the heart. But in
the accompaniment, where the instrumental parts need so much
interpretation, nothing can be begun unless I am there: a few notes
must be drawn out, others accented, some played *mezzo forte*, others louder or softer, to say nothing of the importance of indicating
the speed; playing a little slower or faster can ruin a whole piece . . .
[*Lappenberg: 294*]

By the time Gluck finally arrived in Paris, about the middle of March,
there was only a little over a month to go before the opening night. In
spite of his recent illness, he threw himself into rehearsals with his usual
energy, accompanied, as he had been for *Iphigénie*, by Mme Gluck, and
returning home 'bathed in sweat from the exertion' to be revived 'with hot
towels and a change of clothing'. But by now the eccentricity of his conduct at rehearsals was well known, and the latest reports from the select
members of the public who were permitted to attend them circulated

among the chattering classes of Paris and left a trail of gossip that was still being recalled fifty years later.   [*Mannlich: 164*]

Fétis   When [the rehearsal] was over one could see great noblemen, even princes, eager to present him with his overcoat and his wig, for he was accustomed to throw all these off and put on a night-cap before beginning rehearsals, just as if he were about to retire for the night at home. . . .   [*Fétis: 356*]

As always, Marie Antoinette, now Queen of France, lent her personal support and with it that of her influential entourage. Yet the première on 23 April was a disappointment. '*Alceste* had no success at its first performance', wrote Corancez:

Corancez   . . . I met M. Gluck in the corridors, and found him more concerned with looking for the cause of an event which seemed to him so extraordinary than distressed by the lack of success. 'It would be ridiculous', he said to me, 'if this work failed. That would mark an epoch in the history of your country's taste. I can understand that a work written in a purely musical style might or might not succeed; that would depend on the taste of the audience, which is very unpredictable. I can even understand that a work of this kind might have a wild success to begin with, only to fail later, as it becomes more familiar, with those who originally admired it. But that I should see the failure of a work based entirely on the truth of nature, in which all the passions have their precise expression—this worries me, I confess.' [*Corancez: 1022*]

Though much of the hostility was aimed at a perceived foreign intruder by supporters of the old French operatic tradition, and though rumour attributed some of the antagonism to the fury of Sophie Arnould at being passed over for a younger rival in the title role, for the bulk of the audience the trouble lay in the work itself. 'Her Majesty did her best to support the Chevalier Gluck's alleged masterpiece, but all the efforts of this German's partisans could not defend the poor effect of the third act, which received no applause at all'.   [*Howard: 157*]

It was the problem of the dénouement again, and Gluck and du Roullet took the hint. Within a couple of weeks they had worked out a compromise which was to become definitive. Hercules, who had been deliberately cut out by Calzabigi, was re-introduced early in Act III and undertakes to snatch Alceste from the jaws of death—it is not, after all, his first confrontation with the gods. After a brief display of heroics he drives the infernal deities back into the underworld and restores Alceste to her husband, who leads her, without any recourse to Apollo's magic arts, to a reunion with her children and her people. It is curious that Gluck and du Roullet had not settled for this solution earlier: it is closer to Euripides, it is dramatically more effective, and Hercules' breezy presence introduces a breath of the outside world into an act that Parisian audiences found gloomy and claustrophobic. And it is, after all, a dénouement brought about by human power, not divine intervention—for Hercules, though the son of Jupiter, was a hero and not a god—and in this sense it is perhaps the final symbol of Gluck's struggle to humanise the austerely classical stance of his original Italian masterpiece, and create from it 'a music fit for all nations'.

After a controversial start the French version of *Alceste* ran for thirty-six performances with increasing success; in October, Gluck wrote from Vienna: 'they write from Paris that almost everybody is pleased with *Alceste*', and to the musicians of the Paris Opéra he sent a warm tribute:

[*Gluck, 1914: 11*]

Gluck   They write to tell me that you perform *Alceste* with singular perfection, undertaking it with extraordinary enthusiasm. I cannot tell you how much pleasure this evidence of your friendship on this occasion has given me, and I beg you to believe that I shall lose no opportunity to prove my gratitude. Meanwhile, my dear friends and companions, please accept my heartiest thanks.

[*Prod'homme, 1912: 411–12*]

But by this time Gluck had become reluctantly involved in the famous contest with the Italian composer Niccolò Piccinni, a contest which was to vitiate the rest of his Parisian career. He won it, in 1779, with the last and most successful of his *tragédies-lyriques*, *Iphigénie en Tauride*—the work that came closest to the operatic ideal which he had first envisaged twelve years earlier, and with which he had never lost faith.

'If my [ideas] succeed', he wrote to du Roullet in 1775, 'your old music will be destroyed for ever'. But it didn't turn out quite like that. Times were changing: only ten years separated the first performance of *Iphigénie en Tauride* from the storming of the Bastille, and the growing need for more directly human subject matter was fed by the undercurrent of pre-revolutionary unrest. By the time Gluck died in 1787, Beaumarchais's subversive comedy *Le Mariage de Figaro* had already been transmuted into an altogether new form of musical drama in Vienna, and as the nineteenth century approached, the way forward in the German-speaking countries lay through Mozartian *opera buffa* and the romantic opera that grew out of Beethoven and Weber. Italy, the country at which the reform of *opera seria* had originally been directed, bypassed Gluck entirely and, reluctant to shake off old habits, adapted and re-adapted for another half century the conventions of an earlier age. Only in France did Gluck have any appreciable influence, his Parisian operas paving the way for nineteenth-century French grand opera and eventually providing the direct inspiration for the greatest of them all, Berlioz's classical epic *Les Troyens*.   [*Gluck, 1914: 6*]

But in the end, Gluck's reforms had come too late. Eighteenth-century classical tragedy had had its day, and died with its aristocratic patrons. Yet he achieved in his own operas a balance between drama and music that had no parallel in its time and has remained valid ever since. And of this achievement the cornerstone was *Alceste*—a powerful survivor from a period on the edge of extinction that, whether in the Italian or the French version, stands or falls on its own merits. '*Alceste* is a complete tragedy', he wrote to du Roullet, 'and I confess to you that I think it very little short of perfection'.   [*Nohl:* 33]

Gluck   [It] ought not to please only now, while it is new; it is not a work for any particular moment in time. I warrant that it will please as much in two hundred years, if the French language has not changed by then, because I have grounded it wholly in nature, which is never subject to fashion.   [*Corancez:* 1022]

Mozart at twenty-seven, an unfinished portrait by his
brother-in-law, Josef Lange

Idomeneo

'To write operas is now my one burning ambition', Mozart wrote to his father from Mannheim in February 1778. *'. . . I envy anybody who is composing one. I could really weep for vexation when I hear or see an aria. But an Italian opera, not German; seria, not* buffa*'.*

[*Anderson: 468, 462*]

AT JUST TWENTY-TWO, Mozart already had half a dozen operas to his credit. But because the Archbishop of Salzburg, his employer for the last ten years, possessed no standing opera company of his own, they had been mainly associated with his visits to Vienna or his travels in Italy and Germany. So it was natural enough that now, as he set out on what was to be the last of his big European tours, his hopes should be high. But the months passed, and in Munich, in Mannheim, in Paris, in Munich again, the longed-for opportunity refused to materialise. He returned to Salzburg dissatisfied and discouraged. He loathed the provincial life of the Archbishop's court, doubly dreary after the friends he had made and the standards he had become used to during his travels; he missed his mother, who had died in his arms in Paris only six months earlier, and he tore himself to bits over Aloysia Weber, with whom he had fallen passionately in love in Mannheim on his way to Paris and who had turned him down flat in Munich on his way back. For many reasons he was an exceedingly frustrated young man.

He could not keep his mind off the theatre. He rehashed some old incidental music for a straight play, Gebler's *Thamos, König in Ägypten*, and started on a German singspiel (known today as *Zaide*) which he may have intended for local performance by a travelling opera company, or even by the National Singspiel in Vienna, but left unfinished. In any case, it was not in the end Vienna that provided the chance he was waiting for.

Though Mozart had been well received during his visit to Mannheim by the Elector Palatine, Karl Theodor, he had been disappointed in his hopes of securing a Court appointment. But only a couple of months after his arrival Karl Theodor had succeeded to the Electorate of Bavaria and moved his Court to Munich, where it was soon joined by the bulk of the Mannheim theatrical and musical staff. Amongst these were many of the friends Mozart had made on his Mannheim visit, and it may well have been that support from this quarter worked quietly in Mozart's favour. Whatever the reason, after an interval of two years the good impression he had made on the Elector at last bore fruit, and in the autumn of 1780, Mozart was commissioned to write an opera for the Munich Carnival Season of 1781.

The subject was decided by the Court, and the libretto entrusted by Mozart to another employee of the Archbishop of Salzburg—his Court Chaplain, the Abbé Giambattista Varesco. It was not a happy choice. Varesco was pompous, verbose and difficult to deal with, and though he had no doubt read his Metastasio, it had left him with little or no understanding of the stage. He was to give Mozart endless trouble. Yet in his way Varesco did realise where the essence of his poem lay, and sum-marised it in the introduction to his libretto:

Varesco   The differing emotions awakened in father and son by their recognition of one another; the paternal affection of Idomeneo and his duty towards Neptune; the unhappy position of Idamante, who is unaware of his fate; the mutual passion of the two lovers and their bitter grief when Idomeneo is forced to disclose his secret and fulfil his cruel vow; the jealousy and despair of Elettra—this is the stuff of the present drama . . . as it may be read in the French tragedy which the present Italian poet has in part imitated, and for which he has supplied a happy, instead of a tragic end.   [*Varesco*: 3]

The tragedy which Varesco 'in part imitated' was an early-eighteenth-century drama by Antoine Danchet, originally set to music in 1712 by André Campra as a *tragédie en musique* in the style that had dominated French opera from Lully to Rameau. In his search for ideas Varesco borrowed incidents from various sources (chief among them, perhaps, the oracle as *deus ex machina* at the end from Gluck's *Alceste*), but it was from the French tradition, with its dramatic use of the chorus, its love of the *merveilleux* and its passion for spectacular effects, that he took most of the business with which he decked out his classical tale to provide the large-scale canvas that Mozart needed.

The result was not particularly inspiring. And yet the composer, full of youthful enthusiasm and enterprise, was determined to turn it into a work which would put into the shade every other operatic tragedy ever written. Nowadays we think of Mozart mainly as a composer of what is generally seen as comic opera—even though *Figaro, Così fan tutte, Don Giovanni,* and even more *Die Zauberflöte,* go far beyond comedy in what they tell us about ourselves. But in 1780, Mozart had not yet reached the point where he could relate music, drama and the depths of everyday humanity in so relaxed and informal a manner. His refuge was still the framework: serious opera—which in the eighteenth century meant *opera seria*—was a formal business, something which the Italians had perfected to the point of ossification, and which Gluck had taken over, rejuvenated but not wholly supplanted. Varesco's libretto, whatever its faults, provided him with such a framework while offering him the opportunity for expansion as well. It is the interaction of established Italian formality with the flexibility of French *tragédie en musique* and the reforms of Gluck, combined with the pent-up energy of genius at twenty-two, that gives *Idomeneo* its peculiar qualities.

Mozart was lucky in his commission. There were very few, if any, other cities in Europe which would have been capable of putting on the opera that was in his mind. But with the transfer of the Electoral Court, the company of the Neues Kurfürstliches Opernhaus in Munich had been enormously strengthened by the influx of artists from Mannheim—including the bulk of the famous Mannheim orchestra, for many years without a rival in Europe. The celebrated English music historian and traveller Dr Burney had heard it in 1772 and wrote:

Charles Burney   I found it to be indeed all that its fame had made me expect; power will naturally arise from a great number of hands; but the judicious use of this power, on all occasions, must be the consequence of good discipline; indeed, there are more solo players, and good composers in this, than perhaps in any other orchestra in

Europe; it is an army of generals, equally fit to plan a battle as to fight it. . . . Every effect has been tried which such an aggregate of sound can produce; it was here that the *Crescendo* and *Diminuendo* had birth; and the *Piano,* which was before chiefly used as an echo, with which it was generally synonymous, as well as the *Forte,* were found to be musical *colours* which had their shades, as much as red or blue in painting.   [*Burney:* 34–5]

So Mozart had every reason for thinking orchestrally about his new opera, and he already had many friends among the Mannheim players including the director, Christian Cannabich and his family. And among the singers too. Dorothea and Elisabeth Wendling, his two female artists, were married to brothers who were both members of the orchestra (one of them had accompanied the composer and his mother to Paris in 1778). Vincenzo dal Prato, the young castrato cast for the role of Idamante, was an unknown quantity, but Mozart had made a particular friend, first in Mannheim and later in Paris, of the principal tenor at the Electoral Opera, Anton Raaff. On grounds of seniority, celebrity and diplomacy Raaff had to be given the title role in the new opera, though there is later evidence to suggest that Mozart might have preferred a bass for his Idomeneo. In any case, the famous tenor was now in his middle sixties (Idomeneo in fact turned out to be the last role he was to perform in public) and was beginning to show his age.

Mozart   You will remember, no doubt, that I did not write too favour-
ably about him from Mannheim. . . . But when he made his début
here in the Concert Spirituel . . . and for the first time I really heard
him sing—he pleased me—that is, in his particular style of singing, although the style itself—the Bernacchi school—is not to my
taste. He is too much inclined to drop into the cantabile. I admit
that when he was young and in his prime, this must have been
very effective and have taken people by surprise. I admit also that
I like it. But he overdoes it and so to me it often seems ridiculous.
What I do like is when he sings short pieces, as for example, some
andantinos. . . .
    I fancy that his forte was bravura singing—and, so far as his age
permits, you can still tell this from his manner; he has a good chest
and long breath; and then—these andantinos. . . . In bravura sing-

ing, long *passages* and roulades, he is an absolute master and he has moreover an excellent, clear diction which is very beautiful.

[Anderson: 551–2]

It was the singers who provided the main interest in a new opera for an eighteenth-century audience, and popular judgment was based largely on the opportunities which the composer provided for these public idols to display their gifts. 'I like an aria to fit a singer like a well-made suit of clothes', Mozart had written only a year or two earlier, and it was clearly to his advantage, both from a practical and a dramatic point of view, to give his singers the kind of material they could handle well.

However, these were matters best handled in collaboration with the performers in person, and immediately after the libretto was finished, Mozart set off for Munich, taking with him the music for most of Act I and probably parts of Act II as well. There were still almost two months to go before the projected date for the première, and he used the time, following the almost invariable custom of the period, to complete his composition on the spot, as well as to supervise rehearsals, prepare the singers, and work out the production in cooperation with the designer and the stage manager—in this case, Lorenzo Quaglio—and the ballet-master, Claude Le Grand.

The separation from his librettist (who remained in Salzburg), though probably nothing but a relief from a personal point of view, meant that every alteration in the text which the composer needed had to be asked for in writing, with Mozart's father acting as an interested but rather grumpy go-between in the not-always-simple negotiations. Mozart was too instinctive an artist to be given to theorising about his music or opera at any stage in his life, and certainly these letters do not provide anything like a comprehensive expression of anyone's dramatic principles. Nevertheless here, for once, he was obliged to set down on paper his detailed opinions, and set them down in such a way that they would convince both his father and Varesco: as a result, *Idomeneo* is his one major work for which we possess real comments on the process and problems of its composition. He started the moment he was in Munich.

Mozart 8 November 1780 Mon tres cher père! My arrival here was happy and pleasant—happy, because no mishap occurred during the journey; and pleasant, because we could hardly wait for the moment to reach our destination. . . . Why, that carriage jolted the very souls out of our bodies—and the seats were as hard as stone! For two whole stages I sat with my hands dug into the upholstery and my behind suspended in the air . . . We arrived here at one o'clock in the afternoon and on the very same evening I called on Count Seeau. . . . With regard to the libretto the Count says that Abbate Varesco need not copy it out again before sending it—for it is to be printed here— but I think that he ought to finish writing the text, and not forget *the little notes* [presumably stage directions], and send it to us with the synopsis as quickly as possible. . . . Some slight alterations will have to be made here and there, and the recitatives will have to be shortened a bit. But *everything will be printed*.

I have just one request to make of the Abbate. Ilia's aria in Act II, Scene 2 should be altered slightly to suit what I need. '*Se il padre perdei, in te lo ritrovo*'; this line could not be better. But now comes what has always seemed unnatural to me—I mean, in an aria—and that is *a spoken aside*. In a dialogue all these things are quite natural, for a few words can be spoken aside hurriedly; but in an aria where the words have to be repeated, it has a bad effect, and even if this were not the case, I should prefer an uninterrupted aria. The beginning may stand, if it suits him, for the poem is charming and, as it is absolutely natural and flowing and therefore I have not got to contend with difficulties arising from the words, I can go on composing quite easily; for we have agreed to introduce here an aria andantino with obbligatos for four wind instruments, that is, a flute, oboe, horn and bassoon.   [*Id*: 659–60]

Mozart had clearly lost no time in getting in touch with his orchestral friends in Munich. But in spite of his evident wish to please, he was too good a dramatist to let his music exist in a vacuum, and the solo instruments in *Se il padre perdei* have their place in conveying the emotional confusion that underlies Ilia's words. An aria like this, or Ilia's exquisite *Zeffiretti lusinghieri* which opens Act III, with their eloquent introductions and poetic repetitions, may seem to hold up the action unduly—and it is true that as he grew to maturity Mozart discarded formal elaboration of this kind. But here he is still working within a convention and style that thrives upon such musical richness, and these moments of Italianate expansion need to be felt as points of repose, rather like the soliloquies of spoken drama, in his dignified overall conception of *opera seria*.

And there were theatrical practicalities to discuss as well.

Mozart   13 November 1780. I write in the greatest haste, for I am not yet dressed and must be off to Count Seeau's. Cannabich, Quaglio and Le Grand are lunching there too in order to make the necessary arrangements for the opera. . . .

To Act I, Scene 8, Quaglio has made the same objection that we made originally—I mean, that it is not fitting that the king should be quite alone in the ship. If the Abbé thinks that he can be reasonably represented in the terrible storm, forsaken by everyone, without a ship, alone and exposed to the greatest peril, then let it stand—only in that case please cut out the ship, for he really cannot be alone in one. If the other situation is adopted, a few generals, who are in his confidence, must land with him. Then he must address a few words to his people and desire them to leave him, which in his present melancholy situation is quite natural.   [*Id:* 662–3]

The scene in which Idomeneo lands on Cretan soil, having saved himself from shipwreck by vowing that he will sacrifice to Neptune the first living thing that he meets on landing, obviously had to be carefully organized in order to give full effect to the protagonist's first appearance in the opera. After referring the matter to Varesco, Mozart's father replied:

Leopold Mozart   Idomeneo must land from the ship with his retinue. Then follow the words which he speaks to them, upon which they withdraw. You will remember that I sent off this objection to Munich; but your reply was that storms and seas pay no attention to the laws of etiquette. This, I admit, would be true, if a shipwreck were to take place. But the vow has released them. This landing will produce a very fine effect.   [*Id:* 666]

At this point, however, it was the scene that followed Raaff's entry— the fatal meeting between Idomeneo and his son—that was the focus of the composer's anxiety. This was the moment on which the whole of the rest of the drama depended, and Raaff's ability to carry it off was of crucial importance. But Mozart was no doubt haunted by memories of the first time he had seen the old man in rehearsal at Mannheim, 'in his everyday clothes, with his hat on and a stick in his hand', singing his arias carelessly, and in the recitatives 'every now and then giving a kind of shout which I could not bear', and he had no reason to be optimistic about his handling of the long recitative which Varesco's libretto here required.   [*Id*: 551]

Nor, apparently, could he hope for much help from the other participant in the scene.

Mozart   I have not, it is true, the honour of being acquainted with the hero Dal Prato; but from the description I have been given of him I should say that Ceccarelli [the Salzburg castrato] is almost the better of the two; for often in the middle of an aria his breath gives out; and, mark you, he has never been on any stage—and Raaff is like a statue. Well, just picture to yourself the scene in Act I.   [*Id*: 660]

Leopold Mozart   What you say about the singers is really distressing. Well, your musical composition will have to make up for their deficiencies. . . .   [*Id*: 661]

And indeed, wherever possible, Mozart did make an effort to meet his singers half-way.

Mozart   There is still one more alteration, for which Raaff is responsible. He is right, however, and even if he were not some courtesy ought to be shown to his grey hairs. He was with me yesterday. I ran through his first aria for him and he was very well pleased with it. But the man is old and can no longer show off in an aria like the one in Act II—*Fuor del mar ho un mar nel seno*. So, as he has no aria in Act III, and his first act aria cannot be as cantabile as he would like owing to the expression of the verses, he wishes to have a pretty one to sing [at the end of the opera] after his last words 'O Creta fortunata! O me felice!'   [*Id*: 664]

Like his first recitative, Raaff's last aria was to haunt Mozart's correspondence for nearly two months: Varesco only produced it with great reluctance, and in the end it was cut because there simply wasn't room for it. But for the time being Mozart was concentrating on the completion of Act II. *Fuor del mar*, the great virtuoso aria in which Idomeneo, saved from the sea, faces the storm raging in his soul, was only written after the composer's arrival in Munich, and at this stage Raaff had not yet seen it. Mozart himself was delighted with it, and later called it 'the most superb aria in the opera. . . . [It] is very well adapted to the words. You hear the *mare* and the *mare funesto*—and the musical *passages* suit *minacciar,* for they entirely express the idea of "threatening"' Yet in spite of its impressive display of coloratura, the piece was carefully tailored to exhibit Raaff's failing powers to best advantage and, when he did see it, it evidently went down well. [*Id: 698*]

Mozart   Yesterday morning Mr Raaff came to see me again in order to hear the aria in Act II. The fellow is as infatuated with it as a young and ardent lover might be with his fair one, for he sings it at night before going to sleep and in the morning when he awakes. . . . He said to Herr von Viereck, the Chief Equerry, . . . '*Hitherto both in recitatives and arias I have always been accustomed to alter my parts to suit me, but here everything remains as it was written, for I cannot find a note which does not suit me, etc.*' *Enfin,* he is as happy as a king. [*Id: 677–8*]

And Mozart was equally prepared to accommodate the other senior member of the cast, Domenico de' Panzacchi, who was to sing the minor role of Arbace.

Mozart   Come in! Why, it's Herr Panzacchi, who has already paid me three visits and has just invited me to lunch on Sunday. . . . He has enquired very meekly whether instead of 'se la sa' he may not sing 'se co la'—Well, why not 'ut re mi fa sol la'? . . .

We must do what we can to oblige this worthy old fellow. He would like to have his recitative in Act III lengthened by a couple of lines, which owing to the *chiaro e oscuro* and his being a good actor will have a capital effect. . . . [*Id: 669, 682*]

The female members of the cast, on the other hand, seem to have provided no problems.

Mozart   Now for a cheerful story. Madame Dorothea Wendling [Ilia] is *arcicontentissima* with her scene [*Padre, germani,* at the beginning of Act I] and insisted on hearing it played three times in succession. . . . [*Id:* 660]

Lisel Wendling [Elettra] has also sung through her two arias half a dozen times and is delighted with them. I have it from a third party that the two Wendlings praised their arias very highly—and as for Raaff, he is my best and dearest friend! But to my molto amato castrato Dal Prato I shall have to teach the whole opera. He has no notion how to sing a cadenza effectively, and his voice is so uneven! [*Id:* 664]

The day before yesterday he sang at the concert—most disgracefully. I bet you the fellow will never get through the rehearsals, still less the opera. The rascal is rotten to the core. . . . When he comes here I have to sing with him . . . as if he were a child. He hasn't got a farthing's worth of method. [*Id:* 669]

Meanwhile, Mozart's work on the score had reached the finale of Act II; Neptune, his patience running out, sends a storm and a terrible monster to exact the fulfilment of Idomeneo's vow, and the people of Crete demand a victim. One of the touching aspects of the exchange of letters between Mozart and his father is Leopold's evident delight in the more spectacular aspects of his son's opera, but like many another eighteenth-century musician, he was unable to see much beyond their purely static effect. For the composer these were dynamic scenes and his whole concern was their dramatic impact. At the critical moment when Idomeneo confesses that it is he who is responsible for the fury of the gods, Varesco had followed the usual Metastasian formula and allowed the composer space for lyrical expansion. But Mozart would have none of it.

Mozart   In the last scene of Act II Idomeneo has an aria or rather a sort of cavatina between the choruses. Here it will be *better* to have a mere recitative, well supported by the instruments. For in this scene which will be the finest in the whole opera (on account of the action and grouping which were settled recently with Le Grand), there will be so much noise and confusion on the stage that an aria at this particular point would cut a poor figure—and moreover there is the thunderstorm, which is not likely to subside during Herr Raaff's aria, is it ? The effect, therefore, of a recitative between the choruses will be infinitely better. [*Id:* 664]

'A mere recitative' sounds odd to a musical generation that has come to regard the accompanied recitatives of *Idomeneo* as one of the glories of the work. Never again, except occasionally in *Don Giovanni,* did Mozart manage this type of orchestral declamation with such intensity and resource. Clearly, the model of Gluck—with the music of whose *Alceste* he was quite as familiar as Varesco was with the libretto—was of crucial importance, but the recitatives of *Idomeneo* inhabit a more direct, newer world than the statuesque utterances of the older composer.

And the 'noise and confusion on the stage'? It was not long since Mozart had described choral writing as his 'haupt-favorit-Composition', and in a scene like this the chorus plays a real part in the action. Working together with Le Grand, Mozart did not place the chorus in the middle of the stage as a stylised, compact body in the accepted Italian manner. He divided them visibly into two sections, detached and opposing each other, to give the naturalistic impression of a passionate, excited mass of people, and he added at the end a transforming touch in the panic-stricken flight of the Cretan people and the wonderful dissolving close to the act. It is a scene that must have exceeded the wildest of Leopold Mozart's expectations.

Indeed it seems that the reach of Mozart's youthful imagination was sometimes a source of nervous concern in Salzburg, and certainly the fierce intensity with which his son was living and working prompted Leopold to offer anxious fatherly advice.

Leopold Mozart   Take care of your health, and do not go to bed too late. Young people, particularly when they are engaged in mental work, must have their proper amount of sleep. Otherwise their nerves become weak, their stomach gets out of order and they fall into a decline. If people come in and settle on you in the morning, just stop it. That sort of thing is no joke, for in the end you will have to compose until you are half dead—and how can you know how much you may not have to alter? [*Id: 673*]

I advise you when composing to consider not only the musical, but also *the unmusical public.* You must remember that for every *ten real connoisseurs* there are a *hundred ignoramuses.* So do not neglect the so-called *popular* style, which tickles *long ears.* [*Id: 685*]

But Mozart showed no signs of slowing down, and in the end the only way in which he followed his father's advice was the one least likely to find favour with that crusty old gentleman—the humouring of the longer-eared ignoramuses by the continual removal from Varesco's libretto of whatever he thought they might find tedious.

Mozart   The scene between father and son in Act I and the first scene in Act II between Idomeneo and Arbace are both too long. They would certainly bore the audience, particularly as in the first scene both the actors are bad and in the second one of them is; besides they only contain a narrative of what the spectators have already seen with their own eyes. These scenes are being printed as they stand. But I should like the Abbate to indicate how they may be shortened—and as drastically as possible—for otherwise I shall have to shorten them myself.   [*Id:* 693]

Once again it was a question of Idomeneo's landing and the fatal meeting with Idamante—a scene that was not only long, but written entirely in recitative and therefore specially vulnerable to poor acting. But Leopold Mozart, who did not have to deal personally with Raaff and Dal Prato, was incensed by this summary treatment of Varesco's drama.

Leopold Mozart   I sent for Varesco at once, for I received your letter only at five o'clock this evening, and the mail coach leaves tomorrow morning. We have considered the first recitative in all its bearings and we both find no occasion to shorten it. . . . If you consult the draft, you will see that it was suggested that this recitative should be lengthened a little, so that father and son should not recognise one another too quickly.   [*Id:* 694]

After grudgingly suggesting a possible cut, he adds:

Leopold Mozart   In this way the recitative will be shortened by a *minute*, yes, in puncto, by a whole minute. Great gain, forsooth! Or do you want to make father and son run up to one another like Harleqin and Brighella disguised as servants in a foreign country, meeting, recognising and embracing each other all in a moment? Remember that this is one of the finest scenes in the whole opera . . . on which the entire remaining story depends.   [*Id:* 695]

Not, perhaps, entirely unreasonable. But Mozart was realistic.

Mozart   In regard to the scenes which are to be shortened, it was not
my suggestion, but one to which I have consented—my reason being
that Raaff and Dal Prato spoil the recitative by singing it without any
spirit or fire, and *so* monotonously. They are the most wretched actors
that ever walked on a stage.   [*Id:* 697–8]

This scene was obviously sacrificed to the ineptitude of its first performers, but in general Mozart's cuts were based on a shrewd understanding of dramatic necessity. He knew instinctively what Varesco never
understood: that music, whatever it may add, is bound to slow up words
and action, and that the validity of opera depends always upon a proper
relation between the idea and its musical expansion. And so he continued to jump at every opportunity to tighten and compress, particularly in
the last scene of all, with its sudden interruption by the voice from the
underworld, where any dragging out could be fatal.

Mozart   The second duet is to be omitted altogether—and indeed with
more profit than loss to the opera. For, if you read through the scene,
you will see that it obviously becomes limp and cold by the addition
of an aria or a duet, and very *gênant* for the other actors who have
to stand about doing nothing. Besides, the noble struggle between
Ilia and Idamante would be too long and thus lose its whole force.
                                                              [*Id:* 662]

Leopold Mozart   For a long time Varesco refused to touch the duet. But
I have persuaded him. Idamante and Ilia have still a very short discussion consisting of a few words in recitative, which is interrupted,
as it were, by a subterranean rumbling, and then the utterance of the
subterranean voice is heard.   [*Id:* 666]

But before long Mozart was getting worried about the subterranean
voice as well.

Mozart   Tell me, don't you think that the speech of the voice is too long?
Consider it carefully. Picture to yourself the theatre and remember
that the voice must be terrifying—must penetrate—that the audi-

ence must believe that it really exists. Well how can this effect be produced if the speech is too long, for in that case the listeners will become more and more convinced that it means nothing. If the speech of the Ghost in Hamlet were not so long, it would be far more effective. [*Id:* 674]

Mozart's father agreed, and gave Varesco his 'candid opinion'. His own enthusiasm for this scene is very touching.

Leopold Mozart   It can be a masterpiece of harmony. . . . I assume that you will choose very deep wind-instruments to accompany the voice. How would it be if, after the slight subterranean rumbling, the instruments sustained, or rather began to sustain, their notes *piano* and then made a crescendo such as might almost inspire terror, while after this and during the decrescendo the voice would begin to sing? And there might be a terrifying crescendo at every phrase uttered by the voice. Owing to the rumble, which must be short and rather like the shock of a thunderbolt, the attention of the audience is aroused; and this attention is intensified by the introduction of a quiet, prolonged and then swelling and very alarming wind-instrument passage, and finally becomes strained to the utmost when, behold! *a voice* is heard. Why, I seem to see and hear it. [*Id:* 666, 700]

In spite of such seductive promptings, Mozart kept his feet firmly on the ground. The use of trombones, which were not at this period normal members of the orchestra (he had a job getting Count Seeau to pay for them), and were mainly confined to church ceremonial, automatically gave him an atmosphere of solemnity and the supernatural; so he later used them in *Don Giovanni*, so Gluck had used them in the oracle scene of *Alceste* (where Mozart no doubt got the idea). But the seventy bars he originally composed had to be reduced again and again before he was satisfied, and only ten days before the first performance he wrote:

Mozart   The speech of the oracle is still far too long and I have therefore shortened it; but Varesco need not know anything of this because it will all be printed just as he wrote it. [*Id:* 708]

Rehearsals with orchestra had begun on 1 December and on the 16th the first two acts were tried out in 'a spacious room at court'. The Elector took a personal interest and was present at several rehearsals.

Mozart   After the first act [he] called out to me quite loudly, 'Bravo!'. When I went up to kiss his hand he said: 'This opera will be charming and cannot fail to do you honour'. As he was not sure whether he could remain much longer, we had to perform the aria with obbligatos for wind-instruments [*Se il padre perdei*] and the thunderstorm at the [end] of Act II, when he again expressed his approval in the kindest manner and said with a laugh: 'Who would believe that such great things could be hidden in so small a head?' . . .

   . . . I have heard too from a very good source that on the evening after the rehearsal he spoke of my music to everyone with whom he conversed, saying: 'I was quite surprised. No music has ever made such an impression on me. It is magnificent . . .'.   [*Id: 698, 701*]

But Mozart was still at work on his third act.

Mozart   My head and my hands are so full of Act III that it would be no wonder if I were to turn into a third act myself. This act alone has cost me more trouble than a whole opera, for there is hardly a scene in it which is not extremely interesting. . . .

   No doubt we shall have a good many points to raise when it is staged. For example, in scene 6, after Arbace's aria, I see that Varesco has 'Idomeneo, Arbace, etc.' But how can Arbace reappear [when he has only just left]? Fortunately he can stay away altogether. But for safety's sake I have composed a somewhat longer introduction to the High Priest's recitative. After the mourning chorus the King and all his people go away; and in the following scene the directions are, '*Idomeneo in ginocchione nel tempio*'. That is quite impossible. He must come in with his whole suite. A march must be introduced here, and I have therefore composed a very simple one for two violins, viola, cello and two oboes, to be played *a mezza voce*.   [*Id: 703–4*]

But the most persistently recurring problem in the final scene was Raaff's last aria, the 'pretty one' that he wanted to sing at the very end. Varesco's first verses had met with scant approval.

Mozart   The aria for Raaff which you have sent me pleases neither him nor me. . . . It is not at all what we wished it to be; I mean, it ought to express peace and contentment . . . for we have seen, heard and felt throughout the whole opera quite enough about the misfortune which Idomeneo has had to endure. . . . We should like to have a peaceful, quiet aria. Even if it only has one part—so much the better; in every aria the second part has to take the form of a middle section—and indeed it often gets in my way.   [*Id:* 674, 678]

Nor did the second attempt fare much better.

Mozart   Raaff is the best and most honest fellow in the world, but so tied to old-fashioned routine that flesh and blood cannot stand it. . . . The other day he was very much annoyed about some words in his last aria—*rinvigorir*—and *ringiovenir*—and especially *vienmi a rinvigorir*—five *i*'s. It is true that at the end of an aria this is very unpleasant. . . .

I have just had a bad time with him over the quartet. The more I think of this quartet, as it will be performed on the stage, the more effective I consider it, and it has pleased all those who have heard it played on the clavier. Raaff alone thinks it will produce no effect whatever. He said to me when we were by ourselves: '*Non c'e da spianar la voce. It gives me no scope*'. As if in a quartet the words should not be spoken much more than sung. That kind of thing he does not understand at all. All I said was "My very dear friend, if I knew of one single note which ought to be altered in this quartet, I would alter it at once. But so far there is nothing in my opera with which I am so pleased . . . and when you have once heard it sung as a whole, you will talk very differently. I have taken great pains to serve you well in your two arias; I shall do the same with your third one. . . . But as far as trios and quartets are concerned, the composer must have a free hand".   [*Id:* 698–9]

Despite his insistence on dramatic economy, Mozart was clear in his mind about the places where musical expansion was essential to his purpose. In fact, the turn in the plot which gives rise to this ensemble— Idamante's exile and the permanent separation of father from son, of mistress from lover—never takes place: Idomeneo is a tragedy which by the intervention of supernatural powers ends happily. Though this was a normal convention of eighteenth-century opera, it inevitably deprived the composer of the tragic climax which the drama demanded, and in this harrowing piece of music Mozart seems to have found a moment of truth where he might for once sum up the emotions by which all his four main characters are oppressed. He himself preferred it to any piece in the opera; he took special care over its performance (one evening at the Wendlings he rehearsed it no less than six times in succession), and it is said that, in his later years, he found it so disturbing that he could hardly bear to hear it sung.

Meanwhile, however, Mozart's letters were getting a tetchy reaction in Salzburg.

Leopold Mozart   Signor Raaff is far too pernickety. I needn't say anything about the quartets and so forth, for which diction and action are far more essential than great singing ability or his everlasting '*spianar la voce*'. . . . In regard to '*vienmi a rinvigorir*' it is true there are five *i*'s, but it is also true that I can pronounce the phrase twenty times without any inconvenience, in fact with the greatest rapidity and ease. . . . Basta! To please everyone the devil himself may go on altering and altering.   [*Id:* 700]

Varesco later complained that he had copied out his entire libretto four times, and even then been asked to make further changes. But by now the third act really was done, and on 18 January, Mozart wrote to his father:

Mozart   The rehearsal of Act III went off splendidly. It was considered much superior to the first two acts. But the libretto is too long and consequently the music also (as I have been saying all along). Therefore Idamante's [last] aria is to be omitted; in any case it is out of place there. . . . The removal of Raaff's last aria too is even more to be regretted.   [*Id:* 708]

One can only imagine how this last piece of news went down in Salzburg.

In the end, it was sheer lack of time that precipitated the cuts which saved *Idomeneo* from the longueurs of the conventional eighteenth-century finale and forced upon Mozart a dramatic economy for which he was anyhow feeling the need. After all, once the oracle has spoken, there is little left for the principal characters to do but express their joy and wonder at this miraculous outcome, and in a few brief rapturous phrases over a single sustained chord they do just this, accepting without fuss and without emotional elaboration a conclusion inspired by love. Even so, Mozart must surely have regretted the loss of Idomeneo's aria, at last completed to Raaff's satisfaction after so much discussion, and even more perhaps Elettra's, which was deleted during rehearsals because it was difficult to stage. Elettra is the one character for whom the opera ends in genuine tragedy. Continually thwarted in her love for Idamante, she has existed throughout mainly as a vehicle for the expression of tragic intensity, and in this capacity Mozart provided her with some of the most violently passionate music he was ever to write: in her last, savage outburst of fury and jealousy he finds a final release for the tragic emotions implicit, though divinely evaded, in the conclusion of his drama.

After the première of *Idomeneo*, which took place on 29 January 1781 (with Leopold Mozart as an enthusiastic but perhaps embarrassingly paternal spectator), six further performances were scheduled in Munich of which only two seem to have taken place. In fact, during Mozart's lifetime the opera had a limited success. In Vienna the composer could obtain only a private performance, though he rewrote the role of Idamante for a tenor, and made various revisions. In his own heart, however, the opera always retained a special place. Many years later, when Vincent and Mary Novello visited his widow, she told them that the happiest time of his life was when he was in Munich writing *Idomeneo*, and that this, of all his works, was the one he preferred 'perhaps most of all'.

[Novello: 76]

In his enthusiasm at this first great operatic opportunity, and with an outstanding body of musicians at his disposal, Mozart had been able to satisfy his 'burning ambition'—pouring into this exuberantly youthful work musical ideas in abundance, perhaps more, sometimes, than were demonstrably called for by the dramatic situations of his libretto. He never (with the exception of the hurriedly written *Clemenza di Tito*) attempted another tragic opera on this scale. But from the nobility and high pathos of *Idomeneo* he gained an insight into classical, tragic beauty which enriched all his later works. The opera of his maturity in which he came closest to the spirit of tragedy is *Don Giovanni*, but there the framework of emotions is expanded to include many other facets of the human condition. *Don Giovanni* is a superb—some might say *the* superb—instance of Mozart's capacity to span the whole range of human feeling. But *Idomeneo* remains the place where his music explores, as never before or after, the essence of classical passion.

W. A. MOZART

Doris Stock del. 1789   *Eduard Mandel sc. 1853*

Verlag und Eigenthum von E.H.Schroeder in Berlin.

Mozart in 1789

Le Nozze di Figaro

In October 1781, Mozart was again in trouble with a librettist. He had arrived in Vienna in March, hopeful, ambitious, and flushed with the success of *Idomeneo* only six weeks earlier. True, he was still an employee in the household of the Archbishop of Salzburg, but he was thankful to be rid of the stifling atmosphere of Salzburg itself, and in any case his years of servitude were nearly at an end; less than three months later, after a shocking display of unarchiepiscopal behaviour, he was quite literally kicked out of the archbishop's antechamber and found himself, at the age of twenty-five, for the first time in his life free, independent of his family—and wholly unsupported.

In the new world that lay before him opera, as usual, was his prime target. But the rich tradition of Viennese theatre, with its heady mixture of Italian opera, French plays, Viennese pantomimes and German musical comedies, had recently succumbed to the reforming zeal of the liberal Emperor Joseph II; the popular theatre, and with it the Italian operatic company, had been banished from the Burgtheater and a German-speaking national company established in its place. As a result, Mozart's first Viennese opera, at least since his childhood days, was the German singspiel *Die Entführung aus dem Serail*—and it was trouble with the libretto of *Entführung* that prompted reflections which, with hindsight, look almost prophetic.

Mozart   I don't know—but I think that in an opera the poetry must be absolutely the obedient daughter of the music. Why are Italian comic operas so successful everywhere—in spite of those wretched librettos? . . . Because in them the music reigns supreme, and you forget everything else. Certainly an opera will always be more enjoyable when the plan of the piece has been well worked out—but the words must be written expressly for the music and not just stuck in here and there for the sake of some miserable rhyme; that way, God knows, whatever their literary merits, they contribute nothing to the success of a theatrical performance—on the contrary, they can do it a lot of harm—I mean when words, or even complete strophes, ruin the composer's whole idea. Verses are no doubt the indispensable element for [operatic] music, but rhymes—simply for the sake of rhyming—can certainly be the most damaging. Those gentlemen who go to work in this pedantic fashion will always come to grief, and the music with them.

The best thing of all is when a good composer, who understands something about the stage and is capable of making a few useful suggestions, collaborates with an intelligent poet, that true Phoenix. . . .

[*Mozart, III: 167*]

It was only a couple of months later, in the last weeks of 1781, that the true Phoenix arrived in Vienna.

Lorenzo Da Ponte was thirty-two years old, penniless, unknown, and so far without a libretto or even a play to his credit. Born Emanuele Conegliano, he came from a Venetian Jewish family which had converted to Christianity for practical reasons, had received a thorough education as the protégé of his local bishop and been ordained a priest at the end of it. An attractive, witty and plausible young man, with a growing reputation as a poet and a taste for liberal politics and married women, he never once allowed his priestly vocation to interfere with his amorous adventures, which were numerous, complicated and risky, and it was in fact as the result of a particularly tangled affair that he had been banished from Venice in 1779. After a period of literary and amorous dalliance in Gorizia and a brief but disappointing stay in Dresden, he turned up in Vienna bearing a letter of recommendation to Antonio Salieri. It was a valuable introduction, for Salieri, who had until recently been in charge of the Italian opera company, was a favourite with the Emperor. For the time being, however, his influence on the operatic scene was limited by Joseph's enthusiasm for the German theatre, and during his first few months in Vienna, Da Ponte was obliged to kick his heels and do his best to make influential friends (like the eighty-three-year-old Metastasio).

Meanwhile *Entführung*, given at the Burgtheater in July 1782, scored an immediate hit with the Viennese public, and Mozart gleefully wrote to his father that the first two performances had brought in more than 1,200 gulden. But its success did not go uncontested: Mozart reported a cabal against it on the first two nights—which his Czech friend and biographer, Franz Niemetschek, attributed to the supporters of the rival Italian operatic faction—and the Emperor is reputed to have delivered himself of the famous dictum 'Too beautiful for our ears and an extraordinary number of notes, dear Mozart'. 'Just as many, Your Majesty, as are necessary', replied Mozart, with what Niemetschek calls 'that noble dignity and frankness which so often go with great genius', but what we might be more inclined to regard as typically cocky self-confidence.

[*Niemetschek: 34*]

In any case, the triumph of *Entführung* turned out to be an exception in the brief history of the National-Singspiel at the Burgtheater; Joseph's reforms had not been universally popular, and less than a year later he tacitly accepted failure and re-established the Italian opera with Salieri again as its director. By the end of 1782 change was already in the air.

Mozart   . . . At Prince Galitzin's Count Rosenberg [the High Chamberlain and Director of Court Theatres] spoke to me himself and suggested that I should write an Italian opera. I have already arranged to get the latest opera buffa texts from Italy to choose from, but I haven't received any yet. . . . Some Italian singers are coming here at Easter. . . .   [*Mozart, III: 244*]

But he was still uncertain—'I don't believe the Italian opera will keep going for long,' he wrote a few weeks later, and he flirted with the idea of another German libretto. Only when the Emperor's new operatic initiative actually got off the ground, in April 1783, does he seem to have been convinced.

Mozart   The Italian opera buffa has started again and it's very popular. The buffo [bass] is particularly good—his name is Benucci. I have gone through at least a hundred libretti—probably more—but found practically nothing that satisfies me. At the very least a lot of alterations would have to be made, and even if a poet would agree to do them it would probably be easier for him to write something completely new—and new, in my opinion, is always better in the end.

Our poet here is now a certain Abbate Da Ponte. For the time being he has a tremendous job revising pieces for the theatre, and he has to write *per obbligo* an entirely new libretto for Salieri which he won't finish for two months. He has promised after that to write a new one for me. But who knows whether he will be able to keep his word—or will want to? As you are aware, these Italian gentlemen are very civil to your face. Enough, we know them! If he is in league with Salieri, I'll never get anything out of him.   [*Id*: 268]

When asked by the Emperor at his first interview how many plays he had written, Da Ponte answered frankly 'None, Sire'—a reply which seems to have amused Joseph, though it is true that at this stage Da Ponte had everything to learn. The pieces he had to revise, at least ten of which were put on in the first nine months of the new company's existence, gave him no very high opinion of the competition.

Da Ponte   Poor Italy, what stuff they were! No plot, no characters, no interest, no scenic effects, no grace of language or style, and though they were intended to make people laugh you might have thought they were better suited to make them weep. There wasn't a line in these miserable concoctions that contained any touch of charm, any show of fancy, any elegant witticism that could in any way induce a desire to laugh. They were so many masses of insipid conceits and fatuous tomfoolery.   [*Da Ponte, 1918, I:* 96]

It was of course Salieri's influence which had obtained for Da Ponte the position of poet to the new Italian company, and as its director it was in fact perfectly natural that he should have first claim on Da Ponte's time. But Mozart always regarded Salieri with deep suspicion, and certainly his position in Vienna made him a formidable adversary; he was a crafty operator whose penchant for intrigue found ready material in a society teeming with rivalries and conflicting personalities—from the Emperor and Count Rosenberg to the theatrical functionaries, singers, librettists and composers who lived in, visited or just passed through this restless city. And it was a society in which Da Ponte was soon cutting a distinctive figure: 'small, slender, with quicksilver movements and dark, fiery, southern eyes', a chance observer remembered years later, '[speaking in] a broken German that showed he was Italian . . . he seemed always to be watching to see what impression he was making'. He must have been an easy target for caricature, and the young Irish tenor Michael Kelly, one of the singers Joseph had engaged for his company, was unable to resist the temptation.   [*Hodges: 86–7*]

The setting is the performance of an opera for which Da Ponte himself had written the libretto.

Kelly   In his opera, there was a character of an amorous eccentric poet, which was allotted to me; at the time I was esteemed a good mimic, and particularly happy in imitating the walk, countenance and attitudes of those whom I wished to resemble. My friend, the poet, had a remarkably awkward gait, a habit of throwing himself (as he thought) into a graceful attitude, by putting his stick behind his back and leaning on it; he had also, a very peculiar, rather dandyish, way of dressing; for in sooth, the Abbé stood mighty well with himself, and had the character of a consummate coxcomb; he had also, a strong lisp and broad Venetian dialect.

The first night of the performance, he was seated in the boxes, more conspicuously than was absolutely necessary. . . . As usual, on the first night of a new opera, the Emperor was present, and a numerous auditory. When I made my entrée as the amorous poet, dressed exactly like the Abbé in the boxes, imitating his walk, leaning on my stick, and aping his gestures, and his lisp, there was a universal roar of laughter and applause; and after a buzz round the house, the eyes of the whole audience were turned to the place where he was seated. The Emperor enjoyed the joke, laughed heartily, and applauded frequently during the performance; the Abbé was not at all affronted, but took my imitation of him in good part, and ever after we were on the best of terms.   [*Kelly*, I: 235–6]

A nice example of diplomatic dissimulation, to judge from Da Ponte's testy reaction when this description was published in Kelly's *Reminiscences* many years later. But for a man to whom personal appearances were so important, the temptation to be all things to all men was never far away, and Mozart seems to have sensed this from the start.

In any case, nothing was to be expected from Da Ponte for the time being, and in his frustration Mozart made the surprising suggestion that his father should turn once more to the librettist who had given them so much trouble with *Idomeneo*, the Salzburg Court Chaplain Abbate

Varesco. The one essential condition was 'that the whole story should be really comic . . . , for I know the taste of the Viennese'—though quite why Mozart should have thought Varesco was likely to produce anything even remotely comic is a mystery. The outline he received six weeks later bore the unpromising title *The Goose of Cairo* (*L'oca del Cairo*), but Varesco had hardly begun work on it before Mozart was grasping at yet another operatic straw, this time from an unidentified 'Italian poet' (not Da Ponte) for whose libretto *Lo sposo deluso* he drafted an overture and four numbers before he lost interest. For *L'oca del Cairo* he completed almost the whole of the first act before deciding that a scenario in which the union of two loving couples is achieved by the introduction into an impregnable fortress of the hero concealed inside a mechanical goose was not worth pursuing. 'I should have thought that far more natural and amusing results might be produced if he were to remain in human form', he commented to his father. One cannot but agree.   [*Mozart, III:* 294]

As a step in the direction of *Figaro*, however, both projects gave him valuable practice in handling the conventions of *opera buffa* which were being so successfully exploited by his Italian contemporaries in Vienna and Italy. But in the end, lack of human content consigned them both to oblivion. Besides, his popularity in Vienna as a keyboard player was now at its peak and for financial reasons he needed to exploit it while it lasted; in the two months after laying aside the *Goose* he gave twenty-two concerts, and during the next year produced and performed eight new piano concertos—all this as well as being newly married with two rapidly produced children (of which the first died after only three months). His father, visiting him in Vienna early in 1785, found the pace more than he could take and wrote to his daughter back in Salzburg:

Leopold Mozart   We never get to sleep before one o'clock—don't get up before nine—and eat at two or half past. Horrible weather! Every day there are concerts, and always teaching, music, composing and so on. Where do I fit in?

If only the concerts were over! It is impossible to describe all the rushing and bustling about. Since I got here your brother's fortepiano has been taken at least a dozen times to the theatre or to some other house. . . .   [*Id:* 379]

Nevertheless opera was never far from Mozart's thoughts and he followed events in Vienna attentively. Among the operas put on by Joseph's new company in the first years of its existence, the most successful and popular was a setting of Beaumarchais's comedy *Le barbier de Séville*, which had been given at the Burgtheater in the summer of 1783. Its composer, the celebrated Italian Giovanni Paisiello, was a musician Mozart particularly admired; he was by far the most accomplished of the many foreigners whose works competed for success in Vienna, and when it became known that he was to visit the city, on his way back to Naples after eight years as court composer in St Petersburg, Mozart was eager to meet him.

Kelly   I had the pleasure of seeing him introduced to Mozart; it was gratifying to witness the satisfaction which they appeared to feel by becoming acquainted, the esteem which they had for each other was well known. The meeting took place at Mozart's house; I dined with them, and often afterwards enjoyed their society together.

[*Kelly, I: 238*]

Mozart was clearly determined to make the most of this distinguished connection.

Mozart   Herr Ployer, the agent, is giving a concert in the country . . . where Fräulein [Ployer] is playing her new concerto in G [K453] and I will play in the quintet [K452]; the two of us are then playing the grand sonata for two claviers. I shall pick up Paisiello in my carriage, so as to let him hear both my pupil and my compositions. . . .

[*Mozart, III: 318*]

And when Paisiello's new opera *Il Re Teodoro in Venezia* was given at the Burgtheater in August, Mozart was there.

Leopold Mozart   My son has been very ill. . . . At a performance of Paisiello's new opera he sweated so much that his clothes were drenched, and in the cold air outside he had to search for the servant who had his overcoat, as an order had meanwhile been given not to let servants into the theatre by the ordinary entrance. So not only my son, but a lot of other people caught rheumatic fever, which turned septic when not dealt with at once.   [*Id: 331*]

It is probable, however, that the effect on Mozart was more than merely physical. *Il Re Teodoro,* to a libretto by Da Ponte's rival Giambattista Casti, is remarkable for the vein of seriousness that is threaded through an essentially comic story, and it offered yet another angle on the unexplored possibilities of traditional *opera buffa*. But it was to be a year and more before Mozart's instrumental activities receded enough to allow for the ideas thrown up by *L'oca del Cairo*, *Lo sposo deluso*, Casti and Paisiello himself to bear fruit.

At last, on 3 November 1785, Leopold Mozart wrote to his daughter, now married and living in St Gilgen:

Leopold Mozart   I haven't had a single line from your brother. His last letter was dated September 14th. . . . The journalist I met a few days ago said: 'It is really astonishing to see how many compositions your son is publishing. In all the announcements of musical works I read nothing but Mozart . . .'. I couldn't say anything in return, as I knew nothing. . . . He said something too about a new opera. Basta! No doubt we shall hear about it.   [*Id: 439*]

And a week later:

Leopold Mozart   At last I have received a letter—a full twelve lines— from your brother. . . . He thanks us both for our good wishes and asks me particularly to make his excuses to you and tell you that he hasn't time to answer your letter at once. . . . He begs to be forgiven, but he is up to his eyes in work as he has to finish his opera *Le Nozze di Figaro*.   [*Id: 443*]

Pierre-Augustin Caron de Beaumarchais's comedy *La folle journée, ou Le mariage de Figaro* was written as a sequel to *Le Barbier de Séville* and deals with the later activities of mainly the same set of characters. Though it had been completed in 1781, public performance was banned by Louis XVI on the grounds of its persistent disrespect for authority, as a result of which it obtained a wide reputation for subversiveness in the years leading up to the Revolution. But there was nothing to stop people reading it, and in printed form it achieved a *succès de scandale* which was confirmed at the immensely successful first performance in 1784. When its production was proposed in Vienna soon afterwards, Joseph II, a more progressive monarch than his French brother-in-law, appears to have been concerned about the morals rather than the politics of the play, and the letter he wrote to his chief of police stops short of an outright ban.

Joseph II I understand that the well-known comedy *Le mariage de Figaro* is being proposed in a German translation for the Kärntner-thor Theatre. As this piece contains much that is offensive, I assume that the censor will either reject it altogether, or require such altera-tions as will enable him to take responsibility for its performance, and for the impression it makes on the public. [*Payer von Thurn:* 60]

As in Paris, however, the unexpurgated version was printed, and Joseph himself seems to have enjoyed the play in this form; Niemetschek says that he actually proposed it as a subject to Mozart (censorship in Vienna not being applied to operas with the same strictness as to plays). In any case, Mozart cannot have been blind to the attractions of a sequel to Paisiello's *Barbiere*, nor perhaps to the publicity offered by the con-troversial nature of the new play. Unfortunately he makes no mention of *Figaro* in the very few letters that have survived from the period of its composition—he had no need to write to his librettist, whose office in the Burgtheater was only a few streets away. Da Ponte, on the other hand, is full of information, laid out in the memoirs that he wrote (in two versions) more than thirty years later—after he had become (rather sur-prisingly) a grocer and general merchant, and (more credibly) a teacher of Italian, in Philadelphia and New York—and it is on this somewhat pre-carious source that we have to lean for the main contemporary evidence on the origins of the opera.

Da Ponte's first libretto for Salieri had been a disastrous failure, but during the ensuing two years the Emperor had continued to encourage him, directing his attention to the young Spanish composer Vicente Mar-tín y Soler, newly arrived from Italy, who was soon to become the most popular opera composer in Vienna. Da Ponte seems to have agreed to write a libretto for Martín, *Il burbero di buon cuore*, at about the same time as he began work with Mozart—or 'Mozzart', as he insisted on call-ing him to the end of his life—with whom he had already collaborated briefly in a text for the cantata *Davidde penitente*.

Da Ponte There were only two [composers] in Vienna who seemed worthy of my respect, Martín, the composer at this time favoured by [the Emperor] Joseph, and Volfgango Mozzart, whom I now had the opportunity of getting to know. . . . Although he was endowed with talents perhaps superior to those of any other composer in the world, past, present or future, [Mozzart] had always been prevented by the intrigues of his enemies from giving proof of his divine genius in Vienna, and remained obscure and unknown, like a precious jewel that hides the brilliance of its splendour buried in the bowels of the earth. I can never remember without joy and satisfaction that it was in large part due to my own perseverance and determination that Europe and the whole world owe the exquisite vocal compositions of this admirable genius. . . .

After the success of *Il burbero*, therefore, I went to Mozzart and . . . asked him if he would like to compose the music for a play that I would write for him.

'I should like to very much,' he replied at once, 'but I'm sure I would never get it accepted'.

'I'll look after that,' I said.

And so I began to think about the choice of two subjects which would be suitable for two composers, who were both of the highest genius but almost diametrically opposite to one another in their styles of composition. . . .   [*Da Ponte, 1918, I: 109–10*]

There was a brief interruption while he dealt reluctantly with an unavoidable call for another libretto, which he dashed off with little interest; its failure didn't surprise or discourage him, and he returned as soon as possible to Mozart and Martín.

Da Ponte   As regards the former, I saw at once that the immensity of his genius demanded a subject that was ample, wide-ranging and exalted in style. When we were talking it over one day, he asked me if I could easily adapt Beaumarchais' comedy *The Marriage of Figaro* [as a libretto]. I liked the idea a lot, and I promised to do what he asked. But there was a very great difficulty to be overcome. Only a few days before, the Emperor had forbidden the company at the German theatre to perform this very piece, which he said was too outspoken for a polite audience. So how could it now be suggested to him for an opera? . . . [In the end] I proposed that we should write both words and music secretly, and wait for a favourable opportunity to show it to the directors of the theatre, or even to the Emperor—which I boldly undertook to do myself. Martín was the only person I let into the secret, and because of the regard he felt for Mozzart he generously agreed to my putting off the writing of his opera until I had finished *Figaro*.

So I set to work, and as I wrote the words he composed the music for them. In six weeks it was all done. [*Id: 110–11*]

Though 'obscure and unknown' may seem a bit extreme, it is true that Mozart's reputation in Vienna, as an adult at least, was of relatively recent origin and still largely confined to concert appearances at the piano. And whatever we may think of Da Ponte's self-congratulations, we have to admit that without him 'Europe and the whole world' would never have seen three of Mozart's greatest masterpieces. But it is also clear that Da Ponte, in later years, took every opportunity to inflate the role he had played in Mozart's life—and that his memory is distinctly shaky in matters of detail.

To begin with, the Emperor's embargo on the play, which was anyhow not as absolute as Da Ponte claims, was dated 31 January 1785, so that Da Ponte's 'few days before' implies that his talks with Mozart began in early February. But Mozart's father was staying with his son in Vienna until the end of April and knew nothing about the project when he left, and a letter he received from Mozart as late as mid-September still makes no mention of an opera (though it is possible that the plan of secrecy had been extended to the not-always-discreet Leopold) And *Il burbero* was not performed until January 1786, which puts it well outside the framework of dates provided from other sources.

On the other hand, it is probably true that Mozart was the first to suggest Beaumarchais's play as a subject (Da Ponte would hardly have concealed the fact if he had done so himself), and it is not impossible that he drafted his score in six weeks, particularly if he had already had discussions with Da Ponte about the structure of the piece and any points of character and action that would affect the musical treatment. On the whole it seems likely that it was the commission to write *Il burbero*, rather than its performance, which first encouraged Da Ponte to approach Mozart, and that talks between the two men in the summer of 1785 led to a bout of intense composing activity towards the end of the year. 'No doubt according to his charming habit [my son] has kept putting things off and letting the time slip by', wrote Leopold irritably in November. 'So now he must get to work seriously, for Count Rosenberg is nagging him'.

[*Mozart, III: 444*]

Leopold Mozart   I know the piece; it is a very tiresome play and the translation from the French will certainly have to be altered freely if it is to be made effective for an opera. God grant the text turns out well; I have no doubt about the music. But there will be a lot of running about and discussion before he gets the libretto adjusted in the way he wants it.   [*Id: 443–4*]

In a rambling preface Beaumarchais introduces his work as 'a play that combines moralities of general effect and of detail spread on a sea of inalterable gaiety', and describes the basic plot in terms that suggest the traditions of *commedia dell'arte* from which ultimately it derives. But this is disingenuous.

Beaumarchais   I have always thought, and I still think, that it is impossible to obtain great pathos, or profound morality, or good, true comedy in the theatre without the strong situations that always arise from a clash of social principles in the subject being treated. . . .
Vices, abuses—they never change, but disguise themselves in a thousand forms behind the mask of a prevailing morality; to tear off this mask and reveal them for what they are—that is the noble task of the man who dedicates himself to the theatre. . . .

[*Beaumarchais: 110, 111*]

The subversive reputation of *Le mariage de Figaro* was to a great extent a product of the politically unstable times in which it appeared. The true core of the play is social rather than political satire, round which Beaumarchais weaves a drama that is fast-moving, funny and complex; a mixture of comedy, romance and trenchant social criticism that certainly needed pruning to make a workable operatic libretto.

Da Ponte   The limitations of time laid down for use in dramatic representations, the number of characters habitually employed, and various other prudent considerations of convention, place and public, are the reasons why I have not made a translation of this excellent comedy but rather an imitation, or let us say an extract.

I have therefore been obliged to reduce the sixteen actors of the play to eleven . . . and to omit not only an entire act but a number of delightful scenes as well as many of the witticisms and other pleasantries with which the original teems.   [*Da Ponte, 1956: 53*]

'Prudent considerations' presumably dictated the removal of the famous trial scene, in which Beaumarchais ridiculed the corruption and petty-mindedness of the French judiciary in the shape of the stuttering judge Brid'oison (reduced to Don Curzio in the opera). But the underlying conflict between force and cunning remains, and beneath the wit and the laughter the emphasis of the opera is squarely on the human predicament in a world dominated by rigid social distinctions: *Se vuol ballare, Signor Contino*, sings Figaro in his first aria, 'dance if you want to—but I'll play the tune'. And in this context one has to admire the adroit way in which Da Ponte side-steps the most contentious piece of all, Figaro's celebrated attack on Count Almaviva in Act V of the play.

Figaro   Just because you are a grand Seigneur you think yourself a god. Nobility, fortune, rank, position—how proud these things can make a man! But what have you done to deserve all this? You've gone to the trouble of being born, nothing more—for the rest you're just a man like any other! Whereas I, for God's sake, lost in the obscurity of the crowd—I have had to make use of more skill, more cunning, simply to survive than it has taken in the last hundred years to govern the whole of Spain. . . .   [*Beaumarchais: 224*]

These few sentences, however, form only a small part of a long and hopelessly unoperatic monologue; faced with the problem of reducing it to aria proportions, Da Ponte concentrated instead on the diatribe against women with which the same speech opens, and Figaro, his anger channeled in a less controversial direction, relieves his pent-up emotions in a bitter outburst against the deceitfulness of the female sex—*Aprite un po' quegli occhi*.

Da Ponte's view of the librettist's role was in fact remarkably like Mozart's own.

Da Ponte   Mozart knew very well that the success of an opera depends, FIRST OF ALL, ON THE POET: that without a good poem an *entertainment cannot be perfectly dramatic*, just as a picture cannot be good without possessing the merit of invention, design and a just proportion of the parts: that a composer, who is, in regard to a drama, what a painter is in regard to the colours, can never do that with effect, unless excited and animated by the words of a poet, whose province is to choose [though in this case of course he didn't] a subject susceptible of variety, incident, movement, and action; to prepare, to suspend, to bring about the catastrophe; to exhibit characters interesting, comic, well supported, and calculated for stage effect; to write his *recitativo* short, but substantial, his airs various, new, and well situated; *in fine*, his verses easy, harmonious, and almost singing of themselves, without all which requisites, the notes of the most sublime and scientific composer will not be felt by the heart. . . .

[*Della Chà*: 58–60]

And in the end it is to the heart that *Figaro* goes. Reframed by Da Ponte, the brilliant but artificial figures of Beaumarchais's comedy take on in Mozart's hands a totally new dimension. In Paisiello's opera Rosina, despite her elegance and charm, is still a sentimental girl in love with a man she believes to be a poor student. As the Countess Almaviva, she is a young wife whose natural high spirits are stifled by her husband's philandering; her disillusion cries aloud for stronger treatment, and with her first aria Mozart expresses real suffering.

The fact that there are details in *Porgi, amor* that recall Paisiello's cavatina for Rosina in *Il barbiere* only emphasizes the gulf that lies between the two composers. Such reminiscences may of course have been intended as a compliment to an admired colleague, or even a shrewd reference to a popular predecessor, and the same may be true of the similarity between Cherubino's *Voi che sapete* and the Count's serenade in *Il barbiere* (though here Mozart so far outstrips the simplicity of his model that any intended tribute rather backfires). The fact is that there are echoes of Paisiello, conscious or unconscious, scattered through the score of *Figaro,* and in any case, Mozart had a wide experience of contemporary music and an acquisitive musical memory—it doesn't greatly signify that the perky little rhythm which accompanies Susanna's emergence from the closet in the Countess's bedroom in Act II had appeared in a similar situation in Grétry's opera *L'amant jaloux,* given in Vienna four years earlier, or that a phrase from Gluck's ballet *Don Juan* was evidently the first thing that came into his head when he needed a fandango in Act III. Mozart was simply using the accepted musical language of his day—it's just that his handling of it is so much richer and more subtle that any scraps of remembered material are transmuted in his hands.

More revealing than any passing reminiscence is a self-quotation at the very heart of the Countess's role: the almost note-for-note transposition, at the beginning of *Dove sono,* of the opening of an *Agnus Dei* written six years earlier. Certainly no such feeling character as the Countess had appeared in *opera buffa* before. But it is evident from Da Ponte's introduction to his libretto that he and Mozart were aware they were doing something unusual in *Figaro.*

Da Ponte   In spite of all the care and the efforts of the maestro and myself, the opera will not be the shortest to be seen on [the Viennese] stage; for which we hope a sufficient excuse will be found in the breadth and grandeur of the drama, in the variety of the threads from which the action is woven, in the great profusion of musical numbers that were needed to give the actors enough to do, reduce the boredom and monotony of long recitatives, and express in varying colours the diverse passions that surface as the action develops—but above all, in our desire to offer what is almost a new form of theatre to a public of such refined taste and understanding.

[*Da Ponte, 1956: 53*]

It was a public to which the artists of the Italian company were already familiar. Luisa Laschi, an Italian soprano in her early twenties, had been 'much applauded' as Rosina in Paisiello's opera a year earlier, and her reappearance as the Countess promised a reassuring sense of continuity for the same audience. Both Francesco Benucci (of whom Mozart had a high opinion) and Stefano Mandini were old hands whom Joseph II had engaged for his original company in 1783, along with Michael Kelly and the 'English' soprano, Nancy Storace. In the words of the chronicler Johann Pezzl:

Pezzl   The performers at the opera are carefully chosen, but also well paid. Mandini and Benucci are the two most accomplished buffo actors to be seen anywhere. The star of this comic Pantheon has been, up until now, La Storace, a singer of Italian descent but born in London. She earned more than a thousand ducats a year. Though in fairness it has to be said that she sings very well, her figure is not to her advantage—a dumpy little person without any physical feminine charms except for a pair of large but not particularly expressive eyes. . . .   [*Pezzl*, 3: 421]

On the physical attractions of Nancy Storace, however, there were those who felt differently. The dilettante aristocrat Count Karl von Zinzendorf, noted in his diary:

Zinzendorf   The *inglesina*, Mlle Storace, pretty voluptuous figure, fine bosom, beautiful eyes, white neck, fresh mouth, lovely skin, the naivety and petulance of a child . . . sings like an angel. . . .
                                                   [*Landon:* 243]

Storace was the first Susanna, the crowning example of a type of soubrette role already well known to *opera buffa* audiences. And although Laschi, as the Countess, had the big arias and the final word, Storace was given the last aria, the infinitely touching *Deh vieni, non tardar*, and appeared in more scenes than anyone else as the pivotal figure in the three-way tug of war between Figaro, the Count and the Countess.

The joker in the pack is of course Cherubino, another survivor from the *commedia dell'arte* tradition but given a new lease of life, as well as a discreet but explicit sexual dimension, by Beaumarchais.

Beaumarchais   Still guided by nature, everything he touches has the power to agitate him. Perhaps he is no longer a child, but he isn't yet a man—and this is the moment I have chosen in order to engage the feelings of the audience without obliging anyone to blush. . . .
                                                   [*Beaumarchais:* 120]

For Cherubino's first aria, *Non so più cosa son, cosa faccio*, Da Ponte in fact did little more than adapt Beaumarchais's words into decent verse; it is Mozart's setting that finally transforms the traditional page of French farce into a boy palpitating on the brink of adolescence. We do not know whether Mozart had any particular singer in mind for the role because Dorotea Bussani, who eventually sang it, was a late addition to the company. She was the twenty-three-year-old wife of Francesco Bussani, the stage manager and general factotum of the Italian troupe, who was at a loss to find a fifth female singer and no doubt saw this as an opportunity to promote his new wife's career. Da Ponte, who regarded Francesco as a scheming opponent (which he probably was), allowed his distaste to rub off on Dorotea,

Da Ponte . . . who, though awkward and of little merit, by dint of grimaces and clowning, and perhaps by means more theatrical still, built up a large following among cooks, grooms, lackeys and wigmakers, and was therefore considered a jewel. [*Da Ponte, 1918, I: 139*]

Others were more charitable, allowing her 'a beautiful low voice' and 'a lovely figure', but she was not an experienced singer, and it is possible that her difficulties with *Non so più* resulted in its removal during the first performances of the opera—a cut that must have distressed Mozart, whose widow told Vincent Novello that it was one of his favourite arias. Francesco Bussani, on the other hand, as well as being the stage manager, was an experienced *buffo* bass and sang Doctor Bartolo, the role that most nearly follows the old traditions of *opera buffa*.

Bartolo had in fact been the chief comic role in Paisiello's *Barbiere*, and as such it had been taken by Francesco Benucci, the acknowledged star of the group and one of the great buffo actors of the late eighteenth century. His original inclusion in the company had been a matter of particular importance to Joseph II who, though a devoted admirer of the *inglesina*, told Count Rosenberg that Benucci was 'worth more than two Storaces'. But the role to which he now moved was a different proposition, for Mozart's Figaro soon reveals himself as very much more than the comic servant his first audience would have been expecting; if it is difficult to see the Count taking Cherubino seriously as a sexual rival, Figaro represents throughout a serious obstacle to the Count's amorous ambitions. And by the end of the opera, in spite of the misunderstanding with Susanna in the final scene, it is clear that Figaro's marriage is going to last—whereas we can't help wondering, for all the passionate expression of the Count's penitence and the moving generosity of his wife's forgiveness, whether the Almaviva marriage, in the long run, is going to change that much.

In some ways Stefano Mandini, who played the Count, had the most difficult role of all. A versatile singer who had sung Almaviva as a tenor in Paisiello's opera, he now repeated the role as a baritone for Mozart—

a switch from love-struck youth to domestic tyrant that presented him with a very different musical profile, ranging from the nearest that *Figaro* comes to the nobility of *opera seria* to a tenderness that, whatever its ultimate object, is for the moment touchingly sincere. Kelly remembered calling on the composer one evening:

Kelly   He said to me, 'I have just finished a little duet for my opera, you shall hear it'. He sat down to the piano, and we sang it. I was delighted with it, and the musical world will give me credit for being so, when I mention the duet, sung by Count Almaviva and Susan, *Crudel perchè finora farmi languir così*. A more delicious morceau was never penned by man, and it has often been a source of pleasure to me, to have been the first who heard it, and to have sung it with its greatly gifted composer.   [*Kelly, I*: 258–9]

The actual composition of *Figaro* had to be sandwiched, often hurriedly, between other pressing musical, social and domestic activities, and in circumstances of great financial stress. The young Thomas Attwood, who had recently arrived in Vienna as Mozart's pupil, recalled that 'in consequence of being so much over the table when composing he was obliged to have an upright Desk and stand there when he wrote. . .'. And one of Mozart's earliest biographers, Edward Holmes, drawing on equally personal sources, records that the finale of Act II, an ensemble over 900 bars long, 'occupied him for two nights and a day, during which he wrote without interruption', and that 'in the course of the second night he was seized with an illness which compelled him to stop'.

[*Landon*: 157; *Holmes*: 219]

The Act II finale in *opera buffa* was a sacred convention with which Da Ponte was already well acquainted.

Da Ponte   The finale, besides being intimately connected with the rest of the opera, is a kind of little comedy or drama in itself, and has to provide some new development of the plot which gives it special interest. It is here that the genius of the composer and the abilities of the singers must combine with the greatest dramatic effect. There is no recitative, everything is sung, and every kind of singing has to be included—adagio, allegro, andante, amabile, armonioso, strepitoso, arcistrepitoso, strepitosissimo—with which the finale almost always concludes. . . . By a law of theatrical dogma, the finale must provide for the appearance on the stage of all the singers, even if there are three hundred of them, one at a time, or in groups of two, three, six, ten, sixty, to sing solos, duets, trios, sextets, sessantets—and if the plot of the drama doesn't allow for this, then the poet has to find a way to make it allow for it, regardless of common sense, reason, and all the Aristotles on earth. . . .

[*Da Ponte, 1918: 97–8*]

But by the time he wrote *Figaro*, Da Ponte had learned from practical experience how to handle this complex art with mastery; the succession of scenes he produced gave Mozart the framework he needed to create a continuous movement that, for dramatic ingenuity, richness of comic invention and variety of musical texture—not to mention length—was in a different class from anything in the operas of his contemporaries or predecessors. And if this ensemble is the prime instance in *Figaro* of dramatic action continuously unfolding against an unbroken flow of music, the sextet in the following act is equally remarkable for the compactness with which it resolves a single confrontation. Figaro's discovery that he doesn't have to marry a woman old enough to be his mother by the discovery that she *is* his mother is an *opera buffa* situation of which Paisiello, or any of Mozart's contemporaries, would no doubt have made something very funny—as Mozart does. But at the same time he seizes this moment of high farce and expands the range of emotions to embrace the astonishment and pathos of a family reunited, and a general reconciliation from which only the Count is excluded in baffled frustration. In fact, so fully does he resolve the complexities of Figaro's family history that there is little left for Marcellina or Bartolo to do in the rest of the opera—though Marcellina, like Basilio (whose role is similarly dwindling), gets an aria in the last act out of deference to established *opera buffa* tradition. This is the only dramatic miscalculation in the opera, and a justifiable cut usually removes these superfluous additions to the wonderful, half-lit garden scene of Act IV, whose real and only purpose is to lead, through a last twist of intrigue, to the reconciliation of the Count and Countess themselves in the infinitely touching confrontation with which the opera ends.

What Mozart and Da Ponte set out to write may have been a comedy—the longest and most complicated comedy written till then, but a comedy none the less. What Mozart's music gives us, for the first time in the history of opera, is a group of human beings with whom we can really identify, in whose behaviour—good, bad, silly or simply expedient—we recognise characteristics that we know all too well in ourselves. *Don Giovanni* may be grander, *Così fan tutte* more sophisticated, *The Magic Flute* something else altogether; behind the laughter, there is no more human opera than *The Marriage of Figaro*.

By October 1785, whatever point its composition may have reached, *Figaro* had already been accepted for performance at the Burgtheater at an unspecified date in the future.

Da Ponte   As Mozart's luck would have it, there was a shortage of new scores at the theatre, and I seized the opportunity; without saying a word to anybody I set off to offer *Figaro* to the Emperor in person.

'What!' he said, 'Don't you know that Mozzart, though he is excellent in instrumental music, has only ever written one opera—and that wasn't anything much?'

'Without the favour of Your Majesty', I replied humbly, 'I too would not have written more than one drama in Vienna.'

'That's true,' he answered, 'but I have already forbidden this *Marriage of Figaro* to the German company.'

'Yes,' I said, 'but as I had to write a drama for music and not a play, I have had to leave out many scenes and shorten a lot of others, and I have omitted and shortened whatever might offend the decorum of an entertainment over which Your Sovereign Majesty presides. And as for the music, as far as I can judge it seems marvellously beautiful.'

'Very well,' he answered, 'if that's how it is, I'll trust your taste as to the music, and your discretion as to the morals. Have the score sent to the copyist.'

I rushed off to see Mozart, but I hadn't even finished giving him the good news before a footman from the Imperial Household arrived with a note requiring him to go at once to the palace with his score. He obeyed the royal command and arranged for the Emperor to hear several pieces, which pleased him tremendously—in fact, without exaggeration, astonished him.   [*Da Ponte, 1918, I: 111*]

The years have surely added glamour to this no doubt often repeated story—and quite how much of the score was at this stage in a condition to be played to anybody is questionable. But Da Ponte had made a point of ingratiating himself with Joseph II, and probably did act as intermediary between Mozart and the Emperor.

It seems that the first performance was originally intended for some time in January 1786—which would account for Count Rosenberg's 'nagging' in November. Why the performance was put back by three months is not known: possibly Luisa Laschi was late in getting back from Naples, where she had been allowed by Joseph to return for the Carnival season, or possibly there was some intrigue working against Mozart in Vienna. Kelly's story, however, that there were three operas 'now on the tapis', and that Mozart was 'as touchy as gunpowder and swore he would put the score of his opera into the fire if it was not produced first', is not supported by the facts; of the two competing operas that Kelly names, one had been performed in the preceding October and the other was not given until the following July. The opera that took *Figaro's* place in January was Da Ponte's own *Burbero di buon cuore* with music by Martín, whose relations with Mozart at this stage seem to have been perfectly amicable.

In any case, Mozart was busily engaged during the intervening period with the little operatic squib *Der Schauspieldirektor*, given at the Schönbrunn palace in February, and a revision of *Idomeneo* for private performance in March. Rehearsals for *Figaro* eventually started in April and continued for the best part of a month.

Kelly   It was allowed that never was opera stronger cast. I have seen it performed at different periods in other countries, and well too, but no more to compare with its original performance than light is to darkness. All the original performers had the advantage of the instruction of the composer, who transfused into their minds his inspired meaning.   [*Kelly, I: 258*]

Mozart's assistant, the young Joseph Weigl, later observed that 'to hear Mozart play the most difficult scores with that skill that was unique to him, and at the same time sing, and correct the mistakes of others, could not but excite the greatest admiration . . .', though it seems that in this case Weigl actually played the harpsichord himself for many of the rehearsals—presumably to allow the composer to give his full attention to the singers.   [*Deutsch: 446*]

Kelly   I remember at the first rehearsal of the full band, Mozart was on the stage with his crimson pelisse and gold-laced cocked hat, giving the time of the music to the orchestra. Figaro's song, 'Non più andrai, farfallone amoroso', Benucci gave with the greatest animation and power of voice. I was standing close to Mozart who, *sotto voce*, was repeating, Bravo! Bravo! Benucci; and when Benucci came to the fine passage 'Cherubino, alla vittoria, alla gloria militar', which he gave out with Stentorian lungs, the effect was electricity itself, for the whole of the performers on the stage, and those in the orchestra, as if actuated by one feeling of delight, vociferated 'Bravo! Bravo! Maestro. Viva, viva grande Mozart'. Those in the orchestra I thought would never have ceased applauding, by beating the bows of their violins against the music desks. The little man acknowledged, by repeated obeisances, his thanks for the distinguished mark of enthusiastic applause bestowed upon him.

The same meed of approbation was given to the finale at the end of the [second] act; that piece of music alone, in my humble opinion, if he had never composed any thing else good, would have stamped him as the greatest master of his art.

In the sestetto, in the [third] act, (which was Mozart's favourite piece of the whole opera), I had a very conspicuous part, as the Stuttering Judge. All through the [scene] I was to stutter; but in the sestetto, Mozart requested I would not, for if I did, I should spoil his music. I told him, that although it might appear very presumptuous in a lad like me to differ with him on this point, I did, and was sure, the way in which I intended to introduce the stuttering, would not interfere with the other parts, but produce an effect; besides, it certainly was not in nature, that I should stutter all through the part, and when I came to the sestetto speak plain; and after that piece of music was over, return to stuttering; and I added (apologizing at the same time, for my apparent want of deference and respect in placing my opinion in opposition to that of the great Mozart), that unless I was allowed to perform the part as I wished, I would not perform it at all.

Mozart at last consented that I should have my own way, but doubted the success of the experiment.   [*Kelly*, I: 259–60]

Meanwhile it was becoming clear that forces in Vienna were working against Mozart's opera. At the end of April, Leopold Mozart wrote to his daughter:

Leopold Mozart   Today, the 28th, your brother's opera *Le nozze di Figaro* is being performed for the first time. It will be surprising if it is a success, for I know that immensely powerful cabals are ranged against it. Salieri and all his supporters will again move heaven and earth to bring it down. Herr and Mme Duschek told me recently that it is because of the great reputation your brother's exceptional talent and ability have won for him there is so much plotting against him.

[*Mozart, III:* 536]

In any discussion about the intrigues that surrounded Mozart in Vienna it is invariably Salieri who is cast as the villain. But there were plenty of others in Court circles who had no wish to see *Figaro* succeed. Though the composer himself stood in good favour with the Emperor, Da Ponte—whose technique of ingratiation was not to everyone's taste—had already crossed swords with Count Rosenberg, and Rosenberg's protégé Casti was Da Ponte's chief rival and particular bête noire. Among the artists of the company one at least was in sympathy with this group, and Bussani, 'a man', says Da Ponte, 'who could turn his hand to any trade save that of gentleman', precipitated at the last moment a bizarre incident that according to Da Ponte threatened to disrupt the whole performance.

One of Joseph II's recent reforms in the theatre had been to forbid ballet in all opera performances. When Bussani discovered that Da Ponte had included a (very brief) ballet at the end of Act III of *Figaro*, he immediately reported the matter to Count Rosenberg, who sent for the librettist and subjected him to a grilling that loses nothing in Da Ponte's telling of it. At the end of an angry exchange Rosenberg 'tore two pages out of my play, threw them calmly into the fire and handed the libretto back to me saying: "You see, *signor poeta*, there is nothing I cannot do."'

[*Da Ponte, 1918, I:* 118–19]

Not to be defeated, Da Ponte took prompt action. The dress rehearsal was due the same evening, and the Emperor, who made a habit of dropping in at rehearsals, was present along with Rosenberg, Casti and 'half the nobility of Vienna'. The first acts were received with universal applause, but at the end of Act III, where the fandango should have accompanied the incident of Susanna's note and the Count pricking his finger with a pin, 'all you saw was the Count and Susanna gesticulating like puppets in a puppet show while the orchestra remained silent'.

Da Ponte   'What is the meaning of this?' said the Emperor to Casti, who
was sitting next to him. 'You will have to ask the poet,' replied Casti,
with a malicious smile. So I was sent for, but instead of answering
the question put to me I simply produced my manuscript in which
I had replaced the scene. The Emperor read it, asked me why there
was no dance and, realising from my silence that something was
wrong, turned to the Count and asked him for an explanation. The
Count, half mumbling, said that the dance was missing because the
theatre had no dancers. 'Aren't there any in the other theatres?' said
the Emperor. They told him that there were. 'Well then, give Da
Ponte as many as he needs'—and in less than half an hour twenty
four dancers had arrived. The missing scene was repeated, and the
Emperor called out 'Now it's fine!'   [*Id: 119–20*]

It is possible that Rosenberg was simply trying to reduce expenses,
and in any case he was only implementing the Emperor's own instructions (if rather maliciously). But the story at least suggests the difficulties of dealing with a theatrical bureaucracy peopled with dubious
friends, and may explain why the first performance was further put
back from 28 April to 1 May. Whether Bussani, or any of the other
members of the company, would have gone to the length of sabotaging
the actual performance of the opera is more doubtful. Niemetschek,
writing less than twelve years after the event, believed they did.

Niemetschek   If it is true, as has been widely reported—and it is difficult to question the absolute certainty of so many reliable witnesses—
that the singers, out of hate, envy, and a taste for base intrigue, made
every effort to wreck the opera by making deliberate mistakes at the
first performance, the reader may appreciate how much this faction
feared the superiority of Mozart's genius (and how true were my earlier observations about *Die Entführung aus dem Serail*). . . . It is said
that the singers were given a stern warning and recalled to their duty
by the late monarch, after Mozart had come to his box in dismay during the first interval and drawn attention to what was happening. . . .
                                                    [*Niemetschek: 37*]

But Niemetschek was writing after the overwhelming success of
Figaro in Prague seven months later, and his informants may have been
biased against the Italian faction in Vienna. Michael Kelly's memory of

the occasion, by contrast, veers towards the rose-tinted, partly perhaps because of the success of the stuttering.

Kelly   Crowded houses proved that nothing ever on the stage produced a more powerful effect: the audience were convulsed with laughter, in which Mozart himself joined. The Emperor repeatedly cried out Bravo! and the piece was loudly applauded and encored. When the opera was over, Mozart came on the stage to me, and shaking me by both hands, said: 'Bravo! young man, I feel obliged to you; and acknowledge you to have been in the right, and myself in the wrong'.

[*Kelly, I: 261*]

'At the end of the opera', Kelly recalled, with characteristic enthusiasm, 'I thought the audience would never have done applauding and calling for Mozart, almost every piece was encored . . .'. But in fact the behaviour of the first-night audience seems rather to have justified the predictions of Mozart's father. An article that appeared in the *Wiener Realzeitung* later in the run of the opera gives a more balanced view:

Wiener Realzeitung   Already at the first performance Herr Mozart's music was widely admired by connoisseurs . . . [but] it is true that the public didn't really know, on that first day, what to make of it (a position in which the public often finds itself). It heard many a *bravo* from unbiased connoisseurs, but a gang of rowdy thugs in the upper tiers of the gallery strained their hired lungs with all their might to deafen both singers and audience with their *St!* and *Pst!*—and consequently at the end of the opera opinions were mixed.

In addition it is fair to say that, owing to the great difficulty of the composition, the first performance was not of the best.

[*Deutsch: 244*]

Kelly may have been remembering the later performances: at the second, five numbers were encored, at the third, seven—and in fact on the day following the third performance the Emperor was moved to write to Count Rosenberg:

Joseph II   In order to prevent the duration of the operas from becoming excessive, and yet at the same time avoid prejudicing the glory which singers often seek by repeating their solo arias, I consider the accom-

panying notice to the public . . . to be the most reasonable course of
action.   [*Id*: 241]

And an announcement appeared at the Burgtheater:

NB   It is hereby made known to all members of the public that from
now on, in order not to overrun the prescribed duration of the operas,
no piece composed for more than a single voice will be repeated.
                                                                          [*Id*: 241]

Nevertheless the Viennese public didn't really take to *Figaro*. 'The
opera bored me,' noted Zinzendorf, 'Mozart's music singular, hands without head'. Perhaps it was the old story—'too beautiful for our ears, and an
extraordinary number of notes'; in any case, *Figaro* had nine performances
only in 1786 and wasn't revived in Vienna until 1789, being roundly put in
the shade by Martín's *Una cosa rara* which followed six months later and
had some forty performances over the same period.   [*Id*: 240, 243]

But in Prague that December there was a different story to tell. 'No
piece . . . has ever caused such a sensation as the Italian opera *Le Nozze
di Figaro*', wrote the critic of the *Prager Oberpostamtszeitung* enthusiastically, and a few days later, 'it still hasn't been heard enough, for the theatre was again crammed with spectators . . .'.   [*Id*: 246–7]

Mozart's father was exultant.

Leopold Mozart   [Your brother's] opera has been performed in Prague
with such immense success that the orchestra and a company of
important connoisseurs and lovers of music have sent him letters of
invitation, as well as a poem composed in his honour. . . . He and his
wife must be in Prague by now. . . .   [*Mozart, IV*: 7]

Arriving early in January, they were immediately fêted, welcomed
everywhere, and invited to the grandest balls of the season. Happy but
exhausted, Mozart wrote:

Mozart   I watched with absolute delight as all these people, with such
evident pleasure, whirled about to the music of my *Figaro* arranged
for contredanses and German dances. . . . On Wednesday I am going
to see and hear *Figaro*, if I haven't become deaf and blind before

then. . . . For here they talk about nothing but *Figaro*. Nothing is played, blown, sung or whistled but *Figaro*. No opera is drawing like *Figaro*. Always, always *Figaro*. . . .   [*Id: 9, 10, 12*]

When his presence was spotted in the theatre on Wednesday, the audience burst into clamorous applause after the overture. A few days later he conducted a performance himself, and when he left Prague in February, he had a contract for a new opera in his pocket.

It was only nine months before he was back in Prague again. The new opera was *Don Giovanni*.

Beethoven in 1814, considered by contemporaries
one of the best portraits

Fidelio

I<small>N</small> J<small>UNE</small> 1814, a month after the first performance of *Fidelio,* Beethoven and the Viennese Court librettist, Georg Friedrich Treitschke, wrote to the Intendant of the Court Theatre at Karlsruhe:

> This opera appeared a few weeks ago at the Imperial Royal Court Opera Theatre here; it had the good fortune to meet with greater than usual applause and continues to attract full houses. The libretto and music are not to be confused with the opera of the same name which was performed several years ago at the I.R.Theater an der Wien. . . . The whole piece has been remodelled in accordance with altered notions of theatrical effectiveness, and more than half of it has been newly composed. [*Brandenburg, III: 36*]

Beethoven and Treitschke were understandably anxious to dissociate the latest version of *Fidelio* from its predecessors. This was the third form in which it had appeared (and the one in which Beethoven's only opera is normally heard today); the two earlier versions, which are now usually, though inaccurately, referred to as *Leonore,* had been performed in 1805 and 1806 respectively and had met with little success. But at that time, at the age of thirty-four, Beethoven's experience of vocal composition had been limited, and with the single exception of the oratorio *The Mount of Olives* he was known in Vienna as a virtuoso pianist and composer of instrumental music—1805, after all, saw the first public performance of that great 'fling at the universe' the *Eroica* Symphony.

All the same, as for many composers at the turn of the eighteenth century, it was opera that seemed to promise the greatest scope to his creative ambition, as well as the best road to worldly success. Yet for the last four years both ambition and success had been imperilled by a growing threat that up until now he had kept secret from all but a few of his closest friends.

Beethoven   How could I declare myself deficient in the very sense which
I ought to possess in greater perfection than anyone else, which I did
once possess in the highest perfection? . . . If I tried to ignore my
infirmity, I was driven back the more harshly by the misery of my
defective hearing—and yet I could not bring myself to say to people:
"Speak louder—shout—for I am deaf."   [*Kerst, II: 335*]

Beethoven's deafness is something we accept today as a historical
commonplace, even though its bitter thread runs pitilessly through every
aspect of his character, health and behaviour. But at the time his refusal
to accept defeat was absolute, and he was certainly not the man to let
physical disability stand between him and his artistic purpose.

Seyfried   He enjoyed going to the opera and went often, especially to the
then flourishing Theater an der Wien, . . . where he was particularly
fascinated by the works of Cherubini and Méhul, at that time beginning to rouse the enthusiasm of all Vienna. He would plant himself
hard against the orchestra rail and stand there mute as a statue until
the very last stroke of the bow. But this was the only sign he gave of his
interest in the performance; if it didn't appeal to him he would about
turn briskly at the end of the first act and stump out. It was difficult,
indeed impossible, to see in his face any indication of approval or displeasure; he would be always the same, apparently unmoved, giving
away no opinion of what he heard. Only his mind worked ceaselessly;
the physical shell was inanimate marble.   [*Kerst, I: 77*]

Though the latest importations from Paris no doubt provided a stimu-
lant to his theatrical imagination, for Beethoven the basic operatic problem was always the libretto. What he needed, in fact demanded, was a
subject he could approach 'with love and tenderness', that he could relate
to the lofty if sometimes imprecise ideals of the dawning romantic movement. 'I could not compose operas like *Don Giovanni* and *Figaro*', he said:
'I have an aversion to both of them'. But the high moral tone he was looking for was not easy to find, and he certainly didn't find it in the first
opera libretto that came his way. *Vestas Feuer* was written by Emanuel
Schikaneder, the artistic director of the Theater an der Wien, and as Schikaneder had been the librettist of *Die Zauberflöte* (the one Mozart opera
of which Beethoven did approve), Beethoven probably hoped for another

success in the *Zauberflöte* mould. But times were changing and the project was abandoned before composition had got beyond the first scene.

Beethoven   I have now broken completely with Herr Schikaneder, whose empire has in any case been entirely overshadowed by the brilliance of the clever and well thought out French operas. Meanwhile he has held me up for a full six months, and I have let myself be deceived simply because no one can really deny his success in creating stage effects, and I hoped he would come up with something even cleverer than usual. But how I have been misled! . . . Just picture for yourself a Roman subject (of which I had been told nothing, either about the plot or anything else) with language and verses that sound more as if they came from our local *apple-women*—Anyhow, I have had an old French libretto quickly adapted, and am starting work on it at once.   [*Brandenburg*, I: 205–6]

So *Fidelio* first enters history as a *pis aller*—though it seems that a favourable change in the management of the Theater an der Wien soon conferred official status on the project.

Treitschke   [Early in] 1804 Baron von Braun, the new proprietor of the Theater an der Wien, commissioned Ludwig van Beethoven, then in the full strength of his youth, to write an opera for his playhouse. Ever since his oratorio, *The Mount of Olives*, it was believed that the master might show himself to be as great in dramatic music as he had already done in instrumental works. As well as a fee he was offered free lodging in the theatre building. Joseph Sonnleithner [the secretary of the Court theatres] undertook to provide the text and chose the French libretto [*Léonore, ou*] *L'amour conjugal*, although this had already been set to music by Gaveaux. . . .   [*Treitschke*: 258]

Pierre Gaveaux's opera, to a libretto by Jean-Nicolas Bouilly, belonged to the French tradition of *opéra-comique*—which by this stage in its history frequently treated subjects that were far from *comique*. The main lines of the plot were therefore laid out in spoken dialogue, and in his German adaptation of Bouilly's text Sonnleithner followed the same structure. But Beethoven was impatient to get his hands on the verses that he needed for the musical sections of the opera.

Beethoven   Dear Sonnleithner . . . I beg you most earnestly to make
sure that the text, as far as concerns the poetical part, is completely
finished by the middle of April, so that I can get straight down to
work on it and the opera can be produced in June at latest—by which
time I will be able to help produce it myself.   [*Brandenburg, I:* 207]

June, however, was always a hopelessly optimistic target, even if it
had not been for other, non-musical problems. A close friend, Stephan
von Breuning, wrote to Franz Wegeler in November:

Breuning   You cannot conceive, my dear Wegeler, what an indescribable, I might say, fearful effect the gradual loss of his hearing has
had upon him. Think of the feeling of unhappiness in one of such
violent temperament; in addition reserve, mistrust, often towards his
best friends, in many things want of decision! For the greater part,
with only an occasional exception when he gives free vent to his feelings on the spur of the moment, association with him demands a
real effort, to which one can never resign oneself. From May until
the beginning of this month we lived in the same house. . . . He had
scarcely arrived before he became severely, almost dangerously ill,
and this was followed by an intermittent fever. Worry and the care of
him used me rather severely. . . .   [*Breuning:* 37]

Nor can the restlessness of Beethoven's living arrangements have
helped. He had moved in with Breuning because he had taken against
his rooms at the Theater an der Wien—which, according to Wegeler, 'he
was not satisfied with because they faced the courtyard'—but at once
rented summer lodgings in the country at Döbling as well and then, after
quarrelling with the long-suffering Breuning, took yet another apartment
on the city ramparts. In such circumstances work on *Fidelio* progressed
slowly and didn't pick up again until the summer of 1805, though notes
and sketches from 1804 already give the first glimpses of a process of
composition that was to continue, on and off, for the next ten years.

Like his libretto for Cherubini's *Les deux journées* (a work that
Beethoven particularly admired), Bouilly's *Léonore* is a version of the 'rescue' theme popular in post-revolutionary France. It is based on a true
incident at Tours during the Reign of Terror in which Bouilly himself had
been involved (he calls it a 'fait historique' on the title page): a well-born
lady had disguised herself as a man and liberated her aristocrat husband

from the gaol in which he was being held as a political prisoner—Bouilly, in an official capacity, appearing in the role of Don Fernando. This dramatic tale was set against a characteristically French bourgeois background, and Sonnleithner, who expanded Bouilly's two acts into three, not only retained this but added to it. Beethoven, by nature a symphonist and influenced by the expansive operatic style of Cherubini, was tempted into spreading himself in the first scenes, which became even longer than they are today with an extra trio and duet that add detail to the emotional complications of life in Rocco's family circle (as if they weren't complicated enough already) but do nothing to advance the true plot of the opera. Even the sublime canon quartet, which went through thirteen drafts before reaching its final form and was later transferred to the final version almost intact, is essentially a domestic piece.

It is not until Pizarro's entry in Act II that the opera shakes off its leisurely pace and the drama begins to move forward. In Bouilly's play Pizarro had been a speaking character only; Beethoven introduces him musically with a powerful opening aria and gives musical (rather than spoken) form to the scene with Rocco that follows. But it was above all the figure of Leonore and the idea of womanly heroism that had originally attracted Beethoven to the story—it had been his intention to name the opera after its heroine if the Italian composer, Ferdinando Paer, who produced his own version of the subject in Dresden in October 1804, hadn't got in with the title first. Leonore's opening recitative may now seem overshadowed by the familiar 'Abscheulicher' version, but the original at this point still sounds the first unmistakable note of heroic pathos in the score—although in his anxiety to give full operatic status to his heroine Beethoven loads her first appearance with a display of rather awkward coloratura, and defies dramatic economy with rich thematic elaboration that makes for an aria some fifty-five bars longer than its later counterpart.

The qualities which Beethoven admired, however, did not endear Sonnleithner's textbook to the Imperial authorities in Vienna, and at the last moment the first performance of the opera, originally scheduled for 15 October, was held up by a ban from the Viennese censorship. Sonnleithner made an immediate personal appeal to a Councillor of State, describing the subject as 'moral in the highest degree', resolutely denying any association with current events, and playing a lucky Imperial card.

Sonnleithner   I made this libretto primarily for two reasons: first, because the subject is excellent, and is dramatic and suitable for musical setting in the highest degree; second, because Her Majesty the Empress repeatedly told me that no opera subject had ever interested her as much. The music has been composed . . . the rehearsals have begun; the preparations are made—and, on the 30th September, I received the libretto back with the ban on performance. I leave to your imagination the thunderstroke this was for me. . . .

I submitted the opera again yesterday with a most deferential introduction . . . and now request you, Herr Court Councillor, to do what you can for the attainment of my wish. You will eternally oblige Her Majesty the Empress (who particularly loves this piece as composed in Italian by Kapellmeister Paer . . .), the public (which . . . has already waited a long time for an opera by Beethoven), and the Theatre (which always regards it as its duty to obey most vigorously all the wishes of the higher authorities). It is true that a Minister misuses his power, but only for private revenge—in Spain in the 16th century—and he is punished, punished by the Court, and confronted by the heroism of wifely virtue.   [*Albrecht, I: 171*]

As it turned out, the censorship eventually passed the libretto with minor modifications. But by that time new difficulties had arisen.

Treitschke Though the female roles could be satisfactorily filled by Mlles. Milder [Leonore] and Müller [Marzelline], the casting of the men left much to be desired. And there were a number of shortcomings in the adaptation of the text that had still not been put right. Meanwhile from the distance the storm of war rolled towards Vienna and robbed audiences of the calm necessary for the enjoyment of a work of art. Yet for that very reason every possible effort was made to enliven the sparsely attended opera house. *Fidelio* was thought likely to achieve this best, and so under far from happy auspices the opera was set down for performance on November 20th. [*Treitschke: 258–9*]

By now the Empress, the Austrian nobility, the wealthy patricians, the great bankers and merchants, virtually the entire public on which the opera house relied for support, had fled the capital. A week before the première, the defenceless city capitulated to Napoleon, and on the next day the Emperor of the French hoisted the tricolor surmounted by a golden eagle on the Palace of Schönbrunn. And so it came about that the audience at the first performance was thin and heavily sprinkled with French officers in uniform, 'more familiar with the thunder of cannon than with sublime musical conceptions', and hardly in a fit state to appreciate the new opera. Joseph Carl Rosenbaum, one of the few property owners to remain in the city, noted in his diary:

Rosenbaum In the evening I went to the W[iedener] Th[eater] to hear Louis Beth.'s opera. . . . The piece has attractive, skilful, and weighty music, with a tedious libretto of little interest. It had no success and the theatre was empty.   [*Radant: 129–30*]

Professional criticism was no more enthusiastic.

Critic The whole thing, impartially judged, is outstanding for neither inventiveness nor execution. . . . The vocal numbers are not generally based on any new ideas, and are for the most part too long; the text is full of monotonous repetitions, and the characterisation is sometimes gravely at fault. . . . The choruses are ineffective and one of them, in which the delight of the prisoners in the enjoyment of fresh air is depicted, obviously misses fire.   [*Allg. Mus. Zeitung, 8.1.1806*]

This seems a curious reaction to a chorus that was hardly changed in the later versions of the opera and has always been regarded as deeply moving. Perhaps it was taken too slowly; the tempo indication was twice upgraded in the revised scores. In any case, there was greater justification for criticism at the other end of the second act finale. Admittedly the libretto was at this point no great help: the return of the prisoners to their cells *before* the reappearance of Pizarro (whose anger is here instead occasioned by Rocco's delay in digging the grave), and the dismissal of Marzelline, Leonore and Rocco as soon as he does reappear, leaves only Pizarro himself, with a chorus of guards, to conclude the act. Even so, the aria Beethoven gave him is surprisingly commonplace, ending in a sixty-bar orgy of tonic and dominant for orchestra alone—a blazing exhibition of symphonism but a sad contrast to the wonderful pianissimo close of the later score.

As for the third act, in which the grave-digging scene ran straight into the finale, and Don Fernando and the chorus had to crowd into the confined space of Florestan's dungeon for the final ensemble of the opera, it got short shrift from a correspondent in the *Zeitung für die elegante Welt* who found it was 'over long, the music being without effect and full of repetitions, and did nothing to improve the impression I had formed from his [oratorio] of

Beethoven's talent in vocal composition'. Not unfair, at least as far as the dramatic structure was concerned—though Treitschke saw it differently.

Treitschke   We realised with regret that the work was ahead of its time and met with little understanding from friends or enemies.

[*Treitschke: 259*]

In the end the first *Fidelio* had to be withdrawn after only three nights. But within less than a month the combined Austrian and Russian army was decisively beaten by the French at Austerlitz, and the final acceptance of defeat brought back peace and more normal conditions to Vienna. To give the opera another chance on the stage, Beethoven's friends now decided to tackle the composer and try to persuade him to revise his score. Two separate descriptions of this confrontation were written in later life by Joseph August Röckel, the young tenor who was going to take over the part of Florestan (Fritz Demmer, the creator of the role, having failed to meet with Beethoven's approval).

Röckel   It was in December 1805 that [Sebastian] Mayer, brother-in-law to Mozart and Regisseur of the opera An-der-Wien, came to fetch me to an evening meeting in the palace of Prince Karl Lichnowsky, the great patron of Beethoven. . . . The few friends who had ventured to hear the opera . . . were now at the soirée, to bring Beethoven about, to consent to the changes they wanted to introduce in the opera in order to remove the heaviness of the first act. The necessity of these improvements was already acknowledged and settled among themselves. Mayer [who had sung the role of Pizarro] prepared me for the coming storm, when Beethoven should hear of leaving out three whole numbers of the first act.   [*Thayer, I: 388*]

In his later, more elaborate account of the evening, Röckel remembers that he was so nervous at having to sight-read his new part in the presence of the composer, whom he had never met, that he made excuses and dawdled on the way. When they were confronted on the monumental staircase of the palace by liveried servants carrying away empty tea trays, Mayer made a sour face and muttered: 'I fear your hesitation has produced a delicate situation for our stomachs'. Which indeed turned out to be the case, for the assembled company were waiting for them when they were shown into the music room. In this account the whole cast of

the opera were co-opted for the occasion ('Beethoven carelessly reclin-
ing in an armchair, the thick score of his unfortunate opera across his
knees'—which sounds likely enough), but the earlier version gives a more
credible list of friends and artists.   [*Kerst, I: 113*]

Röckel   At the soirée were present Prince Lichnowsky and the Princess,
Beethoven and his brother Kaspar, [Stephan] von Breuning, [Hein-
rich] von Collin, the poet, the tragedian Lange (another brother-in-
law to Mozart), Treitschke, Clement, leader of the orchestra, Mayer
and myself; whether Kapellmeister von Seyfried was there I am not
certain any more, though I should think so. . . .

As the whole opera was to be gone through, we went directly to
work. The Princess played on the grand piano the great score of
the opera and Clement, sitting in a corner of the room, accompanied with his violin the whole opera by heart, playing all the solos
of the different instruments. The extraordinary memory of Clement
being universally known, nobody was astonished by it, except myself.
Mayer and I made ourselves useful by singing as well as we could, he
(basso) the lower, I the higher parts of the opera. Though the friends
of Beethoven were fully prepared for the impending battle, they had
never seen him in *that* excitement before, and without the prayers
and entreaties of the very delicate and invalid Princess, who was a
second mother to Beethoven and acknowledged by himself as such,
his united friends were not likely to have succeeded in this, even
to themselves, very doubtful enterprise. But when after their united
endeavours from seven till after one o'clock, the sacrifice of the three
numbers was accomplished, and when we, exhausted, hungry and
thirsty, went to restore ourselves by a splendid supper—then none
was happier and gayer than Beethoven.   [*Thayer, I: 388–9*]

In the later account the 'delicate situation' of Röckel's stomach had
reduced him to such a state of hunger that he bolted his first plateful of
food like a starving man—which inspired Beethoven to point out that this
explained the verisimilitude of his performance as Florestan: 'It was no
credit to your voice or your head, but simply to your stomach. So—make
sure you always starve conscientiously before the performance, and we
needn't worry about the outcome'. As Röckel dryly remarked, the assembled company 'perhaps took more pleasure in the fact that Beethoven had
managed to make a joke at all, than in the joke itself'.

The three condemned numbers were the superfluous trio and duet in the first act and Pizarro's aria in the second, but in the end only two numbers were cut entirely (Rocco's aria and the melodrama in the dungeon scene), neither of which were on the Lichnowsky hit list—Beethoven having cunningly salvaged the trio and duet by quietly shifting them to a later position where they held up the action even more. The opera was recast in two acts, though as the new first act was simply a combination of the original Acts I and II with a scene change at the old act break, this made little practical difference. But Beethoven did make many cuts and modifications throughout the score, considerably shortening the opera and entailing changes in the libretto which, as Sonnleithner was by now at work on his text for Cherubini's latest Viennese opera, the composer undertook himself.

Beethoven   When I made the alterations, you were hard at work on your *Faniska*, so I did them myself. You would not have had the patience to deal with them, and it would have put back the production of our opera still further— So I thought that by keeping quiet about it I might hope to have your consent. Three acts have been reduced to only two. In order to achieve this, and to give the opera a quicker sense of movement, I have shortened everything as much as possible, the prisoners' chorus and mainly other numbers of that kind— All this simply meant rewriting the first act; and that's what the revision of the libretto amounts to.   [*Brandenburg, I: 277–9*]

Beethoven no doubt felt it wiser to play down the real extent of the revision, most of which had anyhow been the work of Breuning who, in his own words, 'remodelled the whole libretto for him, quickening and enlivening the action'.

Röckel   A few weeks later the members of the cast already had their parts in the new version. We were all astonished at Beethoven's hard work, and that in so short a time he had completed the recasting of his score. *Fidelio* was performed again on the 29 March 1806, hardly more than four months after its first brief appearance on the stage— but this time before a comfortable 'Viennese' audience. [*Kerst, I: 117*]

If the audience was better, the opera in this second, mutilated version was not. Though Beethoven and Breuning saw part of what was

needed and in fact made several improvements that are generally attributed to the final version, other changes were less well advised and upset
the careful structure of the original without compensating advantages.
There was also a new overture, the one now known as *Leonore* No. 3.
This was a vastly extended version of the 1805 overture (*Leonore* No.
2)—magnificent, but far too long for its purpose and fatally flawed as
an introduction to the drama by its anticipation of the off-stage trumpet
call that subsequently precipitates the emotional climax of the opera.
(Beethoven later realised this and replaced it with two simpler pieces: the
first, confusingly known as *Leonore* No. 1, for a projected production that
never took place, the second for the opera in its final version).

To prepare all this material for performance Beethoven was only
allowed two piano rehearsals and one for orchestra, and this was simply
not enough for a cast or players confronted with a score full of tricky
alterations—not to mention the overture.

Critic   The effect of the whole work cannot have been quite what the
composer intended, since meaningless dialogue ruined wholly or to
a large extent the beautiful impression created by the sung passages.
Herr Beethoven certainly does not lack high aesthetic insight into
his art and knows extremely well how to express the emotions which
are in the words, but he appears to lack utterly all capacity to see the
story from the point of view of its overall effect and to judge it rightly.
The music however is masterly, and Beethoven has showed what he
will be able to achieve in future in this field which he has newly
entered. . . . The overture is displeasing on account of its constant
dissonances, and the overcharged bustling of the violins, and must be
regarded as artifice rather than art in the true sense. [*Zeitung, 1806*]

Nor was Beethoven happy. After the first performance he wrote to Mayer:

Beethoven   Baron Braun has informed me that my opera is to be given
[again] on Thursday. . . . I do earnestly beseech you to see to it that
the choruses are even better rehearsed, for last time they went terribly
wrong. And on Thursday we must have one more rehearsal with full
orchestra in the theatre. True, the orchestra did not make mistakes,
but the performers on the stage did so repeatedly—though that was
only to be expected, as the time was too short.   [*Brandenburg, I: 281*]

Perhaps the prisoners' chorus had still missed fire? In any case, by the morning of the second performance Beethoven's frustration had grown to something near despair.

Beethoven   Please request Herr von Seyfried to conduct my opera today. I want to see and hear it myself from a distance. At least my patience will not then be put to such a trial as it would be if I had to listen to the massacring of my music from close by!—I cannot help thinking that this is being done to me on purpose. About the wind instruments I shall say nothing, but—that all the *pianos, pianissimos* and *crescendos*, all *decrescendos* and all *fortes* and *fortissimos* should have been struck out of my score—or at any rate disregarded! All desire to compose anything any more disappears completely when I have to hear things like that!   [*Id*: 282]

Breuning was quick to justify Beethoven's suspicions.

Breuning   There were enemies of his in the theatre and he clashed with some of them, especially at the second performance, and they brought things to a point where the work was no longer given after that. Even earlier, many difficulties had been put in his way. A single example as evidence of these is the fact that at the second performance he could not get the announcement of the opera to be made with the revised title [*Leonore*], as it is given in the French original and as it appeared on the printed version after the changes had been made. In violation of all the promises made, the first title, [*Fidelio*], was found on the posters for the performances. What made the intrigue all the more disagreeable for Beethoven is that he has been set back financially by non-performance of the opera, for which he was to be paid on the basis of a percentage of the receipts.   [*Breuning*: 41]

Röckel, however, took a different view.

Röckel   The opera might well have become a favourite if the evil genius of the composer had not prevented it. . . . Having had no theatrical experience, he estimated the receipts of the house much higher than they really were; he believed himself cheated in his percentage and, without consulting his real friends on such a delicate point, hastened to Baron Braun—that high-minded and honourable nobleman—and submitted his complaint. The Baron, seeing Beethoven excited and conscious of his susceptibility, did what he could to cure him of his suspicions. . . . He hoped that the receipts would increase with each representation; until now, only the first ranks, stalls and pit were occupied; by and by the upper ranks would likewise contribute their shares.

'I don't write for the galleries!' exclaimed Beethoven.

'No?' replied the Baron, 'my dear Sir, even Mozart did not disdain to write for the galleries.'

Now it was at an end. 'I will not give the opera any more,' said Beethoven. ' I want my score back.'

Here Baron Braun rang the bell and gave orders for the delivery of the score to the composer, and the opera was buried for a long time.

[*Thayer, I:* 397–8]

With the revised version of his opera laid to rest after only two performances, Beethoven returned to instrumental composition with characteristic energy; from these years come the fifth, sixth and seventh symphonies, the *Emperor* Concerto, the Mass in C, the String Quartets Op. 74 and 95, the *Archduke* Trio, and the music for Goethe's *Egmont*. But in spite of all the dealings with the outside world which it involved, the operatic stage still represented the ultimate prize, and on one of his musical sketches from this period there is a scribbled note: 'Even as you have plunged into the whirlpool of society, so will you find it possible to compose operas regardless of social obstacles.' Indeed, early in 1807, a change in the management of the Theater an der Wien gave him the opportunity to address the new directors with a proposal for permanent engagement. In return for a fixed salary he undertook 'to compose every year at least one grand opera, and to deliver gratis each year a small operetta, divertissement, and choruses or occasional pieces according to the wishes of the Worshipful Directors'. No final answer seems to have been vouchsafed to this application which, given the character of the composer, was probably just as well.

At the beginning of 1814, however, an unexpected request reached Beethoven. It clearly took him unawares, and he wrote to Count Lichnowsky:

Beethoven   Dear Count. You would do me a very great kindness *if you would lend me the score of my opera 'Fidelio' for a few days.* I know, of course, that your copy is not entirely correct, but it is still better than none at all. *They now want to perform it here in the Court Theatre, but I cannot find my score.* I believe *I sent it to Leipzig,* but it would take too long to have it sent back. . . .   [*Brandenburg, III: 7–8*]

Treitschke   [Three officials] of the Court Opera had been granted a performance for their benefit, the choice of work being left to them. To find something suitable was not easy: there were no new German compositions readily available, and the older ones did not promise any great profit. The latest French operas were no longer as good, nor as popular, as they had been, and the performers lacked the courage as singers to plunge into Italian works. . . . In this predicament *Fidelio* was suggested and Beethoven was approached for the loan of his opera. Most unselfishly he agreed, but on the strict understanding that many changes would be needed, and at the same time proposing my humble self as the person to make them. I had enjoyed his friendship for some time, and my double position as opera-poet and stage-manager turned his wish to a pious duty. With the permission of Sonnleithner I first took up the dialogue and wrote it almost entirely afresh, as short and clear as possible.   [*Treitschke: 259–60*]

After an interval of eight years the problem now facing Beethoven was a considerable one, and not one that he altogether relished. Only a year earlier he had written adamantly to the Scottish publisher George Thomson:

Beethoven   I am not in the habit of revising my compositions [when they are finished]; I have never done it, being firmly of the opinion that a change in any part of a composition alters its character as a whole.   [*Brandenburg, II: 321*]

In this case, however, it was in fact the very character of the composition that was to be changed. The original *Fidelio,* written by a young man building on the conventions of an essentially French tradition, is about personal relationships and personal courage, and the drama that arises from them. The 1806 version had disturbed the calculated structure of the original but not changed the basic message. But by 1814 the composer's view had expanded beyond the purely personal to encompass a wider vision of humanity. Beethoven was an idealist, and during the years that separated the first *Fidelio* from its final version, the hopes of freedom that had swept across Europe in the wake of the French Revolution had been all but lost in the flood of French imperialism. Not for nothing had he ripped the dedication from the title page of the *Eroica* when he heard of Napoleon's coronation as Emperor. It was a profound sympathy for all oppressed peoples, and a resolute belief in the triumph of right over might, that now inspired the definitive revision of his opera.

To be fair, Treitschke didn't actually rewrite as much as he claimed— there is plenty of Sonnleithner and Breuning left in his final text. But the changes in structure and emphasis that he recommended gave his collaborator the stimulus he needed. The first task was to tighten up the first act, and bring the domestic opening scene out of Rocco's family quarters and into closer relationship with the rest of the drama.

Treitschke   The whole of the first act was [now] transferred to an open courtyard. The duet 'Jetzt, Schätzchen' became my opening number and Marzelline sang her aria immediately after it. . . . Leonore's aria received a new introduction, and only the second part of the *allegro* ['Ich folg' dem innern Triebe'] was retained. The scene and duet which followed in the [1806] libretto Beethoven tore out of the score; the former, he said, was unnecessary, the latter a concert piece, and I had to agree with him, as our purpose was to save the opera as a whole. A little trio for Rocco, Marzelline and Jaquino which came after it fared no better, since it lacked action and had left the audience cold. . . .   [*Treitschke: 260–1*]

The duet and 'little trio', which had been retained against the advice of Beethoven's friends and merely relocated in 1806, were at last excluded altogether. Leonora's new recitative, with its opening cry of 'Abscheulicher!' ('Villain!') presents her at once as a figure to be reckoned with, and in the aria that follows, as well as the cut made by Treitschke, Beethoven drastically reduced the excessive coloratura of the first version. (He may have received a prod from outside here: Anna Milder, the original Leonore, is reported to have said that 'she had severe struggles with the master, chiefly about the unbeautiful, unsingable passages, unsuited to her voice, in the adagio of [her big aria]—but all in vain until, in 1814, she declared that she would never sing the air again in its then shape. That worked'.)   [*Thayer, I: 399*]

Pizarro's first aria, on the other hand, was lengthened by a brilliant and effective new coda, and Beethoven now felt the need to strengthen his reappearance at the end of the act.

Treitschke   New dialogue was needed to motivate the first finale better—for my friend rightly insisted on a different ending. I made many suggestions, and in the end we agreed to arrange for the return of the prisoners to their cells at Pizarro's command, together with their plaintive lament as they re-enter the prison.   [*Treitschke: 261*]

And so the conventional villainies of the first version at last gave way to one of the most deeply felt ensembles in the score.

Once the general reshaping of the drama had been agreed, the rewriting of the libretto was quickly done—though the bulk of the text required for musical setting must surely have been in Beethoven's hands well before the date that Treitschke later remembered.

Treitschke   As soon as the libretto had been put together—towards the end of March [more likely February]—I sent Beethoven a copy, and as proud evidence I quote here what he wrote to me a couple of days later:
'Dear, worthy T . . . I have read with great pleasure your improvements to the opera. They strengthen my determination to rebuild the desolate ruins of an old castle. Your friend, Beethoven'.   [*Id: 262*]

But work was still subject to frequent interruptions.

Beethoven   That damned concert, which I admit I was partly compelled to give because of my wretched circumstances, has put me back in regard to the opera. . . . Now, of course, everything must be done at once, and I would write something new more quickly than I now add the new to the old. The way I write, even in my instrumental music, I always have the whole thing in my mind; but here the whole has already been laid out once in a particular manner, and I am obliged to think myself into it all over again. . . . Before my concert I had only made a few sketches here and there . . . and it wasn't until a few days ago that I was able to begin working them out—The score of the opera has been copied as wretchedly as anything I have ever seen; I have to check it note by note. . . . In short, I assure you, dear T, this opera is gaining for me a martyr's crown. If you had not taken so much trouble over it and reworked everything to such advantage, for which I am eternally grateful to you, I could scarcely bring myself to do it! You have thus saved a few good remnants from a stranded ship.
[*Brandenburg, III: 20*]

So thorough and determined was Beethoven's attack on the final
version of *Fidelio* that there is hardly a page of his opera that he did
not subject to major or minor alterations, carrying out modifications and
improvements of every kind, right down to countless details that tauten
and intensify the musical fabric by altering single notes in a vocal line,
adding or subtracting a phrase, or making small suppressions of sometimes not more than a bar at a time. Early in March he wrote:

Beethoven To give the opera in fourteen days is certainly impossible—
I still believe it will take up to four weeks. Meanwhile the first act
will be finished in a few days. But there is still much to be done in
the second act, as well as a new overture—though I admit this is the
easiest job because I can write an entirely new one. . . . Anyhow, if
you think the delay is becoming too great, then postpone the opera
yourself to some later date. I shall now go on working until the whole
thing is finished, and do so exactly in the way that you have altered
and improved it—which I recognise every moment more and more.
But it doesn't go as quickly as if I were composing something new—
and to finish in a fortnight is out of the question. Do whatever you
think best, but as a friend of mine too. My zeal will not fail.   [*Id*]

Treitschke The second act presented a serious difficulty right from the
start. Beethoven, for his part, wanted to distinguish the unfortunate
Florestan with an aria, but I objected that a man nearly dead of hunger could not possibly be allowed to sing *bravura*.   [*Treitschke: 261*]

It is at the beginning of Act II that Florestan first appears on the stage.
This scene, which provides the one opportunity for a full expression of his
character and situation, is therefore of crucial importance, and nowhere
is the detailed care of the musical revision more subtly displayed. Though
the oppressive melancholy of the original orchestral introduction needed
little changing, from the first note of Florestan's recitative the emotional
level of the later version is at a different pitch. The aria that follows was
always in two sections, beginning with the A flat *adagio* ('In des Lebens
Frühlingstagen') that we know today. But, to be technical for a moment,
where in the original the four symmetrical phrases of the melody closed
regularly in the dominant and tonic keys, in the revision a twist of harmony carries the second phrase into the remote key of C flat; the last note

of the vocal line is only raised by a semitone, but to the listener it inhabits a new world of sound and feeling, and the rest of the aria continues at a new level of intensity. For by 1814, Florestan had become the symbol of a universal condition. The nostalgic and touching *andante* which had originally followed at this point allowed him to dwell sadly upon his lost happiness and the wife he would never see again. In some ways it tells us more about his character than the radiant, breathless *allegro* that replaced it. But personal resignation now had to give way to something at a more exalted level—though whether Beethoven ever really intended to give 'poor Florestan' a bravura aria in the conventional sense seems highly unlikely, and Treitschke somewhat ingenuous in suggesting that he did.

Treitschke   We tried one idea, then another, and at last he felt that I had hit the nail on the head. . . . What I am now going to relate will live forever in my memory. Beethoven came to see me towards seven o'clock in the evening. After we had discussed various other things he asked me how the aria was getting on. It was just finished, so I handed it to him. He read it, ran up and down the room muttering and humming as he always did, rather than singing, and wrenched open the fortepiano. My wife had often vainly begged him to play; now he put the text in front of him and began to improvise marvellously—a fantasy which sadly no magic could preserve, but out of which he seemed to conjure the theme of the aria. The hours passed but Beethoven played on. The supper he had intended to share with us was served, but he was not to be disturbed. It was late before he embraced me and hurried home without his meal. The next day this admirable composition was finished.

Practically all the remaining changes in [the first part] of the second act were limited to cuts and altered verses (as I think that a careful comparison of the printed texts will confirm). I interrupted the grand quartet 'Er sterbe!' with a brief pause in which Jaquino and others announced the arrival of the Minister, who immediately summoned Pizarro to his presence and thus prevented the murder. After the next duet Rocco reappeared to fetch Florestan and Leonore up to the Minister as well.   [*Id:* 261–2]

The quartet is a prime example of the extraordinary way in which a series of small, seemingly inconsiderable musical changes can convert what was already a high point of drama into a climax of incomparable power. In the scene that follows, however, Treitschke's alterations resulted in what is probably the greatest musical loss in the final revision of the opera. In 1805, at this point, Leonore fell in a swoon, and the dawning joy in the long recitative as she awoke made a wonderfully expressive preparation for the love duet that follows. But now this was felt to delay the action at a critical juncture; a ruthless cut therefore replaced it with a few words of dialogue, the introduction to the duet was halved, and the duet itself (a survival from the abandoned music for *Vestas Feuer*) stretched out into the impetuous, overlapping melodic line that we know today.

It was at this point that Treitschke made the most far-reaching of his proposals.

Treitschke   It had always seemed to me a great defect that [in the original *Fidelio*] the second act was played throughout in a gloomy dungeon, in which, at the end, the Minister, his retinue and the mass of the public had to be most unsuitably accommodated and the liberation of Florestan from his bonds be celebrated by the light of a few torches. The problem of the stone bench, the grave and so on remaining on the stage I solved by having them all disappear through [traps in] the floor; at the same time the walls vanished upwards or sideways, so that mobile scenery and other props could open the way out of the abyss. (I would like to recommend a similar procedure in many other cases; it is certainly a better arrangement than having servants, or disguised stage hands, come on to change the set.)   [*Id:* 260]

Treitschke was evidently making good use of the technical equipment at the Theater an der Wien—which was, after all, the theatre where Schikaneder had produced the stage effects for which he was famous.

Treitschke   The closing scene of my version was played in broad daylight, in a green and cheerful courtyard of the castle. First the guards marched in; then the Minister approached with numerous attendants, and the prisoners of state, led by Jaquino, threw themselves on their knees before him. But through the open gate the crowd of the common people pressed into the courtyard, and so a chorus opened the new finale—which only returned to the music of the earlier version at the words 'Bestrafet sei der Bösewicht'.   [*Id:* 260]

Treitschke's revision of this scene switches the emphasis away from the cries for vengeance by the chorus (and a good deal of wordy exculpation by Rocco), which characterized the earlier versions, to broader themes of brotherhood and benevolence. But the return to the music of the original version comes in time to preserve what was always the heart of Beethoven's finale: a last, eloquent re-arrangement of the earliest musical idea in the score. As Leonore, at Don Fernando's bidding, unlocks the chains that have bound her husband, an ecstatic oboe melody provides a moment of rapturous stillness ('O Gott! O welch' ein Augenblick!')—a touching survival from a cantata on the death of the Emperor Joseph II, written nearly a quarter of a century before. Then all further recitative is banished, and the music plunges into a final ensemble in praise of Goethe's 'ewig weibliche' that can only be compared, in nobility and power, to the closing pages of the Ninth Symphony.

But for Beethoven the struggle continued to the last moment.

Treitschke   Those for whom the benefit performance was to be given urged the completion of the opera so as to take advantage of the favourable [spring] season. But Beethoven made slow progress. When I too wrote to him he retorted: [*Id*: 262]

Beethoven   This whole opera affair is the most tiresome business in the world; I am dissatisfied with most of it, and there is scarcely a number in which I have not been compelled, here and there, to patch some satisfaction onto my present dissatisfaction. This is a very different matter from giving oneself up to free reflection and inspiration.   [*Brandenburg, III*: 24]

Rehearsals eventually began in the middle of April 1814. The première was announced for 23 May, but less than a week before it the composer had still not finished his revisions. These included his fourth attempt to write an overture for the opera, which was planned in a lighter vein better suited to the style of the opening scene and, being 'the easiest job', was left to the end. Only a night or two before the dress rehearsal Beethoven was about to leave a restaurant, where he had been dining with his friend Dr. Bertolini, when he suddenly exclaimed 'No, wait a little; I have the idea for my overture', and began sketching notes on the back of the bill of fare. Unsurprisingly the piece was not ready in time.

Treitschke   The orchestra was called for [further] rehearsal on the morning of the première itself. But Beethoven did not turn up. After a long
wait I went to fetch him—and found him in bed, fast asleep, a glass of
wine and a biscuit beside him, the pages of the overture strewn over
the bed and the floor. A burnt out candle showed that he had worked
far into the night. It was obviously impossible to complete the piece,
so his overture to [*Die Ruinen von Athen*] was played on this occasion; the announcement that "due to unforeseen circumstances the
[new] overture would not be heard today" allowed the large audience
to guess the real reason without too much trouble.   [*Treitschke: 263*]

As Beethoven later remarked, 'The people applauded but I was
ashamed; it did not belong to the rest'. Nevertheless the applause was genuine, and the 'full houses' which Beethoven and Treitschke reported in their
letter to Karlsruhe were not an exaggeration. There was no comparison
now with the empty theatre that had greeted the first version of the opera
in 1805; the desolate city of those days had been transformed by the news
of Napoleon's defeat, Vienna was celebrating, and in this new atmosphere
of optimism and relief the final version of *Fidelio* found its true audience.

The performance, too, seems at last to have been worthy of the
occasion.

Treitschke   The opera was excellently prepared. Beethoven conducted
and although his impetuosity often imperilled the beat, Kapellmeister Umlauf, from behind his back, guided everything to success with
his eyes and hands.   [*Id: 263*]

Who really conducted the performance, Michael Umlauf or the
composer? Indeed, how much of his opera, at least in its final form, did
Beethoven ever hear? Descriptions of his conducting on other occasions
at this period suggest that it cannot have been very much, and what he
did hear was almost certainly dim and distorted. But he was always to
hold *Fidelio* among all his compositions most worthy of preservation and
most dear, because it had cost him 'the worst birth-pangs and the deepest
sorrow'. And when he found at the end of the newly prepared piano score
the copyist's closing inscription '*Fine,* by the help of God', he added the
words, 'O Man, help yourself!'.

Gioachino Rossini in his middle twenties

Il Barbiere di Siviglia

THE FIRST PERFORMANCE of Rossini's *Barber* was one of the great fiascos of operatic history. Yet only eight months earlier its composer had taken the first big step in what was to be the most dazzling operatic career of the early nineteenth century.

When Gioacchino Rossini arrived in Naples on 27 June 1815, he was twenty-three years old, he had fourteen operas to his credit, and he had never been this far from home in his life. Born in Pesaro and brought up in Bologna, his early successes had been largely confined to Venice and Milan, and the political divisions of the peninsula, recently reinstated after the Napoleonic interregnum, imposed at least two national borders between the Hapsburg regions of Lombardy and Venetia and the Bourbon Kingdom of the Two Sicilies. But the Italian passion for opera had no respect for political frontiers and already Rossini was being spoken of across Italy as the latest operatic phenomenon. Since Naples had been for a century and a half one of the most important, perhaps *the* most influential, of Italian centres of operatic activity, the appointment of this stripling from the north as director of its royal theatres raised eager anticipation (and not a few eyebrows) as well as opening a new chapter in Rossini's life.

But Italian opera in the early nineteenth century was a cutthroat business. The Neapolitan contract did not tie him exclusively to Naples, and now that he had freed himself from the Venice-Milan axis of earlier years, Rossini was keen to exploit the new possibilities of his position. For some time he had had his eye on Rome, where *Tancredi* and *L'italiana in Algeri* had already been enthusiastically received; in December the previous year he had signed a contract for a new opera with the impresario of the Teatro Valle, and he had been encouraged by his reception there during a brief stopover on the way down to Naples. He wrote to his mother back in Bologna:

Rossini   If you could see the welcome that I am getting in this place you
would be delighted. . . . Everybody wants to meet me and I have been
to see them all, bestowing my favours like a benevolent monarch. . . .
[*Rossini*, 2004: 82]

So when his first Neapolitan opera, *Elisabetta, regina d'Inghilterra*,
had been successfully launched at the San Carlo at the beginning of
October, and a revised version of *L'italiana in Algeri* put safely on its way
at the Teatro dei Fiorentini later in the month, Rossini lost no time in
heading back towards the Papal States.

Rome was not the operatic capital that Naples could claim to be,
and certainly did not have the same musical standards. The overall control of the royal theatres by the Bourbon monarchy had no equivalent in
a city where the Papal authorities tolerated rather than controlled places
of secular entertainment. Apart from occasional moral intervention they
were content to leave the management of the theatres to their (usually aristocratic) owners; it was an arrangement that conferred desirable
social prestige, though at the same time straining the financial resources
of even the wealthiest families, and the rarity of government subsidies,
combined with the exorbitant fees demanded by the most sought-after
singers, meant that funds were not always forthcoming for employees of
lesser importance. These unfortunately included orchestral players—a
field in which the available talent in Italy was anyhow limited. Even
Stendhal, that most passionate apologist for the Italian operatic scene,
was forced to admit that, in the provinces at least, some instrumentalists made mistakes: 'their fingers simply do not have the necessary
dexterity to strike a particular note correctly'. Being Stendhal, he was
prepared to put up with a little inaccuracy for 'the fire! the delicacy!
the soul! the musical feeling!' that went with it. But the violinist and
composer Louis Spohr, being German, found that the situation in Rome
entirely lacked the charm that so enchanted his French contemporary.
[*Stendhal*, II: 39]

Spohr   The orchestra, which was made up of the best musicians in
Rome, was nevertheless the worst of all that had accompanied me in
Italy till now. The ignorance, lack of taste, and impudent arrogance
of these people is beyond all description. Of the nuances of *piano*
and *forte* they know absolutely nothing. . . .   [*Spohr*, I: 330]

As to the theatres themselves, the Irish novelist Lady Morgan, visiting Rome in 1820, was frankly shocked.

Lady Morgan   The Roman theatres, in consequence of the modified toleration under which they exist, are dark, dirty, and paltry in their decorations; but what is infinitely worse, they are so offensive to the senses, so disgusting in the details of their arrangement, that to particularize would be impossible. . . .   [*Morgan, II: 443*]

The Teatro Valle was singled out by Lady Morgan as 'a very small, mean and dirty theatre'. Rossini's first task, when he presented himself there at the beginning of November, was to supervise a revised version of *Il turco in Italia*. This was to be followed by the agreed new opera, *Torvaldo e Dorliska. Torvaldo,* to a libretto by Cesare Sterbini, a Vatican official with cultivated tastes in literature and philosophy, had a mixed reception. But on the day of its first performance Rossini signed a contract for another opera, this time with Duke Francesco Sforza Cesarini, the owner of the Teatro Argentina. This was a step up, because the Argentina was the largest and most important of Rome's opera houses— not that this saved it from Lady Morgan's censure:

Lady Morgan   Suffice it to say, that the corridors of the Argentina exemplify the nastiness of Roman habits and manners more forcibly than volumes could describe. It is in this *immondezzaio* that one is taught to feel how closely purity in externals is connected with virtue in morals. . . .   [*Id: 443–4*]

Nevertheless it was in this 'garbage heap' that Rossini's most famous opera was scheduled to receive its first performance at the beginning of February 1816. The date on the contract was 26 December 1815.

Sforza Cesarini   Signor Duca Sforza Cesarini, Impresario of the [Teatro Argentina], confirms the appointment for the coming Carnival season in 1816 of Signor Maestro Giovacchino Rossini, who promises and undertakes to stage the second *dramma buffo* to be given during the said Carnival season at the aforementioned theatre, in conformity with the libretto, whether old or new, which shall be provided by the Sig. Impresario at the beginning of January, and which the said Sig. Maestro Rossini must set to music suited to the character and abilities of the Signori Cantanti [singers], undertaking at the same time to make any adjustments that may be necessary as and when they arise, either for the better outcome of the music or to suit the needs and convenience of the Signori Cantanti, and this at the sole request of the Sig. Impresario—because it must be thus and not otherwise etc. . . .

Sig. Maestro Rossini equally promises and undertakes to be in Rome in order to carry out the aforesaid task not later than the end of the month of December in the present year, and to deliver the first act, fully completed, to the copyist on the 16th day of the month of January 1816; I say the 16th January in order to allow adequate time for rehearsals and ensemble practice, and to be ready to go on stage on a date to be decided by the Sig. Impresario, though not later than the 5th February . . . , which means that the Sig. Maestro must also deliver the second act to the copyist in time to allow for it to be learnt, rehearsed and put in good order for performance on the aforesaid evening, otherwise the Sig. Maestro will be subject to full penalties—because it must be thus and not otherwise etc. . . .

Sig. Maestro Rossini is also required to undertake the direction of his opera and to be present personally at all rehearsals and ensemble practices, as many times and whenever it may be necessary, either in the theatre or elsewhere, at the pleasure of the Sig. Impresario, and similarly to be present on the first three consecutive evenings that his opera is staged and to direct it from the keyboard—because that is the agreement and not otherwise etc. . . .

As fee for his skilled activities the Sig. Impresario promises and undertakes to pay Sig. Maestro Rossini the sum of four hundred Roman scudi as soon as he has completed the three evenings of direction from the keyboard—and not otherwise etc. . . .

. . . And in addition the Sig. Impresario will provide him with lodgings for the duration of the present contract in the same house that has been granted to Sig. Luigi Zamboni.   [*Rossini, 1992: 124–6*]

Next morning Rossini sent his mother an account of the day's work that was characteristically understated.

Rossini   The outcome of [*Torvaldo*] was good. . . . The audience didn't laugh because the opera is a sentimental one, but on the other hand they applauded, and that's enough. I am going to write another one straight away for the Teatro Argentina; it will be *buffa*, because my good friend Zamboni will be singing in it and I shall be sure of a good result.   [*Rossini*, 2004: *113*]

Luigi Zamboni, a well-established and much-admired bass baritone some twenty-five years older than Rossini, was of Bolognese origin and on friendly terms with Rossini's family. He was already in Rome when Rossini arrived and had at once welcomed the younger man into his own lodgings 'with a thousand kindnesses', so that the provision in the last clause of Rossini's contract with the Duke presumably confirmed (and no doubt subsidised) an existing arrangement—though it is also possible that Cesarini may have seen in the solid figure of Zamboni a potentially restraining influence on the wayward temperament of the young composer.

By the terms of his contract Rossini received substantially less for writing *Il barbiere* than the two leading singers did for singing it, though it is only fair to add they were paid for the entire season, whereas—apart from the little matter of its composition—Rossini was only required to direct three performances in person. The terms were in fact fairly normal for the period, and by this point in his career Rossini knew what to expect. Many years later, in a famous conversation recorded by the amateur musician Edmond Michotte, he told Wagner:

Rossini   I hardly ever got to choose the librettos, which were imposed on me by the impresarios. How often did it happen that to begin with I would receive only part of the scenario—an act at a time, for which I had to write the music without knowing either how the plot continued or how it was going to end! When I think about it now . . . !—but it was up to me to provide for my father, my mother and my grandmother! Travelling from town to town, like a nomad, I wrote three, four operas a year. And believe me, that didn't give me the means to live like a *grand seigneur*. For the *Barbiere* I received 1,200 francs, in a single payment, plus a hazel-coloured coat with gold buttons which was given to me by the impresario so that I could appear decently dressed in the orchestra. This coat, it is true, could have been worth 100 francs. Total: 1,300 francs. I only took thirteen days to write the score, so that it worked out at 100 francs a day all told. So you see I got a substantial salary all the same. I was very proud of it in front of my father, who was only paid 2 francs 50 a day when he had the job of municipal trumpet player in Pesaro.   [*Rognoni*: 404]

For the moment, however, Cesarini was still desperately occupied with singers, and far too busy trying to get his company together to give any thought to librettos. It was an uphill struggle and the stakes were high; earlier in the month he had admitted to his friend the Vatican deputy secretary of state that if he hadn't managed to engage the rest of his singers by the 18th 'he would be looking out his passport because he would certainly have to get out of Rome', and as late as the 16th he was still in 'a desperate state of agitation' about the lack of a second *buffo*—'if we don't find one it will make a laughing stock of Rome for evermore. . .'. [*Rinaldi, I: 494, 496*]

Meanwhile the first *buffo*, Zamboni, was hoping that his sister-in-law, the mezzo-soprano Elisabetta Gafforini, could be persuaded to lead the company. She had achieved great success as a comic *prima donna* in Milan, and would be a great catch for Cesarini, who was to spend much time and effort in trying to persuade her to sign a contract. At the same time, Rossini had been putting pressure on his friend the Spanish tenor Manuel García, of whom he seems (perhaps understandably) to have been rather in awe; some seventeen years Rossini's senior, hot-tempered and unpredictable, García had delayed the first performance of *Elisabetta* in Naples by quarrelling with the management and having to be forced to attend the final rehearsals by the threat of imprisonment. But he was amenable to persuasion, and on the same day that Rossini signed his own contract, he wrote to García with amendments for his role in *L'italiana* (which was now to open Cesarini's season).

Rossini   . . . Please forgive me for not sending them sooner, but you know that a young maestro who has to put a new opera on the stage [*Torvaldo* was opening that evening] is under such pressure that it can even happen that he fails his friends. I hope that, since I am one of that small number, you will understand and forgive me, and get ready to leave [for Rome] as soon as you possibly can.   [*Rossini, 1992: 123*]

But negotiations with Gafforini continued to meet with delaying tactics, and the Duke's agent in Bologna was impatiently urging him to consider an alternative *prima donna*—the contralto Geltrude Righetti-Giorgi; as she, too, was Bolognese, and a childhood friend of Rossini's, he urged Cesarini to apply to Rossini for information about her.

Sforza Cesarini   I have been unwell and confined to my bed, so I have not been able to see Maestro Rossini, and hence unable to obtain information on the subject you raise. . . . But I know that, this lady's husband being a [successful lawyer], it is a long time since she last appeared in the theatre, and if she is returning to it for reasons of her own I should not like to find that, whatever merit she may have had in the past, she is now out of practice or of advanced age. . . . And though I cannot bring myself to believe that [Gafforini's] contract will eventually be returned unsigned, if such a disaster should how-ever occur, and if Sig. Righetti-Giorgi is *really of good quality, not old, and prepared to commit herself firmly to this undertaking,* then in the absence of Gafforini (something that hardly seems possible) I would have no difficulty in engaging her.   [*Id: 119–20*]

The agent hastened to send reassurances—'although she may have given up her theatrical career, she has not given up vocal studies and has frequently appeared at the principal musical occasions in this city'— and when it finally became clear that Gafforini's demands were going to put too great a strain on Cesarini's limited budget, he agreed to engage Righetti-Giorgi *faute de mieux.* On 28 December he wrote to Cardinal Consalvi announcing her imminent arrival in Rome: [*Id: 120n*]

Sforza Cesarini   From what Maestro Rossini and the *buffo* Zamboni, both of whom know her personally, have told me about her, she is an attractive woman, as much in her personal appearance as in her style of singing, so that, although she may not be a Gafforini, and although without hearing her one cannot be sure that she will be well received, at least one can assume that she will do better than the *prima donna* at the Valle—who is a beginner of very little ability. . . .   [*Id*]

Meanwhile 'a mediocre *buffo cantante*', Bartolomeo Botticelli, had been found to play second *buffo*, and with the bass Zenobio Vitarelli the company was at last complete. But the long delay had put Cesarini in a difficult position, and the hassle that ensued in getting *L'italiana* onto the stage in time to open the season less than two weeks later had a disas-trous effect on his ailing health.

Sforza Cesarini   The life I'm living is enough to make a man spit blood, and it's one that I mean never to do again as long as I live. . . . I am holding a knife to everyone's throat in order to get [the opera] onto the stage by Wednesday. . . .

Certainly, having to do things this way—rehearsals, scenery, staging, and all at a moment's notice—is something I do not at all enjoy.
As a result we shall go on the stage unprepared, with the actors totally
exhausted, and if the opera gets sent up, or makes little effect, or is
a complete flop, then everybody will be shouting at me. Last night,
after wearing myself out during the day, I spent from one o'clock at
night until five [in the morning] at a rehearsal of the first act under
the direction of Maestro Rossini . . . , and standing about in a theatre
in this degree of cold is as bad as being on an Alpine pass, with the
result that Rossini, the *prima donna*, the tenor and everybody else
were shivering the entire time, and I got home so numb with cold
that it took me more than an hour to warm up again.   [*Id: 130*]

Nevertheless, *L'italiana in Algeri* opened the Carnival season at
the Teatro Argentina on 13 January. It had a stormy reception. Cesarini
reported 'a terrible uproar' made by the supporters of the Teatro Valle,
'who did their damnedest to silence the people who wanted to applaud'.
All the same, Rossini was called out in front of the curtain at the end of
the first act, and the singers—even the second *buffo*—acquitted themselves to the evident satisfaction of the Duke.

Sforza Cesarini   Botticelli turned out well. He was applauded in the
    Introduction and was called out with the tenor after their duet; he
    forced his voice a bit in the Act 2 quintet, but he did his other pieces
    well and besides his appearance and acting are very good. It is a case
    of contenting ourselves with the mediocre, because neither I, nor any-
    one, could find anything better in the middle of December. The *prima
    donna* made more of a success than I thought she would, and has an
    excellent contralto voice. The *buffo* Zamboni warmly welcomed. The
    tenor beyond praise from every point of view. . . .   [*Id: 133*]

'Geltrude sings and acts to prodigious effect,' wrote Rossini, 'and is
called out to receive universal applause after every piece she sings'. Indeed
her success almost got out of hand at the second performance, when the
audience demanded an encore of one of her arias—'and, as encores are
not permitted here, it became necessary to reinforce the guards in the pit
in order to put down the tumult that had arisen among the spectators'.
However, the season was under way and the cast that was to introduce
Rossini's next opera had been tried out and proved equal to the task.

The trouble was that the next opera was still unwritten, and not even a libretto to show for it.   [*Rossini, 2004: 115*]

There had been a false start. Stendhal, who as Rossini's first and most influential biographer was later responsible for a good deal of unreliable (if entertaining) information about the composer's early life, attributed it to trouble with the Roman censorship—a hare he started in an article, written under a pseudonym, which originally and confusingly appeared in an English magazine published in Paris in 1821.

Stendhal   The impresario had agreed a contract for Rome, and after having several dramas turned down by the censor eventually proposed to Rossini that he should write new music for *Il barbiere di Siviglia*. . . .   [*Rognoni: 356*]

When the article was republished in an Italian translation in Milan in the following year, it caught the eye of Righetti-Giorgi, who decided to set the record straight by publishing her own comments on selected passages.

Righetti-Giorgi   Here, Mr English Journalist, speak I—for whom Rossini actually wrote the part of Rosina in *Il barbiere di Siviglia.*

The censorship didn't have anything to do with it at all. The poet Ferretti was given the job of writing a libretto for the Teatro Argentina, of which the principal role would be for the tenor Garzia. Ferretti proposed a plot in which an officer became enamoured of an innkeeper's wife and was crossed in his affections by a pettifogging lawyer. But the idea seemed to the Impresario rather too commonplace, so he abandoned Ferretti and turned his attention to another poet, Sig. Sterbini. Sterbini, who had been unfortunate with his libretto for *Torvaldo e Dorliska*, wanted to try his luck a second time; he considered with Rossini the choice of a new text, and by common consent they decide on *Il barbiere di Siviglia*.   [*Id: 357*]

In fact, it is probable that, for once, Rossini himself proposed the subject of his opera, and indeed he may have had Beaumarchais's comedy in his sights for some time. *Le barbier de Séville, ou la précaution inutile,* had originally been designed as an *opéra comique* and had only been rewritten as a straight play after its rejection by the Comédie-Italienne—though even in this form it retained a number of interpolated songs, as well as a closing vaudeville with music by Beaumarchais himself. The first truly operatic version had been written in St Petersburg in 1782 by the Neapolitan composer Giovanni Paisiello. It had rapidly become an international success and an established favourite of the Italian repertory, but more than thirty years later Rossini could reasonably feel that such an ideal subject for *opera buffa* could do with fresh treatment. He was not the first to do so (four other operatic versions, now forgotten, had been produced in the intervening years) nor was he to be the last, and in any case, according to the conventions of the time, there was no earthly reason why he should have kept off the subject—many of Metastasio's libretti had been set by fifty or sixty composers and were still being recycled.

Nevertheless, Paisiello, now a Grand Old Man of seventy-five living in semi-retirement in Naples, was known to be cantankerous and jealous in his dealings with other musicians, and this may be one reason why Sterbini was actually less keen to take on the job than Righetti-Giorgi would have us believe. Besides, when he took over from Ferretti (who redeemed himself brilliantly, incidentally, with *Cenerentola* the following year), he had to accept the same deadlines as his predecessor but with almost no time left in which to meet them. He later complained that he had accepted the commission 'reluctantly' and 'against my will', after being begged to do so by both Rossini and the Duke—the latter in his turn complaining bitterly that, the very morning after the exertions of the *Italiana* first night, he had been obliged to 'engage in exhaustive discussions with the poet about the new libretto to be written for Rossini, which has been held up through no fault of mine'.   [*Rossini, 1992: 145; 133–4*]

In any case, three days later Sterbini provided the Duke with a rough scenario.

Sterbini   Introduction. First act.

Scene I. Tenor, Serenade and Cavatina with introductory chorus.

Scene II. Cavatina Figaro, Cavatina Tenor. Another for the Prima Donna.

Duet [Prima] Donna and Figaro—Scene—Figaro tells [Prima] Donna about the Count's love for her. Big duet between Figaro and the Count. Aria, Vitarelli. Aria, Guardian, with intervention. Finale with a full stage and plenty of action.

Second act.

Tenor disguised as the music master gives a lesson to the [Prima] Donna, followed by the aria for her that occurs in the same scene.

Aria second Donna. Quartet. Subject of the quartet: Figaro pre-
pares to shave the Guardian while the Count flirts with the [Prima]
Donna; the Guardian believes he is ill and leaves. Terzetto Figaro,
[Prima] Donna, Tenor. Big aria for the Tenor. Brief finale.

I, the undersigned, promise and undertake to adapt the libretto of
the *Barber of Seville* as above, and to finish the first act within eight
days, and the second within twelve days, of the date of the present
[agreement], and also to assist the Maestro at rehearsals on the stage
and when necessary make any changes to give it greater theatrical
effect.   [*Id*: 135–6]

Sterbini and Rossini were aware of the risks of courting comparison
with such a celebrated predecessor, and determined to take all possible
precautions. According to Stendhal, these included a direct personal
approach to Paisiello.

Stendhal   [Following the proposal] to write new music for *Il barbiere di
Siviglia* the maestro was at first doubtful; he then wrote to Paisiello
to obtain his consent, which Paisiello gave, saying that he had no
doubts as to the success of the enterprise. Rossini showed this reply
to all lovers of opera, and in addition published a notice of explanation in the libretto.   [*Rognoni*: 356]

Forty years on, Rossini himself lent support to this story, claiming in
a letter to a friend that he had written to Paisiello 'declaring that I did not
wish to enter into competition with him, being aware of my inferiority, but
wanted only to treat a subject that gave me pleasure, while avoiding as far
as possible the same situations as those in his libretto. . .'.   [*Pougin*: 44]

But the statement has been received with some scepticism; Rossini's pronouncements in old age were notoriously unreliable, often being
designed to entertain rather than provide accurate information, and in
any case his memory may have confused the personal letter with the
public announcement which he did actually make. Certainly no such letter has survived, let alone any reply; only Stendhal otherwise records its
existence—and Righetti-Giorgi makes short shrift of that.

Righetti-Giorgi   Rossini did not write to Paisiello, as is generally supposed, since he felt that the same plot could be treated with success

by more than one composer. . . . [But] he did include, in the public announcement [of the opera], a declaration saying that he had no intention of offending Paisiello. . . .   [*Rognoni*: 357]

Notice to the Public   The comedy of Signor Beaumarchais entitled *Il barbiere di Siviglia, o sia l'inutile precauzione* will be presented in Rome in the form of a comic opera under the title of *Almaviva, o sia l'inutile precauzione*; this is done with the intention of convincing the public once and for all of the sentiments of respect and veneration felt by the author of the music of the present drama towards the greatly celebrated Paisiello, who has already treated this subject under its original title.

Being called upon to assume this difficult task, Signor Maestro Gioacchino Rossini, in order not to incur the reproach of foolhardy competition with the immortal author who has preceded him, expressly stipulated that *Il barbiere di Siviglia* should be versified entirely anew, and that a number of new situations for musical treatment should be added—which were in any case required by a modern theatrical taste that has changed significantly since the days when the renowned Paisiello wrote his score.

A number of other differences between the composition of the present drama and that of the French comedy have been occasioned by the necessity of introducing choruses in the course of the play, partly because they are required by modern usage, partly because they are indispensable for the musical effect in a theatre of considerable size.   [*Radiciotti, I: 192*]

As if to make the point straight away, Sterbini already has his chorus on the stage when the curtain rises and opens *Almaviva* with a scene that has no place in either Beaumarchais or Paisiello. Instead of entering alone, the Count is surrounded by a group of musicians who not only accompany his serenade to Rosina but follow it with an embarrassingly rowdy chorus of thanks for payment received—a typically Rossinian scene for which the composer, never one to waste a good idea simply because it had misfired elsewhere, recycled music from two of his rare failures, *Aureliano in Palmira* and *Sigismondo* (he was a great self-borrower). The pace and musical energy at once create a comic mood very different to Paisiello's, and with Figaro's entry the focus sharpens more dramatically still. In both earlier versions the barber wanders on stage carrying his guitar, caught rather charmingly in the process of composing a song of his own. But Rossini's barber, after announcing himself, even before he appears on stage, as a force to be reckoned with, embarks on an aria that in its sheer boisterous vitality blows Paisiello straight out of the water. *Largo al factotum* was unlike anything that had appeared in *opera buffa* before, and has remained a classic of the *buffo* style ever since. What on earth can Zamboni's feelings have been when Rossini first sang it to him—as, living in the same house, he surely did?

With such a protagonist it was clear that Rossini's Rosina was going to have to be a very much more assertive figure than Paisiello's heroine. In her first aria, *Una voce poco fa*, she may claim to be 'docile, respectful, obedient', but after only a few bars she pauses and begins again with devastating precision: '<u>but</u>—<u>if</u>—<u>they</u>—touch me on my weak spot it's a <u>viper</u> I shall be', and the ensuing flood of musical bravura leaves no doubt as to her ability to cope with Bartolo, and indeed with Figaro and Almaviva too. Righetti-Giorgi, being a woman of determined character, was well suited to the role; she was also a contralto, and though the range recorded by Spohr of her 'full, powerful voice of rare compass' (two and a half octaves from the F below middle C to the B flat above the stave) rather suggests what we would now call a mezzo-soprano, it was certainly a voice of very different quality from the legion of twittering coloratura sopranos who hijacked the role later in the century, and for years created an altogether false impression of Rossini's resourceful heroine.   [*Spohr, I: 309*]

In general, Sterbini and Rossini were less faithful to Beaumarchais than their predecessor, and in one case even avoided a scene that could have provided Rossini with a magnificent opportunity for fun—the depiction of Bartolo being driven to distraction by his yawning and sneezing servants. Paisiello's *terzetto* at this point invariably brought the house down, so Sterbini and Rossini tactfully dispatched the incident in a few bars of plain recitative—so plain, in fact, that one rather wonders why they bothered to include it at all. But elsewhere Rossini seized gleefully upon every opportunity to develop duets and ensembles, and when the inevitable similarities occur—in the second act particularly—the older score is simply too fragile to bear the comparison. The complexity, teeming invention and cumulative drive of Rossini's ensemble writing are something altogether new in Italian opera; the drunken irruption of Almaviva into the Bartolo household at the end of Act I is turned into a scene of incomparable hilarity, extending into a vast finale (the 'full stage and plenty of action' promised by Sterbini) that inhabits a wholly surreal world of fantasy and ends with what is probably the most exhilarating *stretto* that Rossini ever wrote.

By contrast, the great arias for Figaro, Rosina, Bartolo and Basilio are 'stand and deliver' set pieces, expertly tailored to portray character, and providing static points of reference in the surrounding chaos of unpredictable comedy. In Basilio's celebrated description of the subtle effects of calumny, Rossini, whose use of the orchestral crescendo eventually became so famous that it earned him the nickname of Signor Crescendo, deployed his favourite device with pin-point relevance—an achievement in no way diminished by the fact that the musical terms used by Beaumarchais himself to describe the spread of rumour, '*pianissimo . . . piano, piano . . . rinforzando . . . un crescendo public . . .*', more or less dictated the musical treatment, or that the actual music of the crescendo was simply another exhumation from the score of *Sigismondo*. In any case, the great explosion at the words *come un colpo di cannone* is an altogether new stroke of genius that extinguishes all earlier comparisons.

The companion piece for Bartolo, *A un dottor della mia sorte*, had a curious fate; it opens with spacious self-satisfaction only to break later into some of the most dizzyingly fast patter writing in all opera, and when the *Barber* was first given in Florence, the bass singing Bartolo was totally unable to manage it. A much easier aria, *Manca un foglio*, written by the local maestro Pietro Romani, was therefore substituted, which somehow became permanently adopted, at least in Italy, and continued to be included in standard editions of the score until late in the twentieth century, when it was finally banished in favour of Rossini's original masterpiece.

Only the 'big aria for the Tenor' promised by Sterbini for the final scene of the opera is a dramatic miscalculation. Certainly, in the right hands (or larynx), *Cessa di più resistere* can become the ultimate show-stopper, a brilliant display piece for a star tenor, but in an act that, after an eventful first half, is now mainly concerned with tying up the plot, it delays the action when there is most need to move on quickly, and was only included out of deference to the original Almaviva, Manuel García. For García was clearly regarded as the star of the company—he had not sung before in Rome and was being paid three times what Rossini was getting; he was an experienced musician, possessed of a fine voice somewhat baritonal in quality but of quite exceptional agility, and was able to bring unique elegance and style to the torrent of brilliant vocalization with which Rossini provided him. At his first appearance as Almaviva in London a couple of years later, *The Times* recognised his extraordinary qualifications for the role.

His style is the florid, and carried to a degree which probably has never been exceeded; but his singing is the perfection of that style. . . . To try Signor Garcia as a sentimental singer, would be to destroy his merits altogether. He disclaims that school, we apprehend, upon principle, and should be judged only by those laws on which he has formed himself. . . . [*The Times*]

It is a comment that could well be applied to the opera as a whole. Rossini's florid writing is not simply decorative, as vocal embellishments had been in eighteenth-century opera, but an inherent part of his musical characterization and an integral part of its expressive strength. In no other opera is the passion of virtuosity and the celebration of sheer physical vitality launched with such unflagging power. Though the *Barber* is often thought of as the climax of a long tradition of Italian comic opera, its tough exuberance is far nearer to the robust *commedia dell'arte* origins of Italian comedy than it is to the inherited traditions of *opera buffa*. Rossini was a devoted admirer of Mozart, whose scores he had studied fanatically in his youth, and whom he placed all his life at the undisputed head of his operatic pantheon. Nevertheless it is impossible to imagine Rossini's Almaviva and Rosina turning into the Count and Countess of *Le nozze di Figaro*. For the human breadth and warmth of Mozart's opera Paisiello is a much more likely starting point. In the *Barber* there is room for every sort of comedy, from satire to sly wit to broad humour to gut-wrenching farce, but of human warmth there is an absolute minimum. Nor had Rossini any illusions about the essential artificiality of the operatic medium in the early nineteenth century. Many years later he replied to Wagner's exposition of his theories of music drama:

Rossini   But how is it possible for the independence demanded by the literary conception [of opera] to be maintained, when it has to be combined with musical form, which is pure *convention*? If we have to remain strictly within the limits of logic, we have to admit that people simply don't sing in normal speech: the angry man, the conspirator, the jealous husband—they don't sing! . . . Does anyone really burst into song on his death bed? . . . There is an exception perhaps for lovers, who can be allowed a bit of billing and cooing at a pinch. . . .
[*Rognoni: 410–11*]

Even when Almaviva and Rosina, in the final trio of Act II, are allowed a little billing and cooing, there is Figaro standing behind them, mocking their endearments and nagging them on to make their escape. In opera at least, romantic love was simply not Rossini's strong point.

Sterbini's scenario was dated 17 January. Owing to the delays over the libretto, the opening night had now been put back to 20 February, but even so, if Sterbini handed over the two acts at the intervals agreed (which he appears to have done), Rossini had only a little over three weeks to write his opera, rehearse it, and put it on the stage. So that his own memory of thirteen days for the actual composition cannot have been far wide of the mark. Even if he had been turning the subject over in his mind for some time, this is still a staggering achievement, particularly given the detailed and unprecedented complexity of his orchestration (an aspect of his operas that unfailingly shocked early-nineteenth-century ears). But in spite of his reputation for high spirits and a laid-back attitude to his work—a reputation much encouraged by Stendhal and later biographers—Rossini could be a prodigious worker when the occasion demanded, often regardless of circumstances.

Righetti-Giorgi   I was in Rome with Rossini for the Carnival seasons of 1816 and 1817, during which he composed *Il barbiere di Siviglia* and *Cenerentola*, and I can assert that the first of these operas cost him hard work and study. . . .

The facility with which Rossini composes is unbelievable. . . . When [he] is fired by genius he races along at tremendous speed. The noises that go on around him help rather than hinder him in writing his score. . . . The din made by his friends throws up new ideas. . . . In Rome I saw him composing *Cenerentola* in the midst of the most appalling racket. But he begged his friends to help him in this way: 'If you go away' (he would sometimes say) 'I miss the support and my inspiration goes flat'. Bizarre eccentricity! People would talk, laugh, even sing jolly little songs—though this a little way off. And Rossini, driven on by the pressure of his genius, would get up every so often and, crossing to the pianoforte, play through the latest samples of what he had written.   [*Rognoni: 354, 367–8*]

It was in similar surroundings, and much the same company, that the *Barber* had been composed only a few months earlier.

The score was probably still unfinished when rehearsals began in February, though whether or not the orchestral musicians had 'sufficient dexterity to strike the right notes' when eventually faced with Rossini's instrumental demands we can only guess. In any case, the overture will have been left until the last moment as was Rossini's invariable habit—in fact, it is possible that in this case he never wrote an overture at all: the famous one that is so familiar today was actually written for *Aureliano in Palmira* and had already made a second appearance in Naples with *Elisabetta, regina d'Inghilterra* before becoming attached (definitively) to *Il barbiere* sometime during the course of the original run in Rome. Towards the end of his life Rossini said in a letter that he had originally composed another overture—which some (though not Rossini himself) have claimed was based on Spanish themes provided by García—but, if he did, nothing that looks authentic, and certainly nothing with any Spanish flavour, has survived.

Meanwhile rehearsals continued, no doubt in the same icy conditions that had upset rehearsals for *L'italiana* a few weeks earlier. And in fact the unfortunate Duke Sforza Cesarini, whose weak health had been so severely tried on that occasion and so continually sabotaged in the weeks that followed, was unable to withstand this latest assault on his constitution; after attending a rehearsal on the morning of 16 February he died suddenly that night of a violent seizure at the age of only forty-four. With only four days to go before the first night, his place was taken by the secretary of the ducal household, and the first performance of *Il barbiere di Siviglia* took place as arranged on 20 February.

But for some days it had been clear that other troubles were brewing. The attempt to pacify Paisiello's admirers had backfired, and the obsequious style of the 'Notice to the Public', when the new libretto went on sale, only added fuel to the fire.

Righetti-Giorgi   Oh, what didn't they say about it in the streets and cafés of Rome! The jealous and the ill-disposed wanted to believe that Rossini had already exhausted his youthful inspiration, and displayed the greatest surprise that the Noble impresario of the Teatro Argentina should have asked him to write an opera. So they prepared to make a thorough sacrifice of him, and for a start began by criticizing him for having taken on a subject already treated by Paisiello: 'Just look at this', they cried out in their clubs and bars, 'where is it going to end, the arrogance and lack of judgment of this young man? He has taken it into his head to wipe out the immortal name of Paisiello. You'll see, you idiot, you'll see!'.   [*Id:* 357]

When the night of the performance arrived, the audience was well stocked with Paisiello supporters (who may well have had the tacit—or not so tacit—encouragement of the old man himself), and the first night of *Almaviva, o sia l'inutile precauzione* was one of the great fiascos of operatic history. So much so that descriptions quickly acquired decorative details that are almost certainly fictitious. The one contemporary report that deserves serious attention is that of Righetti-Giorgi herself, though her opening assertion—that, 'by an inauspicious act of courtesy' towards his friend, Rossini had allowed García to replace the second of Almaviva's serenades in the first act with 'ariette' in the Spanish style to his own guitar accompaniment—is open to doubt. The story was accepted as true by most subsequent biographers, but there is no other evidence that it took place; the words of *Se il mio nome saper*, the ravishing Neapolitan *canzone* that Rossini himself provided, are printed in all three editions of the libretto published at the time of the Rome performances, and the vocal line appears in its proper place in the autograph score—though significantly with a guitar part not in Rossini's hand, which suggests that what Rossini may have done was leave the accompaniment to García, an accomplished guitarist, but not the tune. In any case there is no reason to doubt Righetti-Giorgi's account of what followed, when she made her first quick rejoinder before the brusque closing of the shutters.

Righetti-Giorgi   Garcia, after having first tuned his guitar on stage (a proceeding which itself provoked laughter from the mob), sang his [*ariette*] to such poor effect that they were received with contempt. After this I was ready for anything. I climbed nervously up the steps to the balcony, where I had to sing the few words: *Segui, o caro, deh segui così* ['Continue, oh dearest, continue like that']. The Roman audience, accustomed to greeting me in *L'italiana in Algeri* with tumultuous applause, expected me to earn it once more with some pleasing, amorous *cavatina*. When all they heard was those few words, they burst out into screeches and whistles.

After that things developed much as might have been expected. Figaro's cavatina, magnificently sung by Zamboni, and the beautiful duet between Figaro and Almaviva . . . , were scarcely accorded a hearing. At last, no longer at my window, and backed by the reassuring success of thirty-nine previous appearances [before the same public], I appeared on the stage.   [*Id: 358*]

At this point opinions differ.

Stendhal   The opening of this opera made a poor impression on the Romans, who thought it much inferior to Paisiello's version. An aria sung by Rosina [*Una voce poco fa*]—the pretentious cries of a woman advanced in years in place of the sweet lamenting of a young girl in love—was received with displeasure.   [*Id:* 356]

Righetti-Giorgi   Mr Journalist, I was not advanced in years. I had scarcely reached the age of twenty-three. My voice was admired in Rome as the most beautiful that had ever been heard there. Being always ready to give of my best, I had become the protégée of the Roman public. So they quietened down now and prepared to listen to me. I recovered my courage—and the way in which I sang the cavatina of the Viper the Romans themselves will tell you, and Rossini too. They honoured me with three consecutive salvoes of applause, and Rossini even got up from his seat to thank them . . . Turning to me from the keyboard he said jokingly—'Ah! The gifts of Mother Nature!' 'Be grateful to her', I replied with a smile, 'for without her favour you would not be rising to your feet at this moment!'
After that we thought the opera saved. But it wasn't like that. When Zamboni and I sang the fine duet for Figaro and Rosina, jealousy in its most malevolent form brought out all its tricks. Whistles came from every corner of the theatre.   [*Id:* 358]

To add to the merriment the elderly Vitarelli, who was singing the role of Don Basilio, is said to have tripped over a trap door as he came on to the stage and broken his nose—after which it seems doubtful whether *La calunnia* can really have received even the moderate success that Stendhal attributes to it. By the end of the act, with or without the help of a cat which apparently wandered nonchalantly across the stage and had to be summarily ejected into the wings, the situation had evidently become out of hand.

Righetti-Giorgi   We came to the [first act] finale, which is a classic composition that would do honour to the greatest composers in the world. Laughter, catcalls and piercing whistles, with no respite except to hear the very loudest passages. When we reached the [solemn] ensemble passage *Quest'avventura* a raucous voice from the gallery shouted out

'Here's the funeral of D[uke] C[esarini]!' That was the end. It would be impossible to describe the abuse which was showered on Rossini, who remained throughout impassive at the keyboard, as if to say: 'Apollo, pardon these people, who know not what they do'.

When the first act was finished Rossini made a point of applauding with his hands—not his own opera, as many people thought, but the artists who, in all honesty, had really tried to do their best. Many [of the audience] were offended by his behaviour.

That should be enough to give some idea of the fate of the second act.   [*Id*: 358–9]

It seems that about the only thing left to happen in the second act did happen, and Rossinists and anti-Rossinists came to blows. 'As I sat at the keyboard . . . I had to protect myself from an audience that was completely out of control', Rossini told Wagner. 'I really thought they were going to assassinate me'. Nevertheless at the end of the opera he repeated his demonstration of gratitude to the performers.   [*Id*: 397]

Righetti-Giorgi   Rossini left the theatre looking for all the world as if he had merely been some casual spectator. Much moved by the whole occasion I went to his house to offer him comfort, only to find that he had no need of my consolations and was already sound asleep.

[*Id*: 359]

This does sound unlikely, because Rossini, a man of intensely nervous, excitable temperament, was throughout his life acutely sensitive to critical opinion. But he would adopt any artifice to hide his feelings, and it is at least possible that Righetti-Giorgi was on this occasion the victim of an innocent deception that he is known to have practiced later in similar situations. At any rate the following morning he wrote to his mother:

Rossini   Last night my opera went on stage, and was solemnly booed— oh what extraordinary, crazy things are to be met with in this ridiculous town. I can tell you that, in spite of it all, the music is very beautiful, and already people are beginning to talk more optimistically about the second performance this evening, when they will actually hear the music—something that never happened last night because there was a continuous hubbub accompanying the performance from beginning to end.   [*Rossini*, 2004: 119]

Righetti-Giorgi   The next day Rossini removed from his score everything
that seemed to him justifiably criticized. After that, perhaps in order
not to have to reappear at the keyboard, he pretended to be ill. But the
Romans had meanwhile indulged in a change of mind and decided
that it was at least necessary to hear the whole opera with attention in
order to judge it fairly; so they filled the theatre again on the second
night and listened in the most absolute silence.   [*Rognoni: 359*]

Pace Righetti-Giorgi, Rossini in fact changed very little after the first
night, apart from (at some point in the Rome run) substituting the *Elisabetta* overture, and probably cutting altogether the Count's second serenade after the disastrous reception of whatever it was that García had sung
at the first performance. But the change in the audience was dramatic.

Righetti-Giorgi   The opera was now crowned with universal applause. As
soon as it was over we all rushed off to the dissembling invalid, only to
find his bed already surrounded by many distinguished Roman citizens
who had come to compliment him on the excellence of his work.   [*Id*]

Rossini, who had spent the evening in his room anxiously imagining the
progress of his opera in the theatre, was now receiving the reassurances
of his guests. He described the conclusion of the evening to a Bolognese
friend who published it in his biography twenty years later:

Zanolini   While they were conversing together they heard loud shouts
and saw the flames of torches approaching the house. When they distinguished among the uproar the name of Rossini the company grew
pale—but then, recognizing the voices of a number of the maestro's
friends, they threw open the gates to a crowd of spectators from the
Argentina who were transported with enthusiasm and called for Rossini to appear. He did so, to find himself crowned with triumph and
showered with *vivas* and applause. . . .   [*Zanolini: 19*]

Many years later still, Rossini remembered the occasion rather differently, saying that he had been so terrified by the noise outside that he
had tried to hide, and that García had begged him in vain to put in an
appearance for the benefit of crowd. 'Tell them', I replied, 'that I f . . .
them, their bravos, and all the rest. I'm not coming out of here'. I don't
know how poor García presented my refusal to that turbulent crowd—in

fact, he was struck in the eye by an orange, tumefied traces of which formed a black circle visible for several days.'   [*Weinstock: 125*]

In any case, from that moment onward Rossini's illness ceased abruptly, and subsequent performances were greeted by a crescendo of applause. He sent his mother another letter:

Rossini   I wrote to tell you that my opera was booed, and now I write to say that the same piece has met with the happiest possible fate—because on the second evening and at all the later performances [the audiences] have done nothing but applaud my work with an indescribable fanaticism, obliging me to appear five or six times on stage to receive applause of a kind that is entirely new to me and which has made me cry with pleasure. . . . My *Barbiere di Siviglia* is a masterpiece, and I am certain that if you were to hear it you would like it, because it is music that springs directly from the action and follows it with almost excessive care.   [*Rossini, 2004: 121*]

Among all the chaos and fury of those early days, it was an acute self-judgment, which was echoed many years later by the greatest of all Rossini's Italian successors. Along with 'abundance of musical ideas and comic verve', Giuseppe Verdi singled out 'truthfulness of declamation' as a cardinal virtue of the *Barber*, which he called quite simply 'the finest *opera buffa* in existence'. Nor was he alone in this opinion: Beethoven was vigorous in his approbation—'give us more *Barbers*,' he growled as he said goodbye to Rossini after their meeting in Vienna—and Wagner admired without reserve. For in spite of the many rich qualities and sometimes genuinely powerful drama of his later works, and the phenomenal succession of serious operas that ended in the triumph of *Guillaume Tell*, there is always a sense that with comedy Rossini is on his home ground. 'J'étais né pour l'*opera buffa*, tu le sais bien!' he wrote in the famous letter to God at the end of his *Petite messe solennelle*, and to Wagner he admitted: 'To tell the truth I always felt more aptitude for *opera buffa*. I was happier treating comic subjects than serious ones'. But Rossini was never easy to know, and happiness is a fragile state; it was Beaumarchais's Figaro who famously declared 'je me presse de rire de tout, de peur d'être obligé d'en pleurer', and it is perhaps no chance that, of all Rossini's operas, it should be this beautifully constructed and brilliantly artificial comedy that weathered all the ups and downs of his posthumous reputation and was always accepted as the classic Rossini masterpiece.

It took time to reach that status. Perhaps the very directness that Verdi so admired and the utter lack of sentimental appeal disappointed audiences who still hankered (like Doctor Bartolo) after the simpler charms of eighteenth-century *opera buffa* and the elegant emotional world it inhabited. Not many performances passed, however, before the title *Almaviva* was dropped and all invidious comparisons with Paisiello were swept into history. As for Paisiello himself, it would be nice to exonerate him from any part in the uproar on the first night, for he died only four months later; the case against him has never actually been proved, but his reputation is against him and it seems likely that the behaviour of his supporters received encouragement in some form or other from Naples. Whatever the truth of the matter, Rossini was not the man to bear a grudge. In the year of his death, when he was old and immensely famous, he received a letter from a young Italian composer—now quite forgotten—who had had the 'audacity' to set Beaumarchais's comedy to music once again. Replying, Rossini gracefully accepted the dedication of the young man's score:

Rossini   Passy, 8th August 1868. . . . This word 'audacity' is the only one that I find superfluous in your charming letter. I certainly didn't regard myself as audacious when, after Papa Paisiello, . . . I set Beaumarchais' delightful subject to music. So why should you be if, after half a century and more, you bring a new style to the musical setting of the *Barber*?

Not long ago Paisiello's version was revived at a theatre in Paris: sparkling as it is with spontaneous melody and theatrical invention, it obtained a brilliant and well-deserved success. Many polemics and many disputes have arisen, and still arise, between the admirers of the old music and the new, but you should remember (at least I advise you to) the ancient proverb which says *Fra i due litiganti il terzo gode* [When two dispute it's the third who benefits]. Please be assured that it is this third whom I should like to see the beneficiary.

And so may your new *Barber* join [your earlier works] in assuring imperishable glory for its author and for our common homeland. Such are the cordial wishes offered to you by the old man of Pesaro whose name is

Rossini.   [*Mazzatinti*: 328–9]

Hector Berlioz at the time of the first
performance of *Les Troyens*

Les Troyens

FOR BERLIOZ the story of Troy was a lifelong obsession: Virgil was an unfailing source of inspiration, and the *Aeneid* one of the few books he kept always at his bedside. The imagery of those heroic days of antiquity pervaded his dreams and fantasies:

Berlioz   If I were rich, very rich, . . . I would go to Mehemet-Ali and I would say to him: 'Highness, sell me the island of Tenedos, sell me Cape Sigeum and the Simoïs, the Scamander *et campos ubi Troja fuit*. Don't be alarmed; it has nothing to do with war or commerce, it's not going to upset your operations on the Hellespont; it's a matter of music and poetry—but that needn't concern you. . . .'

    Once I had become master of those places consecrated by the Muse of antiquity, of those hills, those woods where flowed the tears of Andromache and Briseis, the blood of Hector and Patrocles . . . I would fit out a vessel and embark a great orchestra . . . and set sail for Troy. And when I arrived in that sublime country I would create a place of solitude. I would build a temple of sound at the foot of Mount Ida. . . .   [*Revue, 28.1.1841*]

It was a passion that had been formed in his earliest years.

Berlioz   I was ten years old . . . when my father decided to take over my education himself, but to begin with he was unable to inspire me with any taste for the classics. Above all I hated having to learn passages of Horace and Virgil by heart every day; it was only with agonies of mental effort that I memorised this glorious verse, and my thoughts wandered off impatiently in other directions. . . . [But slowly these dreams] faded before the beauties of poetry. It was Virgil who revealed to me the epic passions for which instinct had already prepared me, Virgil who first found the way to my heart and kindled my smouldering imagination.

How often, construing to my father the fourth book of the *Aeneid*, have I felt my breast heave, my voice falter and break! One day. . . . I was struggling bravely on to the crisis of the drama and came to the scene where Dido, surrounded by the gifts and weapons of her perfidious lover, pours out the bitter torrent of her lifeblood upon her bed—*that bed, alas, so full of memories*; when I found myself forced to recite the despairing cries of the dying Queen, 'thrice raising herself upon her elbow and thrice falling back', to describe her wound and the fatal passion which ravaged her breast, to echo the lamentations of her sister and her women, to depict that terrible agony which moved the gods themselves to pity . . . then, indeed, my lips trembled and the words fell from them indistinct and incoherent. At last came the line: '*Quaesivit coelo lucem ingemuitque reperta*'. At this sublime image, as Dido 'sought light from heaven and groaned at finding it', I was seized with violent agitation; unable to read further, I stopped dead. . . . My father, pretending not to notice my emotion, rose and shut the book. 'That will do my boy, I'm tired!' he said. And I rushed away, far out of sight, to indulge in solitude my Virgilian grief.   [*Mémoires*: 42–4]

It was this scene, this grief—and the desperate music that it eventually tore from him—which was to crown and close the last great work of Berlioz's career. But it was not until fifty years after the tranquil childhood described in his *Memoirs* that *Les Troyens* made its long-awaited appearance, in sadly truncated form, before an uncomprehending Parisian public.

In the years between, the growing composer found other gods to worship. Gluck, Beethoven, above all Shakespeare, were the heroes to whom he turned as he struggled to match reality with his dreams and ambitions. But they were years, too, of frustration and disappointment; his best work was repeatedly misunderstood, his only opera, *Benvenuto Cellini*, a failure that closed the doors of the Paris Opéra to him for ever. His work as a music critic became a drudgery from which he could not escape, and his natural exuberance and romantic enthusiasm hovered continually on the brink of despair. In October 1854, at the age of nearly fifty-one, he wrote the closing pages of the *Memoirs*.

Berlioz And now here I am, if not at the end of my career at least
upon its last steep decline—tired, burned up and yet still burning,
filled with an energy that sometimes bursts out with such violence
that it almost frightens me. I begin to know French, to be able
to write a decent page of music, or verse, or prose; I can direct
an orchestra and give it life; I worship art in all its forms. But I
belong to a nation that no longer cares for the noble expressions
of the mind, whose only god is the golden calf. The Parisians have
become a barbarian people. . . . The industrialisation of art, swollen
with imbecile vanity and followed by all the base instincts to which
it panders, marches at the head of its ludicrous procession. In Paris
I can do nothing.

    I know well enough what I could accomplish in dramatic music,
but the attempt would be both useless and dangerous. Our lyric theatres are houses of ill fame musically speaking, the Opéra above all.
And I could only give free rein to my ideas in this type of composition
if I could be sure of being in absolute control of a great theatre, as
I am in control of an orchestra when I conduct one of my symphonies. . . . An opera house, as I conceive it, is before everything else
a vast musical instrument; I know how to play it, but if I am to play
it well it must be entrusted to me without reserve. And that's something that will never happen.

    For the last three years I have been tormented by the idea of an
enormous opera, for which I would write both words and music. . . .
To me the subject seems magnificent and deeply moving—which
clearly means that the Parisians would find it flat and dull. And
even if I were mistaken in this, I should never get a woman intelligent and devoted enough to interpret the chief part, for it needs
beauty, a great voice, real dramatic talent, perfect musicianship and
a heart and soul of fire. . . . The very thought of encountering, over
such a work, the senseless obstacles which I have endured in the
past, and which I see daily endured by others who write for our
noble Opéra, makes my blood boil. . . . I am resisting the temptation to realise this project, and I shall continue to resist it, I hope,
until the end. [*Id*: 547–50]

And so he might have done, but for a conversation which took place in
February 1856.

Berlioz   I happened to be in Weimar with the Princess Wittgenstein, Liszt's devoted friend, a woman of sympathy and intelligence who has often comforted me in my darkest hours. Something made me speak to her of my admiration for Virgil, and of the idea I had conceived of a great opera, on the Shakespearian plan, based on the second and fourth books of the *Aeneid*. I added that I knew too well the inevitable miseries of such an undertaking ever to attempt it. 'But,' said the Princess, 'your passion for Shakespeare combined with this love of classical antiquity would certainly produce something new and splendid. Come, you must write this opera, this lyric poem or whatever you like to call it. You must begin it—and finish it.' I continued my objections. 'Listen,' she said, 'if you shirk the difficulties which this piece can and must bring you, if you are so feeble as to fear braving everything for Dido and Cassandra, then never come back here. I will not see you again.'

This was more than enough to decide me. On my return to Paris I set to work on the verses for *The Trojans*.   [*Id:* 567–8]

The story of the wooden horse and the sack of Troy does not appear in its chronological place in Book 1 of the *Aeneid*, but is related to Dido by Aeneas after his arrival in Carthage in Book 2. It is this tumultuous description that Berlioz took as the basis of his first two acts—though he vastly expanded the character of Cassandra, from a few lines in Virgil, to the Sibylline protagonist who despairingly watches the unfolding tragedy and becomes its ultimate victim. He dispensed entirely with Aeneas's account of his adventures before he reached the African coast (which fill Book 3), and turned back briefly to Book 1, with its depiction of Dido in her newly founded city and her reception of the Trojan refugees, for the first of his Carthage scenes. But the bulk of the last three acts, the love of Dido and Aeneas, the hunt, the storm, Aeneas's departure for Italy and Dido's final immolation, came entirely from Virgil's fourth book, sometimes with details that are lifted almost verbatim from the original.

Thanks to his long familiarity with the *Aeneid*, Berlioz was able to construct much of his libretto from actual translation or paraphrases of Virgil's text, using the spoken dialogue where possible and elaborating it with material gleaned from the narrative. As a model for structure and style, he looked back to the great classical dramas of Gluck, a composer he had always worshipped, though he added elements of spectacle—

crowd scenes, ballet and an important role for the chorus—that suggest
a debt to the Parisian grand opera of his own day. And there is the inevitable influence of Shakespeare, not only in moments of poetic ecstasy,
but in the human contrasts and variety of the action. For this is a very
human interpretation of Virgil. Apart from the recurrent insistence on
Aeneas's destiny in Italy, there is no overt presence of the gods whose
intrigues and favours control the development of the Latin epic; this is a
story of classical antiquity seen through the eyes of a man for whom its
participants were real, live beings—often more real and more live than
their counterparts in the world around him.

Berlioz   Paris, April 12th, 1856. My dear Liszt . . . I have already started
working out the main lines of the great dramatic business which the
Princess is so interested in. It's beginning to take shape—but it's
enormous and therefore dangerous. I need plenty of spiritual calm,
which is precisely what I haven't got. It will come, perhaps. Meanwhile I am ruminating, and gathering my strength like a cat before a
desperate spring. I am trying above all to resign myself to the agonies
which this work cannot fail to bring me. . . . Anyhow, whether I succeed or not, I shan't tell you any more about it until the whole thing
is finished. And God alone knows when that will be—I am under no
obligation to do it quickly.   [*Correspondance, V: 286*]

From the beginning, Berlioz was anxious to keep his new project a
secret, away from publicity and the unwanted curiosity of strangers. But
to the Princess Sayn-Wittgenstein he confided his hopes and fears in
a series of letters that chart the progress of the work, and bear witness
to the 'ardent, exalted existence' that he led during the two years of its
composition.

Berlioz   May 17th, 1856. Dear Princess . . . I wanted to be able to send
you some positive news about the great enterprise which *you* have
inspired. Only the day before yesterday I finished versifying the first
act. It will be the longest, and took me ten days to write—the first I
have had free since I got back from Weimar.
    I cannot tell you what moods of discouragement, joy, disgust, plea-
sure and fury I have passed through during those ten days. Twenty
times I've been on the point of chucking the whole thing into the fire

and giving myself up for ever to the contemplative life. But now I'm sure of the courage to reach the end; the work has got hold of me. Besides, I re-read your letter every so often to spur myself on. It's usually at night that I feel discouraged, but in the morning, in the youth of the day, I return once more into the breach. And now I can hardly sleep; I think of nothing else, and if only I had the time to work at it in two months the whole mosaic would be complete.

But how to find the time! . . . Always these infernal reviews to write—recitals by débutants, recitals by débutantes, revivals of antiquated operas, premières of antiquated operas, concerts of antiquated music which go off like forgotten squibs at the end of a firework display. . . . And now I've got to rush about Paris from morning till night, seeing all and sundry (mostly sundry) and busying myself with my election to the Institute. . . .   [*Id: 300–1*]

Berlioz's activities as a musical journalist, though financially necessary, were a constant source of irritation to him, and now there was a new distraction to add to his problems. The death of Adolphe Adam had left a vacant seat at the Institut de France, and Berlioz with nine others was nominated for election. It was a belated sign of recognition, but as a result he found himself forced into the customary campaign of wearisome private visits to solicit votes.

Berlioz   I'm spending today on a round of the academic shrines. Believe it or not, M. Ingres himself has unbent and promised me his vote— on the second ballot, if his own little Benjamin, Gounod, is not elected on the first. The musicians are for me, including Halévy, in spite of my last article on his *Valentine*. But Auber remains placidly determined to side with the biggest guns. . . .   [*Id: 310*]

I am enormously busy and, to tell you the truth, thoroughly ill— without in the least knowing what's wrong with me. An extraordinary sense of *malaise*: I fall asleep in the street and so on. Perhaps it's the spring. . . . And everybody's dying; I'm never out of a cemetery. The good Lord is mowing us down. . . .   [*Id: 303, 308*]

June 24th. A thousand apologies, Princess, for not replying until today. As you will have guessed, the *Aeneid* and the Academy have been the cause of the delay, but the *Aeneid* far more than the Academy. Every morning I got into a cab, visiting book in hand, and as I

continued my pilgrimage I dreamt not of what I was going to say to
the next Immortal on my list, but of what I was going to make the
characters say in my opera.

But now at last that dual preoccupation is over. As you know, I
have been elected to the Institute. . . . And so here I am, a respectable
person at last—no longer a Bohemian, a vagabond! What a comedy!
I don't despair of being Pope one day. . . . My apartment is never free
of visitors; letters of congratulation come pouring in. Such transports
of delight as you simply can't imagine—and I certainly didn't foresee.
I still have twenty-two colleagues to call upon and thank; I saw fifteen this morning and was obliged to suffer the embraces of several
who voted against me. . . . Never mind! In three weeks I shall have
finished chiselling my libretto and I shall set to work on my score. . . .

Forgive the triviality and coldness of this letter. Can it be that
already I . . . ? But no, surely not—my Institute uniform hasn't even
been ordered. . . .   [*Id*: 329–30, 322]

The poem of the opera is very nearly finished. I'm at the last scene
of the fifth act. I get more impassioned about the subject than I
should, but I'm resisting continuous appeals for attention from the
music. I want to get everything properly finished before I begin on
the score. And yet, last week, it simply wasn't possible not to write
. . . the music *as well as* the words for the great duet in the fourth act,
a scene stolen from Shakespeare and Virgilianised which reduces me
to the most absurd state of emotion:

> '. . . In such a night as this
> When the sweet wind did gently kiss the trees . . .'

I've really had to think only about the *arrangement* of this immortal
ecstasy of love, which raises the last act of *The Merchant of Venice* to
a level with the sublime hymns of *Romeo and Juliet*. It is Shakespeare
who is the real author of both words and music. Strange that he, the
poet of the North, should have intervened in the masterpiece of the
poet of Rome. . . . What singers, these two!   [*Id*: 329, 317]

So the music for this 'litany of love', the passionate outpouring of melody
that closes the fourth act of the opera, was the first part of *Les Troyens*
to be composed.

Only a week later he sent the completed libretto to the Princess.

Berlioz   I would have sent you the manuscript already, but for my fear of finding you disappointed in it. However, you'll have to decide sooner or later what you think of this amateur poetry; in two or three days *The Trojans* will leave here by train. Would you be kind enough to let me have them back as soon as possible, and show them only to intimate friends on whose discretion one can count? When I say *The Trojans* I don't mean that this title is settled. But it's the one which seems best at the moment. All the others—*Aeneas, The Aeneid, Dido, Troy and Carthage, Italy!*—have been adopted and rejected in turn. . . . But that's no great matter. The thing now is the music, and you will see what an enormous score this libretto presupposes.

You laugh at my plans for seclusion, my hankering for deserts, etc. None the less it's true that for eight days I've been unable to snatch a single hour's freedom to think over my ideas, and all next month is being torn from me in shreds. . . .

And then . . . and then . . . Will you believe that I have fallen *in love*, but utterly in love, with my queen of Carthage? I adore her passionately, this beautiful Dido! . . .   [*Id:* 337–8]

The Princess (whose letters to Berlioz have not survived) sent sixteen pages of comment and congratulations. Berlioz replied from Baden, where he was conducting.

Berlioz   How can I thank you, Princess, for your goodness in writing me so precious a letter! What an analysis! This is really entering into the spirit of the thing! . . . But your object was to encourage me, and I shall not be deluded by your words; you even credit me with the beauty of Virgil's poetry and praise my thefts from Shakespeare. Don't worry—it wasn't necessary to lure me on with eulogies I don't deserve. It's beautiful because it's Virgil; it's striking because it's Shakespeare; I know it. I'm nothing but a plunderer; I have ransacked the garden of two geniuses and cut there a swathe of flowers to make a couch for music: God grant she will not perish, overcome by the fragrance. . . .   [*Id:* 350]

When I am back in Paris I shall try to shake off all other business and begin my musical task. It will be hard: may all Virgil's gods come to my aid, or I am lost. What is so terribly difficult is to find the musical *form*—that form without which music does not exist, or at most exists only as the humble slave of the words. There lies Wagner's crime; he wants to dethrone music, to reduce it to *expressive accents,* thus going even further than Gluck (who most fortunately *did not succeed* in following his own ungodly theory). I am for the kind of music which you yourself call *free.* Yes, free and proud and sovereign and conquering. I want it to grasp everything, to assimilate everything. . . . How to find the way to be *expressive, true,* without ceasing to be a musician; how to endow music, instead, with new means of action—that is the problem. . . . And there's another rock in my way: the feelings that must be expressed move me too deeply. That's useless. One must try to do coolly things that are fiery. It was this that held me up so long in the adagio of *Romeo and Juliet* and the finale of reconciliation; I thought I would never see my way.

Time! . . . Time! . . . He is the great master! Unfortunately, like Ugolino, he eats his children. . . .   [*Id*: 352–3]

In fact, Berlioz had already made a start on the music of his opening scene. On the way to Baden he had spent a fortnight at Plombières, the fashionable spa in the Vosges, and for the first few days had dutifully taken the waters as a restorative for his health. But before long he had been unable to resist the call of his score; one day, 'dreaming in the woods', he had plunged straight into Act I with the opening chorus for the Trojan crowd and the scene for Cassandra that follows it. (Contrary to nearly all French precedent, he wrote no overture for his opera, a fact on which he later commented in a letter to Liszt.

Berlioz   The reason I didn't write an overture is an orchestrator's reason. During the crowd scenes at the beginning, the Trojan mob is accompanied solely by the wind (woodwind); the strings remain silent and don't make an entry until the moment when Cassandra first speaks. It is a special effect which would have been ruined by an overture, because I wouldn't have been able to do without the strings. . . .)
                                                        [*Correspondance*, VI: 316]

The return to Paris brought the usual distractions and worries, as well as increasing pain from what he described as his 'malaise'—the intestinal condition from which he suffered for the rest of his life; to his sister, Adèle, he wrote with an intimate desperation that contrasts with his manner to the Princess.

Berlioz   I had to write to you today. . . . I am in a state of internal agitation, and I feel I might calm the fever if I talk to you for a moment. . . . I am trembling from head to foot, from head to heart with impatience, agony, enthusiasm and too, too much life. I cannot write my score quickly enough; it needs a huge, a disastrous amount of time. And what of its future? There's no one to perform it. The Opéra is in the hands of the enemy. The Emperor knows nothing, understands nothing—nothing is written or played in this little world but imbecilities and platitudes. The buffoons and cretins gain the day. And time passes. . . .

I saw Robert yesterday. He says I have neuralgia of the intestines. He has prescribed six drops of laudanum every morning, to be taken in a spoonful of water. I began today: the relief is immediate, but it leaves an internal trembling which is rather unpleasant. . . .

[*Correspondance, V:* 378–9, 386]

November 14th. I owe you many excuses, Princess, for being so late in replying. . . . I haven't ceased one day from my Phrygian task, in spite of the ugly moods of disgust into which my health has plunged me. I found then that everything I had done was cold, flat, insipid and worthless; I wanted to burn it. . . . But the human machine is strange and unpredictable. Now that I'm better, I re-read my score and it seems to me not so stupid as I thought.

I compose a piece in two days—sometimes one—and then take three weeks to think it over, polish it and orchestrate it. I am still at the big ensemble:

> Châtiment effroyable!
> mystérieuse horreur!

after Aeneas has described the fate of Laocoön. . . . The account of the disaster, and even more the ensemble which follows, are two tremendous horrors which I think will make your heart miss a beat. . . .

[*Id:* 382, 693]

By a mixture of luck and good management Berlioz was free of foreign travel and virtually all conducting engagements until his next trip to Baden the following summer, so that, apart from the incessant demands of concerts and reviews, he could devote every available moment to his score. He felt more confident of his material. 'I'm beginning to be able to prevent myself being carried away by my subject,' he wrote; 'that's an important step in becoming master of it'.   [*Id: V, 388*]

To begin with he divided his attention between the first act and the music for Act 4—which he still found impossible to resist.

Berlioz   25th December. You ask me news of Troy. I only got back there tonight. Yesterday I was in Carthage, completing the instrumentation of the great duet of the lovers and the finale of Act 4. But this doesn't mean that the preceding pieces are done. I am working now at the end of the first act (the scene of the procession with the wooden horse)—all the rest of this act is finished. . . . I retouch the poem again and again. . . . But when I think of what is to become of all this my heart grows cold.   [*Id: 401*]

I am always ill; yesterday I suffered particularly, but it was the day after a big dinner at which no doubt I committed some indiscretion of diet. . . . There's another banquet tomorrow—I shall only eat sardines. . . .   [*Id: 412*]

26th January. I have this moment completed the full score of the monster finale to the first act. Until yesterday I was very much worried because of its size. But I sent Rocquemont [Berlioz's copyist] to the Conservatoire to find me the score of Spontini's *Olimpie*, which contains a triumphal march in the same movement as mine, and in bars of the same length. I counted the bars: he has 347 and I have only 244. What's more, there is no action at all during the vast processional development of his march, whereas I have Cassandra to occupy the stage while the cortège of the wooden horse passes in the background. So I think it will do. . . .   [*Id: 418*]

5th February. Five days ago I was on the point of writing you a long letter which, fortunately, I didn't send off. . . . I was in a ferment of joy; I had just played through my first act mentally from one end to the other. Now there is really nothing so ludicrous as an author who, imitating the good Lord, considers his work on the seventh day and *finds it good*.

But just imagine: apart from two or three pieces I had *forgotten the whole thing!* With the result that in reading it I actually made discoveries. . . . Hence raptures! . . . I had left out only the mime scene for Andromache—its importance terrified me. But now that's done too, and of the whole act I think it's the piece that comes off best. . . . I've wept buckets over it already. Imitating the good Lord again, you will observe—though a lively sensibility was not his strong suit if one is to believe that appalling old rogue Moses. . . .   [*Id:* 424]

[Just as I had finished it] I had a visit from the cornet player, Arban, a man with the most precise sense of melodic expression; he began singing the clarinet solo, perfectly, and there I was in the seventeenth heaven. Two days later I sent for the clarinettist of the Opéra, a first-class virtuoso but cold. He tried his solo, phrasing it *approximately,* and found it very *pretty* . . . and there I was in hell, fed up with Andromache and Astyanax and ready to chuck the whole thing into the fire. What a crime is this *approximately* in musical performance! However, I think the young man will end by understanding his solo, if I make him study it bar by bar. . . .   [*Id:* 428]

And so here I am with an act and a half of the music behind me. My score is building itself up like a stalactite in a damp cave, almost without my knowing about it. Given time, perhaps the rest of the stalactite will form in the same way—that is, if the cave itself doesn't collapse. . . .   [*Id:* 419]

A new stimulus came from readings of the libretto to groups of friends and colleagues. To his sister he wrote on 25 February:

Berlioz   The other day I had an immense pleasure. Baron Taylor (the president of the Artists' Association, who used to be director of the Théâtre-Français) had often asked me at the Institute to read him my poem, but I was desperately nervous of doing so. At last I gave in, and I scarcely dare repeat what he said. He was overwhelmed. 'There hasn't been an opera poem like it since Quinault's *Armide*. It's superb! If I became Director of the Opera I'd put it on tomorrow and I'd spend a hundred thousand francs on it.'

It is true that, since I read it to you, the whole poem has been much cut and improved. The advice and criticisms of friends have not fallen on deaf ears.   [*Id:* 433]

Legouvé [dramatist and close friend] gave up a full half day to studying it in detail. As a whole he was delighted, but he made four important observations on the development of the action with which I agreed. Three corrections were quickly done, but the last, at the beginning of the fifth act, has made me sweat. It's finished now. Only, as it entails another change in the finale of the fourth act, for which the music is already written, I've had a few pages of score to rework.   [*Id:* 424–5]

Since completing the first act, Berlioz had been concentrating entirely on the fourth, 'the act of tenderness, of love, of fêtes and hunts and the starlit African night'. Having already begun at the end of it, with the love duet, he had worked backwards.

Berlioz   It's coming in floods, but in thoroughly disorganised floods. The end and the middle are done, and I am about to begin the beginning. . . . The last piece I have written is the ensemble which comes before the duet of the lovers·

> 'Tout n'est que paix et charme autour de nous,
> La nuit étend son voile et la mer endormie
> Murmure en sommeillant les accords les plus doux'

It seems to me that there is something new in this evocation of happiness at *seeing the night* and *hearing the silence,* and in finding sublime expression for the sound of the sleeping sea. What is more, this ensemble links onto the duet in a wholly unexpected way—which came about by chance, for I hadn't thought of it when writing each piece separately. . . .

As to my feelings about the music, they vary according to my mood, according to the sunshine or the rain, according to whether or not I have a headache. The same piece that yesterday threw me into transports of delight inspires me today with cold disgust. I can only comfort myself by remembering that it's always been like this with all my works. . . .   [*Id:* 428–9]

March 12th. What a joy! A letter from you this morning, dear Adèle! Just what I needed to pull me up a bit. My neuralgia pains are worse than ever. The cause, I think, is the agony I have suffered at not being able to work on my score for the last eleven days. I am in an absolute wasp's nest of concert-givers: they come and wake me when I'm still asleep, to hear their masterpieces in *my house*, or want to drag me off to *their houses*, and all of them expect me to go to their performances, advertise them, talk about them in my articles—it's enough to drive one mad. . . .

A few days ago I gave a solemn reading of *The Trojans* at M. Bertin's house—the director of the *Journal des Débats*. Most of my colleagues were there. . . . The success was great; everybody was struck, almost frightened by the immensity of the musical under-taking, by the force of such epic passions and the grandeur of this Virgilian-Shakespearian canvas. They begged me to leave everything, forget everything for the sake of my score. You can see just how easy it is to follow such advice. . . .

But I'm back at it again today, and I'm about to attack the big scene of the royal hunt, when Dido and Aeneas are overtaken by a storm in the forest. I've finished the scene of the ring—do you remember? The one where Ascanius in play pulls from Dido's finger the ring of Sychaeus, her former husband. The idea is borrowed from a picture by Guérin. It's a quartet [eventually a quintet, with the addition of a part for Aeneas] of fine proportions: above all there is a phrase for Dido, 'Tout conspire à vaincre mes remords, et mon coeur est absous', which seems to me extremely moving—for anyone capable of emotion.

I have got to find a way of speaking about this work to the Emperor (for the distant future). The Opéra at the moment is in a state of utter chaos, and nothing would be more impossible than to put on *The Trojans* with the dilapidated means available there.   [*Id*: 436–8]

Berlioz's first contact with the Opéra about his new work had not been encouraging. As early as September, 1856, he had spoken in confidence to Royer, the newly appointed director . . .

Berlioz   . . . but he's like all the other directors have been, a musical Hottentot. He looks on me as a symphonist who ought to stick to symphonies and doesn't know how to write for voices. He has heard neither *Faust* nor *L'enfance du Christ*; he knows nothing whatever about it—he's just got this idea fixed in his head. . . .   [*Id*: 366]

Even at this date the idea of approaching the Emperor directly was already in Berlioz's mind: now that he had reached official eminence as a member of the Institute, he naturally hoped for a share of official recognition. But it soon became evident that access to Court circles did not necessarily solve anything.

Berlioz   I went to the Tuileries last Monday: the bore of these soirées is having to put on a uniform and a sword, and then all these crosses, big as your hand, which make a noise like an ironmonger's shop in a high wind. . . . I couldn't get a word in with the Emperor; he only talked to *useful* people. . . . If he would help me that would be something. But it looks as if I might as well try moving mountains! His horror of music grows from day to day—and the Empress is worse. It's unbelievable, this harmoniphobia! Still, the Minister of State has just subscribed for ten copies of my *Te Deum,* and the Kings of Prussia, Saxony and Hanover have done the same. I have hopes of Russia; but of Prince Albert, to whom the work is dedicated, I have no hope at all. He is perfectly capable of sending me what he sent Meyerbeer on a similar occasion—*his own complete works.* . . .   [*Id:* 438, 434]

March 24th. Dear Princess . . . I leave Ascanius and the Trojans in the Africa forest, with the trumpets sounding and the thunder rolling, to give myself the pleasure of talking to you. . . . I have now opened the fifth act with a scene for the Trojan chieftains—'Each day sees the wrath of the gods increase'—then the entry of Aeneas, his monologue and the appearance of the spectres.

And I have added another great tirade for Cassandra during the finale of the first act, as the cortège with the wooden horse moves away after crossing the back of the stage. . . . This adds a new touch of excitement to the scene, and is declaimed (in music, of course) over the processional march as it fades into the distance.

It would take too long to tell you all the small changes I have made here and there. Only when the score is finished shall I be able to regard the libretto as finished too. At the moment I'm looking for ways to save time. It's too long. And I've got to find twenty-five minutes for the ballet.

I spent yesterday evening at the Tuileries and was able to speak for quite a long time about *The Trojans* to the Empress. . . . To my great surprise I found her well versed in the poets of the classical period; she knows the *Aeneid* down to the last detail. My God, how beautiful she is! Ah, if only I had a Dido like that—but no, it would wreck the piece; the audience would throw eggs at an Aeneas who could for one instant contemplate deserting her. . . . [*Id*: 445–6]

This long interview was a source of great curiosity to the spectators, as you can imagine. My colleagues of the Institute, above all, amused me afterwards with their questions: 'But what the devil did you have to say to the Empress, talking to her so long?'. . . When I took leave of her I made a point of asking permission to read her my poem—later on, when I'm further ahead with the score. The idea seemed to please her; at least she agreed readily enough. . . . I hope it will come off, but I shan't hurry myself. [*Id*: 451]

April 9th. The day before yesterday I finished this diabolical scene of the storm during the royal hunt, where there are so many stage pictures which the music must absolutely portray: Naiads bathing in the tranquil forest, distant fanfares, huntsmen alarmed by the approaching storm, streams transformed into torrents, cries of ill omen from the distracted Nymphs when Dido follows Aeneas into the cave, grotesque dances of Satyrs and Fauns who wave in their hands the burning fragments of a tree shattered by lightning, etc. etc. Now I must tackle the second act, which I had left behind. . . . [*Id*: 450–1]

During the summer Berlioz had less time for letters, and information on progress is scarcer. There were no further signs of Imperial interest (the promised reading never came off), and his health was worse than ever. Nevertheless he stuck to his score, turning down tempting conducting offers from as far afield as Sweden and even America, and on June 26th was able to report to his sister:

Berlioz   I am just now finishing the music of the second act. It is, I think, the most difficult part of my task; the scene of Cassandra with the Trojan women above all presented enormous problems. But I hope I have achieved my object and really evoked this ceaselessly mounting exaltation, this passion in the end for death, which inspires the heroic virgin and sweeps on to the Trojan women, and which ends by wrenching even from the Greek soldiers a horrified cry of admiration.

Another thing I've done, for the third act, is the national song of the Carthaginians, which will be sung several times to welcome Dido at her entry. It's the *God save the Queen* of Carthage.

So you see I'm getting on, and it looks as if by this time next year everything will be finished. As for the means of staging it, the date of the production, the director who will put it on—all that's in the clouds, better not think about it. . . . [*Id: 470–1*]

And there is an ironic little postscript to his two nieces:

Berlioz I am sending you a manual of harmony in which you can learn the science of chords. Be sure to write each of you, as soon as possible, a little opera in five acts. The need is much felt. . . . [*Id: 472*]

From Plombières, on his way to Baden to direct the only concert he had allowed himself since the same engagement the previous year, he wrote in early August:

Berlioz This terrible heat of which you complain so much suits us admirably; it's a positively tropical climate and I'm already looking for pineapples in the woods. . . . You can have no idea of the beauty of the woods here at sunrise or by moonlight. Three days ago I went out quite alone in the early morning to the spring of Stanislas. I took my *Trojans* manuscript, some music paper and a pencil; the lodge keeper arranged a table for me in the shade and put on it kirsch, sugar and a bowl of milk, and I worked there peacefully, looking out over this beautiful countryside, until nine o'clock. I was writing a chorus for the third act of which the words seemed very much to the point:

> 'Vit-on jamais un jour pareil? . . .
> Quel doux zéphir! notre brûlant soleil
> De ses rayons calme la violence' . . .   [*Id: 475*]

The other day, while I was sleeping in a field under a beech tree (like the shepherd in Virgil), I stumbled on the most wonderful idea for the staging of my finale with Cassandra and the Trojan women. I've had to write a few lines of verse but the music is hardly changed. I cannot resist telling you that it is of a radiant, antique beauty.   [*Id:* 477]

Work on the third act continued through the autumn; at the end of October Berlioz wrote from Saint-Germain where he was staying with friends:

Berlioz   Looking at the countryside seems to bring greater intensity to my Virgilian passion. I feel I have known Virgil; I feel he knows how much I love him. . . . Yesterday I wrote an air for Dido which is really just a paraphrase of the famous line: *Haud ignara mali miseris succurrere disco.* After I had sung it through to myself I was childish enough to say aloud: 'That's it, isn't it, dear Master? *Sunt lacrymae rerum?*'— as if Virgil were there. . . .   [*Id: V,* 502]

On his return to Paris he received a letter from the Princess congratulating him on the tenacity with which he stuck to his task.

Berlioz   No great credit to me if I turned down the American engagement. . . . I should be in a fine mess now if I had accepted. They talk there of nothing but bankruptcies, and all their concerts and theatres are racing towards the Niagara Falls. Ours are in no such danger— there's no cataract without a current. We paddle about on a placid pond, full of frogs and toads and enlivened by the song or the flight of a duck or two, where the only shipwrecks are due to the rotting timbers of the ships. But I live in my score like Lafontaine's rat in his cheese, if you will pardon the comparison.

I am about to begin the fifth act, and in a few months everything will be done. . . . I think of nothing but finishing the work. This month the lyric theatres have given me some respite; I have only had rare interruptions in my composition, and I go at it with a concentrated passion which seems to grow the more it is satisfied. And what will it all be worth in the end? God knows. Anyhow, I find a real happiness in shaping and fitting out and rigging this great Robinson Crusoe's canoe—which I'll never be able to launch if the sea doesn't come to fetch it for itself.   [*Id:* 509–10]

I should be in agonies, now above all, if anything happened which forced me to abandon it. . . . [*Id:* 512]

But even at this late date he was still altering and improving his original design. The opening scenes of the fifth act, coming after the emotional climax of the fourth act and immediately before the final catastrophe of the opera, continued to worry him. His eventual solution was Shakespearian in its simplicity. To his son Louis, a sailor in the merchant navy, he wrote:

Berlioz I've modified this act again. I have made a big cut in it and added [at the beginning] a character piece which is intended to contrast with the epic style of the rest. It's a sailor's song; I thought of you, dear Louis, as I was writing it. It is night, and the Trojan ships lie at anchor in the port: Hylas, a young Phrygian sailor, sings as he rocks at the masthead. . . . He is overwhelmed by nostalgia and dreams with passionate longing of the great forests upon Mount Didymus . . . he loves. [*Id:* 539, 679]

If it is the poetry of Shakespeare that inspired the great love duet in Act IV, it is the historical plays that provided the model for a sudden, simple scene like this, as they did for the touch of popular comedy, a couple of scenes later, which Berlioz had added in the previous year.

Berlioz The scene I have added to the fifth act is between two Trojan soldiers mounting guard before the tents at night, and chatting whenever they approach one another. They complain of their commanders' determination to leave Carthage at all costs and set out for this wretched Italy. They are doing very nicely in Carthage; what folly to face once again storms, hunger, thirst at sea, etc., you know the kind of thing. The tastes and ideas of these two soldiers make a contrast which I think will be a happy one with the passions and heroic aspirations of the other characters. . . . [*Id:* 357]

December 27th. Forgive me, Princess, for not having replied to your last letter. I have been completely absorbed by the last monologue of Aeneas, and I couldn't have put two ideas together until it was entirely done. At times like these I'm like a bulldog that lets himself be cut to pieces rather than give up what he's got between his teeth.   [*Id: 518*]

From the departure of Aeneas onwards the ancient tragedy drove him inexorably forward. To Hans von Bülow, Liszt's son-in-law, he wrote:

Berlioz   You ask me what I am doing. I am finishing *The Trojans*. For fifteen days I've had no chance to work at it. I am at the final catastrophe: Aeneas has left, Dido doesn't yet know, she will soon find out, she has a foreboding of his departure. . . . *Quis fallere possit amantem?* This heartfelt anguish to be expressed, these cries of grief to put into music, they terrify me . . . how am I going to manage? I am especially worried at the moment by the accentuation of a passage for Anna and Narbal during the religious ceremony of the priests of Pluto:

> 'S'il faut enfin qu'Énée aborde en Italie,
> Qu'il y trouve un obscur trépas! . . .'

Is it a violent imprecation or is it dumb concentrated fury? . . . If poor Rachel [the great actress, who had recently died] were not dead I should have gone to ask her. You will probably think that I am taking too much trouble, concerning myself like this with truth of expression, and that it will always be *true* enough for the public. Yes—but for us? . . .   [*Id: 532–3*]

Again and again *truthfulness of expression* recurs as an ideal that Berlioz kept continually before him—one which, in a letter at about this time, he even described as 'in my view the principal merit of the work'. In these final scenes of the drama, he was facing the last and toughest round of a long struggle.

Berlioz   You cannot have any idea, my dear Bülow, of the flow and tide of contrary emotions which have tugged at my heart since I began on this work. Sometimes it's a passion, a delirium, a devotion—like an artist of twenty. And then disgust, coldness, a revulsion from my task which terrifies me. I am never in doubt: either I believe, or I don't believe any more; then I believe again . . . and when it comes to the point I go on shoving at my rock. One more big heave and we'll be there—one carrying the other.

What would be fatal for Sisyphus at this moment would be any kind of discouragement from outside; but there's no one to discourage me, because no one has heard any of my score. . . . Even if you were here I wouldn't show it to you. I'm too much afraid of being afraid. [*Id:* 533]

And to his son:

Berlioz   February 9th. I'm working as hard as I can to finish my score. I am at this moment writing the last monologue of Dido: 'Je vais mourir, dans ma douleur immense submergée'. I am more pleased with what I have just written than with all I have done before. I believe that these terrible scenes of the fifth act will carry in their music heartrending conviction. [*Id:* 539]

He was back, at last, at the scene which had driven him sobbing from his father's side some forty-four years ago. His task was nearly done.

Berlioz   I assure you, dear sister, that the music of *The Trojans* is noble and grand: its truth is poignant, and there are a number of new ideas which, unless I am pathetically mistaken, will make the ears of all the musicians in Europe, and perhaps their hair too, stand on end. It seems to me that if Gluck came back to this world and heard it he would say: 'Truly, this is my son.' That's not modest, is it? But at least I have the modesty to admit that I lack modesty. [*Id:* 551]

Tuesday evening, April 7th. I have not been able to find an instant to write to you in all these last days. And tonight I have no mind for it. I have just written the last bar of my opera. . . . [*Id:* 556]

But it was another five days before he could bring himself to consider it completely finished: the last page of the manuscript is dated April 12th, 1858, just twenty-three days under two years since he had begun work on the libretto.

With the completion of the score, a new chapter begins in the history

of *Les Troyens*, a bitter, frustrating and disappointing chapter which coloured the remaining eleven years of Berlioz's life. During the last months
of his work on the opera he had written to a friend:

Berlioz   It matters little what happens to the work, whether it is ever
performed or not. My musical and Virgilian passions will have been
satisfied and at least I shall have shown what I think can be done
with a classical subject on a big scale.   [*Id: 546*]

Brave words, and necessary ones. It was to be more than five years
before the first performance of *Les Troyens* took place, on 4 November,
1863, and even then it was given incomplete and savagely cut. Meanwhile
he had to suffer the humiliation of seeing *Tannhäuser* put on at the Opéra
at the command of the Emperor, with all the razzmatazz of a Wagnerian
première, while his own masterpiece lay neglected and unperformed. His
health grew steadily worse. 'I have never seen such thinness', wrote the
Princess to Liszt. 'He is no longer a body, he is scarcely anything like a
human being'. Eventually, after frustrations and broken promises, he was
forced to abandon all hope of bringing his work to the Opéra, and reluctantly agreed to a production of the last three acts only at the smaller
Théâtre Lyrique—omitting the Troy scenes altogether, and incidentally
creating the fatal impression that the opera was intended for performance
in two separable parts.

In accordance with Parisian custom the work was conducted by the
permanent conductor at the Théâtre Lyrique, Louis Michel Deloffre,
and the production was in the hands of the theatre's director, the auto-
cratic entrepreneur Léon Carvalho. Berlioz involved himself closely with
every aspect of the preparation during the months of rehearsal, but even
so, and in spite of his protests, the shortcomings of the theatre were made
the excuse for more and more cuts as the première drew near. Nevertheless the singing of Mme Charton-Demeur as Dido was a constant source
of pleasure, and he was at last hearing much of his greatest music for the
first time. Coming out of the dress rehearsal, he called in to see the wife
of one of his oldest friends.

Bernard   He looked to her like a ghost, so pale and emaciated had he
become. 'Whatever is the matter?' she cried in alarm. 'Did something go wrong at the rehearsal?' 'On the contrary' he said, falling

back into a chair, 'it's beautiful, it's sublime!' And he started to cry.

[*Bernard:* 55]

On the first night the Parisian musical world was present in strength, from the oldest of his friends, colleagues and adversaries to the twenty-five-year-old Georges Bizet (whose *Pearl Fishers* had immediately preceded *Les Troyens* at the Théâtre-Lyrique) and though Meyerbeer missed the first night through illness, he came to twelve subsequent performances 'for my pleasure and my instruction'. There was applause for many of the numbers, and the septet had to be repeated in response to vociferous acclamation in which even Berlioz's enemies were observed to be joining. But not everything went smoothly, and a badly organised scene change after the 'Royal hunt and storm' caused a delay of three quarters of an hour; the Parisian audience reacted predictably, Carvalho took fright, and the remaining performances were given without a piece which has since come to be recognized as one of the jewels of the score.

Berlioz   The theatre was not large enough, the singers were not good enough, the chorus and orchestra were small and weak. . . . But I confess that even so I was profoundly moved by certain pieces that were well performed. Aeneas' [last] aria, . . . and above all Dido's monologue 'Je vais mourir', overwhelmed me. . . . Of all the passionately sad music I have ever written, I know of none to compare with Dido's in this passage and in the aria which follows—except for Cassandra's in parts of *The Capture of Troy,* and that has not yet been performed anywhere. . . .   [*Mémoires:* 570, 573–4]

Nor would it be, in his lifetime. Though a run of twenty-two performances can hardly be regarded as a failure, the first performance was certainly not the triumph for which Berlioz had been hoping—and in any case it was only half the opera.

Berlioz   Oh my noble Cassandra, my heroic virgin, must I then resign myself to the thought that I shall never hear you!—and I, like the young Chorebus, *insano Cassandrae incensus amore.*   [*Id:* 574]

The first performance of *Les Troyens* in its entirety did not take place till 1890, twenty-one years after the composer's death—and then not in

France but in Karlsruhe in Germany. Yet there was an innate toughness in Berlioz which saved him from the worst excesses of self-pity.

Berlioz   I am certain that I have written a great work, greater and more noble than anything that has been done till now. . . . Let discouragement and trouble come if they will: nothing can destroy the fact that the work is in existence. . . .

> [*Corréspondance*, VI: 218; V: 555]

He was right: he had written a work which, despite the indifference of his contemporaries, would one day come to be recognised as the passionate, crowning masterpiece that it is. Appropriately it was dedicated to the Princess Sayn-Wittgenstein, though her name never appeared on the title page of the score, which bore instead the heading DIVO VIRGILIO. In a dedicatory preface to the Princess, Berlioz wrote: 'Without you, and without Virgil, the work would not exist'—and in a private letter:

Berlioz   I would like you to be convinced of my gratitude, Princess, for the persistence with which you have urged me to undertake and complete this work. Whatever destiny awaits it, I feel today entirely happy to have brought it to a conclusion. I am sufficiently detached now to judge it, and I think I can say that there are things in the score that are worthy of being offered to you. . . . As for the principal object of the work, the expression of passions and emotions and the musical interpretation of the characters, this was from the beginning the easiest part of my task. I have passed my life in the company of this race of demigods and I know them so well that I feel they must have known me. . . .   [*Id:* 693–4]

He recalls his childhood, and remembers his first experience of Virgil.

Berlioz   Isn't this one of the strangest and most glorious manifestations of the power of genius? . . . that a poet, dead for thousands of years, could overwhelm the soul of a simple, ignorant boy with a story passed on through the centuries and with images whose colours have not been paled by the wings of time. . . . I have often asked myself what is the object of this mystification that we call life. . . . It is knowing what is beautiful, it is loving. People who do not know, who do not love, are the ones who are really lost. But we—we have the right to mock at the great mystifier. [*Id:* 694]

Richard Wagner in Paris, February–March 1860

Tristan und Isolde

As I have never in my life enjoyed the true happiness of love, I mean to raise a monument to this most beautiful of all dreams in which, from beginning to end, that love shall for once be satisfied to the full. I have in my mind the plan for a Tristan und Isolde, *the simplest but most full-blooded musical conception, and with the 'black flag' that waves at the end I shall then cover myself—to die.*

[BWL, II: 43]

DECEMBER 1854 SAW WAGNER well into the most inventive phase of his creative life. After completing the score of *Lohengrin* in April 1848 he had written no music for more than five years, and now at last the pent-up store of musical energy accumulated during that period had found release; work on the immense project of *The Ring* was making good progress—*Das Rheingold* was finished, *Die Walküre* fully sketched. But while his powers as a composer were developing fast, his personal situation deteriorated steadily, and creative work and philosophical brooding were his only refuge from the ever-increasing miseries of his life. As a proscribed revolutionary seeking asylum in Zürich, he had no proper home; he was dependent for his spasmodic and inadequate income on occasional concerts or the charity of friends and, worse still, at the age of forty-one he had come to realize beyond a shadow of doubt that he could never hope to find in his marriage the exalted love for which his 'passionate nature' longed.

Wagner's relationship with his first wife, the actress Minna Planer, had been plagued from the start, as much by the overbearing demands he made on it as by her inability to treat them with the detachment that was her only hope of survival. The last eighteen years had seen quarrels, infidelities, separations and reconciliations, held together through poverty and political danger by financial necessity, shared experience and a certain residual tenderness that he never quite lost. Nor, in spite of the relative stability that Zürich now seemed to offer, was there anything in his artistic surroundings to lift his depression or bring relief to his sense of isolation as a musician and a man. So it is not surprising that when, only a month or so before the first glimmerings of *Tristan*, he was introduced to the work of Schopenhauer, he should have avidly devoured *Die Welt als Wille und Vorstellung* and welcomed that most pessimistic of German philosophers as 'a gift from heaven in my loneliness'.   [*Id*: 42]

Wagner   His chief idea, the ultimate denial of the will to live, is one of terrible seriousness, but it offers a unique means of redemption. . . . When I think of the fierce tenacity with which, against my own judgment, I used to cling to the hope of life, of the fearful convulsions through which my heart has passed, and indeed the storms that still often sweep through me like a hurricane, I have at least found a sedative which helps me to get some sleep on waking nights: it is the sincere and ardent longing for death, for complete unconsciousness, total non-existence, freedom from all dreams—the last and only salvation.   [*Id*: 42]

It was a state of mind perfectly attuned to a story in which the power of love is so overwhelming that its human victims can achieve their hearts' desire only in death.

Not that the Tristan legend, in its pre-Wagnerian form, carried quite this Schopenhauerian charge. The sources of the original story reach back into antiquity (including the black flag on Isoud's ship—which Wagner did *not* in the end incorporate in his adaptation) and seem to have been Celtic and Breton in origin. After generations of oral transmission and rambling improvisations the medieval romance reached literary shape in three French versions during the second half of the twelfth century, but it was in the German version, made about fifty years later by the minnesinger Gottfried von Strassburg, that Wagner had first encountered it. Curiously enough it was an abortive project by one of his musical protégés that now gave him the idea of Tristan as a subject for opera.

Wagner   Although I was familiar with the subject from my Dresden studies, my attention had been drawn to it more recently when Karl Ritter told me of his plan to turn it into a drama. I made no bones about telling my young friend where the faults lay in his sketch. He had confined himself to the lighter aspects of the romance, whereas it was the essential tragedy which impressed me at once, and I felt convinced that all irrelevant details should be stripped away from this central theme. On returning from a walk one day, I jotted down the contents of the three acts into which I imagined concentrating the action, with the intention of working them out more fully later on.

[*ML:* 594]

Franz Liszt, at this time Wagner's closest friend and confidant, greeted the news with characteristic enthusiasm: 'Dearest Richard' he wrote, 'your *Tristan* is a splendid idea; it could become a glorious work. Don't abandon it!'. But for the time being Wagner was too deeply involved in *The Ring* to give more than occasional thought to other projects, and *Tristan* was relegated to the back of his mind, where it underwent for the next three years the kind of poetic and musical fermentation that seems to have been essential to any of Wagner's major dramatic conceptions.

[*BWL, II:* 49]

Ever since his exile from Dresden, Wagner had relied on a succession of friends and admirers for the financial support that enabled him to live in some approximation, at least, of the style to which he felt himself entitled. Now, as he worked at the scores of *Rheingold* and *Walküre*, their number was increased by a new and wealthy admirer, the retired silk merchant Otto Wesendonk who had recently settled in Zürich with his young wife Mathilde. The Swiss novelist Gottfried Keller was one of many recipients of the Wesendonks' hospitality.

Keller   Here in Zürich . . . I have excellent company and meet all sorts of people—a more interesting group than one might find together in Berlin. Among them is a Rhenish merchant family, Wesendonk, originally from Düsseldorf, but who have lived a while in New York. She is a very pretty woman, née Mathilde Luckemeier. These people keep a stylish house and are also building a luxurious villa just outside the town; they have received me very kindly. Then there are excellent supper parties at the house of an elegant government offi-

cial, where Richard Wagner, Semper [the architect], [the philoso-
pher] Vischer, and some local people foregather, and where, after a
discreetly sumptuous meal, one gets a cup of tea and a Havana cigar
at two o'clock in the morning. Wagner himself occasionally gives
substantial lunches where the bottle circulates freely so that I, who
thought I had escaped from the materialism of Berlin, have fallen
from the frying pan into the fire.   [*Keller*: 146–7]

From their first meeting Wagner was deeply attracted by Mathilde
Wesendonk who, at the age of twenty-three, was thirteen years younger
than her husband (and more than fifteen years younger than Wagner); his
evident interest in her did not escape the notice of his Zürich friends, like
Robert von Hornstein, another protégé who was a regular dinner guest
at the Wagners' apartment. On these occasions, says Hornstein, Wagner
often made music and 'could be utterly charming. . .'.

Hornstein   . . . but unfortunately it wasn't always like that. He could
    also be quite insufferable. The presence of Frau Wesendonk always
    made him agitated; he seemed unable to bear it when she didn't pay
    him attention.
        I remember one evening when . . . there was no music [and] we
    all talked with our neighbours. But [Wagner] was used to holding the
    floor. Suddenly, to the astonishment of everybody, he let out a yell. It
    was short and sharp, like a pistol shot. Everyone stared at him, upon
    which he announced with the utmost calm that he was extremely
    fond of *The Golden Pot* by Amadeus Hoffmann, and that he now
    wished to read it to us.
        He read it from start to finish, by which time it was very late. [At
    the end] Wesendonk permitted himself a by no means inappropriate
    comment on this type of Romanticism, for which he had no taste.
    At this Wagner flew into a towering rage and it was only thanks to
    Wesendonk's self-restraint that the evening did not end in a row. But
    there was another surprise still to come. Towards the end [Wagner]
    broke into a great lament about his creditors, who were pursuing him
    because of all the stuff by which he was surrounded. The next day
    Wesendonk paid his bills. It needed all the fanatical devotion char-
    acteristic of young people to forget the impression that this made.
                                        [*Hornstein*: 139–40]

There is not much evidence of Wagner's feelings for Mathilde at this stage. But in a rather bland little memoir written many years later Mathilde revealed a curious reference to herself on the manuscript score of *Die Walküre*: the letters 'G . . . . S . . M . . . .', written at the head of the Prelude, which have been convincingly interpreted as standing for 'Gesegnet sei Mathilde' (Blessed be Mathilde). There are sixteen other annotations of a similar kind, always at emotionally significant moments between Siegmund and Sieglinde, throughout the first act of the opera, from which it seems fairly clear that Wagner was already beginning to see himself and Mathilde in the idealised terms of his own creation.

[*Spencer: 103*]

It was in any case a crucial moment in Wagner's creative career. For years he had been giving much thought to the problems of dramatic expression in musical theatre, and the inadequacies of existing forms of opera. During the fallow period between *Lohengrin* and *Das Rhein-gold* he had produced a number of theoretical writings in which he examined, in language that is complex, repetitive and often impenetrably dense, the historical origins and interrelationships of drama, poetry and music, and the developments to which he had been driven in his attempts to unite the three. Being no longer interested in the tedious historical incidents that made up conventional operatic subjects, he looked instead for dramatic material closer to human experience: 'the only poetic subjects which aroused in me the desire for creative work', he wrote, 'were those that involved primarily my emotional, rather than my intellectual being . . .'

[*MMF: 147*]

Wagner   . . . Only what was wholly human, shorn of the trappings of historical formality, could . . . arouse my interest and spur me to find expression for the vision I had in mind.

Since the whole source of my creative work was the original subject, and that subject as seen through the medium of music, so in working it out I arrived inevitably at a gradual but complete upheaval of the traditional operatic form. By its very nature this had never been a form that embraced the drama as a whole, but was rather an arbitrary stringing together of separate smaller forms of song whose haphazard combination of arias, duos, trios and so on, with choruses and so-called ensembles, made up the conventional edifice of opera. When I came to planning the layout of my material I could no longer consider simply filling these ready moulded forms . . . [and indeed] in the whole course of the drama I now saw no possibility of division or demarcation other than the acts, which indicate a break in place or time, or the scenes, which allow for a change in dramatis personae.

Nor was I any longer interested in writing operatic melodies as such, but only in finding the most fitting means to express the feelings of my characters. . . . In order to provide a true reflection of its emotional content, the dialogue was to be set in such a way that *not the melodic expression in itself but the expressed emotion* should arouse the interest of the listener. The melody must therefore spring spontaneously out of the verse, and attract attention not as pure melody for its own sake, but only as the most expressive vehicle for an emotion already clearly outlined in the words.

As a result of this conception I now completely abandoned the usual mode of operatic composition and no longer tried intentionally for melody as it is usually understood, or in a sense for melody at all, but let the vocal line arise entirely from the expressive delivery of the words. . . . The melody's loss in rhythmic definition—or better *vividness*—I then made good by a harmonic livening of the expression, something that only a man in my particular relationship to melody could feel the need of . . . [and] I heightened the individual character of this expression by a more and more symbolic treatment of the orchestra, to which I assigned the specific task of clarifying the harmonic 'motivation' of the vocal line.

[*Id: 147, 149–50, 154, 155, 156, 157*]

While this new approach to dramatic music, and the concept of 'endless melody' that went with it, was at last being consistently applied in the scores of *Das Rheingold* and *Die Walküre, Tristan* was evidently still brewing away at the back of Wagner's mind. In the process the preoccupation with Schopenhauer, which had so strongly influenced the original conception of the work, had been joined by a growing interest in Buddhism (he even sketched a scenario for an opera on the Buddha early in 1856), and Schopenhauer's negation of the Will, which leads inevitably to ultimate nothingness, was being modified into the rather less nihilistic concept of Nirvana. It was a shift of philosophical attitude that made a good deal more sense of the ultimate union of the lovers in death. And his fascination with other elements of religious mythology continued; in

December 1855 he appears to have elaborated his original idea for the third act with a curious premonition of the future.

Wagner   Tristan, languishing but unable to die of his wound, became identified in my mind with the Amfortas of the Grail romance . . . [and] I wove into the last act a visit to Tristan's sickbed by Parzival, wandering in search of the Grail—an episode which I later removed. . . .   [ML: 594]

The music was showing signs of becoming articulate, too; a year later, while he was in the middle of the first act of *Siegfried*, he wrote to Princess Marie Wittgenstein, the eighteen-year-old-daughter of Liszt's mistress:

Wagner   Today I intended to work on *Siegfried*, and fell unawares into *Tristan*. Music without words for the time being—but for a good many things I would rather write the music than the verse. . . . *Tristan* has come between [me and *Siegfried*] in the form of a melodic thread which, although I would much rather have let it go, kept on spinning itself in my mind so that I could have spent all day developing it. . . .
                                                            [Sternfeld: 4]

A musical sketch, bearing the same date, is headed 'Love scene: Tristan and Isolde' and consists of eighteen bars that open with a clear outline of one of the most important motifs of the love scene in Act II. And even more significantly, on the same page there is another note—a tiny fragment of four rising semitones which seems at first sight trivial enough, but which was to reappear on the oboe in the second bar of the *Tristan* Prelude and be labeled by later Wagner commentators 'the motif of Desire'; the emotional and harmonic implications of this little phrase were to become a crucial ingredient in the rich texture of the *Tristan* score and find their ultimate fulfilment only in the final chord of the opera.

Wagner   In the same way as the joinery of my individual scenes excluded every alien and unnecessary detail, and focused all the interest on the dominant mood, so did the whole building of my drama now coalesce into one organic unity. . . . No mood was permitted to be struck in any scene that did not stand in a weighty relation to the moods in the other scenes, so that the development of these moods out of one another, and the evident logic of this development, itself established the unity of the work. In addition, each dominant mood, in keeping with the nature of its subject, was provided with definite musical expression in the shape of a specific musical theme . . . [as a natural result of which] a characteristic tissue of principal themes spread itself, not just over one scene (as in the old way with separate operatic 'numbers'), but over the entire drama—in intimate connection with the poetic aim.   [*MMF*: 151–2]

The term 'leitmotiv', or leading motif, though it was not originally coined by Wagner himself, later came to be widely used to describe these thematic fragments—short, flexible and often strikingly memorable phrases that became the building blocks of his latest scores, and were to be deployed in *Tristan* with greater subtlety and perception than in any of his other operas.

But for the time being it was the immense undertaking of the *Ring* which occupied him and which, still only a little beyond the half-way mark, might yet take him years to complete and far longer to bring to performance. In the face of ill health and growing depression, he battled on with *Siegfried*, and by the end of March 1857 had put the first act into full score. But a couple of months earlier *Tristan* had cropped up again in a letter to Marie Wittgenstein (with the reservation 'but no more about that for the moment: it's all only music so far'), and when in June he began the orchestral sketch of the second act of *Siegfried*, he added the significant note on the first page: '*Tristan* already decided on'.

[*FZ*: 202; *Strobel*: 55]

Liszt, who of all Wagner's friends was the most active in his efforts to secure performances for his operas, was the first to know when the decisive step was taken. On 28 June, Wagner wrote to him:

Wagner   I have finally decided to give up my obstinate determination to complete the *Nibelungen*. I have led my young Siegfried into the beautiful solitude of the forest and left him there under a linden tree, taking leave of him with heartfelt tears. . . . There was a time when, even without the expectation of seeing the work performed in my lifetime, I could conceive, begin, and half finish it . . . [but since then] my last hopes have vanished, and an overwhelming bitterness possesses me. . . . You, rarest of friends, do everything in your power to rouse my spirits, to cheer me and stimulate my desire to work. But I realise that you must regard this as little more than a *pis aller*, and so I have at last determined to help myself. I plan to complete *Tristan und Isolde* without further delay, on a modest scale that will make its performance easier, and produce it in Strasbourg a year from today. . . . There is an attractive theatre there . . . and I hope that, God willing, I shall once more be able to produce something of my own, in my own way, which will give me back some sense of freshness and restore my awareness of my own being. . . .

[So] I have torn Siegfried from my heart and placed him under lock and key, as if he were being buried alive. . . . Perhaps the rest will do him good; as to his awakening I make no plans. . . . I have had to face a hard and painful struggle to reach this point. Now let us regard it as settled. [*BWL, II: 171–2, 173*]

Liszt   Dearest Richard . . . I can only weep when I think of the interruption of your *Nibelungen*. . . . You certainly have every reason to feel bitter, and if I generally observe silence on the point I feel it none the less deeply. . . . [But] *Tristan* looks to me a very happy idea. No doubt you will make something splendid of it, and then go back refreshed to your *Nibelungen*. [*Id: 176*]

The idea of *Tristan* on a 'modest scale' may raise a smile today, but just how desperately Wagner needed at least a prospect of performance, after eight years of exile from the one country in which performances might most reasonably be expected, is clear from the eagerness with which he clutched at an unlikely straw that now blew in his direction—an invitation from the Emperor of Brazil to produce his operas in the new opera house at Rio de Janeiro. As only Italian was sung there, everything would have to be translated, and any new work composed in that language.

Wagner   Curiously enough, this prospect actually struck me as very agreeable; I felt that I could very well bring off an impassioned musical poem that would turn out excellently in Italian, and my thoughts turned again with ever-renewed enthusiasm to *Tristan und Isolde*. [*ML: 637*]

Even Liszt was shocked at the idea.

Liszt   But how, by all the gods, can you turn it into an opera for *Italian singers* as I hear . . . you intend to do? Well, you have already made the incredible and impossible your own elements, and perhaps you will manage even this. Certainly the subject is splendid and your conception of it wonderful.   [*BWL, II: 179*]

As things turned out, Wagner never heard any more about the Brazilian adventure, and in any case the step of placing *Siegfried* under lock and key was not effected at the first attempt. A couple of months later he confessed to Princess Marie Wittgenstein that, after closing the score and sitting down to begin work on *Tristan* . . .

Wagner   . . . I was suddenly overcome by such a miserable longing for *Siegfried* that I took out [the score] again and made up my mind to complete at least the second act. This is now done. . . . But all this has been a great strain on me, for while I was working at *Siegfried*, *Tristan* would give me no peace. I actually worked on them both at the same time, and as [the music of] *Tristan* took more and more and more definite shape, and I became so passionately involved in it, the double labour drove me in the end to a state of absolute torment.   [*Sternfeld: 5*]

Though the torment was not without its positive side.

Wagner   As I sketched *Tristan und Isolde* I never really felt that I was parting from the world of poetry and myth opened up to me by my work on the *Nibelungen*. The essential connections that exist between all true myths, as they emerged from my studies, had sharpened my eye for the wonderfully varied forms in which these similarities appear. One such struck me, delightfully and unmistakeably, in comparing the relationship of Tristan and Isolde with that of Siegfried and Brünnhilde. . . . Both Tristan and Siegfried, fettered to an illusion which denies them freedom of action, woo, on another's behalf, brides destined by fate to be their own—and in the resulting conflict meet their doom. But where the poet of *Siegfried*, bound by the overall coherence of the Nibelungen myth, could only see the hero's downfall as an integral part of his wife's vengeance and self-sacrifice, the poet of *Tristan* finds the stuff of his drama in the very pangs of love to which the pair, awakened to their true relations, fall victim until their death. [BDW: 237–8]

It was not until late in August that he actually began work on the prose sketch for his drama.

Wagner   I was in the first instance a poet, and only in the complete working out of my poem did I become once more a musician. But I was always a poet conscious in advance of the musical expression that would be available when it came to this final working out. . . . [MMF: 145, 149]

Both prose sketch and a first draft of the full poem were completed within a month, and on 1 October, less than two months after finally abandoning *Siegfried*, he began composing the music for *Tristan und Isolde*.

With the very first bars of his score, Wagner entered a new world of sound, a world in which the keynote was ambiguity. In the opening of his previous operas there had been nothing ambiguous—*The Flying Dutchman*, *Tannhaüser*, the massive tonal foundation stone of the *Ring*—but for *Tristan*, the poem of passion and longing, there is no assertion, only a lingering question whose resolution is constantly deferred. The two tiny individual motifs that make up the opening phrase give rise to a harmonic progression which has since become uniquely famous in the history of music—the notorious 'Tristan chord', which stands at the very outset of the opera as a symbol of the radical approach to tonality that was to make this score a turning point in the history of music. The harmonic question it poses receives no harmonic answer; nor does it for any of the three repetitions that follow, and when it is eventually seized and carried on, it is only in such a way that even now its conclusion is no conclusion, only a sense of half-fulfilment and the start of something new.

From this moment on, the flow of the music is virtually unceasing. In *Tristan*, more than in any of his other works, Wagner was to evolve a continuously chromatic idiom that is ideally suited to his subject, and into the opening prelude he now poured the musical quintessence of a drama that was still to be written.

Wagner   Here, because he felt himself in music's most completely
unfettered element, the composer . . . could let that insatiable longing well up in one long succession of linked phrases, from the first
timid avowal of tender attraction, through tremulous sighs, through
hopes and fears, through laments, longings, joy and anguish, to the
mightiest, most powerful effort to find the breach that will open,
for the infinitely desirous heart, the way to the sea of love's endless
delight.

But to no purpose! Powerless, the heart sinks back to languish in
desire—desire without attainment, for each attainment only renews
desire—, until, to the failing sight on the verge of its final collapse,
there dawns a glimpse of the highest bliss of all: the bliss of dying, of
being no more, the ultimate deliverance. . . .   [*TV*: 62]

Such openly erotic language is not altogether easy to square with
Wagner's admiration for Schopenhauer, whose attitude to sex tended to
the ascetic, but there is little doubt that the composition of *Tristan und
Isolde* was by now motivated less by philosophical theory and associated
ever more intimately with the realities of Wagner's personal life. And
there is equally no question that—in one way or another—he was now
very much in love.

The full truth about Wagner's 'affair' with Mathilde Wesendonk—
which coincided almost exactly with the gestation and genesis of *Tristan*,
and ended with it—is still a matter for speculation. Contemporary evidence is patchy; and although for practically all the rest of his life he left
an abundance, almost a super-abundance, of documentation in his auto-
biography, his prose works and his letters, he had every reason, when dic-
tating his life story a decade later to his second wife Cosima von Bülow,
to play down both his domestic squabbles with his first wife, Minna, and
even more the storms of passion to which he had worked himself up over
Mathilde. To read *My Life* alone, the Wesendonk episode which played
so large a part in releasing the tragic love music of *Tristan* might seem, as
Wagner himself put it, 'not really important'. How much, for example, is
missing from his description of the first occasion when the three women
who played so great a part in his life—the hapless Minna, his present 'mistress' Mathilde, and Cosima herself—were all united under the same roof?

Wagner   I had almost finished the first act of my *Tristan* poem when a
newly married young couple turned up in Zürich who had a particu-

larly strong claim on my attention: ... Hans von Bülow and his young wife Cosima, Liszt's daughter. .... I went to meet them and invited them for a lengthy visit to my little house ... [and] we passed September in stimulating activities. Meanwhile I completed the *Tristan* text, of which Hans made a fair copy, ... I read it to my visitors act by act, until I was finally able to arrange a private reading of the whole work, which made a deep impression on the audience who were all close friends. As Frau Wesendonk appeared to be particularly moved by the last act, I said consolingly that there was no reason to sorrow over it because, in so grave a situation, such an outcome was the best that could be expected—and Cosima agreed.   [*ML*: 642]

It was in fact only due to the generosity of Mathilde's husband that Wagner now had accommodation spacious enough to offer hospitality to anyone. To Liszt he had written on 8 May 1857:

Wagner Ten days ago we took possession of the little country house that you know about, close to the Wesendonks' villa, for which I have to thank the great interest shown in me by that friendly family. ... [The removal] took a lot of time ... , but now it's all over ... and everything is in the place where it will remain until my death.

My study has been laid out with the pedantry and elegant comfort that you know; my writing table stands at the large window with a splendid view of the lake and the Alps. .... A pretty and well-kept garden ... will enable my wife to occupy her time agreeably and offer her a distraction from worrying thoughts about me. .... So you see that I have acquired a charming spot in which to live in seclusion, and when I consider how long I have been hoping for such a place, and how difficult it has been to discover the slightest prospect of getting it, I feel obliged to look upon the excellent Wesendonk as one of my greatest benefactors.   [*BWL, II*: 158–9]

Excellent in many respects, but one cannot help wondering whether Otto Wesendonk, in his desire to provide Wagner with the peace and comfort that he needed to complete *Tristan*, was entirely wise to establish him on the very doorstep of his own wife—clearly the cause of Minna's 'worrying thoughts'. When the 'Asyl' ('haven' or 'refuge', as Wagner christened it) had first been offered to him, at a time when he still had hopes of some financial return from negotiations with his publishers, Wagner had shown some compunction on this point—which would have done him credit had he stuck to it.

Wagner   . . . Certain considerations, having their ground partly in my friend's character, partly in other very tender relations, have made me resolve firmly not to take his property unless I can feel pecuniarily quite independent of Wesendonk and can give him convincing assurance of this.   [*Id: 150–1*]

'That my relationship with this couple is a fairly artificial one and not at all easy for me is something I have hinted at sufficiently often in the past,' he wrote to Liszt, and when the Wesendonks eventually moved into their newly completed villa next door, the situation reached a fresh degree of intensity. He saw Mathilde constantly, and when he could not see her sent her little intimate notes, calling her his angel, his darling, his beloved muse—or sometimes simply 'child'—and keeping her up to date with work in progress as fast as it was completed. In a curious sort of letter diary which he later addressed to his by-then-absent 'beloved', Wagner maintained that Mathilde had first confessed to him that she returned his love on the very day—most appropriately—when he had delivered to her the completed poem of *Tristan*.

Wagner   On that day, at that moment, I was born anew. . . . I had been painfully detaching myself more and more completely from the world. I was all negation, all rejection. . . . I longed to find something affirmative, personal, some union with a kindred soul. That instant gave it to me, with such infallible certainty that a hallowed stillness came over me. A lovely woman, shy and diffident, had thrown herself bravely into a sea of griefs and sorrows in order to give me that precious moment when she said: I love you. Thus did you consecrate yourself to death, to give me life, and thus did I receive your life, from then on with you to leave the world, with you to suffer, with you to die.   [*MW: 96–7*]

It is so close to the mood, even to the words, of *Tristan* that is impossible not to believe that Wagner's fantasy had now inextricably identified his romantic attachment to Mathilde with that of the ill-fated lovers in his opera: Wagner, Mathilde and Otto seem irrevocably cast as Tristan, Isolde and Marke.

Just what Mathilde's reaction to all this may have been is difficult to gauge; no letters or notes from her side appear to have survived, and the memoir that she wrote many years later suggests nothing more than admiration and affection for Wagner. 'It is to him alone', she wrote, 'that I owe all that has been best in my life'. It is extremely doubtful whether she was the kind of person to follow him all the way in the exalted flights of his imagination, and her only tangible contributions to the work in which he traces the sweep of the most adventurous, destructive and absolute passion in the world were five rather mediocre poems in the *Tristan* manner containing veiled allusions to their secret feelings. But even these were grist to Wagner's mill. He turned them into songs, two of which, *Träume* and *Im Treibhaus*, contain thematic material that he subsequently used in *Tristan* and were later described as 'Studies for *Tristan und Isolde*'. Characteristically he arranged for *Träume*, which later reappeared at the heart of Tristan and Isolde's love scene in the second act, to be performed by a small orchestra under Mathilde's window as a birthday greeting (a trick that he was to repeat with the *Siegfried Idyll* for Cosima's benefit thirteen years later).

The question of whether or not Wagner and Mathilde were ever lovers in the physical sense has been the subject of much dubious speculation, but given Mathilde's upbringing and moral background, and the tolerance with which Otto Wesendonk tacitly accepted the situation, it seems unlikely. Just because the music of *Tristan* is so powerfully and openly erotic in expression, it seems more probable that it was Wagner's sexual frustration that was here translated into musical terms; certainly this is the explanation that best fits the prevailing mood of resignation and renunciation—and indeed the romantic hyperbole of his letters.

In any case, at this pitch it could not last. At the end of December he put the finishing touches to Act I: 'the great duet outburst between Tristan and Isolde has turned out beautiful beyond words' he wrote. 'Just done—in a great flood of delight'. But only days later he felt obliged to absent himself from Zürich for a while in order to assuage the ruffled feelings of his friend Wesendonk. After four weeks in Paris he came back and resumed work on *Tristan* once more, but the end was near.   [*Id: 73*]

It was foolish and commonplace rather than tragic. Minna, suspicious for some time, intercepted a letter to Mathilde enclosed in a roll of music—the pencilled first draft of the prelude to *Tristan*. It was an eight-page letter, largely taken up with an unexceptionable discussion of Goethe's *Faust*. But it opened with an apology for an earlier display of jealousy, and one can hardly blame Minna for her feelings as she read it.

Wagner   . . . and out of this there grew a figure in which I recognised all the misery in the world as mine. And so it went on all through the night. In the morning I returned to my senses, and was able to pray to my angel from the very depths of my heart—and this prayer is love! Love!—the deepest joy of my soul, the source of my redemption! But then came the day, with its wretched weather; the joy of your garden was denied me, and I couldn't get on with my work either. So my whole day became a struggle between ill-temper and my longing for you. . . .

When I look into your eyes, then I just can't speak any more—anything I could think of saying simply becomes worthless! One look, and everything is indisputably clear to me; then am I sure of myself; that wonderful, holy gaze rests upon me and I submerge myself within it! Then subject or object no longer exists; everything is one united, deep, vast harmony! Oh, there is peace, and in that peace the highest, the most perfect life!   [BC: 510, 511]

This is, of course, Schopenhauer, or even the Buddha, as much as anything else—but Minna wasn't to know that. Like a bull in a delicately balanced china shop, she insisted on seeing Otto and accused Mathilde of breaking up her marriage. She was obviously ill (in fact, she had a serious heart condition), and was persuaded by Wagner to go away for a cure at Brestenberg. Appearances were preserved—Wagner stayed on alone and completed the full score of Act I, but when he began the composition sketch of Act II a month later, he headed it, significantly, 'Still at the Asyl'. Minna returned in time for the visit of the Bülows in July, but in August, Wagner himself bowed to circumstances and in turn departed for an uncertain destination. To Mathilde a last note said, in English, 'It must be so'.

Early in the second act the orchestral sketch of *Tristan* was broken off. Less than two months later Wagner took it up again—in Venice. To a Zürich friend he wrote:

Wagner   I have been looking for a place where I could live quite unnoticed and completely retired, and work without any disturbance. A small, dull town would not have made this possible. But here [in Venice] I have everything I want; a very quiet flat (naturally without any streets or the noise of carriages) on the Grand Canal where I spend the greater part of my day. Then a promenade through the incomparable, ever new parts of Venice between St Mark's Square and the public gardens, with their view across the lagoons and out to sea; the lively bustle of the crowds which, however, always remain quite alien, quite 'objective' to me—all this is quite enough for me and falls in exactly with my present mood.   [FZ: 241–2]

It was a mood, aggravated by ill health, of depressed resignation. He confessed to von Bülow:

Wagner   My last heart-rending experiences of life have made me more and more negative in my attitude to the world; I feel myself now almost entirely free from all longings or desires; I only want to cause others as little suffering as possible. . . . If I were not an artist I could become a saint, but this redemption is not prescribed for me. . . .
                                                                    [BHB: 106–7]

All the same, the separation from Mathilde did not imply the end of the state of exaltation into which he had plunged himself in Zürich; on the contrary, since correspondence between them was for the time being ruled out, he poured his feelings into a sort of letter-diary which he kept for her in his Venetian solitude (and later sent to her in batches). In it he was able to speak of their mystical union and their act of renunciation in even more high-flown terms.

Wagner   On the last night in the Asyl I went to bed at 11 o'clock. . . . As I closed my eyes the thought passed through my mind, that I had always lulled myself to sleep in this room with the idea that one day I would die here in this same place; like this I would be lying when you came to me for the last time, when you would fold my head in your arms, openly, before the whole world, and receive my soul with one last kiss! To die like this was the fondest of my dreams. . . . Thus you would wrap your arms about me, thus gazing up at you I would die. And now? Had even that chance of death been taken from me? Coldly, like a hunted animal, I was leaving this house in which I had been imprisoned with a daemon that I could no longer banish except in flight—But where? Where now should I die? And so I fell asleep.
                                                                    [MW: 85]

In October he took up the score of Act II again: 'I am now returning to *Tristan*,' he wrote, 'to let the deep art of its sounding silence speak to you for me . . .'.   [*Id: 119*]

Wagner   What music it is going to be! I could spend my whole life working on this music alone. Oh, it grows deep and beautiful—the most
sublime wonders mould themselves so supply to the sense of the
words. I have never done anything like this before. . . .   [*Id: 134*]

22 December. A lovely morning, dear child! For three days I had
been stuck at the passage 'Wen du umfangen, wem du gelacht' and
'In deinen Armen, dir geweiht' etc. . . . I had been interrupted for a
long time, and I couldn't remember the way I meant to work it out. It
really worried me, and I couldn't get any further—when suddenly my
good imp knocked, appeared in the form of my gracious muse, and in
an instant the passage was clear. I sat down at the piano and wrote
it out as quickly as if I had known it by heart for ever. A severe critic
might find a touch of reminiscence in it—the ghost of *Träume* hovers
close by. But you will forgive me that, my darling!   [*Id: 134–5*]

As he approached the shattering interruption that catastrophically
cuts short the climax of Tristan and Isolde's love, he became more and
more involved in the intensity of his own creation. But a couple of months
were still needed to complete the noble monologue of King Marke, the
lingering farewell of the lovers and at last the fatal wound dealt by Melot.

Wagner   10 March 1859. Yesterday at last I got the second act done, the
biggest, and in that way a precarious, musical problem, and I know I
have solved it in a manner never achieved before. . . . All my earlier
works, poor things, are completely put in the shade by this one act!
. . . It is the summit of my art until now.   [*Id: 163, 157*]

'There is a quality that my art has acquired', he wrote revealingly to
Mathilde a few months later, 'of which I am becoming increasingly aware
since it affects my life as well. It has always been natural for me to swing
rapidly and abruptly from one extreme mood to another . . .'

Wagner   . . . and I realise now that the fabric of my music . . . owes
its characteristic structure above all to an extreme subtlety of feel-

ing which involves the constant process of mediating and knitting together successive steps in the transitional passages that link extremes of mood. Perhaps I might describe this, the most delicate and profound aspect of my art, as the art of transition—for the whole texture of my work depends on such transitions. I have come to dislike everything abrupt or hurried; this is often unavoidable and necessary, but even then should not occur unless any sudden change has been so unmistakeably prepared in advance that it seems to happen as a natural development. My greatest achievement in subtle, gradual transition is unquestionably the big scene in the second act of *Tristan und Isolde*. The beginning of this scene evokes the fullness of life in all the violence of passion, the close a most dedicated, heartfelt longing for death. These are the two pillars—and now, child, you can see how I have joined these pillars together, how one of them is led across into the other. This, then, is the secret of my musical form, and I make bold to claim that it has never before been dreamt of in such full and clear continuity, with such agreement between every detail. . . .   [*Id:* 232–3]

In the end, Wagner was allowed little more than six months to find rest in Venice before being forced to move on again. As an ex-revolutionary, he was still wanted by the police, and in October an official memorandum from Vienna had recommended that the Venetian authorities 'should keep a careful eye on the state of his health and, so soon as an improvement sets in, take the proper steps to procure his departure from Venice and from Austrian territory altogether'. Reports went back to Vienna in December and January.

In consequence of [recommendations received] Richard Wagner, the political refugee from Saxony, has been kept under close observation. He is lodged in the Palazzo Giustiniani . . . where his conduct, so far, has given us no cause for remark. He lives a very retired life and is employed solely with his musical compositions. . . . He makes it clear that he intends to make very few new acquaintances. . . .

[*Lippert:* 120]

[Wagner] continues his retired mode of life, spending many hours a day at home composing new music, and does not seem to have received any visitors. A week ago he sent [the poem of] his new opera *Tristan* to Baden, with a dedication to Her Highness the Grand

Duchess of that state, who not only deigned to accept the dedication but was further pleased to express her gratification. . . . Wagner has quite recovered from the infection in his foot, which obliged him to keep his room, and can now be seen at midday on fine days walking on the Riva degli Schiavoni . . .'.   [*Id: 121*]

The final outcome was a courteous but firm request that he should leave Venice without delay, and although he managed to obtain a post-ponement, he eventually decided to leave after the completion of the second act rather than start the last in unsettled conditions. And so in March he returned to neutral Switzerland, this time to Lucerne.

On his way he visited the Wesendonks for a night, and saw Mathilde, as it seemed to him, 'only through a mist'. But if the great flood of passion had now largely spent itself, it was still she who, in the correspondence that they resumed, received the first news of the renewal of composition.

Wagner   Lucerne, 10 April 1859.

I have begun the third act! It is clear to me now that I shall never again invent anything new; out of this one supreme blossoming so many buds have sprung that all I now need to do is reach back into my store and tend the flower with gentle care. And I believe, too, that this most sorrow-laden act of all will not so sorely distress me as one might expect. The second act still taxed me severely. Life's most ardent fire flamed up in it with such unimaginable power that it burned and consumed me almost personally. The more it cooled down towards the end of the act, and the soft radiance of the last transfiguration emerged from the glow, the calmer I myself became. . . . Now all I hope for is a good ending!   [*MW: 168*]

If the second act of *Tristan* is unremittingly concerned with passion in the modern sense of the word, the third act presents it in all the pain of its original meaning. For the orchestral introduction Wagner drew on another of his settings of Mathilde's poems, *Im Treibhaus*, and from it distilled a sense of grief and desolation which offers little hope that what follows would 'not so sorely distress' him.

Wagner   Child! Child! Tears have just been streaming down my face as I wrote the music for Kurwenal['s reply to Tristan:

'Now are you home in your own land, the land of your
    fathers,]
among your own meadows and delights,
where the old sun is shining, and where from
death and from your wounds you will blessedly be saved'.

It will be deeply harrowing—above all because it makes no impression on Tristan, only passes over him like an empty string of sounds.
There is immense tragedy in it! Unbearable!   [*Id: 170*]

Child! This *Tristan* is becoming something terrible! . . . I fear the
opera will be forbidden—unless of course the whole thing is turned
to parody by a bad performance—only mediocre performances can
save me! Really good ones are bound to drive people crazy—I don't
see how it can be otherwise. So this is what I have come to! . . . !
                                                        [*Id: 169–70*]

Only a month after starting work on Act III he wrote to Liszt from
his Lucerne hotel room:

Wagner You know, or you can imagine, that this is no 'life' I am liv-
    ing; the only thing that could help me now—art, art to the point of
    drowning and utter forgetfulness of the world—of that I have even
    less than I do of life, and this state of things has already been going
    on for so long that I shall soon be counting in decades! Except for
    the servants, I see and speak to no one. . . . People say to me: 'Get
    Tristan finished, then we shall see!'. That's all very well—but what if
    I don't get *Tristan* finished because I can't? I feel as if I might at last
    run out of strength, and collapse within sight of my goal. I look at my
    poem at least once a day with the best of intentions—but my head is
    confused, my heart empty. . . .   [*BWL, II: 264–5*]

And to Mathilde next day:

Wagner Yesterday's attempt at work was lamentable. My temper was
    awful, and I gave vent to it in a long letter to Liszt. . . . Today I have
    been staring with utter desolation into the grey vault of the sky, sim-
    ply looking for something to hang my bitterness on. It is eight days

now since I was able to make any progress with composition—stuck at the transition from 'vor Sehnsucht nicht zu sterben' to the sick man's [memory of his] voyage [to Ireland]. So I left it, and instead went back to working out the beginning. . . . But today I couldn't get any further with that either, because I felt I'd done it all much better before, but couldn't any more remember exactly how. . . .   [*MW*: *180*]

But the whims of genius are unpredictable. With her last letter, Mathilde had sent Wagner a consignment of biscuits, of a kind of which he was particularly fond.

Wagner   When the biscuits arrived I realised immediately what had been wrong; the ones I got here were far too sour, so that nothing decent could occur to me. But the sweet, familiar biscuits, dipped in milk, put everything back on the right track at once. So I put the working out aside, and went on composing. . . . And now I am perfectly happy: the transition has succeeded beyond belief, with a quite wonderful combination of two themes. God, what a proper biscuit can do!   [*Id*: *181*]

Thus fortified, Wagner was able to face the scene in which Tristan curses the love potion that has brought him to this pass, and his last, terrible climax of self-reproach before the arrival of Isolde.

Wagner   It takes me a great deal of time to get through the passages of suffering; even when it's going well I can get very little finished at a sitting. But the fresh, fiery, faster moving parts get done far more quickly. And so, even as I work at this technical 'completion' I'm living it out 'painfully and joyfully' all through, and am entirely at the mercy of my subject. For this last act is a state of intermittent fever—the profoundest, most unheard of suffering and anguish, and then immediately the most unheard of joy and exultation. God knows, no one has ever yet taken the thing in such earnest. . . .   [*Id*: *190–1*]

There are some for whom the philosophical ramblings of Wagner's libretto seem to drag themselves out to unnecessary lengths, and the constant mood of yearning becomes otiose. Nevertheless the relentlessness with which he clings to the inner meaning of his drama makes it difficult, if not impossible, to disengage, and the new and subtle use of leitmotivs—no longer in the outspoken, heroic manner of the first half of the *Ring*, but woven into a constantly shifting tapestry of intimate associations and inner relationships—creates a continuous symphonic development that rarely relaxes its grip.

'What the public will think remains to be seen', he wrote to Marie Wittgenstein . . .

Wagner . . . but one objection is sure to be raised: that this work is too full, too continuously filled with its subject at its highest pitch, too incessantly given over to unrelentingly strong expressions of the most erotic passion, of the most intimate relations. At the first glance people will see that [my latest] scores are infinitely richer, more lavish, more densely woven than all my earlier scores taken together. . . .

[FZ: 252–3]

Did he have an inkling of the problem when, arranging for a musical evening with the Wesendonks, he promised Wesendonk 'to put plenty of nice full closes into my playing—every eight bars a small gratification'?

[MW: 174]

Indeed in the last act such gratification is almost continuously denied, and with the arrival of Isolde the harmonic buildup reaches a last climax of expectancy. The death-intoxicated love music of the second act—there cut short at its natural climax by the intrusion of King Marke in a dramatic stroke that has inevitably been identified with *coitus interruptus*— is taken up and carried to its ultimate fulfilment.

Wagner Lucerne, July 1st.

  . . . On my walk the other day a sudden powerful scent of roses burst upon me; to one side stood a little garden, where the roses were just in full bloom. It brought back to me my last enjoyment of the Asyl garden; never have I been so affected by roses as I was then. Every morning I picked one, and put it in a glass beside my work. I knew I was bidding farewell to the garden. And with those feelings this perfume has now become wholly interwoven—the sultry heat, the summer sun, the scent of roses, and—parting. This is how it was when I sketched the music for the second act.

  What surrounded me in those days with such an almost intoxicating presence now lives again as in a dream. . . . Yet the anxiety, the anguish, has been cleared away: everything is transfigured. This is the mood in which I now hope to bring my third act to a close.

[*Id*: 204]

By this time Wagner was working on the final pages of his score—the vast, embracing music of Isolde's *Liebestod,* which finds its ultimate resolution as the tiny motif of Desire vanishes at last into the great, calm chord of B major that ends the opera.

Wagner   And so what fate divided in life now lives on transfigured in death: the gate of union is thrown open. Over Tristan's dead body the dying Isolde grants the blessed fulfilment of ardent longing, eternal union in measureless space, without limits, without fetters, insepa-rable. . . .   [*TVS*: 63]

He put the finishing touch to the full score of *Tristan und Isolde* at four-thirty in the afternoon of 6 August 1859.

Attempts to bring *Tristan* to performance were met with constant disap-pointment and lack of comprehension. When the Prelude was played for the first time, in Paris in 1860, it was greeted with perplexity by the public and hostility by the press: even Berlioz, that most perceptive of critics, saw it only as 'a slow movement, without any other theme than a sort of chromatic sigh', and many listeners felt much as Otto Wesend-onk had done: 'with scrupulous avoidance of all closing cadences,' wrote the Viennese critic Eduard Hanslick, 'this boneless tonal mollusc, self-restoring, swims ever on into the immeasurable. . .'. From Paris, Wagner wrote to Mathilde:

Wagner   *Tristan* is and remains to me a miracle! How I could have pos-sibly have done such a thing becomes more and more incomprehensi-ble: as I read it through again my eyes and ears reeled with the shock! How terribly I shall one day have to atone for this work, if I want to perform it complete: I can see quite clearly the most unheard of suf-ferings ahead of me, for I cannot deceive myself, I have in every way far exceeded the limits of what we can possibly hope to achieve in performance; only the most amazingly gifted artists would be equal to the task, and they are incredibly rare in this world. And yet I can't resist the temptation; —if I could only hear the orchestra!!—

[*MW*: 286]

But when the whole opera was put into rehearsal in Vienna in 1862, it was abandoned after seventy-seven sessions (and not attempted again in Vienna for another twenty years).

Meanwhile, Wagner's fortunes dipped and twisted in their usual way. He revised *Tannhäuser* for Paris, and completed the poem of *Die Meistersinger*—though of the music he composed only the Prelude and the first scene. On the remainder of the *Ring* he did nothing. His marriage dragged on and relations with Minna became more and more strained; he saw her for the last time in November 1862, but still couldn't bring himself to end it in divorce (she died a little over three years later). The desire for female company and the urgent need for financial support continued, and the inevitable cooling of his friendship with the Wesendonks removed a valuable source of both. Nor did his straitened circumstances diminish his passion for comfort and luxury: 'I must have beauty, splendour, light', he famously declared to Eliza Wille; 'the world owes me a living! I can't live the wretched life of a local organist, like your Master Bach!'

[*Wille: 104*]

But in 1864, suddenly, everything changed. In March the young king Ludwig II, a starry-eyed admirer of Wagner's work and person, ascended the throne of Bavaria, and two months later summoned Wagner to a private audience in Munich. It was the beginning of an extraordinary relationship, and a blatantly romantic one—though Wagner was certainly no homosexual, there is a remarkable similarity between the language of his letters to Ludwig and his outpourings to Mathilde. In any case, the king's extravagant generosity at last provided Wagner with the financial support for which he had been searching all his life. In a matter of days his debts had been paid off, and he found himself rehoused in comfort on the shores of the Starnbergersee. It was here that he received, at the end of June, a visit from Cosima von Bülow, with whom he had been falling progressively in love ever since the Bülows' visit to the Asyl in the summer of 1858. Now, owing to the unexpected absence of her husband, she and Wagner were alone together for the first time, and the following spring she gave birth to a daughter, Isolde (thus precipitating the most notorious divorce in nineteenth-century music). But unlike Wagner's subsequent marriage to Cosima, which lasted to the end of his life and well beyond it, the honeymoon with Ludwig II proved of short duration. Only eighteen months after his arrival Wagner's behaviour, and even interference in affairs of state, obliged the king to bow to the demands of his ministers and banish him from Munich.

But one solid musical ambition was achieved during this brief visit: the first performance of *Tristan und Isolde* on 10 June 1864, under the baton of Hans von Bülow.

The date originally fixed had been 15 May. Having secured, in the young tenor Ludwig Schnorr von Carolsfeld, the only artist whom Wagner considered capable of singing the role of Tristan, daily rehearsals began on 10 April; Bülow rehearsed the orchestra in the theatre in the mornings, Wagner coached the singers at home in the evening, and on 11 May the opera was given for the first time in full dress before the king and an invited audience of six hundred. Wagner, appearing on stage to introduce his work, regretted that his poor health did not allow him to conduct it himself but expressed his confidence in Bülow, whom he described, somewhat ironically under the circumstances, as his 'second self'. His growing unpopularity in Munich made an unqualified success unlikely: 'On Friday next', wrote the *Münchner Volksbote*, 'adultery with drums and trumpets, complete with the entire Music of the Future, is to appear at the Court and National Theatre—[though] some, it is true, take the liberty of saying that it is neither courtly nor national to extol a breach of the seventh commandment with glitter and with glory. . .'. And when in the afternoon of the 15th news arrived that Schnorr's wife, Malvina, who was to sing Isolde, had suddenly lost her voice, the inevitable postponement encouraged every kind of malicious gossip about Wagner and his 'unperformable' music.

At the performance itself there were none of Wagner's Zürich friends; the Wesendonks were invited but did not come, and Minna was by now terminally ill in Dresden. But Cosima was there, and Bülow directed three performances which gave Wagner, for the first time in his life, the ecstatic pleasure of hearing one of his own works in a near-ideal interpretation. With a few exceptions the press was predictably hostile, and the tragic death of Ludwig Schnorr only a month later allowed the more ill disposed to blame it once again on the strain of singing Wagner's music (he actually died of gout).

But it was not any danger to the human voice that caused the uneasiness of the first *Tristan* audience—though it is true that not every singer is wise to attempt either of the main roles. What was really upsetting was the astonishing novelty of the harmonic and thematic structure of the music: Hanslick's 'boneless tonal mollusc' was not so wide of the mark after all, and it was certainly towards the immeasurable that *Tristan* pointed the way. If the completion of the *Ring*, and the amazing achievement of Bayreuth, represent the summit of Wagner's life work in a worldly, personal sense, it is the intricate, radically chromatic idiom of the *Tristan* score that marks the real turning point in the history of music. For by fatally blurring the outlines of traditional tonality it began a process that led progressively but inexorably, over the next half century and more, to the birth of atonality, the theories of Schoenberg, and the principles of dodecaphonic composition in all its forms. Its effects are with us still.

Wagner himself was never in doubt about the significance of what he had done.

Wagner   As I worked on Tristan's great scene [in the last act] . . . I could not help asking myself, time and again, whether I was not mad to want to give such a work to a publisher for performance in a theatre. Yet I would not have sacrificed a single one of those accents of suffering, even though the whole thing tortured me to the last degree. . . . It became finally clear to me that in this opera . . . I had embodied the most daring and original conception in all my writings.   [*ML*: 683]

   [Here] all my theories were forgotten; . . . here at last I moved with the fullest freedom and the most utter disregard of every theoretical scruple, to such an extent that during the actual composition I became aware how far I was outstripping my own system. Believe me, there is no greater sense of well-being for the artist than this complete lack of hesitation in creative work, as I felt it while composing my *Tristan*.   [*ZM*: 206]

But Wagner's memory was often selective, particularly after he was married to Cosima. Perhaps he came nearest to admitting the true source of *Tristan* in a letter he sent to Mathilde while he was working on the passionate scenes of the second act. 'Never,' he wrote, 'did an idea so surely enter into experience'.

Georges Bizet in the year of *Carmen*

Carmen

'COMPLETE CHANGE OF PLAN!' wrote Bizet to his friend and pupil Edmond Galabert in February 1869:

Bizet   The new management at the Opéra-Comique have asked me for a work—I have it in writing! We're looking for a big piece—three or four acts. . . . I really want to do it, and should be delighted to have a go at changing the style of opéra-comique. Death to *La Dame Blanche!*'. [*Galabert: 176*]

In contrast to the Opéra, which by this time was little more than a salon for the elite of Parisian society, the Opéra-Comique was the theatre of the bourgeoisie. For thirty years it had supplied its audiences with a stream of works whose plots, mostly sentimental, were laid out in a succession of conventional numbers linked by easily understood spoken dialogue and could be relied on to provide a happy ending and a good evening out for family and friends. *La dame blanche*, the masterpiece of Adrien Boieldieu, epitomized a tradition that, at least in the opinion of the younger generation of French musicians, had long outstayed its welcome. But after well over a thousand performances since its first success in 1825 its position in the operatic hierarchy seemed unassailable. An early conversation between Bizet and his teacher, the distinguished composer Fromental Halévy, is revealing.

Bizet   What I said was the simple truth: 'It's a detestable opera, without talent, without ideas, without wit, without melodic invention, without any merit whatever. It's stupid, stupid, stupid! . . .' Halévy, turning towards me with his subtle smile, said (and I have a witness): 'Well, yes, you're right, its success is incomprehensible, it's a worthless piece. Only, *one mustn't say so'*. He was no doubt right too. . . .   [*Ganderax: 321*]

As both the Opéra and the Opéra-Comique were bound by tradition and deeply suspicious of anything new, Bizet's earlier operatic appearances had been made elsewhere—first with the prize-winning operetta *Docteur Miracle* at the Bouffes-Parisiens, and later with two full-length operas at the more liberal Théâtre-Lyrique. *Les pêcheurs de perles*, an exotic and adventurous score for a young man of twenty-four, got a stuffy reception from the critics, who complained of noisy instrumentation, strange harmonies, and the noxious influences of Wagner and Verdi, and *La jolie fille de Perth*, which marked a step towards a lighter form of lyric drama, did only marginally better. But the right libretto was never easy to find; Bizet's life was littered with projected, hardly begun or nearly completed operas on a mixture of subjects—twenty or so tantalising might-have-beens to half a dozen finished scores—and now, at the age of thirty, the invitation from the Opéra-Comique seemed to offer something solid in a shifting world.

The new management was the result of the appointment as director of Camille du Locle, thirty-seven years old and a poet and orientalist of refined taste who was later to be one of the librettists of Verdi's *Don Carlos*. He shared the position with the existing director, Adolphe de Leuven, an elderly aristocrat of Swedish descent whose father had fled to Paris after being implicated in the assassination of Gustav III, and a prolific librettist of the old school with a horror of anything new. In the words of the writer and critic Henri Blaze de Bury, 'de Leuven's contemporaries were old, but he was archaic'.   [*Blaze de Bury: 279*]

It was of course du Locle who suggested the idea of an opera from Bizet. But a libretto acceptable to both directors as well as the composer proved elusive, and external circumstances prolonged the delay. Bizet's struggle to marry Geneviève Halévy (the daughter of his old teacher) against her family's wishes made for a stressful emotional situation, and Napoleon III's war with Prussia (during which Bizet briefly enrolled in the National Guard) and the uneasy birth of the Third Republic hardly provided a tranquil working environment. So the 'big piece in three or four acts' was eventually shelved; a shorter text was provided by Louis Gallet, the librettist of an earlier unfinished project, and Bizet made his début at the Opéra-Comique in May 1872 with the one-act oriental fable *Djamileh*.

Gallet   Bizet's score entered the sanctuary of the Opéra-Comique with an air of independence hardly likely to recommend it to the powers that be. There was the old stage-manager Avocat, known to everybody as Victor, a diehard traditionalist who . . . watched Bizet with an expression both resentful and distressed as he listened from a corner in the wings to this music of which he could make no sense, and stumped off to his office with a shrug of his shoulders and a growl that boded ill. And there was de Leuven, . . . used to the light and familiar music of the operas of his youth, upon whom the inspirations of Bizet, so fine, so richly coloured, so full of seduction and genuine passion, fell like dull rain. . . . There was no way he could use one of those tricks . . . picked up from a colleague of the old days, that he sometimes recommended to me—'Look, when the action shows signs of flagging it's very simple: one of the characters just drops a pile of plates and there's your audience awake again!' In *Djamileh*, unfortunately, there were no plates. . . .

But Camille du Locle was in heaven. With the mischievousness of a Parisian street urchin he delighted in stirring up the indignation of [the theatre staff] and poking fun at the disdainful pomposity of his co-director. The little details of the production enchanted him; . . . very much the artist, he would rush off every morning in search of some fabric, some original embellishment, some authentic garment or piece of furniture. . . .   [*Gallet: 19–20, 24*]

The music that Bizet wrote for this little tale of love in the Cairo marriage market was original and imaginative, but all du Locle's efforts at décor could not prevail against a mixture of poor singing and the uncomprehending hostility of the Opéra-Comique audience. 'There you are—a complete flop', said Bizet to Gallet as the curtain came down on the first night, and once again he found himself faced with a chorus of critics talking of harmonic confusion, lack of melody and boredom.

Bizet   All the same I am satisfied with the overall result. The press has been very interesting—never has an opéra-comique in one act been more seriously, I can honestly say more passionately, discussed. The old fuss about Wagner continues. . . . But what gives me greater satisfaction than the opinion of all these gentlemen is the absolute certainty that I have found my way. I know what I am doing.

[*Galabert: 199*]

And then, almost as a throw-away at the end of the letter, comes the first hint of *Carmen*:

Bizet   They have just asked me for a three act piece at the Opéra-Comique. Meilhac and Halévy are going to write it for me. It will be gay, but of a gaiety that allows for style. . . .   [*Id: 199–200*]

Henri Meilhac and Ludovic Halévy (nephew of Fromental and cousin of Bizet's wife) were the most talked-of theatrical partnership in Paris. It was they who had provided the sparkling librettos for the great Offenbach hits from *La belle Hélène* onwards, Halévy being responsible for the verses and the dramatic structure, Meilhac for the dialogue—and pretty well exclusively for the dialogue it seems, to judge from the words of a contemporary theatrical chronicler:

Mortier   Meilhac likes neither music nor scenery—those two rather important features of opéra-bouffe. When he goes to the première of a musical comedy he positions himself at the back of a box, listening to the dialogue. In vain the audience swoons with rapture at the varying beauties of the score, in vain they encore the songs, applaud the sets and the costumes—if the dialogue hasn't amused him, 'there's a success that won't last!' he says.   [*Mortier, 1875: 381–2*]

Clearly de Leuven hoped that Meilhac would be able to infuse something of the spirit of traditional *opéra-comique* into whatever subject this unpredictable young composer might choose. To make doubly sure, he provided the librettists with three scenarios of his own in the best de Leuven manner. But this was not the path that Bizet was 'certain of having found', and it is no chance that the one important work he completed while discussions about the new opera hung fire was the incidental music for a drama of real life, Alphonse Daudet's *L'Arlésienne*. For a man whose origins were firmly northern French, the wild, sun-baked region of Provence, with its strange customs and speech, and the obsessive passions of the people who gave Daudet the stuff of his play, offered an exotic background every bit as remote as the Spain of Prosper Mérimée's *Carmen*.

The starkly unforgiving world from which *Carmen* itself is drawn was described by Mérimée in a letter to a friend written just after he had finished writing his tale in 1845.

Mérimée   It's about a peasant from Malaga who has killed his mistress because she offered her charms too freely to the public. . . . As I have been making a close study of the gipsies for some time, I have made my heroine a gipsy girl. . . . Now in my day, in Seville or Cadiz or Granada, there were gipsy women whose virtue wouldn't have withstood a farthing. There was one, very pretty, in the prison house by the Alhambra, who was more hard-hearted, but even she could be tamed in the end. Most of the women are horribly ugly. . . . In the wild state, they are beasts of burden and so badly treated that they become ugly by sheer force of misery. . . . They sleep under the open sky, carry their children on their backs, eat the scraps that their men leave them and are entirely innocent of soap and water.

[*Mérimée*, I: 134–5]

Mérimée's interest in the gypsies was not limited to Spanish sources; his reading had led him to George Borrow in England and Pushkin in Russia and particularly to Pushkin's narrative poem *Tsygany* (The gypsies). In this short but passionate little tale Aleko, a young man escaping from city life, becomes the lover of a gypsy girl, Zemfira, lives with her and her companions until she can no longer bear the constraints he places upon her freedom and, when she takes another lover, stabs them both and gives himself up to the gypsies. There are obvious parallels here with *Carmen*, and Mérimée, who regarded the poem as Pushkin's masterpiece, had probably read it before he wrote his own story. In any case, he made a prose translation of it soon afterwards which was published, as *Les bohémiens*, in the same volume as the very successful second edition of *Carmen*; the two works continued to appear together in all the editions that were available to Bizet and his collaborators, and *Les bohémiens* left its mark, sometimes even in the form of direct quotation, on the libretto of Bizet's opera. When Carmen teases Zuniga, in Act I of the opera, the words '*Coup-moi, brûle-moi, je ne [te] dirai rien*' are taken verbatim from Zemfira's song over the cradle of her baby, and the angry confrontation with Aleko which follows contains the seeds of Carmen's '*Je chante pour moi-même*' as she tempts Don José into letting her escape. Throughout the opera there is an immediacy in the dialogue between Carmen and José, and a pervading sense of fatality, that suggests the influence of Pushkin, and certainly the last scene with its rapid dramatic confrontation is nearer in spirit to Pushkin than to the lonely, drawn-out close of Mérimée's tale.   [*Briggs*]

Whatever its sources, *Carmen* was a very different subject from any that Bizet's two librettists had tackled before, and from the beginning they must have realised they would have a difficult course to steer between the traditional expectations of the Opéra-Comique and the demands of dramatic realism. One cannot help wondering whether they were quite as positive about it as Halévy later remembered.

Halévy   Meilhac and I immediately shared Bizet's enthusiasm for Méri-mée's splendid story. So did Camille du Locle when I spoke to him about it, but at the same time he was anxious and said: 'There's de Leuven. . . . A subject like this will terrify him. Go and see him—he's very fond of you—perhaps you'll manage to convince him'.
    . . . De Leuven was an old friend of my father's and had known me as a child. . . . I went to see him and, in fact, he interrupted me after my very first sentence. '*Carmen*! . . . Mérimée's *Carmen*! . . . But isn't she murdered by her lover? . . . And all that *milieu* of robbers, and gypsies, and cigarette-girls! . . . At the Opéra-Comique! . . . the fam-ily theatre! . . . the theatre that parents use to interview prospective sons in law! . . . Why, every night we have five or six boxes taken for these interviews! . . . You are going to put our audience to flight! . . . it's impossible!'
    I persisted. I explained to M. de Leuven that this would be *Car-men*, certainly, but a *Carmen* softened and watered down . . . that in addition we had introduced into the piece new characters in the purest *opéra-comique* tradition, one of them a most innocent, chaste young lady. . . . We had, it is true, some gypsies, but they were comic gypsies (which they certainly were not!), and the death, the unavoid-able death at the conclusion, would be, as it were, hurried over at the end of a very brilliant, lively act, on a feast day in bright sunlight, with processions and ballets and jubilant fanfares.
    In the end M. de Leuven resigned himself to the idea, but only after a hard struggle, and as I left his office he said to me: 'I beg you, try to avoid her dying. Death at the Opéra-Comique! . . . such a thing has never happened . . . do you hear, never! Don't make her die! . . . I beg you, my dear child'.
    I was, at that time, a child some forty years of age.

[*Halévy, 1905: 5–8*]

Halévy's object may have been to pacify de Leuven, but it is true that he and Meilhac had made substantial changes in Mérimée's plot. The original story is narrated by the author in the first person and concentrates entirely on the two central characters, Carmen and Don José. It is a story seen through the eyes and emotions of one man, and it portrays an internal passion; for the theatre it had to be given visible presence, with singing roles that allowed for musical development, and a structure to provide dramatic impact on the stage. Meilhac and Halévy, working closely with Bizet, set about this task like the professionals they were. They compressed the action by removing all reference to Carmen's husband and other lovers, thus eliminating two earlier murders that José commits in the novel. The gypsies and smugglers provided a ready-made chorus, and the dialogue follows Mérimée in filling in details of José's background. José's comrades Zuniga and Morales and Carmen's companions Frasquita and Mercedes are new, and the indistinct off-stage picador Lucas, whose gallantry towards Carmen in the bull-ring at Cordova was the last straw that drove José to murder in the novel, reappears elaborated out of all recognition into the glamorous, macho figure of the toreador Escamillo. And then, as promised to de Leuven, there is 'the innocent, chaste young lady', Micaela.

To all this Bizet made his own contributions, and it was probably he (rather than his two more business-like collaborators) who was responsible for the traces of Pushkin in the text. The result may not be Mérimée's *Carmen*: the story is stripped of much of its mystery and violence; Don José is not a committed bandit and murderer, but rather the reluctant victim of circumstances that have run out of his control (and as such more Pushkin than Mérimée); Carmen has become a less depraved figure, no longer a compulsive liar and thief, and there are touches of Meilhac's knock-about humour in the exchanges between Le Dancaïre and Le Remendado that would certainly have had no place in Mérimée's view of the gypsy world. But as a libretto it is brilliant. Above all, the invention of Micaela as a contrast to Carmen (strengthened by the off-stage presence of José's mother—a mere hint in the novel) is a crucial addition that establishes the innocence of José at the beginning of the story, runs like a nagging thread through the struggle with his growing passion, and loses itself at last in one of the most heart-breaking dramatic climaxes in all opera.

On this rich and promising material Bizet set to work early in 1873, with a private determination effectively masked by the easy-going manner that his friends knew so well.

Gallet   There was a mild but penetrating look behind those irremovable eye-glasses and a lip almost continually arched in a smile of distant mockery; with that air of detachment that I always knew in him he talked modestly, in a slightly whistling tone of voice. . . . [In the country] he would wear a straw hat and a loose jacket and stroll with the casual assurance of a country gentleman, smoking his pipe, chatting happily with his friends and welcoming them to his table with a *bonhomie* touched with characteristic banter. . . .   [*Gallet: 8, 13–14*]

Yet 'I was afraid of him', wrote one of his piano pupils, a young American girl:

Stuart Henry   Not that he ever scolded, but the way he would look at you through those eye-glasses! . . . He was as uneasy as a lion in a cage during the lesson; . . . I often thought he was paying no attention . . . and sometimes would make little slips in fingering. Then he would say savagely: '*Je ne dors pas! Je ne dors pas!*' . . .

He was full of the airs of *Carmen* at this time, so I heard most of them sooner than almost anyone, but of course I did not know what they were. We only knew he was at work on an opera. . . . He would excuse himself during the lesson and go in to the piano in the study, close the door and work over some strain that was running in his head. . . . He would hum the melodies and develop them on the piano. I recall particularly the Toreador song and '*J'irai danser la séguedille/Et boire du Manzanilla!*'   [*Henry: 193–200*]

Bizet generally made few preliminary sketches for his operas, simply noting down the vocal lines with occasional indications for harmony or orchestration. So it is difficult to be sure just what it was that the twelve-year-old Stuart Henry heard through the closed door. But whether in his head or on paper, by May 1873 he had enough of *Carmen* worked out to be able to write to one of his pupils: 'I have finished the first act and I'm reasonably pleased with it'.   [*Imbert: 193*]

It is a long act and it was originally longer (fifty-eight minutes at the first performance). Rather like Beethoven in *Fidelio*, Bizet was tempted by a succession of relatively traditional 'numbers' to indulge in an expansive presentation of the background against which the drama was to develop. Dramatically, the most significant difference bewteen the original version and its revision was in the quarrel scene after the knife attack in the cigarette factory; the two halves of the chorus were originally linked by fifty-three bars of purely orchestral music, and it was at this point that Carmen made her appearance from the factory, rather than at the end as in the final version. Later he added a pantomime scene at the beginning of the act, very much in the *opéra-comique* manner, to strengthen the role of Morales when it was taken over by the baritone Duvernoy.

By the end of August he had made sufficient progress to start thinking about an interpreter for the role of Carmen. The first two suggestions, no doubt prompted by de Leuven, were the popular Offenbach singer Zulma Bouffar, who was turned down by du Locle, and Marie Roze, a current favourite at the Comique, who seems at first to have been approved by Halévy and Meilhac. But after a meeting with the composer, at which he made it clear that there was no intention of modifying 'the very scabrous side' of Carmen's character but that instead it was to be 'scrupulously respected', she declined the role. It is clear that Bizet's view of the opera was already rather different from that of his collaborators.

[*Curtiss:* 355]

As soon as he heard of Marie Roze's refusal, du Locle wrote offering the part to the mezzo-soprano Célestine Galli-Marié, a singing actress who had been making a brilliant name for herself at the Opéra-Comique since her début in 1862.

Paul de Saint-Victor   She is small and alluring, moves like a cat with an expression at once rebellious and full of mischief—there is something capricious, impudent about her whole manner and personality. . . .

[*Soubies:* 44]

. . . with a wayward temperament that the actor Pierre Berton remembered.

Berton   She had not read Mérimée's novel and knew absolutely nothing about this immortal character of which she was none the less to become the perfect incarnation. She was in Spain when the first proposal from the management of the Opéra-Comique arrived. A few days later her friend and colleague [Paul] Lhérie [later to be Don José] received from her a letter which began with the words 'My dear Director'. Lhérie, who realised at once what had happened, chanced to meet du Locle at the theatre the same day and told him that, due to an error, he had a letter which was meant for him. 'As a matter of fact I have one for you, too' replied du Locle, in a voice so strange that Lhérie wondered anxiously what Galli-Marié could possibly have written to him. The two men exchanged letters and as soon as he was alone, Lhérie hastened to look at his. 'My dear friend', he read, 'your little marmoset of a director has written asking me if I would like to create *Carmen*. What is it?'   [*Berton:* 237]

Du Locle appears not to have taken lasting offence; at any rate he engaged Galli-Marié—and was somewhat mollified a few months later when she appeared at a rehearsal stroking and kissing a pet marmoset which she carried in her muff. But this was in the future; for the time being the Opéra-Comique was still mired in financial problems, and a long series of haggling letters took place before Galli-Marié's engagement was confirmed. She wrote to Bizet:

Galli-Marié   M. du Locle talks about *Carmen* . . . but in the long run comes to no conclusion, and the fundamental question still remains in doubt. I know that M. du Locle is only $\frac{1}{2}$ director, as he writes to me, which is all the worse for me. . . . You ask me if I value you at all. You know very well that I understand and like your school and I should be very happy to interpret a work . . . signed by you, whose last two scores I know almost entirely by heart, both voice and accompaniment. The best proof I can give you is my *waiting* as I am doing until the thing is decided in your favour.   [*Curtiss:* 361–2]

'*Carmen* is nearly finished', wrote Bizet sometime in the late summer of 1873, adding 'I begin rehearsals in December'—though this was optimistic, given that the work was still in short score and it was not until 18 December that Galli-Marié wrote du Locle:

Galli-Marié   Yes, *cher Monsieur*, I accept—2,500 francs a month—four months—October 1874, November, December and January—12 times a month—to create *Carmen* by MM. Bizet, Meilhac and Halévy—Is that it, are you satisfied? That will make nice little performances at 208 francs 33 centimes a time! . . . But at what a price to my *amour-propre*! And how you despise the Good Lord's poor actors! . . .

My best regards to M. Bizet (I'm sure he will dine well tonight!)   [*Delmas:* 51–2]

Even so, the directors of the Opéra Comique continued to drag their feet, and in January de Leuven resigned his position—largely because of his antipathy for the subject of Bizet's opera, which he clearly felt to be beyond the help of even the most liberal application of crockery. With du Locle now in sole charge the situation might have looked more hopeful, but in the following spring rehearsals were again put back. Bizet's marriage, and health, were going through a difficult phase, and after an acute bout of his recurring tonsillitis he decided to get out of Paris. 'I've found a pleasant, peaceful little place by the river at Bougival', he wrote to a friend. 'I am going there to finish *Carmen*, which goes into rehearsal in August. . .'.

But August passed, too, and it was late September before he wrote again. [*Imbert: 194*]

Bizet Rehearsals start in a few days' time. *Carmen* will have its first performance at the end of November or the beginning of December. I have just spent two months orchestrating the 1200 pages of my score. [*Id: 196*]

This was an even bigger job than it sounds: since the opera so far existed on paper only as a draft piano score with a few instrumental reminders, this was the first time the full orchestral accompaniment had been put on paper in any form. But at least the later acts had turned out to be shorter than the first; the onward pressure of the drama had gradually swept away the remaining vestiges of traditional *opéra-comique* and found expression in a new continuity of texture that made musical expansion for its own sake utterly irrelevant. It is the unique quality of *Carmen* that the gradual transformation of the musical form exactly matches the growing intensity of the narrative.

At only two points in the last three acts does the original score contain anything of significance that doesn't appear in its successor: first, the duel between Escamillo and José in Act III is substantially longer, with a first section in which Escamillo has José at his mercy but spares his life—an episode that lends a welcome touch of magnanimity to the Toreador's character, while at the same time underlining the moral degradation of José, who would none the less have taken mortal advantage of a slip by his opponent had Carmen not intervened in time; and second, at the end of the opera, after being stabbed by Don José, Carmen falls on her arm and, as she dies, repeats '*d'une voix éteinte*' the same words that had earlier been wrung from her when she saw her death foretold in the cards.

Meanwhile Bizet had re-established communication with Galli-Marié, meeting her in Paris in June for a preliminary run through of some of her music, and on July 9th she wrote briskly:

Galli-Marié   I am waiting impatiently for the pieces we read at sight recently. If you will have them sent to 18 Cité Malesherbes. . . . I shall have the time to study them and tell you if anything troubles me.   [*Curtiss: 368*]

It has of course been suggested that during the months before the first performance of *Carmen* Bizet and Galli-Marié indulged in the inevitable love affair, but there is little evidence that this was other than theatre gossip—and in any case Galli-Marié had for some time had a permanent lover. If Bizet felt, as he very probably did, a more than purely artistic attraction for his capricious and warm-hearted interpreter, the tone of her letters suggests that she kept him firmly at bay; when he proposed delivering the rest of her music in person, at the château near Bordeaux where she was on holiday, her reply was uncompromising:

Galli-Marié   Monsieur . . . I wish absolutely to work only on the difficult passages in my role and not on the role as a whole, which I shall read at sight on October 1st, the day my contract starts. So if you would be kind enough to send me *by mail* . . . the pieces I went over with you, and any others that are difficult either in intention or execution, I shall be most grateful. I shall get a metronome at Bordeaux. I am no less grateful for your offer, and remain, Monsieur, sincerely yours, Galli-Marié.   [*Id: 368–9*]

Galli-Marié made the role very much her own, and the composer Ernest Guiraud, one of Bizet's closest friends, claimed that Bizet was obliged to 'rewrite' her opening aria thirteen times before she was satisfied with it. This is no doubt an exaggeration, but the leading soprano's entry aria is an important moment in any opera, and the lilting $\frac{6}{8}$ tune used at the first rehearsals was probably (and rightly) thought tame. It was eventually replaced by a tune that Bizet came across by chance and took for a Spanish folk song—a romance in *habanera* rhythm by the

Spanish composer Sebastián Iradier (as Bizet later acknowledged in a footnote to his score).

Bizet had never been to Spain (he is reputed to have said that it would be 'tiresome and unnecessary') and he had no firsthand knowledge of Spanish folk music. Apart from a brief snatch of a popular song from Ciudad Real, when Carmen is teasing Zuniga in Act I, there are no Spanish folk tunes in *Carmen* and, apart from the *habanera*, only one borrowing from a Spanish composer—a *polo* by the Spanish tenor Manuel García which forms the prelude to Act IV. But in both cases the improvement on the original, though minimal, is striking, and the changes Bizet made in the *habanera* transform it magically from a rather ordinary little ditty into a hypnotic display of musical sexuality. He kept the words of Halévy's refrain '*L'amour est enfant de Bohème . . .*' and the opening lines of the first verse; for the rest he sent his librettist a draft of what he wanted, with instructions for 'eight more lines in a similar vein, the second, fourth, sixth, eighth, tenth, and twelfth lines to begin with a vowel!!!'—to which mathematically rather confusing demand Halévy replied:

Halévy   Here are the twelve lines you wanted. Do they have the right feeling? I did some that were rather more tender, but I think we mustn't give Carmen too melancholy a tinge at the beginning, and a touch of wry humour won't do any harm.   [*Malherbe. 181*]

But they were not Bizet's idea of Carmen; the remainder of the words in the final version are his own, and the one change in the refrain—substituting for the airy indifference of Halévy's '*Si tu m'aimes, tant pis pour toi*' the thinly disguised menace of '*Si je t'aime, prends garde à toi*'—indicates the difference between his view of his heroine and that of his librettists. He was always having to defend the tougher aspects of Mérimée's story and resist the efforts of his collaborators, particularly Meilhac, to water it down to Opéra-Comique standards.

Not that they can really be blamed; their experience until now had been confined to a very different style of theatre, and one in which they were still deeply immersed. Nevertheless, Halévy's strong sense of identification with the characters he created—'for me they're not the least imaginary' he wrote, 'they're more real and more alive than many flesh and blood individuals'—and his long experience of what was needed to make a scene 'go' provided Bizet with a type of theatrical support that he had never received before. Though it is perhaps difficult to accept at its face value Halévy's story about the origin of the Toreador's famous entry aria in Act II.

Halévy   I was the one who was responsible for that. Bizet had played me the act, and, speaking as a man of the theatre, I said to him 'There, in the middle of the act, there's something missing'. 'No, there's nothing missing', he replied. And I insisted. Then one day he said to me: 'Listen'. And he played me the whole piece—the aria, the refrain. I said to him, 'That's it, that's what was needed'. 'Too bad!' he replied. And that's the exact truth.   [*Halévy, 1938: 131*]

It is highly unlikely that Halévy's original libretto failed to provide an aria to mark the first appearance of the Toreador, and in any case words must have existed for the music that Bizet eventually wrote. But Halévy may well have felt (as Galli-Marié had with the *habanera*) that Bizet's first effort did not make enough of the opportunity. That could hardly be said of its replacement. There have always been criticisms of this brilliantly showy piece, and certainly it is easy to see it as a concession to the style that Bizet was trying to avoid—indeed his laconic reaction recorded by Halévy may be the origin of the oft-quoted (and apparently unsubstantiated) tale that after writing it he remarked, 'Well, they asked for rubbish and they've got it'. But the whole point of Escamillo is that he is a showy figure—just as the point of Micaela is that she is an innocent little *opéra-comique* miss—and the direction *'avec fatuité'* over the music of the refrain gives a clear indication of Bizet's intention. It is after all this conflict between the *opéra-comique* milieu of Escamillo and Micaela and the savage world of Mérimée's story that gives Bizet's drama its essential point of departure.

Rehearsals began, at long last, at the beginning of October. They were to drag on for five difficult and, for Bizet, often agonising months. If the departure of de Leuven had removed a dinosaur at the head of the organisation, it had made little difference to the atmosphere in the theatre into which Bizet was now plunged. Unfortunately, Halévy, who kept a diary throughout this period, later cancelled many entries and so mutilated the rest that much of it is completely unreadable. Why he did this is not clear—perhaps to eliminate embarrassing references to Bizet's matrimonial difficulties (he was after all a member of the family), possibly to safeguard his subsequent literary reputation or simply to suppress his first thoughts about a work that had meanwhile become an international success. One of the few entries that survived, dated thirteen days after the première of the opera, suggests that he had at first sympathised with the difficulties experienced by the principal singers.

Halévy   During the rehearsals I went through a series of widely differing impressions. I adored this score. Georges had played me each number in his own inimitable manner. At first the music appeared tortuous and complicated, but little by little the clouds dispersed and the artists began to see their way clearly through all the delicate and original things which fill this curious and very unusual score.
[*Halévy, 1937: 830*]

They certainly felt the difficulties of interpreting a work so new in character but rapidly, from day to day, they found their way into the beauties of the score and became passionately attached to their roles.
[*Halévy, 1905: 8*]

Berton   To be fair, the director hadn't fallen again into the unforgivable error that had stifled the success of *Djamileh*. All the interpreters of *Carmen* were fully up to their roles: everyone, from the admirable quartet of Galli-Marié, Chapuy [Micaela], Lhérie, Bouhy [Escamillo], down to the humblest of their colleagues. In them Bizet found not only all the talent he could need, but devotion and faith as well. Three of them were friends of mine, and everything that they said to me about the work during the rehearsals would have been music to the ears of the composer.
[*Berton: 241–2*]

Halévy   The real obstacle came with the performance of the choruses. The majority of the chorus members, finding themselves completely out of their depth, threatened to go on strike. After a full two months of rehearsal the choruses in the first act, at the entry of the cigarette girls and during the brawl surrounding the officer when Carmen is arrested, were still declared 'unperformable'. It is true that these choruses are very difficult to realise on the stage—the singers not only had to sing, they had to move around, act, come and go . . . be alive, in fact. But that was something unprecedented at the Opéra-Comique. The members of the chorus were accustomed to singing their ensembles standing still in neat lines, their arms dangling loosely at their side, their eyes fixed on the conductor and their thoughts elsewhere.
[*Halévy, 1905: 8*]

Mortier   . . . You can't believe what's asked of them; they dance, they fight one another, and—unheard of audacity—they smoke cigarettes! There are some among them who must have been in the chorus at the première of *Richard Coeur de Lion* [1784!], and who turn a terrible shade of grey every time they blow out a puff of smoke.   [*Mortier, 1876: 87*]

Bizet's struggle to get the performance that he visualised out of such unpromising material was observed by the young Vincent d'Indy, then a student at the Conservatoire, who slipped into rehearsals and later recalled the battle in which Bizet was constantly involved with the producer, Charles Ponchard, a professional of the old school who defended the conventions of the Opéra-Comique with an authority that nobody dared to question.   [*Malherbe: 201–2*]

And then there was the director himself. Curiously, in spite of his professed affection for Bizet as a man and the fact that he had been the original instigator of *Carmen*, du Locle's attitude towards the opera seems to have become inreasingly hostile as rehearsals progressed.

Vallas   The incomprehension he showed made [d'Indy's] blood boil. Bizet provided him with ideas designed to give more life to the production, especially in the first act, where he wanted the chorus to enter in little groups and not in a solid mass. But du Locle turned a deaf ear to all Bizet's requests, preferring to remain faithful to the absurd and much loved traditions of his theatre. The composer was disconsolate when he realised, that despite all his efforts, his interpreters were not being allowed to escape from the ruts carved out by generations of mediocre artists.   [*Vallas: 135*]

Berton   From all I had heard about [du Locle] I took him to be a man of refined tastes and progressive ideas, very ready to break with the routine formulas of the old Opéra-Comique and therefore well suited to putting on a work like this and making a success of it. Unhappily, all this was no more than a kind of dilettantism, a superficial veneer and not a matter of deep conviction. In reality he was a sceptic who lacked entirely any genuine basis of conviction. I think he was afraid of appearing to believe in anyone or anything in particular, and was less concerned with the welfare of his undertaking than with being regarded as an infallible judge. . . .

That du Locle could actually have disliked a work like *Carmen* seems to me improbable. But he didn't believe in its success and, foreseeing its failure, thought it best to predict it—because above all else he wanted to be seen by the gallery as Monsieur who is never Wrong. He permitted himself disparaging comments, which were repeated in the theatre, offending the librettists, upsetting the composer and worrying the artists. [*Berton:* 239–40]

'It's Cochin-Chinese music', he told Saint-Saëns, and he took sides with the *chef de chant* and other staff musicians in trying to flatten out Bizet's harmonic originality—they had a particular hatred of the magical cadence that closes Don José's aria '*La fleur que tu m'avais jetée*'. Nor did Bizet receive much support from his librettists, who had four pieces in rehearsal at different theatres at the time and had little energy to spare for the rehearsals of *Carmen*. When they did turn up they still exerted themselves to preserve what was left of their own view of the opera—nervous of the realism which, as one of them openly said, they would gladly have toned down, but which the composer 'ferociously' defended. [*Soubies:* 219]

'*Carmen* doesn't allow me a moment's peace', Bizet wrote to Ambroise Thomas; 'I do all the accompanying myself, I am making the piano reduction myself . . .'. [*Wright:* 41]

And the chorus continued to give trouble. To du Locle he wrote in desperation:

Bizet As you are making great sacrifices for *Carmen*, please allow me to do one small thing to assure the proper execution of my women's choruses in the first act. Meilhac and Halévy want faces, and I would like voices! Authorise me to take six additional first sopranos and four second sopranos. . . . What I am asking need not delay you for five minutes. The women are there. I will rehearse them myself tomorrow, *Sunday*, and the *day after, Monday*! They can take their places on stage on *Tuesday*. I shall do *everything necessary* so that the choruses will be ready in three days. Please forgive my frenzy, but don't think that I am selfish; if I were alone before the enemy, I should be less disturbed. But you are with me; you are risking more than I am. I sense a possible victory, I assure you, and I know that you will be repaid by it. It is a matter of honour, and also, *cher ami*, of feeling.
[*Curtiss:* 382]

'What you ask does not seem to me very reasonable', wrote du Locle; 'in spite of what you say you are condemning us to at least a week's delay'. And to Halévy: [*Id: 382*]

Du Locle   My dear friend, Bizet has sent me a note this evening, asking for extra voices for these *diabolical* women's choruses in the first act. . . . But is this absolutely necessary?   [*Halévy, 1905: 8*]

'Bizet insisted', says Halévy, 'and Camille du Locle allowed him the extra voices'. But by now the pressures of the situation were beginning to tell on the composer. Henri Maréchal, a young musician who came to him for advice, remembered sitting with him smoking a pipe till late in the afternoon:

Maréchal   As we talked I would often notice a tear welling in his eye, which he would quickly control and force back into the depths of his being. Because at this time Bizet's work was far from achieving any real success. . . . People had begun to have doubts about him as a composer; he knew it, and there was no way the grief he felt could go unnoticed by his friends. He smiled as he talked . . . but behind the laughter the wound was clear.   [*Maréchal: 233–4*]

Berton   It was the only time that I saw Ludovic Halévy, that most prudent, level-headed, philosophical of men, lose a little of his *sang froid*. But he felt what we all felt, Bizet more than any of us, that the test for Bizet was decisive—a turning point in his career. The emotion of the composer was all the greater because his hopes were so high. The slightest shock set him vibrating like an over taut wire, and all this backstage chatter, seeping through the half-open door of the director's office and whistling through the wings and dressing-rooms like a wind of ill omen, . . . shook his confidence for the first time.
                                                      [*Berton: 241*]

The beginning of orchestral rehearsals brought more trouble; this was a very different matter from the routine accompaniments of *La dame blanche*, and some of Bizet's more imaginative passages were declared 'unplayable'. But the loyalty of his principal singers, at least, was not in question. In the face of opposition from the theatre staff, Lhérie and Galli-Marié stood by Bizet to the point of threatening to resign their parts, and when a concerted attempt was made to persuade him to shorten the great duet between Carmen and Don José in Act II, and break it up to allow for applause, Bizet was able to stand firm and refuse to mutilate this disturbingly 'naturalistic' scene (*or* weaken the Cochin-Chinese harmonies at the end of José's aria).

All the same, it is clear from the score and parts used at the first performance that Bizet did revise his music during rehearsals and make a number of significant cuts. Given the atmosphere of hostility existing in the theatre, it has become a matter of debate whether these were made by Bizet himself or forced on him by others. But a composer may often have second thoughts after seeing his work in rehearsal on the stage, and Bizet was not a man who would allow himself to be bullied into compromising his artistic integrity. Nor were the cuts made in any sort of last-minute panic; they began early in the rehearsals. Among the first to go was the reminiscence of the card scene at the moment of Carmen's death—a theatrical conceit that may have looked effective in the libretto but on the stage held back the dramatic impetus at the climax of the drama. On the other hand, the pantomime for Morales in Act I survived for thirty performances before it was dropped as an unnecessary concession to the old *comique* manner, and the longer version of the duel duet lasted well into the public run before being lopped of its first half—either to save time or because of Lhérie's inadequacy as an actor, or both.

The quarrel scene in Act I is a different matter. It had always caused trouble; it was musically and theatrically complex, and Carmen's appearance in the middle rather than at the end meant that she was on stage during the whole second half of the scene—an added distraction which may well have proved the last straw for the hard-tried ladies of the chorus. The removal of the orchestral passage that accompanied her entry certainly alters, perhaps weakens, the musical structure of the piece (it was made up of themes that have already appeared and will appear again at the end of the scene). But in a long act it also held back the dramatic momentum, and by now dramatic momentum was Bizet's constant concern. Throughout rehearsals he made numerous small cuts and worked at revising and tightening the last two finales—drawing together at the end of Act III the disparate strands represented by Micaela, Escamillo, Don José and Carmen into a single powerful ensemble, and cutting and reordering the end of Act IV, so that the Toreador's refrain breaks in with savage irony at the exact moment of Carmen's murder, and Don José's despairing 'Ah Carmen! ma Carmen adorée!', with its unforgettable dying fall, is properly allowed to close the opera.

Halévy   The last rehearsals were excellent. For audience they had the staff of the theatre, who had all lived with this music for three or four months and as a result had time to appreciate its beauties. Slowly, everyone in the theatre had succumbed to the same enchantment.
[Halévy, 1937: 830]

And Bizet himself seems to have regained his composure.

Bizet   They make out that I am obscure, complicated, tedious, more fettered by technical skill than lit by inspiration. Well, this time I have written a work that is all clarity and vivacity, full of colour and melody. . . . Come along; I think you will like it.   [Dean: 108–9]

Halévy   Carmen opens next Wednesday. There are some very, very beautiful and charming things in the score, and I dare to hope for a happy outcome for Bizet. In this case it's only his interest that I worry about—the thing has little importance for Meilhac and me. If Carmen does comes off on Wednesday we shall have a première and a centième on the same evening.   [Halévy, 1937: 830]

'We were full of confidence on the evening of the first performance', Halévy remembered only a fortnight afterwards. But du Locle, who was already on record as regarding the libretto scandalous, now felt it necessary to invite a minister, who had applied for tickets, to come and see the dress rehearsal before deciding whether or not it was a suitable piece to bring his family to.

Berton   The fact that these comments came from the director of the theatre, for whom the success of the opera could hardly be a matter of indifference, lent them an obvious significance and spread legitimate suspicion about the work.   [Berton: 254]

There was even a suspicion that du Locle was behind the reports in some parts of the press on the morning of the first performance that the opera contained 'such scabrous characters and such ambiguous situations that it may very well cause offence'. It was therefore under mixed auspices that the première of *Carmen* took place, before an audience packed with ill-disposed critics and theatre-goers prepared for an evening of enjoyable scandal, on Wednesday, 3 March 1875.

Musically, the performance was a reasonable one, with Galli-Marié outstanding (some thought outrageous) as Carmen, and Escamillo and Micaela receiving good performances from the Belgian baritone Jacques Bouhy and the young and appealing French soprano Marguerite Chapuy. Lhérie was no great actor, and tended to drop in pitch in his unaccompanied entry in Act II ('he begins in G minor and finishes in E, or even, unbelievably, in E flat!!' complained Bizet, who got young d'Indy to provide a discreet harmonium accompaniment for later performances). The ladies of the chorus still had trouble with the realism required of them, but apart from an unfortunate (and loud) false entry by the percussionist there were no mishaps in the orchestra.

Nevertheless most of the audience, relying on the great names of Meilhac and Halévy, had come to the theatre expecting an *opéra-comique* and what they got was *Carmen*. Ironically, but perhaps predictably, the bulk of the applause was aimed at Micaela and Escamillo, the only two characters who came anywhere near the kind of thing that might have been expected by *habitués* of the Opéra-Comique; for later commentators, who wanted to see *Carmen* as pure music drama, they were to become an easy target for criticism, but without them, and the musical and dramatic contrast they supply, there would be no agony or loss of innocence in *Carmen*, and an audience that does not perceive this has little hope of following Bizet into the heart-wrenching finale of his opera.

Halévy wrote to a friend on the following day:

Halévy   First act a success. Galli-Marié's first aria applauded. . . . Duet for Don José and Micaela applauded. Good curtain . . . applause, recalls. . . . A lot of people on the stage after this act. Bizet surrounded and much congratulated. Second act less happy. Very brilliant start. Tremendous effect of the Toreador's entry. After that, coolness. . . . As Bizet, from this point onward, got further and further away from the traditional manner of *opéra-comique* the audience was surprised, disconcerted, puzzled. . . . Fewer people round Bizet during the entr'acte. Congratulations less sincere, anxious, embarrassed.   [*Halévy, 1905: 8*]

During one of the intervals (he says the first, but that seems unlikely) d'Indy and a friend went out into the rue Favart, where they found Bizet pacing up and down with his publisher.

D'Indy   'My poor children,' Bizet replied to our timid offer of praise, 'you are really very kind, but your congratulations are certainly the only ones that I am going to receive this evening. I sense defeat—I foresee a definitive and irremediable flop.'   [*Delmas: 45*]

Halévy   The third act was colder still. . . . The only applause was for Micaela's aria, a piece in the classic traditional style. . . . Still fewer people backstage. And after the fourth act, which was glacial from beginning to end, no one at all except three or four of Bizet's sincere and faithful friends. They all had reassuring words on their lips but sadness in their eyes. *Carmen* had not been a success.   [*Halévy, 1905: 8*]

For Bizet it was a disaster. The press next day, with rare exceptions, was damning—both of the subject, which was shocking, and of the music which, incredible as it seems today, was regarded as utterly lacking in melody. The atmosphere at the theatre became more hostile than ever and d'Indy recalled how everybody 'from the director to the door-keeper' turned their backs whenever the composer appeared. Bizet's chronic throat problem returned and this time would not leave him; though Gallet describes him still 'smiling and talking in that same tone of amused banter that hid from those who didn't know him his sensitiveness and goodness of heart', inwardly he fell into an acute state of depression. He lost his temper in public with one of *Carmen*'s harshest critics, and retired again to the country at Bougival. The throat problem increased, and was followed by a severe heart attack from which he appeared to recover. But on the morning following the thirty-third performance of *Carmen*, du Locle received a telegram:

'The most horrible catastrophe. Our poor Bizet died tonight. Ludovic Halévy'.   [*Pigot: 281*]

He was just under five months short of his thirty-seventh birthday.

––––––––

After narrowly avoiding closure after the first few performances, Bizet's opera achieved a respectable run mainly on its sensation value, although the houses were rarely more than half full. After this, Paris left *Carmen* severely alone for eight years.

But on the day before he died Bizet had signed a contract for its production in Vienna, for which he had agreed to replace the spoken dialogue of the original with sung recitatives. Some five months later it was given at the Hofoper with recitatives by Ernest Guiraud, and was an immediate success; Brahms saw it twenty times and Wagner exclaimed 'Thank God—at last someone with ideas in his head for a change!'. But the new material, though written with pious care by the composer's closest friend, changed the character of the work—not least because the full dialogue, being based directly on Mérimée, made a vital contribution to the atmosphere, the characterisation and the clarity of the action. Most of Meilhac's humour disappeared, and the uniquely hybrid nature of Bizet's original was compromised by its adaptation for performance in a theatre, and an operatic style, very much 'grander' than any that he himself had envisaged.

Nevertheless the transformation made *Carmen* available to many big opera houses that might have baulked at putting on the dialogue version, and it is in the recitative version that the opera achieved its greatest success. It had reached twenty-two theatres in eighteen other countries before it was taken up again in Paris—where ironically, at least until recently, the Opéra-Comique became the only house where the original dialogue could regularly be heard. The situation was complicated further in 1964 by the publication of a controversial score which restored many of the cuts that had been made during the composer's lifetime, whether or not they appeared to have his authority. As a result, the variety of possible versions in which Bizet's opera could be seen became for a while both infinite and unpredictable—a state of confusion which was at last set right by the publication in the year 2000 of a score which, 125 years after Bizet's death, at last presents *Carmen* in the nearest possible approximation to its composer's intentions.

Pyotr Ilyich Tchaikovsky in 1874

Eugene Onegin

Y OU MAY WELL BE RIGHT in saying that my opera will not be effective on the stage', wrote Tchaikovsky to his friend and pupil Sergey Taneyev soon after he had completed the first act of *Eugene Onegin*:

Tchaikovsky   I must tell you, however, that I don't care a jot for such effectiveness. It has long been an established fact that I have no dramatic vein, and now I don't worry about it. If it's undramatic, then don't stage it and don't perform it! I wrote this opera because I was moved one day with unutterable force to express in music everything that seems to cry out for music in *Eugene Onegin*. . . . If my enthusiasm for the subject is evidence of my limitations, my stupidity and my ignorance of theatrical conventions, I am very sorry; but I can at least say that what I wrote *proceeds in the most literal sense from my innermost being,* and is neither fabricated nor forced.

[*TLP, VII: 21, 23*]

Tchaikovsky did not take naturally to opera. At the age of thirty-seven he had already produced several of the works by which he is remembered today—the First String quartet, the Piano Concerto in B flat minor, the fantasy-overture *Romeo and Juliet*, and most recently the ballet *Swan Lake*—but of his three operas only *The Oprichnik* had achieved any critical success, none had made any noticeable impression on the Russian public, and all had left the composer himself dissatisfied.

His attitude to the operatic form was in any case ambivalent, and to begin with had been oddly naïve; 'I simply wrote music for the text provided', he later admitted, 'without really thinking at all about the endless distinctions between the operatic and symphonic styles', [*TLP, VIII: 445*]

Tchaikovsky   In composing an opera, the author must constantly bear
   the stage in mind—i.e. remember that the theatre needs not only
   melodies and harmonies but also *action* so as not to abuse the attention of the opera-goer, who has come not only *to hear but to see*, and,
   finally, that the style of music for the theatre must correspond to the
   style of decorative painting, hence be *simple, clear and colourful*. . . .
   Music abounding in harmonic subtleties gets lost in the theatre,
   where the listener needs sharply drawn melodies and a lucid harmonic design. . . . These conditions to a significant extent paralyse
   the composer's purely musical inspiration. . . . In a symphony or a
   sonata I am *free*; there are no limitations, or constraints on me. . . .
   [*Id*]

So it was to the freedom of the symphony that Tchaikovsky turned to
confront his most personal emotional problems, and in the early months
of 1877 these problems were reaching a crisis. As a composer and teacher,
he could look back on a dozen years of strenuous musical activity and
growing reputation, but as a man his complex neurotic character, his
romantic hypersensitivity and the tensions and ambiguities of a life of
active homosexuality had brought this shy and kindly human being to a
level of emotional stress that sometimes came close to hysteria. It is not
surprising therefore that it should be another symphony that was now
claiming his attention, into the opening movement of which, the longest
and by far the most complex that he had yet written, he could, and did,
pour the agonies of his soul. Even without Tchaikovsky's own description there is no mistaking the sense of the hammering brass fanfare with
which the Fourth Symphony starts:

Tchaikovsky   This is *Fate*, the fatal force which prevents our hopes of
   happiness from being realized, which watches jealously to see that
   our bliss and peace are not complete and unclouded, which, like the
   Sword of Damocles, is suspended over our heads and perpetually
   poisons the soul. . . .   [*TLP, VII: 125*]

The one element that provided a degree of stability in the emotional
turmoil of Tchaikovsky's life was his deep love of his family. But even this
was no substitute for the permanent personal relationship that he really
longed for, and in spite of his sexual inclinations, the idea of marriage

was a recurring theme in his earlier years. In his late twenties he had been briefly in love with the singer Désirée Artôt and actually become engaged to her (though she dropped him a few months later), and in August 1876 he had written to his brother Modest, 'I must tell you that I *have decided to get married*. This is irrevocable'. Comments like this hardly suggest any very passionate approach to matrimony, however, and to his brother Anatoly (Modest's twin), he later wrote in terms that suggest a very different kind of emotional need.　　　　　　　[*TPR*: 253]

Tchaikovsky　There is a certain kind of yearning for tenderness and consolation that only a wife can satisfy. Sometimes I am overcome by an insane craving for the caress of a woman's touch. Sometimes I see a sympathetic woman in whose lap I could lay my head, whose hands I would gladly kiss. . . .　　　　　　　　[*TLP, XI*: 55–6]

It doesn't sound like a good recipe for marriage, and indeed, in the light of later events, it seems likely that the only adult relationship with a woman which could have worked for Tchaikovsky was the improbable one upon which he entered at exactly this time with the wealthy widow Nadezhda von Meck. Mme von Meck, herself an amateur musician, became interested in Tchaikovsky both musically and personally, and during the next thirteen years followed every aspect of his music, his life and his professional career with a passion that was nothing short of obsessive; the prolific correspondence upon which they embarked documents a friendship of sometimes gushing intimacy—but, crucially, they were never to meet. 'There was a time when I very much wanted to get to know you', she wrote, 'but now I feel that the more you fascinate me the more I shrink from knowing you. . . . I prefer to think of you from a distance, to hear you speak and be at one with you in your music. . .'. Nevertheless she provided him with constant financial support, becoming in effect his secret patron, and in gratitude Tchaikovsky made her the dedicatee of the new symphony. It is a curious irony that links some of the most wildly passionate music he ever wrote with a relationship so conspicuously lacking in real-life passion.

[*TPM, I*: 6–7]

However, if it was the symphonic form that Tchaikovsky saw as the vehicle for his most personal musical expression, it was still opera that he regarded as the true measure of a composer's success. Predictably, he had no great sympathy with the new developments that were now occupying the attention of the operatic world. In 1876 he had been to the first complete performance of *The Ring* at Bayreuth.

Tchaikovsky   [Wagner] is gifted with genius, but it has wrecked itself upon its own tendencies; his imagination is paralysed by theories which he has himself invented and which he can't help wanting to put into practice. In his efforts to attain *reality, truth and rationalism* he lets *music* slip quite out of sight. . . . For I cannot call that music which consists of kaleidoscopic, shifting musical phrases which follow one after the other without a break and never come to a close, never give you the least chance to grasp a musical form . . . ; Wotan, Brünnhilde, Fricka and the rest are all so impossible, so non-human, that it is very difficult to feel any sympathy with their destinies. . . . For three whole hours Wotan lectures Brünnhilde on her disobedience. What a bore!   [*TLP, VI*: 262]

Italian opera he loved, Rossini and Bellini in particular, but he had doubts about the subject matter of Verdi's latest opera, whose 'effectiveness' had been cited by Tanayev.

Tchaikovsky   If you are taking *Aida* as an example, I assure you that I could not compose an opera on such a subject for all the money in the world, because I need human beings, not puppets. I would gladly write an opera that was lacking in strong and startling effects, but which offered characters something like my own, whose feelings and experiences I could share and understand. The emotions of an Egyptian princess, a Pharaoh, or some mad Nubian, are something I don't know about or feel. . . .

You ask what I actually require. All right, I'll tell you. I want no kings, no queens, no popular uprisings, battles, marches, speeches—nothing that earns the description *grand opera*. I am looking for an intimate but powerful drama, based on a conflict of circumstances such as I myself have experienced or witnessed, which is capable of moving me deeply. . . .

But I am reaping the fruits of my insufficient erudition. If I had a better knowledge of the literature of other countries I should no doubt have hit upon some subject that was both to my taste and suitable for the stage. Unfortunately I am not able to do this for myself, nor do I know anyone who could lead me to a subject like, for instance, Bizet's *Carmen*,—one of the most perfect operas of our day. . . .

[*TLP VII*, 21–2]

It was on a visit to Paris early in 1876 (a few months before the Bayreuth trip) that he had seen *Carmen* and been bowled over by it. Modest, who was with him, remembered, 'I never saw Pyotr Ilyich so excited by any performance', and Tchaikovsky revelled in a score that, while preserving Latin clarity, made new and original departures in harmony and orchestration.

Tchaikovsky   Here is a Frenchman with whom these savours and spices seem the result not of *fabrication* but pour out in a stream; they gratify the ear but at the same time touch and trouble. . . . *Bizet* is an artist who pays tribute to modernity, but is fired with true inspiration. And what a marvellous subject for an opera! I can't play the final scene without tears. On the one hand, the crowd enjoying itself and coarsely making merry as they watch the bullfight, on the other, a terrible tragedy and the death of the two principals who, through fate, *fatum*, ultimately reach the peak of their suffering and their inescapable end.   [*TLP, IX: 196–7*]

Here at last was an operatic subject offering the kind of dramatic honesty that he had so far been unable to find. And yet such a subject had been there, on his own doorstep, for years.

On 30 May 1877, Tchaikovsky wrote to Modest. He had been at a party at the house of the singer Elizaveta Andreyevna Lavrovskaya.

Tchaikovsky   The conversation turned to subjects for opera. Her stupid husband talked a lot of incredible nonsense and suggested the most impossible subjects. Liz. And. herself said nothing and smiled good-naturedly, but suddenly said: 'What about *Eugene Onegin*?' The idea struck me as wild, and I said nothing. Later, while I was dining *alone* at a restaurant, I remembered about *Onegin*, considered it, began to think Lavrovskaya's idea possible, got carried away and by the end of dinner had made up my mind. I rushed off at once in search of the *Pushkin*. . . . I found it with difficulty, set off for home, and read it with delight for the whole of an absolutely sleepless *night*—the result of which was the *scenario* of a splendid opera on Pushkin's *text*. . . .

The next day I went to see Shilovsky, and he is now working flat out at my scenario.   [*TLP, VI: 135*]

Konstantin Shilovsky, the elder brother of a pupil and intimate friend of Tchaikovsky's, had a country estate at Glebovo not far from Moscow. He had already worked on two operatic scenarios for Tchaikovsky, neither of which came to anything, and though at first there seems to have been an idea that he should write the full libretto for *Onegin*, his contribution to the final text was limited. But now, when Tchaikovsky could only snatch forty-eight hours before returning to Moscow for the last ten days of the Conservatoire term, Shilovsky was given the preliminary job of selecting passages from Pushkin to incorporate in the framework that Tchaikovsky had already outlined.

Pushkin's *Eugene Onegin*, laid out in eight chapters of from forty to sixty stanzas each, was published in instalments between 1825 and 1833. It was described by its author as a 'novel in verse', and its easy, conversational style, braced by verse of strict and subtle construction, is the ideal medium for a tale set among the conventions and attitudes of contemporary Russian society. Pushkin himself, who is vaguely identified with Onegin, drifts in and out of the narration, observing his characters with an often ironical, sometime satirical detachment that allows for passages of intense personal involvement and digressions with a clear autobiographical flavour, while at the same time unfolding the story with charm, humour, and an unfailingly deft poetic touch.

Tchaikovsky   You can't believe how fired I am by this subject. . . . I am not deluding myself; I know that stage effects and [dramatic] momentum will be slight in this opera. But the mixture of poetry, human interest and simplicity of subject matter, united with a text of *genius*, will compensate for what it lacks in other respects. . . .
                                                                              [*Id*]

Not only is *Onegin* Pushkin's masterpiece, it is one of the cornerstones of Russian literature, loved and admired by the poet's countrymen as one of the most personal of their national treasures. So it is not surprising that Tchaikovsky's intention of reducing it to the proportions necessary for an operatic libretto had a mixed reception: 'Everyone I have told has been surprised at first, and then delighted', he told his brothers and Mme von Meck with happy confidence. But criticism was not long in coming.

It came in three forms: simple shock at the misuse of a much-loved masterpiece, objections to the cuts Tchaikovsky was obliged to make in reducing it to a libretto, and complaints that the subject lacked the dramatic effectiveness required for an opera. Anatoly went so far as to say that he couldn't imagine an opera on *Onegin* being any good, and that he was 'very upset' that his brother had chosen the subject. Taneyev, candid as always, was more specific when he later saw the music for the first act.

Taneyev   The one thing that doesn't quite please me is the libretto. There's little action: the whole of the first scene, for example, consists of guests arriving at the Larins and nothing else. . . . Everything corresponds to the 'descriptions' in a novel. You learn from it that in the Larin household there are two daughters, two different characters, that they are acquainted with Lensky, etc. The character of these roles is not explained from the action, and each one talks about herself—Olga [saying] that she is cheerful and without a care, Tatyana that she is a dreamer. . . .   [*TTP*: 22]

Tchaikovsky replied that, though the actions of the girls were 'very simple everyday actions—not theatrical', each of them nevertheless 'acts in the only way of which she is capable'. And certainly there is enough left to identify the two characters who are to be the main representatives of the rural, Larin world. In fact, Tchaikovsky and Shilovsky treated their source material with respect and sensitivity. The descriptions of country and city life and the personal reflections which are so characteristic of Pushkin were clearly not the stuff of opera, and the first and seventh chapters (respectively covering Onegin's early years in fashionable society, and the gap between Lensky's death and Onegin's reappearance in St Petersburg) were cut. But the original scenario—which remained largely unaltered in the finished opera—condenses the essentials of the action into a well-balanced succession of scenes, and the text with which Tchaikovsky later filled it out uses Pushkin's own dialogue wherever possible or, when there is no dialogue, adapts material taken from elsewhere in the poem. The narrative element of Pushkin's rambling masterpiece is presented with a clarity and dramatic coherence that exactly suited Tchaikovsky's purpose—and if in the libretto the ironic detachment of the original is lost, that is because detachment and irony formed no part of Tchaikovsky's emotional needs.

Tchaikovsky   The opera will of course have no strong dramatic movement, but the human side of it will provide interest, and how full of poetry it all is! And what about the scene with Tatyana and the nanny! . . . If only I can achieve that calm state of mind essential for composition, I'm sure that Pushkin's text will be an inspiration to my own kind of inspiration.   [*TLP, VI: 140*]

From the beginning it was the character of Tatyana, rather than Onegin himself, who engaged Tchaikovsky's affections. He had at one time considered setting the famous letter in which Tatyana declares her love to Onegin as an independent vocal piece, and it was to this crucial scene that he now turned in the spare moments of his remaining days in Moscow. The idea of the timid, innocent, romantic girl, struck by love for the cold, elegant intellectual from the sophisticated world, was one that touched him acutely and that he instinctively understood.

Tchaikovsky   *Tatyana* is not merely a provincial young lady who falls in love with a metropolitan dandy. She is a wholly pure feminine beauty, an innocent soul still untouched and unaffected by the realities of life; a dreamy nature, seeking a vague ideal and passionately pursuing it. As long as she finds nothing that resembles her ideal she will remain unsatisfied but tranquil. But it needs only the appearance of a face that—at least externally—stands out from her banal surroundings and she imagines that this is her ideal, and her passion makes her lose her head. . . .   [*TLP, XII: 246*]

It was a view he defended against all criticisms.

Taneyev   It seems to me unnatural that Tatyana should fall in love with Onegin as soon as she sets eyes on him, even before he has begun to speak. In Pushkin it says that Onegin's visit to the Larins provokes rumours among the neighbours that he wants to marry Tatyana; Tatyana hears them and eventually falls in love with him.

[*TTP: 22*]

Tchaikovsky With regard to your observation that Tatyana doesn't fall in love with Onegin at once, I say that you are mistaken. It is at once. *'As soon as you arrived, I recognised you, I was overwhelmed, I was inflamed.'* She doesn't come to love him gradually, you see, she doesn't need to know him to love him. Even before he appears on the scene she is in love with the vague hero of her romance. The instant she sets eyes on him she invests Onegin with all the qualities of her ideal, and transfers to a human being the love she has hitherto bestowed upon the creature of her burning romantic imagination.

[*TLP, VII: 22*]

And when he had finally got away from the Conservatoire and settled at Glebovo, he wrote defensively to Modest:

Tchaikovsky At first your criticism of *Onegin* annoyed me, but that only lasted a moment. Let my opera lack scenic effect, let it have little action, I am in love with the image of Tatyana, I am fascinated by Pushkin's verse, and I am drawn to compose the music as if something is compelling me. I am lost in the composition of the opera.

[*TLP, VI: 141*]

Within eight days of his arrival in the country the music for the Letter Scene was finished. It was to remain the heart of Tchaikovsky's score, from which he drew, as the opera progressed, not only much of the thematic material but the musical warmth and, above all, the extraordinary sense of personal involvement which distinguishes his portrayal of Tatyana.

The extent to which that personal involvement was reflected in Tchaikovsky's own life is a well-trodden byway of musical history. It is easy to over-romanticise the story (as has indeed been done), and certainly Tchaikovsky himself is not a wholly impartial witness. But the surviving letters and known facts speak for themselves, and the coincidence between life and art is so startling that it can hardly have been without an effect on his creative work. The idea of marriage as a kind of dream state, that would provide him with the stability that he lacked, the home that he longed for, and a magical resolution of the tensions and risks inherent in an ambivalent and necessarily secretive life style, was an ever-present panacea at times of deep depression, and only days before Lavrovskaya's party he had confessed to a friend: 'Life is empty, tedious and banal, and I am seriously considering marriage or some other firm relationship' (in itself an ambiguous statement). He later described the events of the next few months to the music critic Nikolay Kashkin.   [*Id, 132*]

Tchaikovsky   In the early or middle part of May 1877 I received a long letter containing a declaration of love. The letter was signed Antonina Milyukova, and the writer explained that her love had originated several years before when she had been a pupil at the Conservatoire. . . . At this very time I was much occupied by the thought of *Eugen Onegin* as an opera, and particularly by the character of Tatyana, whose letter it was which had above all attracted me to this composition. Having no libretto as yet, but only a sort of general plan of the opera, I began to write the music of the letter scene, submitting to an irresistible inward urge in the excitement of which I not only forgot about Miss Milyukova but even lost her letter—or anyhow hid it so well that I couldn't find it—and was reminded of it only some time later by the receipt of a second letter. In this Miss Milyukova complained bitterly of not having received a reply, adding that if the second letter shared the same fate as the first there would be nothing left for her but to put an end to her life.   [*Abraham: 227–8*]

Tchaikovsky's (or Kashkin's) memory is not strictly accurate. Antonina's first letter is lost, but Tchaikovsky was not as callous as he liked to remember; her second letter, which has survived, is a somewhat resigned reaction to an intervening one from him that had evidently been calming in tone, expressing his sense of gratitude but pointing out the defects in his character and perhaps his unsuitability as a husband.

Antonina   I see now that it's time I began to master my feelings, as you yourself said in your letter. I am not able to see you now, but I console myself with the thought that you are in the same city as me; in a month, perhaps even sooner, you will probably leave town, and God knows when I shall see you, as I don't expect to stay in Moscow myself. But wherever I am, I shan't be able to forget you or to stop loving you.   [*TPM, I:* 569]

This arrived only a few days before Lavrovskaya's party, and if it is the week that followed which represents the period of neglect for which he later blamed himself, he had good reason to be otherwise occupied. In any case, Antonina's mood of resignation soon passed; her third letter strikes a very different note.

Antonina   For a whole week I've been in the most agonising state, Pyotr Ilyich, I don't know whether to write to you or not. I see that my letters are already beginning to be a burden to you. But is it possible that you could drop our correspondence before even meeting me? No, I'm sure you won't be so cruel! God knows, perhaps you think me an empty-headed, superficial girl, and because of that don't trust my letters? I wish I could prove to you that what I say is true, that it is impossible to lie. After your last letter I loved you twice as much, and your faults mean absolutely nothing to me. Perhaps if you were perfect I should have remained perfectly cool towards you. I am dying with unhappiness and desperately want to see you, to sit and talk with you. . . .

Do not try to disillusion me further about yourself, because you are only wasting your time. I cannot live without you, and perhaps I shall soon kill myself. So let me see you and kiss you so that I may remember that kiss in the other world. Farewell. Yours eternally, A.M.   [*Id:* 569–70]

Tchaikovsky   In my mind all this became identified with the idea of Tatyana. . . . Completely engrossed in the composition [of my opera] I had so familiarised myself with the figure of Tatyana that she had become for me a living person in living surroundings. I loved her and was terribly indignant with Onegin, who seemed to me a cold, heartless coxcomb. . . . Yet it seemed to me that I had myself behaved incomparably worse than Onegin, and I was sincerely angry with myself for my heartless attitude to this girl who was in love with me. . . .   [*Abraham:* 228]

And so, of course, Tchaikovsky went to see her.

Tchaikovsky   Thus our acquaintance began. At this first meeting I
told her that I could not reciprocate her love, but that she aroused
my sincere sympathy. She replied that my sympathy was dear to
her and that she could be satisfied with it—or words to that effect.
I promised to see her frequently, and I kept my word. . . . In my
mind there was constantly that feeling of indignation at Onegin's
careless, thoughtless attitude to Tatyana. To behave like Onegin
seemed to me heartless, and simply not to be thought of. . . .

[*Id*: 228–9]

The behaviour of Pushkin's Onegin on receiving Tatyana's letter is,
in fact, extremely correct. He is obviously touched by her innocence and
sincerity and offers an equally candid reply. He is not made for domestic
bliss, and is not worthy of her many qualities; he calmly explains the
impossibility of the situation and firmly, but not unkindly, puts an end
to what—from his point of view—must have been a trying and probably
faintly absurd situation.

But Tchaikovsky could only see the matter from Tatyana's point of
view. When he came to write the music for Onegin's reply, he rejected
lyrical expansion in favour of a cool, unemotional tone that gives away as
little as possible of anybody's feelings. Onegin is perhaps a shade patron-
ising, slightly inclined to gratuitous advice and definitely reserved in his
manner. But given his character and social background, he is not unreasonable or unkind and, galling though it must have been to Tatyana, it is
not easy to see what else he might have done.

Not what Tchaikovsky did, anyhow. To Mme von Meck, of whose
opinion about the whole affair he must have been more than a little nervous, he wrote some weeks later:

Tchaikovsky   I told her frankly that I could not *love* her, but that I
would in any case be a devoted and grateful friend; I described to
her in detail my character: my irritability, my nervous temperament,
my unsociability—finally my financial situation. Then I asked her
if she would care to be my wife. Her answer was of course in the
affirmative. I cannot describe to you the agonies I have endured in
the days since that evening. . . . To live for thirty-seven years with
a congenital antipathy to matrimony, and then suddenly, by force of
circumstances, to find oneself *engaged* to a woman with whom one is

not in the least in love, is very painful. . . . I comfort myself with the thought that we cannot escape our fate. . . . If I am marrying without love, it is because circumstances have left me with no alternative. . . . Having once encouraged her affection by answering her letter and visiting her I was bound to act as I have done. In any case my conscience is clear, I have neither lied to her nor deceived her. I have told her what she can expect from me, and what she must not count upon receiving. . . .   [*TLP, VI: 145–7*]

But Antonina was no Tatyana. Tchaikovsky had been warned by a friend that she was unintelligent to the point of stupidity and definitely unbalanced, and although her reputation was 'above reproach', she evidently suffered from the delusion that she was highly desirable to men. Yet he remained blinded by the parallel with his operatic heroine—whom he clearly regarded as more real and more important than her flesh-and-blood counterpart.

Tchaikovsky   Having made this decision, I was perfectly unconscious of its importance and did not even consider what it would mean to me. It was indispensable to remove, as soon as possible, everything that prevented my concentration on the idea of the opera which possessed my whole being, and it seemed to me the most natural and simple way to act. Having entrusted all the trouble and preparation of the wedding to Antonina, I felt as if I had rid myself of a burden and went away to the country, to Shilovsky's. . . . As for the new way of life I was about to begin, I hardly thought of it at all, and only somewhere deep within me stirred an uneasy expectation of something I didn't want to think about, considering it useless to do so—and still worse, disturbing.   [*Abraham: 230*]

Glebovo gave him exactly what he wanted.

Tchaikovsky   When I am writing an opera nothing and no-one must disturb me. For instance, (1) I must not see anybody at all during certain hours of the day, and know that no one can see or hear me; I have a habit when composing of singing very loudly and the thought that someone could hear me disturbs me very much. (2) a *piano* must be at my disposal nearby, i.e. in my bedroom—because I can't write without one, at least not peacefully and easily. . . .

[*TLP, VI: 136–7*]

To tell the truth, there could hardly be a more favourable setting for composition than the one I am in here. I have the full use of a separate, beautifully furnished house; no one, not one human soul, except Alyosha [manservant], appears in the house when I am busy and, above all, I have a piano of which the sound, when I am playing, doesn't reach anyone except Alyosha. I get up at eight, have a bath, drink tea (alone) and then work until breakfast. After breakfast I have a walk and then work till dinner. After dinner I go for an enormous walk and then spend the evening in the big house. . . . Hardly any guests come to visit us—in a word, there's peace and quiet. The country is in every way delightful. But what's awful is the weather: cold morning frosts *every day*. . . . So far there hasn't been one warm summer day.

Thanks to all this my work is going ahead very fast. . . .   [*Id: 141*]

Towards the end of June he wrote to his brother Anatoly, whose doubts about the 'effectiveness' of the opera continued.

Tchaikovsky   Criticize *Eugene Onegin* as much as you like, I shall write my music with great pleasure, and I am certain that the poetic subject and the indescribable beauty of the text will be effective. . . . If I were to remain here all summer there's no doubt that the opera would be finished by the end of the season. . . . The whole of the first act, in three scenes, is already done, and I have started on the second act today.   [*Id: 142*]

The valse and mazurka in the first scene of Act II found Tchaikovsky in his element, like the polonaise in the equivalent scene at the beginning of Act III: he was always at home with dance music (though he does seem to have been at a loss at the St Petersburg production of the opera in 1885, when he was suddenly asked by the director of the theatre to add an *écossaise* to the ball scene in the last act. 'I believe Schubert wrote *écossaises*', he wrote in desperation to his publisher; 'if not, perhaps you can tell me where I can find one for a model . . . I *must* have an *écossaise!*').

Nevertheless, with all his evident delight in the family festivity at the start of Act II, he never loses sight of its dramatic level; compared with the treatment of the St Petersburg ball at the beginning of the third act, this is very much a local, country affair to celebrate the name day of the young Tatyana. The appearance of the elderly neighbour, M. Triquet, to sing his *couplets* in Tatyana's honour could hardly have taken place in the sophisticated surroundings of the city. In any case, this essentially provincial background has already been established in Act I: in the opening ensemble, in Mme Larina's domestic concerns, in the happy chatter of Olga, in the omnipresent figure of Tatyana's old nurse and in the sounds of the Russian countryside—the choruses of peasants, and the magical moment when dawn breaks and the cool piping of the shepherd brings the freshness of the country into Tatyana's bedroom after the heated emotions of the night.

Tchaikovsky   As regards the Russian element in my music—i.e. the relationship between the national songs and my melodies and harmonies—this has developed because I grew up in the backwoods, from earliest childhood saturated with the indescribable beauty of the characteristic traits of Russian folk music, because I passionately love their Russian element in all its manifestations, because, in a word, I am *Russian* in the fullest sense of the term.
[*TLP, VII:* 155]

Tchaikovsky did not flaunt his nationalism in any display of musical ethnicity, and the only piece of actual Russian folk music that can be identified in *Onegin* is the tune in the second part of the chorus that opens Act I. There is nothing to suggest the specifically Russian musical methods of Balakirev or Mussorgsky (whose *Boris,* another Pushkin adaptation, Tchaikovsky regarded with particular contempt), and the Russian nationalists—the 'Mighty Handful'—in fact regarded Tchaikovsky as something of a renegade. But it is true that the Western influences in Tchaikovsky's score are at least as strong as the Russian. Above all, there is the recurring shadow of *Carmen*—Don José's Flower Song behind the impassioned melody of the Letter Scene (in the same 'remote' key of D flat major), Carmen's fate motif in the winding chromatic theme with which *Onegin* opens, Don José's despairing 'Dût-il m'en coûter la vie' as Lensky faces the possibility of his own death. And although there is no whiff of Wagnerian leitmotif, Tchaikovsky makes constant use of thematic reminiscence—a technique common enough in nineteenth-century opera, but used here with a subtlety and ubiquity that almost seems involuntary.

He remained at Glebovo well into July, giving as little thought as possible to his own immediate future, and by his own account completing 'two thirds of the opera'—'very calmly' he told his sister Sasha, though to Mme von Meck he admitted: 'I would naturally have written far more but for my agitated state of mind'. Whichever was the truth, as the month drew on, he could no longer shut his eyes to the outside world; making some sort of excuse to Shilovsky, he abruptly left Glebovo and, after telling his father, brothers and Mme von Meck at the last possible moment, married Antonina in Moscow on July 18th.

What followed was a nightmare. Panic set in at once—even on the train that carried the newly married couple away to St Petersburg.

Tchaikovsky   I was on the point of screaming, choked with sobs. Nevertheless, I had to amuse my wife with conversation as far as Klin, so as to earn the right to remain in my own chair in the dark, alone with myself. . . . My only consolation was that my wife did not understand or realise my ill-conceived misery. . . . She has looked quite happy and content all along.   [*TLP, VI: 151–2*]

A couple of agonizing weeks, first with his own family, then with Antonina's, did nothing to improve matters, and after only a few days back in Moscow he found that he could bear it no longer. Totally unable to work in the company of his wife, he trumped up an excuse that he needed to take a cure and fled to his sister's house at Kamenka in the Ukraine.

Tchaikovsky loved Kamenka, and always enjoyed the company of his sister and her family. Four days after his arrival he wrote to Mme von Meck:

Tchaikovsky   If I were to say that I had got back to my normal frame of mind, I would be lying. . . . But . . . I am at peace here, and beginning to look the future in the face without fear.   [*Id: 165*]

But he still couldn't get down to work—'the idea frightens and oppresses me'—and although he took up the orchestration of the symphony again, it was another couple of weeks before he felt like getting back to *Onegin*. Even then he doesn't seem to have done much new composition for the third of his score that still remained unwritten.

Tchaikovsky   You ask about my opera. It has moved on very little here, but I have completed the orchestration of the first scene of Act I. . . . It seems to me that the first number is not without a certain piquancy of sound, when the two girls sing a sentimental duet at the back of the stage while the two older women chat together, under this music, at the front.   [*Id: 170, 206*]

In any case, he was soon forced back to reality. The Conservatoire term began again at the end of September, and he could no longer avoid returning to Moscow and to his wife. Leaving Kamenka threw him into deep depression . . .

Tchaikovsky   . . . which today is inexpressibly, unspeakably, and infinitely painful. . . . The furnishing of our new home leaves nothing to be desired. My wife has done everything possible to please me. The apartment is cosy and nicely arranged. Everything is clean, new and good. And yet I look at it all with hatred and anger. . . .

Ultimately death is truly the greatest of blessings and I summon him with all my soul. To let you realise what I am going through it is enough to say that my only thought is to find a chance to escape somewhere. But how and where? It is impossible, impossible, impossible!
[*Id: 175*]

After ten days of increasing desperation he actually made a half-hearted attempt at suicide. Wading up to his waist in the freezing waters of the Moskva, he stood there until he could bear it no longer in the hope that he would contract pneumonia. But he didn't—and in the end he wired Anatoly to send a fake telegram requiring his immediate presence in St Petersburg. Meeting him at the station, Anatoly scarcely recognised the man who stepped off the train; once in the privacy of a hotel room 'everything I had been hiding in my heart of hearts for those two endless weeks came pouring out'—and Tchaikovsky, mortally exhausted, collapsed into a deep sleep for the next two days.

A psychiatric consultant was called and made it clear that Tchaikovsky must end his marriage and avoid any further contact with his wife. Anatoly left at once for Moscow to ask Antonina to agree to a divorce—a tricky undertaking in which he was assisted by Tchaikovsky's colleague Nikolay Rubinstein, the director of the Moscow Conservatoire. But when the two men cautiously broached the subject, Antonina calmly offered them tea and agreed to anything that her husband wanted; 'well now,' she observed with a beaming smile when her distinguished visitor had left, 'I certainly never expected that Rubinstein would be taking tea with me this afternoon'. As for the divorce, she soon recanted; she never allowed Tchaikovsky the legal freedom he longed for, but pestered the composer and his family on and off for the rest of their joint lives and eventually died in a mental hospital in 1917. But for Tchaikovsky, in 1877, the marriage was over.

The cost in emotional and physical terms had been appalling, and early in October he left with Anatoly for an extended trip abroad. Settling first at Clarens, on the Lake of Geneva, he gradually recovered sufficient composure to start work on the opera again. He completed the instrumentation of Act I, and even began thinking about a partial performance of the scenes that he had so far finished—a curious idea that can only have arisen from a passionate longing to hear the music that he had written for the young Tatyana. He wrote to Rubinstein:

Tchaikovsky   The first six scenes [of *Onegin*] will be in your hands any day now, and I shall be very happy if they please you; I have written them with great enthusiasm. A performance at the *Conservatoire* would be my fondest dream. [The work] is intended for a modest setting and a small theatre.   [*Id: 193*]

But his moods of depression failed to lift, and he decided to exchange the calm of the Swiss scenery for the livelier distractions of Italy, so it was from Rome that he finally sent off the first act to Rubinstein.

Tchaikovsky   I am terribly agitated whether [it] will please you or not. Please don't give it up on your first impressions, they are often deceptive. I wrote this music with such love, such delight. I am especially pleased with the following: 1, the first duet behind the scenes, which afterwards becomes the quartet; 2, Lensky's *arioso* [at the end of the first scene]; 3, the scene with the nanny; 4, the chorus of country girls. If you can just tell me you have enjoyed it. . . .

I shall be very happy. As soon as I have finished [orchestrating] the first scene of the second act and sent it to you, I will vigorously attack the *symphony*, which I beg you to keep a place for in the coming concerts.

I thank you with all my heart, dear friend, for the many things you have done for me, and for your kind letter in which I recognise your sincere friendship. But for God's sake don't summon me back to Moscow before next September. I know that I shall find nothing there but terrible mental suffering.   [*Id:* 229–30]

The noise and bustle of Rome soon proved too much for Tchaikovsky's nervous condition, and after only four days he abandoned it for the calmer surroundings of Venice, where he finished scoring the first scene of Act II and sent it off to Moscow at the end of November. With a burst of energy he even managed to complete the orchestration of the second scene as well, in time for Anatoly to take it with him on his return to Russia.

Just how much of the opera remained unwritten at this stage is uncertain; apart from scoring, he had done little work on it in the four months since his marriage, though most of it probably existed in the sketch form that he had produced during those first weeks at Glebovo. At that stage the music seems to have come easily; when Mme von Meck later asked him to let her see some of his manuscripts, he suggested the original sketch for *Onegin* 'because none of my works was written with such fluency, and the sketch can be made out quite clearly, with few corrections'. But it also seems that by January 1878 two crucial episodes at least, the duel scene that closes Act II and the final scene between Onegin and Tatyana, were still giving trouble. In any case, now that the opening scenes were safely in Rubinstein's hands, Tchaikovsky laid the rest of the opera aside and turned back instead to the Fourth Symphony, working on it with fierce concentration and finally completing it on 9 January. He despatched it at once to Rubinstein and only a few days later started again on the orchestral score of *Onegin*—though now at the beginning of Act III, having for the time being skipped the duel.

[*TLP, VII:* 321]

Meanwhile the first act had reached Moscow.

Tchaikovsky   I have had some very joyful news—the first act of *Onegin* has been received with *rapture* by my colleagues, beginning

with Rubinstein. I was very nervous of their verdict. It is very, very
pleasing. . . .   [*TLP, VI:* 280]

From some quarters, though, there were the usual complaints about
the lack of dramatic action, and when Taneyev joined his voice to them,
Tchaikovsky burst out in despair:

Tchaikovsky   *Onegin* will never have a success; I already know that. . . .
Yes, this opera has no future, I was aware of that when I wrote it. . . .
[But] I wrote it in obedience to an unconquerable inner attraction. . . . I
did my best, working with indescribable pleasure and enthusiasm, and
thought very little of the treatment, the effectiveness, and all the rest.
After all, what are 'effects'? I spit on them!   [*TLP, VII:* 22–23]

Taneyev replied at once in conciliatory vein.

Taneyev   When I wrote that *Onegin* was not scenic I didn't mean to say
that there were no battles, marches, national uprisings. I meant that
the movement of the drama itself, the action proper, has almost no
interest for the spectator; there are no events on the stage which he
can follow with heightened attention, or visual climaxes to affect him
in one way or another. . . .
   Opera is dramatic action, and in opera any human quality must
make itself apparent through the dramatic action. This plot would be
good in a novel, in a story. That's what I meant when I said it was 'not
scenic'.   [*TTP:* 27]

Tchaikovsky   I really can't argue with you any more about the 'scenic'
or 'non-scenic' qualities of *Onegin*. . . . However I can say that if,
as you maintain, *opera is dramatic action*, and there is none in my
Onegin, then I am ready to call *Onegin* not an opera but whatever
you want: scenes, a scenic presentation, a poem—whatever you
like. . . .   [*TLP, VII:* 69]

And the idea stuck. Later, when the score was being printed, Tchaikovsky wrote to his publisher:

Tchaikovsky   Do you remember my request, when I sent it off to you from
abroad in the winter, about the title page? I asked you to inscribe it

thus: *Eugene Onegin, Lyric Scenes in Three Acts*. This is essential. For many reasons I do not want to call this thing an opera. . . .   [*Id:* 353]

It was a good choice; nothing could better define the intimate, unoperatic quality of Tchaikovsky's treatment of Pushkin. Not that the conception of Lyric Scenes in any way precluded dramatic intensity; though Tchaikovsky's preoccupation with Tatyana undoubtedly tended to shift the centre of gravity of the opera away from Onegin, the episode of the duel with Lensky remains, as in Pushkin's poem, an essential pivot of the drama. To a criticism of the scene from Mme von Meck he replied:

Tchaikovsky   In the duel scene I see something far more significant than you do. Is it not profoundly dramatic and touching that a youth so brilliant and gifted should lose his life from a collision with the demands of a fashionable view of *honour*? Surely there is no more dramatic situation than that in which the bored city lion from *boredom*, from petty irritation, without purpose, led by a fatal chain of circumstances, takes the life of a young man whom, really, he loves? All this, you may say, is very simple, even ordinary, but the simple and the everyday are excluded from neither poetry nor drama.
    [*TLP, XII*: 246–7]

For Lensky's aria Tchaikovsky set the verses written by Pushkin's Lensky on the night before the duel, and the music opens with a typical emotional twist; the theme from Tatyana's letter to Onegin is now ironically transposed into the minor—the expression of love in innocence transformed to evoke the bitterness of love in despair as Lensky faces the tragic absurdity of unnecessary death. The Duel Scene produced from Tchaikovsky some of the most heartfelt music that he ever wrote, and continued to preoccupy him to the very end of his work on the opera. As late as 26 January, he told Mme von Meck that, though the orchestration of the third act was finished, Act II, Scene 2 was 'still in rough draft', and a couple of days later he wrote to Anatoly from San Remo:
    [*TLP, VII*: 49]

Tchaikovsky   Today, after lunch, I went alone into the mountains with notepaper and pencil to finish the scene of the *duel*, which is not yet all composed. With difficulty I found a solitary nook, where there was no-one about, and worked successfully.   [*Id:* 52–3]

As for the end of the opera, the resolution of the situation between the two main characters was never going to be easy; the complexities of Tchaikovsky's own emotional life were too closely interwoven with it. In his new symphony he had confronted those complexities head-on, but the happy, all-embracing resolution he intended in the last movement eluded him. The frenzied exuberance of the music does not carry emotional conviction, and the dramatic return of the Fate motif from the opening bars of the symphony sends a confused message. It sounds like an escape. But there was no such escape for *Onegin*. The need to make a drama explicit on the stage makes cheating impossible—or at least too easily detectable—and Tchaikovsky's sense of identification with his characters precluded anything but absolute honesty. In any case, since the first act Onegin himself had changed. The cold sophistication of the opening scenes had given place in the second act to a fatalistic recognition of tragedy, and now, at the very end of the opera, Onegin suddenly becomes the object of our sympathy: after the chance meeting at the St Petersburg ball, when his suppressed feelings burst out to the same music with which Tatyana had once declared her love for him, he is a genuinely moving figure.

It was in the last act that Tchaikovsky made his one considerable modification of Pushkin's narrative. In the penultimate chapter of the poem Tatyana, dragged from her dreams in the country to become a reluctant debutante in Moscow society, is pictured at a ball, dubiously eying the 'fat general' who is evidently seen as a prospective *fiancé*. It is not until the final chapter, after she has been married for two years, that Onegin reappears in St Petersburg and is introduced to her by her husband. In his original scenario Tchaikovsky compressed all this into a single scene: Tatyana, on her very first appearance at a Moscow ball, meets the general, who promptly falls in love with her and asks her to marry him. But later, recognising the improbability of such a lightning courtship, he cut out Moscow and moved straight to the ball in St Petersburg, where Tatyana is already an established social figure locked into a conventional marriage with the general—now identified as Prince Gremin. The solid, loving, but essentially unromantic nature of the marriage is made beautifully clear in Gremin's single aria, and once again it is to a minor-key version of this music that Tatyana, in the final scene, reminds Onegin of the love she had once felt for him.

From this point on, Tchaikovsky's fidelity to Pushkin begins to waver.

In the poem, though she can barely restrain her tears, Tatyana is calm and resolute:

> 'I love you (why should I dissemble?),
> But to another I belong;
> To him I shall be faithful all my life'.

With these words she leaves, and Onegin stands 'thunderstruck' until Gremin's approaching footsteps are heard. It is 'at this unhappy moment' that Pushkin takes leave of his hero and, three short stanzas later, of his readers as well. But for Tchaikovsky such cool, underplayed tragedy was difficult to accept at the end of an opera in which he felt himself so intimately involved. In his original scenario for the final scene he had written:

Tchaikovsky.   St Petersburg. Tatyana awaits Onegin. He appears. Big duet. After his declaration Tatyana yields to feelings of love for Eugene and wrestles with herself. He implores her. Her husband appears. Duty triumphs. Onegin flees in despair.   [*TLP, VI: 135*]

At one stage he seems to have toyed with the idea of letting Tatyana and Onegin escape together, but in the end he settled for an impassioned love scene in which Tatyana abandoned herself to her feelings and fell into Onegin's arms. He seems to have felt some compunction in diverging from Pushkin at this final moment of truth.

Tchaikovsky   I have been obliged, because of musical and scenic require-ments, to dramatise very strongly the scene of Tatyana's explanation to Onegin. At the end I have made Tatyana's husband appear and order Onegin with a gesture to leave. I found it necessary at this point for Onegin to have something to say, and I have put into his mouth the line: 'O death, O death! I go to seek you!'. It seems to me that this is silly stuff, and that I should think of something else, but what? I can't imagine.   [*TLP, VII: 93*]

Gremin's appearance at the end of the opera in fact survived into the first edition of the vocal score where, on seeing him enter, 'Tatyana . . . lets out a cry and falls unconscious into his embrace'. It was not until the scene was revised for the first professional performance of the opera in 1881 that Tchaikovsky banished Prince Gremin altogether.

But that was still three years in the future. Meanwhile, on 13 February 1878, Tchaikovsky at last wrote from San Remo:

Tchaikovsky   Today I finished the opera, and have already packed it up and sent it off. As a result of which I am in the best of spirits. . . .
[*Id*: 82]

But though he professed himself happy at having completed two important works 'in which it seems to me that I have taken a step forward, and a significant one', his emotional condition was still precarious. Taneyev, after at last seeing the finished scores of both symphony and opera, characteristically had some criticisms. . . .

Taneyev   . . . but don't be cross with me. It's not surprising that the symphony doesn't entirely please me. If you hadn't sent *Eugene Onegin* at the same time in all probability it would have satisfied me. It's your own fault for composing such an opera, after which everything else is bound to seem less interesting. *Onegin* has given me such delight, I've had such pleasure studying the score, that I'm completely incapable of expressing my feelings about it. A wonderful opera!

   And yet you say you want to give up composing. You have never written anything as good! Take credit for having achieved such perfection.   [*TTP*: 32]

For months now Tchaikovsky had been almost entirely concerned with the completion of existing sketches or the development of existing ideas rather than the creation of anything new, and to begin with he found original musical inspiration slow to return. But early in March he was back in Clarens, and by the end of the month had completed the sketches for the Violin Concerto and begun work on a piano sonata. Early in June he wrote to Modeste:

Tchaikovsky   Yesterday evening I played through the whole of *Eug. Onegin*. The author was the only listener. I am ashamed to admit it, but—well, I'll tell you a secret: the listener was moved to tears. . . .

Oh, if only the audiences of the future will be as much moved by this music as the composer! . . .   [*TLP, VII*: 285–6]

He had always been afraid of the wrong impression that could so easily be made in the unsympathetic surroundings of a conventional opera house.

Tchaikovsky   Where shall I find the Tatyana whom Pushkin imagined and whom I have tried to illustrate musically? Where is the artist who can even faintly approach the ideal Onegin, this cold dandy penetrated to the marrow with worldly *bon ton*? Where on earth is there a Lensky, an eighteen-year-old youth with the thick curls, the impetuous and individual manner of a young poet à la Schiller? How Pushkin's captivating picture will be vulgarized when it is transferred to the stage with its routine, its senseless traditions, its veterans of both sexes who, without any shame take on, like Alexandrova, Kommisarzhevsky and *tutti quanti*, the roles of sixteen-year-old girls and beardless youths!   [*TLP, VI*: 309]

It was for this reason that the idea of a performance at the Conservatoire had always attracted him. And his appeal to Rubinstein for a partial performance had not gone unnoticed. Even as he worked at the last scenes of the opera, word had reached him that the first four scenes were already in rehearsal at the Conservatoire, with Taneyev at the piano and a student cast. The idea shocked Mme von Meck.

Tchaikovsky   You lament that *Onegin* will be performed by young people who correspond very little to our idea of the heroes and heroine of *Pushkin's* poem. That's fine, but you know what? Whatever they're like, they're young, they're students, from whom one can't expect a great deal. . . . *Zilbershtein*, of course, won't convey the ideal Lensky, but as a young man he's still better in my view than the pot-bellied *Dodonov*. . . . *Klimentova* is no Tatyana, but I'll find her more acceptable than our state prima donnas, because again she is young and not corrupted by routine. With surprising acumen you call *Gilev* a dandy *du bas étage*, but I'd prefer even him to Melnikov, an excellent singer but an old stuffed-paunch (forgive the expression). And, most importantly, at the Conservatoire the production will be free of the trivial, murderous routine, and those glaring anachronisms and absurdities without which no state production can manage. . . .   [*TLP, VII:* 35–6]

To a colleague he gave a more specific indication of what he wanted:

Tchaikovsky   1, Singers of the middle rank, but well-trained and reliable; 2, singers who can act *simply* and *well*; 3, a setting not too sumptuous, but thoroughly in keeping with the period of the story; the costumes must correspond faithfully to the period (the 1820s); 4, a chorus that is not a flock of sheep like that of the Imperial Opera, but real *people* taking part in the staging of the opera; 5, a conductor who is not a machine . . . concerned only with the fact that a C sharp must not be played as a C, but a real leader of the orchestra. . . .]   [*TLP, VI:* 275]

He insisted that he would never let theatre managements get their hands on *Onegin* until it had first been performed at the Conservatoire—'the Bolshoy stage is simply not necessary to me, with all its conditions and unthinking administration'. And so it was by the pupils of the Moscow Conservatoire, on 29 March 1879, that *Eugene Onegin* was given its first performance, with Nikolay Rubinstein conducting. Tchaikovsky was acutely nervous; he wrote to Anatoly only a few days before the performance to say that he had 'decided to be there, but incognito', and in fact only just made it in time for the dress rehearsal.

Tchaikovsky   I arrived in Moscow before the rehearsal began. They rehearsed in costume with fully lit scenery, but the hall itself wasn't lit. This gave me the opportunity to hide myself in a dark corner and listen to my opera without being nagged. It gave me great pleasure. On the whole the performance was very satisfactory. The chorus and orchestra did their job splendidly, though the soloists, understandably, left much to be desired. . . .

Those hours, spent in a dark corner of the theatre, were the only pleasant ones of my visit to Moscow. Between the acts I saw all my old colleagues. I saw with pleasure that all, without exception, were delighted with the music of *Onegin*. Nikolay Grigoryevich [Rubinstein], who is so parsimonious with praise, told me that he had *fallen in love* with this music. After the first act *Taneyev* wanted to express his feelings, instead of which he burst into tears. I really cannot tell you how this touched me. . . .

Before the [actual] performance began, Rubinstein invited me on to the stage. When I appeared, to my horror, I found myself confronted by the whole Conservatoire, and at the head of the professors Nikolay Grigoryevich himself with a wreath which he presented to me amid loud general applause. Of course I had to say a few words in answer to his speech. What it cost me, God alone knows. Between the acts I was recalled several times. I have never seen such an enthusiastic audience.   [*TLP, VIII: 155–6*]

But the success didn't last, and Tchaikovsky had to wait nearly two years for the first professional performance, which took place at the Bolshoi in January 1881. It was for this production that he modified the last scene into the form in which it stands today—partly, at least, at the insistence of Anatoly, who wrote complaining that 'every time one mentions *Onegin* somebody immediately accuses you of distorting Pushkin'.

Tchaikovsky   You say that you wish I would change the last scene of *Onegin*. Although personally I don't agree with you, because I find that Pushkin, by certain hints and a reluctance to be precise, gives one as it were the right to end it in the way that I have done, I have nevertheless taken your point and tried to change the scene [as follows]. . . .

First of all, . . . instead of the direction that 'Tatyana falls on Onegin's breast' etc., I have written: 'Onegin comes closer'. Then he sings what is printed on this page, still addressing her with the formal 'you'. After that everything continues as before, but at the very end I have changed Tatyana's words; she no longer kneels and starts giving way, but continues to insist on her duty. Onegin does not seize her, but only implores. Then, instead of 'I am dying!', Tatyana sings 'Farewell for ever!' and leaves him, and after a few moments of stupefaction he says his last words. The General must not appear.
                    [*TLP, IX: 301*]

So Tchaikovsky's final version of the last scene came closer to Pushkin than it had ever been: duty triumphs without the intervention of Tatyana's husband, Tatyana's decision to reject Onegin is hers alone, and Onegin's fate is decided by Tatyana's acceptance of the very social code that he is now, for the first time, attempting to break. It was obviously a difficult scene for Tchaikovsky. If Tatyana represented an ideal of womanhood that existed only in his imagination, how does this ideal of womanhood behave when faced with the harsh realities of life, and what should be the fate of the repentant lover—no matter how undeserving? There are no exact parallels, and to draw any would be dangerous, but it is perhaps significant that Tchaikovsky eventually left Onegin in a situation as unresolved as his own. There is no grand operatic climax. As in Pushkin, but perhaps for different reasons, the story simply ends. And if the new words given to Onegin at the very end, 'Disgrace! Anguish! How pitiable is my fate', are no great improvement on the 'silly stuff' of the original version, at least they imply the influence of the same force that had heralded the emotional turmoil of the Fourth Symphony.

The Bolshoy première, though reasonably successful, still made no lasting impression, and the true success of the opera began only with its production on the Imperial stage at St Petersburg in October 1884. St Petersburg was a city that Tchaikovsky had never liked, and whose musical elite held him in low esteem; after the first night the St Petersburg press in general took their tone from César Cui, the petty-minded advocate of the Russian nationalist composers, who found that Tchaikovsky lacked both self-criticism and 'discriminating taste', that the overall effect of the opera was one of wearisome monotony and that the work was 'still-born and absolutely valueless'.   [*Newmarch*: 463]

Nevertheless it was the St Petersburg performance that finally launched *Eugene Onegin* on its career; of the two works of genius that he had written, more or less in tandem, during those agonising and tumultuous years, the Fourth Symphony eventually gave place to the *Pathétique* as his ultimate symphonic statement, but not even *The Queen of Spades*, that later masterpiece from Pushkin, was able to displace *Eugene Onegin* as Tchaikovsky's most popular and most successful opera. And of all Tchaikovsky's creations, Tatyana remained the one closest to his heart.

Tchaikovsky   Pushkin has portrayed the power of this virginal love with such genius that even in my childhood it touched me to the depths of my soul. If the fire of inspiration really burned within me when

I composed the Letter Scene, it was Pushkin who kindled it, and I tell you frankly, without false modesty, that I should be proud and happy if my music reflected only a tenth of the beauty contained in the poem. . . .   [*TLP, XII: 245*]

Those for whom the first requirement in an opera is *theatrical action* will not be pleased with [my work]. But those who are prepared to look for the musical expression of feelings far removed from high tragedy or theatricality—everyday, simple, human feelings—will (I *hope*) be content with my opera. In a word, it is written sincerely, and on this sincerity I pin my hopes.   [*TLP, VI: 170*]

Giuseppe Verdi (right) and Arrigo Boito at the Villa Sant' Agata
(Property of Ricordi & C. Milan)

Otello

I̲N APRIL 1865, piqued by criticism after the Paris première of *Macbeth*, Verdi wrote to his French publisher:

Verdi Some point to one thing, some another. Some find the subject
sublime, some find it impossible to set to music. And some find that
I didn't know Shakespeare when I wrote *Macbet*.

Oh, but in this they are very wrong. Maybe I haven't interpreted
Macbet well, but that I don't know, that I don't understand, don't feel
Shakespeare—that no, for God's sake, no. He is one of my favourite
poets, whom I have had in my hands from my earliest youth, and
whom I read and re-read continually. . . .   [*Prod'homme: 187*]

The Paris *Macbeth* was a revision of an opera first performed in 1847.
It was Verdi's own favourite among the works of those gruelling early
years, and the one in which he had made his most consistent effort to
break out of the rut of early-nineteenth-century operatic melodrama.
'This tragedy is one of the greatest of human creations' he wrote to his
librettist Francesco Maria Piave; 'if we can't make something great out of
it, let us at least try and make something out of the ordinary'.

Verdi I find that our operatic stage is guilty of excessive monotony, so
much so that I would now refuse to compose subjects like *Nabucco*,
Foscari, etc. They provide exciting theatrical moments, but no variety. It's a single string, noble if you like, but still always the same
string. Perhaps I could explain it this way: Tasso's may be a better
poem, but I'd a thousand times rather have Ariosto. And for the same
reason I prefer Shakespeare to all other dramatists, the Greeks not
excepted.   [*Pascolato: 46*]

Macbeth was not the only instance, or even the earliest, of Verdi's preoccupation with Shakespeare in the years before *Otello*; in 1849, *Re Lear*, *Amleto* and *Tempesta* appear at the head of a list of possible operatic subjects in Verdi's hand, and the idea of *Lear* had been in his mind from 1843 at least. In the 1850s he made a sustained effort to get this massive project off the ground: 'obviously you can't give it operatic shape using the forms generally accepted up to now', he wrote, 'it would have to be treated in a manner that is completely new and vast, without regard to conventions of any kind whatever', but as he told his librettist, Antonio Somma, he found the prospect 'frightening':   [*Cesari*: 478]

Verdi   . . . Two things worry me particularly. The first is that the opera will get too long, especially the first two acts. . . . The other is that there are too many changes of scene. One thing that has always held me back from treating Shakespearean subjects more frequently has been precisely this necessity for changing scenes every minute. In the days when I went to the theatre it used to annoy me a lot—I felt that I was at a magic lantern show. . . .   [*Pascolato*: 48, 51]

The correspondence over the *Lear* libretto, which continued fitfully for nearly three years, shows Verdi grappling doggedly with the complexity of Shakespearean drama and coming to many of the same conclusions that he later did with *Othello*.

Verdi   In the first act we could take out part of the first scene up to the entry of Lear. At most . . . give five or six lines of recitative to Kent and Gloster. If we keep the chorus here we shall have to make a musical piece of it, and a musical piece takes time. And I think, too, that to start the opera at once at the rise of the curtain . . . would be more impressive and characteristic.   [*Id*: 65–6]

Whether Verdi ever got as far as putting any music for *Lear* on paper nobody knows with absolute certainty; if he did, he never showed it to anybody, and no identifiable sketches have survived. More significant than any unprovable musical conjecture is his involvement with the characters of Shakespeare's play, particularly with the character of Edmund.

Verdi   Develop this character as much as you like and paint him clearly. . . . Personally I wouldn't make Edmund a man capable of feel-

ing remorse, I would make him a frank villain; not repellent like Francesco in Schiller's *Masnadieri* [*Die Räuber*], but a villain who laughs
and sneers at everything and commits the most atrocious crimes with
perfect indifference. . . . Do it any other way and he would have to sing
big phrases with melodramatic outcries. Contempt and irony can be
expressed (and more originally) with the *mezza voce*; it becomes more
terrible like that, and allows me more variety of colouring.   [*Id: 71–2*]

Here, surely, is the forerunner of Iago—a type that fascinated Verdi, and
continued to do so: it was to be *Iago,* not *Otello,* which was first used as
the title for his penultimate opera.

In the end, *King Lear* was laid aside, though Verdi never quite brought
himself to give up the idea entirely. When Mascagni asked him in 1896
why he had never written the music, he replied, 'the scene when Lear is
alone on the heath terrified me'—though his last letter on the subject to
Somma suggests that the fault lay rather with the libretto: 'I don't know
how to explain it, but there's something there which doesn't satisfy me. It
lacks brevity, certainly, but perhaps also clarity, perhaps truth . . .'.

[*Id: 78–9*]

What was needed, and what Verdi had not yet found, was a librettist
who could produce a text genuinely in a different class from the current
Italian melodrama and convince him that, whatever his disappointments
in the past, his ambition to set another Shakespearean libretto might be
achievable. That librettist was Arrigo Boito, but his association with Verdi
did not begin until it seemed almost too late in the composer's career.

It was in 1871, while Verdi was still at work on *Aida,* that his friend
and publisher Giulio Ricordi had made a first effort to interest Verdi in
this poet, the composer's junior by some thirty years. There was a certain
initial resistance to be overcome: in his earlier days Boito, a member of
the young group of avant-garde Milanese artists known as the Scapigliatura, had published an ode *All'arte italiana* which contained some pithy
comments about the state of Italian music that Verdi had taken as a personal insult. The matter had been patched up, but eight years later Verdi
was still suspicious and all too ready to take offence where young Italy
was concerned. In the intervening period Boito had made a name in the
operatic world, both as composer and poet—in the former capacity with
the opera *Mefistofele,* which created a furore at its first performance in
1868, in the latter with a libretto on *Hamlet* for his friend Franco Faccio,
who was now about to be appointed chief conductor at La Scala.

After finishing *Mefistofele*, Boito had turned his musical attention to the subject of Nero. But Ricordi realised that Verdi, too, was attracted by this subject, and he at once acted with an unscrupulousness that is as staggering as it is characteristic. Taking advantage of the Milanese première of Faccio's opera, he wrote to Verdi on 26 January 1871:

Ricordi   I have sent you a libretto of *Amleto* and take the occasion to broach at once a *Grand Project*!! which as you know I am ruminating worse than an ox!! . . . Now, two or three times you have mentioned *Nerone* to me, and I saw that this subject didn't displease you. Yesterday Boito was here with me, and—*boom*—I fired my shot. He asked for a night to think it over, and this morning was here and discussed the matter with me at length. The outcome is that Boito would consider himself the happiest, the luckiest of men if he were able to write the libretto of *Nerone* for you, and would cheerfully give up any idea of doing the music for it himself. He told me frankly that he feels himself capable of satisfying all your requirements . . . , and it would certainly be difficult to find a writer whose verses, both in form and in substance, are more splendid and elegant than his. . . . I can in all conscience put in a word of recommendation for this quite exceptionally gifted young man, who would thoroughly deserve such a piece of good fortune.   [*Medici, I: xxvi*]

Ricordi's blatant manipulation, and Boito's remarkable generosity, produced an immediate reply.

Verdi   Dear Giulio. Now, about *Nerone*. It is useless to say again how much I love this subject, and I need hardly add how agreeable it would be to me to have as collaborator the young poet whose outstanding talent I have just had occasion to admire in this *Amleto*. But you know my situation and my obligations well enough to realise what a grave step it would be for me to take this new burden on my shoulders. I find myself in a singular position: I have neither the courage to say 'Let's do it', nor do I dare to give up such a beautiful idea. But why not, dear Giulio, leave this matter in abeyance for a while and take it up again later? . . .   [*Id: xxvi–ii*]

The completion of *Aida*, and arrangements for its first performances in Cairo and Milan, kept Verdi occupied for another year. It left him exhausted—and angered by accusations of 'Wagnerism' from a handful of critics: 'a fine outcome, after a career of thirty-five years, to end up as an imitator!!'. In the last days of 1872 he wrote to an old friend, Clarina Maffei: 'Peace is the best thing in this world, and the one I want most at the moment', and as he moved on into his sixties, he repeatedly allowed it to be understood that with *Aida* he had closed his work as an operatic composer. [*Abbiati, III: 749; Cesari: 685*]

Verdi   But do you really mean what you say about my conscientious obligation to write? No, no, you are joking, because you know better than I do that the accounts are closed. That's to say: I have always honestly fulfilled every obligation I have undertaken, and the public in turn has met me with honest hisses, honest applause and so on. So nobody has any right to complain and I repeat once more: the accounts are closed. [*Cesari: 510*]

And so it seemed. Though he produced a string quartet in 1873, and the *Requiem* in 1874, there was no opera. But in July 1879 he conducted a performance of the *Requiem* at La Scala. Its triumphant reception did something to dissipate his usual reserve and put him in a good humour, and he and his wife, Giuseppina Strepponi, entertained Ricordi to dinner.

Giuseppina Verdi   By chance the conversation turned to *Othello*, the marvellous drama by Shakespeare, and how the mediocre bungler who adapted it as an opera [for Rossini] had done so in a manner that everybody knows to be unpoetic, completely undramatic and hope-lessly unshakespearian. [*Medici, I: xxix–x*]

Rossini's opera, an early success which was still being given in Italy, may have been the stalking horse on this occasion, but in a conversation with his biographer, Giuseppe Adami, Ricordi made it clear whose hand had held the reins.

Ricordi   The idea . . . arose during a dinner among friends, when I turned the conversation casually to Shakespeare and to Boito. At the mention of *Othello* I saw Verdi eye me with suspicion, but with interest. He had certainly understood, he had certainly reacted. I felt the time was ripe, and I had a skilful accomplice in Franco Faccio. But I flattered myself too much. Next day, when on my advice Faccio

took Boito to see Verdi with a plan for the libretto already worked
out, the Maestro found it excellent but wouldn't commit himself. . . .

[*Adami: 64*]

And on his return home the composer dug himself firmly into his position, writing to Ricordi:

Verdi Now listen carefully. . . . I warn you once more that I have not
made the slightest commitment, that I do not want to make any,
and that I wish to keep all my freedom. . . . Do you understand? . . .
Addio, and believe me yours, G. Verdi.   [*Abbiati, IV: 86*]

Nevertheless, Ricordi and his accomplices were not going to abandon
what they now referred to as 'the chocolate project'. For six weeks Ricordi
waited, then late in August wrote to Verdi proposing a visit 'with a friend'
to the composer's villa at Sant'Agata. But Verdi was not to be caught.

Verdi It would always be a pleasure to have a visit from you with a
friend—who would be Boito, of course. Allow me, however, to speak
to you quite clearly and frankly about this matter. A visit from him
would commit me too much, and I absolutely do not wish to commit
myself. You know how this chocolate project started. You were having dinner with me and one or two friends. We talked about *Othello*,
about Shakespeare, about Boito. The following day Faccio brought
Boito to my hotel. Three days after that Boito reappeared with a
sketch for *Otello* which I read and found good. 'Write the libretto',
I told him; 'it will always come in for you, or for me, or for someone
else', etc, etc.

But now, if you come here with Boito, he will bring the finished
libretto and I shall find myself unavoidably obliged to read it. If I
think it is good in every respect, I shall find myself in a manner committed. If, while thinking it good, I suggest modifications that Boito
accepts, I shall find myself committed still more. If, however beautiful, it doesn't please me, it would be too hard to have to tell him so
to his face!

No, no—you have gone too far already; we must stop before we
run into wrangling and unpleasantness. In my opinion it would be
best (if you agree, and it would suit Boito) for him to send me the fin-

ished libretto, so that I can read it and express my opinion at leisure, without either of us being in any way committed.   [*Medici, I: xxvii*]

To this rebuff Ricordi replied with the calculated, rather flamboyant deference characteristic of his letters to Verdi.

Ricordi   Ever since *Aida* went onto the stage at La Scala there has been much talk about you between Faccio, Boito and myself, and about how happy Boito would be to write a libretto for Verdi; alas, the years have passed, but the idea has never left us . . . and we longed for a favourable opportunity that never seems to come. . . . Nor have I ever had the courage to speak of it, for when I find myself in Verdi's presence my timidity is such that I lose needle and thread. Besides, to tell you the truth, my situation as your publisher puts me in an ambiguous position! . . . out of a sense of delicacy I am always afraid you may think it is the *business man* who is speaking . . . and that repels me
[*Luzio, IV: 200*]

He refers cautiously and obliquely to the earlier 'misunderstanding' between Verdi and Boito, quotes Boito's own letters to prove his present admiration and desire to help, and slips in a good deal about Verdi's illustrious name and the Glory of Italian Art.

Ricordi   My feelings are shared entirely by Boito and Faccio, and on their daily visits to my office they have never failed to look at your portrait which hangs there and exclaim 'But is it really true that he will write no more?' . . . When all the world is clamouring noisily for another Verdi opera, surely you, Maestro, will not fail to understand the even greater eagerness of three friends. . . .   [*Id: 201, 202*]

But Verdi was nobody's fool. He had been perfectly right in his assessment of his publisher's intentions; for some time past, Boito, subjected to extreme pressure by Ricordi and tormented by acute toothache, had been painfully 'engaged in fabricating the chocolate'—which, since he had no assurance that Verdi would write so much as a line of the music, was a considerable act of faith. 'No other undertaking of my life', he admitted to Ricordi, 'has caused me as much uneasiness and agitation as I have experienced in these months of intellectual and physical struggle'.   [*Id: 203*]

Boito   The most difficult part of the work is to condense into brief dialogue the sublime breadth of the text. Re-reading [my earlier sketch]
I find much to cut, much to reduce to more nimble verses. I know
who I am writing for and I want to do the best I can. . . . I am
applying to the lyrical parts a peculiar rhythmic construction which
I think will excite the Maestro's interest. . . . I believe I have found a
form which will marvellously serve Shakespeare as well as his musical interpreter.   [*Id: 201*]

The job which Boito had hoped to polish off in a few weeks dragged
out over four months, much to the annoyance of Ricordi, who was keen
to strike while the iron was at least still warm. He was wisely restrained
by Giuseppina who, though no less anxious to further the project, understood perhaps better the diverse characters of the two chief players.

Giuseppina   I hope and believe that one can say 'all's well that ends well',
and that this is how it *will* end. So don't write or speak to Verdi of fears,
wishes or uncertainties—nor, I might add, tell him that I have written
to you about this. I believe this is the best way to avoid giving him the
slightest feeling of pressure. Let us leave the stream to find its own
way to the sea. It is in the ample spaces of time that certain men are
destined to meet and understand one another.   [*Medici, I: xxix*]

And when in November Verdi finally received the finished libretto, his
acknowledgment was laconic in the extreme.

Verdi   I have just received the chocolate. I shall read it tonight, because
at the moment my head is spinning with business matters. [*Id: xxix*]

He went to Milan with Giuseppina to discuss Boito's remuneration
with Ricordi, but he still put off a meeting with Boito himself.

Giuseppina   The libretto seems to have pleased Verdi because after
reading it he bought it, but he has put it alongside Somma's *Re Lear*,
and that has lain in his portfolio for thirty years, sleeping the sleep of
the just. What will become of this *Otello*? Who knows?   [*Id: xxx*]

So there the matter rested, and Verdi's obstinate refusal to think seriously about the opera continued. After a couple of months in Paris for

the French première of *Aida*, he was back at Sant'Agata in May, burying himself in work on his estate and his farm, repairing his tenants' houses and 'breathing all the fresh air I need, with nothing to admire but my cows, oxen and horses'.

Verdi   Here I am architect, stonemason, blacksmith, a bit of everything. So goodbye books, goodbye music; I feel as if I had forgotten all about notes and wouldn't recognise them any more. For the time being we don't talk about the perfidious Iago. Boito has done the libretto for me, but I haven't written a note of it.   [*Alberti:* 260]

'Otello sleeps peacefully', he wrote to a German colleague, 'and so far has murdered neither Desdemona nor any audience'.   [*Luzio, II:* 337]

But beneath the surface things were moving. Verdi's pupil and protégé Emanuele Muzio, who had been with the composer in Paris, told Ricordi that Verdi had actually been sketching music for the opera while he was there—and the composer was betraying a tell-tale interest in the subject in other ways. To an old painter friend, Domenico Morelli, who had sent him photographs of a scene he was doing from King Lear, he wrote:

Verdi   As heart-rending as its subject! . . . Why not do a scene from *Othello* as a pair to it? For example, Othello smothering Desdemona— or better still (and more original) the scene where Othello, driven mad by jealousy, swoons and Iago looks down on him with a satanic smile and exclaims: 'Work on, my medicine, work!'. What a figure . . . , this Iago with the face of an honest man!'   [*Cesari:* 693]

In fact, Iago so fascinated Verdi that, in the beginning, it was often his name, rather than Othello's, which cropped up as the title of the opera— and which later became attached to it by eager members of the waiting public.

Meanwhile Ricordi's medicine was working too. He kept up the pressure on Boito, who had been having another shot at the difficult finale of Act III.

Ricordi   We shall have to wake up our friend Verdi a bit. . . . I have the feeling he has rather put the Moor to sleep . . . and that an electric shock from your verses at this point would be a godsend! . . . So for

heaven's sake do me the favour of sending this blessed finale of yours
to [Sant' Agata].   [*Medici, I: xxx*]

Early in August, Ricordi, unable to restrain himself, wrote to Giuseppina, once again testing the ground for a visit to the composer. And once again Giuseppina counselled patience. Apart from anything else she was afraid that the press, who were already chattering freely about the rumoured new opera, would get wind of the meeting and upset Verdi still further. 'All things considered, I believe it best to let the matter rest for the time being, and observe the greatest possible silence about the Moor'.

Nevertheless it was only a couple of weeks later that Boito received Verdi's first letter on the subject of *Otello*. He had just received the new version of the third-act finale.

Verdi   Dear Signor Boito, Giulio will have told you that I received your
verses a few days ago, and that I wanted to study them carefully
before I replied.

Certainly they are warmer in feeling than the earlier ones, but
in my view the theatrical climax is still missing, and it is missing
because there is no place for it. Once Otello has insulted Desdemona there is nothing more to be said—or at most just a phrase, a
reproof, a curse on the barbarian who has insulted a woman. So here
either the curtain must fall, or we must come out with a *trouvaille*
which is not in Shakespeare. For example, after the words 'Devil, be
silent!' Ludovico, with all the pride of a patrician and the dignity of
an ambassador, could turn haughtily upon Otello:

'Unworthy Moor, do you dare to insult a Venetian noblewoman, a
relative of mine, and not fear the wrath of the Senate!' (a stanza of 4
or 6 lines);

Iago gloats over his work (a similar stanza)
Desdemona (a similar stanza)
Rodrigo (a stanza)
Emilia and chorus (a stanza)
Otello silent, motionless, terrible, says nothing . . .

All at once there is a distant sound of drums, trumpets, cannon
shots etc., etc . . . 'The Turks! The Turks!' People and soldiers rush
onto the stage; general surprise and horror! Otello pulls himself
together and rises like a lion, brandishing his sword and turning to

Lodovico: 'To battle! I lead you once more to victory!'. . . . All leave the stage except Desdemona. Meanwhile the women of the city, running in from all sides, fall on their knees in terror while the cries of soldiers, the firing of cannon, drums, trumpet calls and all the fury of battle are heard from the wings. Desdemona, alone, motionless in the centre of the stage, her eyes raised to heaven, prays for Otello. The curtain falls.

The musical set-piece would be there, and a composer could well be satisfied with it. But the critic would have much to say. For instance: if the Turks have been defeated (as we are told at the beginning of the opera), how can they be fighting now? . . . And there is a graver consideration: Otello, frantic with grief, eaten up by jealousy, stricken physically and morally—can he rise up again at a moment's notice and become the hero he was before? And if he can, and if glory still dazzles him and he can forget love, grief, jealousy—then why kill Desdemona, and after that himself?

Are they mere scruples, these, or serious observations? . . . Think about it, and let me know. [*Id*: 1–2]

Boito made some more revisions and returned them to Verdi, but attempted no comment on what he perhaps saw as Verdi's rather naïve suggestions for the end of the act. '*Divinamente bene!*' replied Verdi in a brief note, but then 'what do you think of the scruples I mentioned in my last letter?'. And Boito, unable to prevaricate any further, grasped the nettle with well-judged diplomacy. [*Id*: 3]

Boito 'Serious observations', I should say. You have put your finger on the weak spot. Otello is a man whirled about in a nightmare, and under the increasing and fatal domination of this nightmare he thinks, acts, suffers and accomplishes his appalling crime. If we now conjure up a situation which must necessarily distract and release Otello from this obsession, we at once destroy the whole of the sinister spell created by Shakespeare, and we can no longer arrive logically at the conclusion of the action. This attack of the Turks seems to me like a fist that breaks the window of a room in which two people were dying of suffocation. The intimate atmosphere of death, which Shakespeare creates with such care, is destroyed at a single blow. The breath of life circulates once more in our tragedy, and

Otello and Desdemona are saved. To bring them back on the road to death we should have to imprison them once again in the lethal chamber, recreate the nightmare, and patiently set Iago once again upon his prey—and we only have a single act left to reconstruct the whole of this tragic progression. In other words: we have found a good curtain, but at the expense of the final catastrophe.   [*Id:* 4–5]

Nevertheless he did his best to meet some of Verdi's requirements.

Verdi   Well done for the third act finale! I like Otello's fainting better in this scene than where it was before. Only I still don't feel, I haven't quite got the ensemble as a whole. . . . But we'll talk about this later—for the time being, as Giulio will have told you, we have something else to think about.   [*Id:* 6]

'Something else' was the revision of *Simon Boccanegra*, an earlier opera which had never had much success but was now being considered for revival at La Scala. At Ricordi's suggestion Boito had agreed to make some changes to the text. He was not enthusiastic, describing Piave's libretto as 'a shaky table that remains shaky no matter where you try to prop it up'; in spite of Verdi's insistence that 'it only needs a leg or two straightening to make it stand,' the work was substantial and represented another act of generosity by Boito, who must have regarded this fresh procrastination as the last straw. It is possible that Verdi saw the whole business as a practical test of his young collaborator's good will, and if so it was one from which Boito emerged with flying colours. The collaboration laid the foundations of a warm new personal relationship between the two men, as well as providing, above all in the magnificent Council Chamber scene, a first outlet for the musical impulses that were to crown Verdi's old age.

When the curtain fell at the end of the first performance of the revised *Boccanegra* in March 1881, the Milanese audience leapt to its feet in a tumultuous ovation. But the success of the opera was not maintained and Verdi was not encouraged; there was no relaxation of the deadlock over *Othello*—'why talk of an opera that doesn't exist?'—and when Verdi reappeared nearly three years later in the same place, on the same stage, before the same audience, it was still only with another revision, this time the four-act version of *Don Carlo*. Once again the applause for the composer was tremendous. But Verdi was not deceived.

Verdi   I know what it meant, this clapping. . . . It wasn't for *Don Carlo*, or for the operas I've already written. . . . It was to say: 'However old you may be, you're still of this world; sweat again, even if it kills you, but make us dance once more'. . . . Forward, Pagliaccio, and Viva la Gloria!

[*Alberti: 305*]

It doesn't sound particularly promising. But only a week or two after the first performance of *Don Carlo*, Boito paid a visit to the composer in his apartment at the Palazzo Doria in Genoa. And it was then that he realised that what Verdi had so long resisted was happening at last: at the age of seventy he was sliding into *Otello* because the temptation was too great.

Boito wrote to Ricordi:

Boito   I have good news for you, but for heaven's sake don't breathe a word to anyone—not even in your own home, not even to yourself: already I'm afraid of committing an indiscretion. The Maestro is writing, he has even written a good part of the beginning of the first act—and he seems to me excited. . . .

[*Abbiati, IV: 234*]

Yet at this critical moment Boito unwittingly became the central figure of a newspaper incident which nearly wrecked all the plans so cautiously fostered by Ricordi, Faccio and himself. At a public function in Naples he was reported to have said that 'he had treated the subject of *Othello* almost against his will, but that, now it was finished, he regretted not being able to set it to music himself'. At once Verdi wrote to Faccio.

Verdi   The worst of it is that, if Boito *regrets* that he is unable to set it to music himself, it naturally makes it look as if he doesn't expect to see me set it in the way he would like. I absolutely accept this, I accept it completely, and it is for this reason that I turn to you, as Boito's oldest, most loyal friend; tell him by word of mouth, not in writing, that I will return his manuscript to him without a shadow of resentment, without rancour of any kind—and since the libretto is my property I offer it to him as a gift, to set to music whenever he likes.

[*Cesari: 324–5*]

Faccio   I found your letter waiting for me on Sunday evening, and read it with profound emotion. . . . If Boito has spoken of regrets, I swear to you by all that is most sacred that he was alluding to the regrets which he, and Ricordi, and I, and all of us who love and desire the glory of Italian art, would feel if you should really decide not to write *Otello*. . . . Of course I shall speak to him as soon as he returns [from Naples]. . . .   [*De Rensis:* 225–6]

Boito   Thank you with all my heart, Maestro mio, thank you, but I am embarrassed at even having to tell you seriously that I do not accept your most noble, most generous offer. . . .

You alone can set *Otello* to music: all the theatre you have given us proclaims this truth. If I have been able to divine the potent musical qualities of Shakespeare's tragedy . . . and express this in my libretto, it is because I have seen it in terms of Verdi's art, because in writing these verses I have felt what you would feel in illustrating them with that other language, a thousand times more intimate and powerful, the language of music. And if I have done this, it is because I have wanted to seize the opportunity, in the maturity of my life and at an age when faith no longer changes, to demonstrate more fully than is possible in spoken praises how deeply I love and am moved by the art which you have given us.   [*Medici, I:* 70, 72]

Boito explains that his remarks had been completely distorted, and reminds Verdi of his preoccupation with an opera of his own.

Boito   What you cannot suspect, Maestro, is the irony which, through no fault of yours, seemed to be implied in your offer. Look—for seven or eight years now I have been at work on *Nerone*. . . . I dwell under this incubus: on days when I do not work I accuse myself of idleness; on days when I do, I call myself an ass—and thus life runs by and I continue to exist, slowly suffocated by an ideal too high for me. To my misfortune I have studied my period—I mean, the period of my subject—too deeply, and I am terribly in love with it. . . . I may finish *Nerone* or I may not finish it, but it is certain that I shall never abandon it for another work. . . . Now judge for yourself whether, with this obsession, I could accept your offer. But do not *you* abandon *Otello*, for Heaven's sake do not abandon it. It is predestined for you: do it. You had begun work on it and I was encouraged and already hoping to see it finished at some not distant date. You are healthier than me, stronger than me . . . , you are serene and at peace. Take up your pen and write straight away: 'Dear Boito, please be kind enough to alter these lines . . .' and I will change them at once with joy. I shall know how to work for you—I, who do not know how to work for myself—because you live in the true, the genuine realm of art, and I in the world of hallucinations.   [*Id:* 72–3]

Verdi   From the moment that you did not accept my offer (which was made, believe me, without a shade of irony) the letter I wrote to Faccio has no further purpose or meaning. . . . You say 'I may finish *Nerone* or I may not finish it!' I can only repeat your words with regard to *Otello*. There's been too much talk about it! Too much time has gone by! I'm too old! . . . The conclusion is that all this has poured cold water on this *Otello*, and stiffened the hand which had begun to sketch a few bars. . . .   [*Id:* 73–4]

But any stiffness there may have been soon melted before the warmth and sincerity of Boito's appeal. In December of the same year Verdi wrote:

Verdi   Dear Boito—In which part of the globe are you? . . . It may seem impossible, but it's true, for Heaven's sake!!! I'm busy, I'm writing . . . because I'm writing . . . without purpose, without preoccupations, without thinking about what comes next . . . even with a decided aversion to what comes next. . . .   [*Id:* 78]

Boito   Your letter was a joy that I have kept all to myself. But it didn't surprise me. One can't escape one's own destiny, and by a law of intellective affinity this tragedy of Shakespeare's is predestined for you.   [*Id:* 80]

And so, after nearly five and a half years of teasing uncertainty, the real composition of *Otello* had begun, and Verdi found himself face-to-face with Shakespeare once more. But now at last he had what had been lacking for *King Lear*: a poet who understood what he was doing.

Boito   Everyone knows that *Othello* is a very great masterpiece, and in its greatness *perfect*. This perfection derives (as you know better than me) from the wonderful harmony of the details and the whole, from that unyielding and *fatal* logic which lies behind the succession of incidents, from the way in which the passions stirred up are observed and expressed—above all the terrible passion that dominates the tragedy. . . . But an opera is not a play, and our art draws its life from elements unknown to spoken tragedy.   [*Id: 5*]

The fidelity of a translator must be very scrupulous, but the fidelity of one who illustrates with his own art a work in a different artistic medium need, in my opinion, be less so; . . . his mission is to interpret the spirit. The one is a slave, the other free.   [*Id: 104*]

For operatic purposes Boito had taken a number of carefully calculated liberties, the most drastic of which was the complete suppression of Shakespeare's first act. Curiously enough, he was not the first to come up with this idea; over a hundred years earlier, Dr Johnson observed in his *Notes to Shakespeare*: 'Had the scene opened in Cyprus, and the preceding incidents been occasionally related, there had been little wanting to a drama of the most exact and scrupulous regularity'. For Verdi and Boito, as in the comparable case of *King Lear*, it was rather a matter of getting the opera off to a powerful start. The one serious loss was the love poetry from the Venetian senate meeting, but Boito brilliantly made a virtue of necessity by drawing the essence of these speeches together in a single scene and placing it as a point of repose at the end of his first act. His adaptation of Shakespeare's verse was sometimes remarkably direct, and wrung from Verdi some of the most deeply felt love music he ever composed:

> She lov'd me for the dangers I had pass'd;
> And I lov'd her that she did pity them.

> *E tu m'amavi per le mie sventure,*
> *Ed io t'amavo per la tua pietà.*

In the first draft of the libretto, Iago was to have appeared in the background at the end of this duet as a sinister observer. Verdi abandoned this idea, but it was of course Iago who of all the characters in the play first haunted the composer's imagination, a subtler descendant of the unrealised Edmund in *Lear*.

Verdi   This Iago is Shakespeare, is humanity—he is the ugly part of humanity. . . .

   If I were an actor and had to represent him, I should want him to have a fairly tall, slender figure, thin lips and eyes set close to the nose like a monkey, a high sloping forehead and a head well developed at the back; a distracted, nonchalant manner, indifferent to everyone, incredulous, speaking good and evil pungently but lightly as if with his mind quite elsewhere—so that, if someone were to reprove him, saying 'What you say, what you propose, is infamous', he could reply 'Really? . . . it didn't strike me that way . . . let's not talk of it any more!'. A man like this could deceive anybody, even up to a point his own wife. But a small, malignant figure would put everyone on their guard and wouldn't deceive a soul!   [*Cesari:* 694, 317–8]

For musical treatment Boito was obliged to simplify and re-create the enigmatic, complex creature of Shakespeare's imagination (perhaps taking a hint or two from his own opera *Mefistofele* in the process). Evil is here a more primitive thing than it is in the play, at its most explicit in the great outburst 'Credo in un Dio crudel', which Boito developed out of Shakespeare's 'Divinity of Hell!' and added to Iago's role in the second act of the opera. Though this existed already in Boito's original draft, it was Verdi, sensing its theatrical importance, who urged the librettist to strengthen it and Boito, eager to recover his good relations with the composer after the unfortunate affair of the press report, sent him the revised version as something of a peace offering.

Boito   . . . I remembered that you were not happy with a scene of Iago's in the second act . . . which you wanted in a more irregular, less lyrical form. I suggested that I might do a sort of evil *Credo* and I have tried to write it in a metre that is broken and not symmetrical. . . . If I haven't got it right, blame my haste and my emotional state, I can redo it better whenever you like. . . . I have done it to comfort myself, for my own personal satisfaction, interpret that how you will. . . . So here you are: Iago's *Credo*. See what villainies I have put into his mouth.   [*Medici*, I: 74–6]

Verdi   Bravo. It's beautiful . . . , most powerful, and Shakespearean in every way.   [*Id:* 76]

Powerful it certainly became in Verdi's hands, where its portrayal of Iago's infernal purposes and his own shuddering horror of death found musical expression of jagged intensity. But Verdi was sadly mistaken if he really thought that the text Boito provided could have found a place in Shakespeare's play.

To some extent, at least, Iago needed to be misunderstood for the purposes of opera. But Desdemona was a different story.

Verdi   From a common sense point of view Desdemona, who allows herself to be maltreated and thrown about and then, even when she has been half smothered, forgives her murderer and asks his blessing, seems a silly creature. But Desdemona isn't a woman, she is a type. She is the type of goodness, of resignation, of sacrifice. There are some beings who are born for others, unheeding of their own right to existence, beings who exist in part, and whom Shakespeare has given poetic form and immortalised in creating Desdemona, Cordelia, Juliet—types that only have their counterparts, perhaps, in the Antigone of the ancient theatre.   [*Abbiati, IV:* 332]

Desdemona's essential innocence was allowed musical expression from the very beginning, first in the love duet of Act I, and then (a telling afterthought of Boito's) in the chorus of islanders serenading Desdemona in Act II.

Boito   Look what an effective place I have managed to find for [it]. Towards the end of the first fatal conversation between Iago and Otello, when Iago is craftily guiding the Moor's thoughts towards the precipice of jealousy, . . . the audience hears a soft chorus offstage, which comes slowly nearer while Iago continues his infernal business. A few moments later, through an opening in the centre of the stage which looks out onto the garden, we see Desdemona surrounded by women and children, who scatter flowers and branches in her path and sing serenely around her. At this fatal moment of the drama it will be like a chaste and gentle apotheosis of song and flowers around the beautiful, innocent figure of Desdemona.
                    [*Medici, I:* 51–2]

Verdi found that it 'couldn't be more graceful, more elegant or more beautiful—and what a splash of light amid so much darkness!'.   [*Id:* 57]
For Desdemona's own voice Verdi turned to the pure melodic inspira-

tion which had always been at the source of his art, and of which, perhaps, he was now beginning to see himself as the last repository.

Verdi   We [Italians] are a straightforward people, to a great extent sceptical. We don't believe in much, and we can't believe for long in the fantasies of a foreign art which lacks both naturalness and simplicity. An art without naturalness and simplicity is no longer art! Simplicity is necessary to inspiration. . . .   [*Cesari*: 326–7]

Good operas have always been rare, now they are almost impossible. Why? you will ask. Because we make too much music! We search too much! By peering into obscurity we lose touch with the sun!   [*Alberti*: 310]

Desdemona is a role in which the line, the melodic thread, is never broken from first note to last. I repeat, Desdemona sings from the first note of her recitative, which is also a melodic phrase, right up to the last 'Otello, non uccidermi!' which is another melodic phrase. Just as Iago should only declaim and sneer, so Desdemona must always sing, sing. . . .   [*Abbiati, IV*: 337]

If it was pure lyrical artistry that Verdi wanted above all for the role of Desdemona, the vocal attributes that he expected of Otello were of an altogether different order—'Otello, now warrior, now passionate lover, now crushed to the point of baseness, now wild as an untamed savage, must sing, must shout . . .'. For gradually he had come to realise that in this tormented figure, suspended fatally between the Good of Desdemona and the Evil of Iago, he had the true protagonist of his drama.

Verdi   Everyone writes to me and speaks to me of *Iago*! . . . He is, it is true, the Demon who sets everything in motion, but it is Otello who *acts*—who loves, is jealous, kills and kills himself. And so it seems to me hypocrisy not to call the opera *Otello*.   [*Medici, I*: 99]

It is the terrible disintegration of this central character, the classic instance of the man who kills the thing he loves, which must provide the core of any interpretation of the Othello story. In the opera the turning point comes at the beginning of the third act, where Boito weaves together elements from the last scene of Shakespeare's Act III and the second scene of Act IV to provide the crucial confrontation between

Otello and Desdemona. It is at this point, in the play, that Othello swoons and Iago, standing over him, provides the spectacle that Verdi had recommended to Morelli for a painting. In the difficult process of finding 'a trouvaille not in Shakespeare' for the rest of this act, Boito eventually transferred the swoon to the end, where Iago's savage 'Ecco il Leone!' makes a superbly melodramatic curtain.

Boito   I have been chewing this finale over and over, but it is so big a mouthful that I never succeeded in digesting it fully . . . and I have had a hard job producing the result which you now have, and which is, I think, the outcome of our many discussions at Sant'Agata. As we planned, the ensemble has its lyrical and its dramatic side *fused into one*; that's to say, it is a lyrical, melodic piece beneath which runs a dialogue of drama. The principal figure on the lyrical side is Desdemona, on the dramatic side Iago.

Iago, after finding his plans for a moment disrupted by an event not within his control (the letter recalling Otello to Venice), quickly regathers the thread of the tragedy, turns this unforeseen incident to his own account, and even uses it to accelerate the onrush of the final disaster. All this was in the mind of Shakespeare, all this now appears clearly in our work . . . [and] Iago has the last word, the last gesture of the act. . . .

Otello's attitude is indicated, indeed dictated by the drama. We have seen him slumped beside the table after [he has thrown Desdemona to the ground with the words] 'A terra! e piangi!', and thus he must remain, not getting up even when he replies to Iago, for the whole length of the ensemble. He has no reason to *speak* or to *sing* while Iago mutters to Rodrigo: his silence is grander, more terrible. . . . He only rises to cry out 'Fuggite!—Begone!' and then fall senseless to the ground.   [Id: 58–9]

Scenes like this were going to require considerable acting abilities in the singers of the principal roles, and acting abilities were not in plentiful supply on the Italian operatic stage at the end of the nineteenth century. For the dramatically testing roles of Iago and Otello the most likely candidates were the great French baritone Victor Maurel, who had already won Verdi's praises for his Amonasro and Boccanegra, and the celebrated heroic tenor Francesco Tamagno. Maurel, although he annoyed the composer by attempting to establish a sort of personal copyright over his role, eventually earned from Verdi the comment that 'nobody could do the part better than he'. About Tamagno, who combined a tremendous voice with limited musical intelligence, Verdi was from the outset less sure.

Verdi   In many, many things Tamagno would be excellent—but in very many others no! There are long, broad *legato* phrases which must be given quietly, *mezza voce*—a thing impossible for him. What is worse, he would lack warmth at the end of the first act, and (worse still) the fourth! There are . . . immensely important *mezza voce* phrases (after he has stabbed himself) which we simply can't do without. . . .

He is so inexact in his reading of music that I want him to study the part with a real musician, so as to make sure that he sings his notes with their proper value, and in time . . . Even when he has learned the music there will be much to teach him about expression and interpretation; the comments I should have to address to him— the 5,000 lire tenor—(in front of Maurel particularly) might easily wound his *amour propre*—and then *brrrrr* . . . !!   [*Abbiati, IV:* 273–4: *Morazzoni:* 15; *Abbiati, IV:* 298]

It was with the superb power of Tamagno's voice in mind that Verdi provided Otello with the opening '*Esultate!*', one of the most magnificent entries in all opera—and it only came as an afterthought. In May 1886, when the rest of Act I was already finished, he wrote to Boito:

Verdi   You know that the storm, musically speaking, continues during the entry of Otello. . . . There are too many lines in Otello's solo, and the storm gets interrupted too much. I think this scene would lose nothing if we cut it by four lines, and then I could do a phrase for Tamagno which might have a good effect—in fact it's done already. . . .   [*Medici, I: 105*]

Boito   Bravo!!! I absolutely approve the cut. . . . We weren't satisfied with the entry and have been trying to improve it, and now it's been found, and it's splendid! A powerful exclamation of victory which ends in a burst of the storm and a great shout from the people! Bravo, bravo!   [*Id: 106*]

The role of Desdemona provided another crucial problem. After much discussion, and reports from Boito and Ricordi and Faccio on vari-

ous contenders, the choice fell on the dramatic soprano Romilda Pantaleoni—in spite of Verdi's fears that 'an artist so passionate, so fiery and
violent' would not be capable of 'restraining and containing her emotions
in the calm, aristocratic passion of Desdemona'. To some extent his fears
were confirmed as he worked with her: 'it isn't that she doesn't sing her
solos well, but that she sings them with too much emphasis, too dramatically. . . . But I shall go on working at her until she manages to find the
right accents for the situation and the poetry'.   [*Id: 116*]

   It was not only a question of acting, or even of singing the right notes,
it was the need for a dramatic flexibility new in Italian opera—the difference between Rossini's *Otello* and Verdi's, between the type of vocal art
required for the plaintive static beauty of Rossini's Willow Song and the
graded structure of Verdi's.

Verdi   In the fourth act Desdemona has the biggest part, and the hardest.
   The Willow Song presents very great difficulties, both for the composer and the artist who sings it. The singer must have, like the Holy
   Trinity, three voices—one for Desdemona herself, one for Barbara the
   maid, and a third for the 'Salce, salce, salce . . .'.   [*Morazzoni: 44*]

He might have added a fourth for the astonishing outburst at the end—a
moment of fierce passion when Pantaleoni must surely have come into
her own.

   In the last scene of all, Boito had originally made Otello, after half-
suffocating Desdemona, finish her agonies with a sword (as in fact Rossini's *Otello* does), thus allowing Verdi a brief opportunity to include
something for his heroine to sing as she dies. When he came to the
composition of 'this last, most terrible scene of all', Verdi abandoned the
idea, but Desdemona's death, a stumbling point for many literal-minded
critics, is still more quickly dispatched in the opera than it is in Shakespeare—sixteen suffocated words as against twenty-one.

   In the final pages of the score the singing line for Otello disintegrates
into a succession of apparently disconnected phrases 'which I have intentionally set only with sounds that have almost no musical value':

Verdi   After he has discovered that Desdemona has died innocent
   Otello has no breath left in him: he is worn out, prostrated physically
   and morally; he cannot and should not sing with more than a veiled,
   half-dead voice. . . .   [*Abbiati, IV: 274*]

Not since Monteverdi had there been music in Italian opera of such economy, yet instinct with such dramatic and emotional power.

He was not sure whether he had succeeded.

Verdi   I have found it difficult to avoid too much recitative, and to find rhythms and phrases amongst so much free, broken up verse. But this was the way in which you were able to say everything that had to be said, and I am as happy as can be.   [*Medici, I: 85*]

Boito   I must confess that I have an irresistible desire to hear what you have written on these pages so filled with terror, with the deepest anguish ever conceived by the mind of man. . . . If [the rhythms and accents] you have put on paper have caught the terrible grandeur of the truth with the same power and simplicity as in the earlier scenes then one can only dread to hear them.   [*Id: 89–90*]

On 1 November 1886 the composer wrote to Ricordi:

Verdi   I write to tell you that *Otello* is completely finished!! Really finished!!! At last!!!!!!!   [*Abbiati: 294*]

And to Boito on the same day:

Verdi   Caro Boito. It's done! A health to Us . . . (and also to *Him*!!). Addio.   [*Medici, I: 117*]

Nevertheless he still wasn't quite there; a couple of lines required adjusting by Boito, and final touches were needed in the orchestral score. And he sent an urgent message via Ricordi to Faccio, who was now busily engaged in teaching Tamagno his part:

Verdi   In the third act duet for Otello and Desdemona, tell Faccio not to teach Tamagno the very last phrase on the words '*quella vil cortigiana che è la sposa d'Otello*'. I've done this phrase twenty times and I can't find the right notes . . . perhaps I never shall . . . who knows? . . .   [*Abbiati, IV: 299*]

But on 18 December he sent the last two acts to the copyist—'Poor Otello, he'll come here no more!!!!'.

Boito Caro Maestro mio. So *Otello* exists. The great dream has become reality. Sad, sad! . . . The Moor will not come again to beat on the doors of the Palazzo Doria, but you will go to meet the Moor at the Scala. [*Medici, I: 119*]

With the score completed, Verdi turned his full attention to its practical realisation.

Rehearsals in Milan began early in January, and from the start he laid down his conditions in characteristic terms. He wrote to Ricordi, appointing him his intermediary with the management of La Scala.

Verdi I will be present at all rehearsals that I consider necessary. . . .

As usual, no-one, but absolutely no-one, at rehearsals, and I will have absolute authority to suspend them and forbid the performance, even after the dress rehearsal, if either the execution, or the *mis-en-scène,* or anything else in the running of the theatre is not as I want it.

The personnel involved in the production of *Otello* will answer directly to me . . . the director of the orchestra, of the chorus, of the staging, etc. . . .

The first performance shall not take place without my authorisation, and should anyone take it upon himself to disregard this condition the publishing house of Ricordi will pay me a fine of one hundred thousand (100,000) lire . . . I require musical pitch at the level normal in theatres. . . . A box in the grand tier at the disposal of Signora Verdi. . . . [*Abbiati, IV: 305*]

Though he had just turned seventy-three, he flung himself into rehearsals with an enthusiasm of which the journalist Ugo Pesci left a glimpse.

Pesci The Maestro himself sits at the piano for a run through of the solo numbers and duets giving advice and encouragement and dropping every so often one of those comments that are worth more to an artist than any triumph. He is anxious to fuse singing and action at the earliest possible stage. . . . He demands the greatest possible naturalness and studies every movement and gesture with a critical eye, intent on catching whatever seems to him most natural, most true to life. . . . [*Conati: 179*]

In his determination to get what he wanted from his interpreters he frequently resorted to doing it himself. At the end of the opera he wanted Otello to fall in the manner of the great Italian tragedian Tommaso Salvini, but Tamagno couldn't get it right, and in the end Verdi took over, stabbing himself and rolling down the steps by Desdemona's bed with a realism that astonished the assembled cast. When Tamagno was unwell and had to stay at home for a few days Ricordi briefly substituted for him, sketching in Otello's part in the ensembles *mezza voce*. But he was soon required elsewhere. . . . [*Monaldi*: 226]

Pesci   . . . and Verdi took his place in a scene with Desdemona. But her embrace seemed to him too cold and too restrained and, switching roles for a moment, the Maestro demonstrated to Signora Pantaleoni what a genuinely passionate embrace should be like.   [*Conati*: 179]

As rehearsals progressed, rumours about the opera leaked inevitably to a press avid for the latest gossip; it was fifteen years since Verdi had last produced a wholly new opera and seven and a half since the dinner party at which the idea of *Otello* had first been mooted, and by the time the first performance took place on 5 February 1887, the interest of the whole world, and the excitement of all Italy, had reached fever pitch. Of that day, in many ways the climax of Verdi's career, a wonderfully spontaneous description has been left in the letters of the young American soprano and writer, Blanche Roosevelt.

Roosevelt   Before noon I was in the streets. Streets? There were no streets—at least, no crossings—visible, and had the houses not divided the town architecturally, everything would have been run together, like honey, with human beings, human beings, human beings! . . . Men, women, children, beggars and nursemaids, hand organs pealing forth Verdi tunes—Ernani, Manrico. . . . The windows of the tall houses were a mass of shifting heads: balconies were freighted with excited humanity, and the Italian-terraced roofs, where people were eating and drinking and shouting, were literally black with moving forms . . . The Piazza della Scala was a sight to see, and the cries of 'Viva Verdi! viva Verdi!' were so deafening that I longed for cotton in my ears. . . .

At last we started to the theatre. The carriage had to be sent off long before we reached the door, the horses could not make their way through the crowd. At best, human beings one by one between a line of police could struggle towards the entrance. . . . However, I managed to get in whole, and once there the sight was indescribable. La Scala has never before held such an audience, and although it was fully an hour before the time to commence, every seat was occupied. . . . From pit to dome, the immense auditorium was one mass of eager faces, sparkling eyes, brilliant toilettes, and splendid jewels. The Italian Court was a rainbow of colours, and Queen Margherita's ladies of honour like a hothouse bouquet of rarest exotics. . . . I know of no city in the world which could present a spectacle of similar brilliancy. . . .

   Faccio's appearance in the conductor's chair, which he has filled so long and so well, was a signal for thunders of applause. . . . A few glorious chords representing a tempest were followed by an instantaneous rise of the curtain. . . .   [Roosevelt: 183–6, 189]

Miss Roosevelt's 'few glorious chords' do scant justice to the explosion of sound with which Otello opens, nor to the furious choral and orchestral excitement of the opening scene. But there was no doubt about the excitement of the audience.

Roosevelt   [At the end of the opera] the ovations to Verdi and Boito reached a climax of enthusiasm. Verdi . . . was called out twenty times, and at the last recalls hats and handkerchiefs were waved, and the house rose in a body. The emotion was something indescribable, and many wept.   [Id: 199]

Giuseppina   The enthusiasm was deafening, almost delirious . . . but I confess that the reason it moved me was because this admiration, this passionate demonstration was the outcome a profound esteem, a love and understanding for Verdi that has never faltered in the whole of his long career. He gave in Milan the first proofs of his immense talent, and he wanted to give Milan the last fruit of his genius.
                                                            [Abbiati, IV: 326]

Boito   I was up in a box with Signora Verdi when the maestro sent for us . . . When I heard my name I was strangely touched. I had not thought about it. . . . We went to the stage, and when we were called he started, then turned in a half-dazed way for me. . . . I can never describe to you how he took my hand: his touch—there was something so kind, so paternal, so protecting in it, and yet so delicate . . . I shall never forget it.   [*Roosevelt: 231*]

Outside the theatre the enthusiasm of the Milanese public was redoubled: the crowd unharnessed the horses from Verdi's carriage and dragged him back to his hotel in triumph. As he stepped down from the carriage, he turned to Boito with a bewildered expression, grasped his arm and, with the words 'I leave my wife in your hands', plunged into the seething mob below. Later he appeared with Boito and his singers on the balcony of the hotel, and music continued under his windows until five o'clock in the morning.

It seemed like the last and greatest triumph in a long and passionate career. But for the composer the occasion was not without its undertone of melancholy. 'How sad to have finished it!', he said to the playwright Giuseppe Giacosa . . .

Verdi   . . . How lonely I shall be! Until now, from the moment I woke up, I returned each morning to the love, the anger, the jealousy, the deceits of my characters, and I said to myself: this is the scene I have got to write today—and if it didn't come out as I wanted it I would prepare myself for a struggle, confident that in the end I would win. Then, when the opera was finished, there were the rehearsals, the uncertainties, the job of explaining my ideas to the actors, . . . new suggestions for staging . . . , and I would return home still exhilarated by the glorious life of the theatre, happy at what I had achieved, thinking what more I might achieve tomorrow, not aware of being tired, or of being old. But now? Now that *Otello* belongs to the public it has ceased to be mine; it has been taken from me entirely, and the place it held in my heart has left an emptiness so great that I think I shall never be able to fill it.   [*Conati: 156–7*]

Who could have guessed, that night in February 1887, that less than eighteen months later Verdi would be writing to Boito: 'Did you ever give a thought, while you were sketching this *Falstaff*, to the enormous number of my years?'.

But that is the birth of another opera.

Debussy in Pierre Louÿs's house,
photographed by Louÿs about 1895

Pelléas et Mélisande

I AM NOT AN IMITATOR. *My idea of drama is different: music [begins] where the word finishes. Music is for the inexpressible. It must emerge from the shadows. Be discreet. . . .* [Hoérée: 28]

D
ISJOINTED COMMENTS, these, scribbled in pencil in a notebook by a young student at the Conservatoire de Musique in Paris as he listened to a conversation between Claude Debussy and his teacher Ernest Guiraud. It was the late summer of 1889 and Debussy, twenty-seven years old and just back from Bayreuth, was talking about Wagner, about words and music.

'What kind of poet would you have in mind for yourself?' asked Guiraud.

Debussy One who only half says things. Two dreams linked to one another—there's the ideal. No country, nor time. No big scenery. No pressure on the musician completing the work. Music is insolently predominant in opera. There is too much singing. Musical setting is too heavy. Sing when it's worth singing. . . . No musical development for its own sake. A mistake! Extended development does not fit, cannot fit, the words. I imagine short librettos, constantly changing scenes. To hell with the three unities! Scenes that vary in place and character; people who do not argue with one another, submitting to life, to fate. . . . [Id: 28–9]

It seems almost incredible that three years were still to pass before Debussy even heard of *Pelléas et Mélisande*. But Maurice Emmanuel's notes are perfectly genuine, and there is no reason to doubt that the young Debussy, talented, diffident, enigmatic, with subversive views on harmony and a vision of music that was hopelessly at odds with contemporary attitudes, was already forming a clear idea of the opera he was going to write.

Paris in the late 1880s was in the throes of acute Wagner fever. After the championship of Baudelaire the Wagner cause had been taken up by the generation of Symbolist writers grouped round Mallarmé—a focal point of Parisian intellectual life that became a source for many of the ideas that shaped Debussy's view of the musical universe. He had been a passionate admirer of Wagner as a student, but his admiration was based almost entirely on the printed scores; though he had seen *Lohengrin* in Rome during his brief stay as a Prix de Rome winner, there had been no performance of any Wagner opera in Paris since the *Tannhäuser* debacle of 1861, and when he heard the first act of *Tristan* at a concert in March 1887, the impact was overwhelming. 'For sheer depth of emotion it is absolutely the most beautiful thing that I know', he wrote; 'it embraces you like a caress—it literally makes you suffer'.

[*Lesure, 1993: 56*]

It was the beginning of an obsessive relationship with *Tristan* that was to last until the end of his life. But Debussy never swallowed Wagner whole, and he never lost his critical sense.

Debussy   After [two years] of passionate pilgrimage to Bayreuth I began to have doubts about the Wagnerian formula—or rather, it seemed to me that it could only serve the particular case of Wagner's genius. . . . And, without denying his genius, it is fair to say that Wagner put a full stop to the music of his time. . . . One had to find a way to be 'after Wagner' rather than 'according to Wagner'.

[*Debussy: 62–3*]

In spite of beautiful moments, he thought the *Ring* 'a contraption': 'what a bore these leitmotifs are!' he wrote to Guiraud, and to a later interviewer: [*Dietschy: 53*]

Debussy   Each character has his photograph, his 'visiting card' so to speak . . . by which he is always preceded. I confess that I find this procedure a bit crude. Besides, the symphonic development that he has introduced into lyric drama seems to me constantly at odds with the moral struggle in which his characters are involved—the *action passionelle*—which is the only thing that matters.   [*Debussy: 277*]

But *Tristan* and *Parsifal* were always different. The leitmotivs were less explicit, more subtly absorbed into the emotional content of the drama. 'What I love in *Tristan* are the themes as reflection of the action', he said to Guiraud; '. . . the symphonic texture *does no violence* to the action. . . . The themes provide the orchestral colouring needed to suit the expression of the moment'. And although the dramatic technique that he later developed was to be essentially anti-Wagnerian, it is still true that the thematic reminiscences and continuous orchestral texture of *Pelléas* would have been unthinkable without the experience of *Tristan*. All the same, extracting what he needed, and only what he needed, from that oppressive legacy wasn't easy. About 1890, at one of Mallarmé's famous 'Tuesdays', he met the poet Pierre Louÿs, who questioned him about his feelings for Wagner. Debussy replied without hesitation, 'Tristan'. 'And the rest?' asked Louÿs.
[*Hoérée: 33, 30; Dietschy: 53*]

Debussy   The rest . . . yes, yes and no. . . . It is *Tristan* that gets in the way of our work. One doesn't see . . . I don't see . . . what can be done beyond *Tristan*.   [*Dietschy: 53*]

And Wagner was in any case only a part of the problem.

Debussy   For a long time I tried to write music for the theatre, but the way I wanted to treat it was so unusual that after a number of attempts I almost gave up the idea. My earlier experiences in pure music had left me with a hatred of classical development, whose beauty is entirely technical and can only be of interest to the mandarins of our profession. I wanted for music that freedom of which it is perhaps more capable than any of the other arts, because it is not limited to any exact representation of nature, but can explore the mysterious affinity between nature and the imagination. . . .
[*Debussy: 62*]

It took him time to find his way. The music for *Axël*, a solemnly Wagnerian play by the symbolist writer Auguste Villiers de l'Isle-Adam, got no further than a single scene. *Rodrigue et Chimène,* to a disastrously weak text by the Wagnerphile critic Catulle Mendès, reached three acts of continuously symphonic draft score and occupied him for more than two years before he finally abandoned it; 'the traditional aspects of the subject draw from me music that simply isn't mine', he wrote, 'it's so utterly contrary to everything that I really want to express'.

[*Ingelbrecht:* 71]

In fact, there was material much nearer to his heart in another source currently fashionable with the Symbolists, Baudelaire's translation of Edgar Allan Poe's *Tales of Mystery and Imagination.* Debussy was fascinated by the musical possibilities of two stories in particular, *The Devil in the Belfry* and *The Fall of the House of Usher*; with the latter he was to struggle intermittently throughout his life, but difficulties with the libretto fatally inhibited his work on the music and *La chute de la maison Usher* remains one of the great unfinished torsos of operatic history. In the end, it is the non-operatic works—the String Quartet, the *Cinq poèmes de Baudelaire,* the *Proses lyriques* and the first sketches for the prelude to Mallarmé's eclogue *L'après-midi d'un faune*—that provide a true idea of Debussy's growing powers as a composer during this period.

But in February 1890 a new play by the Belgian poet and dramatist Maurice Maeterlinck was published in Paris. *La Princesse Maleine* was enthusiastically received by the Mallarmé circle—and a subject so haunted by that mysterious sense of fatality in which Maeterlinck was always to specialize, with such similarity to the ideas that Debussy himself was already formulating, must have come as a relief after *Rodrigue et Chimène.* Not only was it far nearer to the spirit of Poe, but it had the added advantage of being already in dramatic form, and Debussy immediately applied to the poet for permission to turn it into an opera. This was refused on the grounds that it had already been promised to Vincent d'Indy (who never in fact made use of it). But Maeterlinck's next play, *Pelléas et Mélisande,* which followed only two years later, delved even more deeply into the tenuous world of symbolism. Debussy bought a copy as soon as it was published, and we know that he was at the single stage performance in Paris on 17 May 1893 because his subscription ticket issued by the theatre still exists.

There is no record of his reaction in the various letters written by contemporaries (perhaps he just left at the end without speaking to anybody, as he often did). But it is not difficult to imagine his feelings on finding himself presented with a set of characters who might have been created expressly to fit the description he had given to Guiraud three years earlier.

Maeterlinck   They live under the spell of overwhelming, unseen and destructive powers whose intentions no-one can fathom . . . , slight, fragile, bewildered beings, involved in a drama played out at the edge of an abyss; the words they speak, the tears they shed, have importance only because they fall into that vast mysterious pit and by their muffled reverberation suggest that everything loses itself there in confusion.   [*Script*]

Debussy   The drama of *Pelléas*, for all its dream-like atmosphere, possesses more humanity than the so-called documents of real life. . . . Its language is evocative, with a subtlety that could be developed still further in a musical and orchestral setting; . . . it seemed to me exactly right for what I wanted to do.   [*Debussy: 63*]

In fact he was so fascinated by the play that he had begun sketching what he later called 'a few secret ideas about possible music' even before he saw it on the stage—though whether he originally intended to make a full-scale opera of it is not certain. In any case, by the beginning of August he had progressed far enough to justify approaching the author for a second time—though now he did so through the good offices of the poet Henri de Régnier.

Régnier   My friend, Achille Debussy, who is a musician of the most clever and delicate talent, has begun some charming music for *Pelléas et Mélisande*, which deliciously garlands the text while scrupulously respecting it. Before going further with this work which is not inconsiderable, he would like authorisation to continue.
                                                                      [*Leblanc: 168*]

Maeterlinck   Dear poet, will you please tell M. de Bussy that I have the greatest pleasure in giving him all the authority he may want for *Pelléas et Mélisande*, and since you approve of what he has done I thank him already for whatever he would [now] like to do.   [*Vallas: 154*]

And less than a month later Debussy wrote to a close friend, the composer Ernest Chausson:

Debussy   Latest news . . . C. A. Debussy is in the process of finishing a scene of *Pelléas et Mélisande*, 'A well in the park' (Act IV, scene 4), on which he would like to have the opinion of E. Chausson.
[*Lesure, 1993: 87*]

But as always, he was in need of encouragement.

Debussy   It remains to be seen whether I have got the wrong number for the omnibus to happiness. . . . Now that the clock has struck on my thirty-first year I'm still not sure where I stand from a musical point of view; there are things that I still don't know! (how to write masterpieces, for example, or . . . how to be entirely serious—I have the bad habit of dreaming too much of my life, and not recognising its realities until they suddenly become insurmountable). . . . In any case I am not happy with what I am turning out, I would like you here for a bit, I'm afraid of working in a void.   [*Id: 85–6*]

No surprise, then, that he wrote again in October:

Debussy   I was too quick to crow about *Pelléas et Mélisande* for, after a sleepless night (the kind that brings wiser counsel) I had to admit that this wasn't it at all. It looked like a duet by Monsieur So-and-So, or anybody, and worst of all the ghost of old Klingsor, alias R. Wagner, peered out from behind the barlines. So I have torn it all up and started off again in search of a more characteristic little chemistry of phrases, forcing myself to be Pelléas as much as Mélisande. . . .   [*Id: 87–8*]

Debussy had begun work on his opera at the end, with the scene in which Pelléas and Mélisande finally declare their love for one another—which they do with the famously reticent (and profoundly Maeterlinckian) exchange 'Je t'aime'—'Je t'aime aussi'. No orchestra, no explosion of passion, just two lonely voices. Anything further removed from the rhetoric of nineteenth-century opera would be hard to imagine, and for the first time he found himself faced with the musical implications of this deliberate renunciation of theatrical effect.

Debussy   I have been searching for the music behind the veils in which [Mélisande] wraps herself, even when she is with her most devoted admirers! And I have come up with something which will perhaps please you: I have made use quite spontaneously of a device that seems to me rather unusual, that's to say silence (don't laugh) as a means of expression—and perhaps the only way to give full value to the emotion of a phrase. Even if Wagner used it, I think it was only for its dramatic effect.   [*Id: 88*]

But in banishing the ghost of Klingsor from his score, he admitted another influence altogether more French—that of the reigning favourite of the Parisian operatic world Jules Massenet (for whose music he confessed 'a perverse affection'). As a result, the emotional climax of Debussy's opera, even after later revisions, was always to retain a degree of melodic lyricism that certainly throws into sharp relief that fleeting moment of revelation, but is scarcely to be found elsewhere in the work.

The new version of the scene must have been quickly completed, because only just over two weeks later the painter Henri Lerolle wrote to Chausson:

Lerolle   I had the idea of going to see Debussy. . . . He has just played me . . . a scene from *Pelléas et Mélisande* . . . it—it's astonishing. . . . I find it very, very . . . and then, it sends cold shivers down your back. In a word it's very good. And he seems content with it too.
                                                    [*Lesure, 1977: 11*]

Now that he was seriously committed to the opera, Debussy decided to pay a personal visit to Maeterlinck in Ghent. Pierre Louÿs, the gifted and highly cultivated young poet who was now to become the most intimate of his friends, went with him.

Louÿs   I was with Debussy on that famous visit when he went to ask Maeterlinck for permission to set *Pelléas* to music. It was I who spoke for him, because he was too timid to speak for himself. And as Maeterlinck was more timid still and made no reply whatever, I had to reply for Maeterlinck too. I shall never forget the scene.   [*Louÿs: 30n*]

But once the ice was broken, the meeting appeared to go swimmingly.

Debussy   Though at first he assumed the airs of a young girl on being
introduced to her future husband, gradually he thawed and was
charming. The way he talked about the theatre showed him to be
a very remarkable man indeed. As for *Pelléas*, he is giving me full
authorisation to make any cuts I like, and went so far as to point out
some very important, *even very useful* ones himself. On the musical
side of things, he says he understands nothing at all—he is lost in a
Beethoven symphony like a blind man in a museum. But honestly,
he's a good fellow, and talks with exquisite simplicity of the extraordinary things he keeps finding out. At one point, while I was thanking
him for entrusting me with *Pelléas,* he did his utmost to prove that
it was he who was indebted to me for my willingness to add music
to it! Since I held diametrically the opposite view, I had to employ
what little diplomacy nature has endowed me with—which isn't a lot.

[*Lesure, 1993: 93–4*]

Just what cuts in the play were discussed during the visit to Ghent
is not known, though it seems likely that they included the omission of
four complete scenes: Act I/1, in which the servants are cleaning the
main gate of the castle in preparation for 'grands événements'; Act II/4, in
which Arkel persuades Pelléas to put off his journey to Marcellus's grave-
side; Act III/1, in which Golaud finds Yniold and Pelléas in Mélisande's
chamber; and Act V/1, in which the castle servants await the moment of
Mélisande's death. In any case, when Debussy set to work on the beginning of the opera, he omitted the first of these and plunged straight into
Golaud's discovery of Mélisande alone in the forest—struggling again to
find a voice for the fragility and mystery of Mélisande to set beside the
heavy tread of Golaud.

Debussy   I have spent days in pursuit of that 'nothing' of which she
is made, and sometimes I lacked the courage to tell you about it.
Besides, you know yourself what these struggles are. But I don't know
whether you have ever gone to bed, like me, with a vague desire to
cry, feeling rather as if the day had gone by and you had not been able
to see someone you deeply love.

Now it is Arkel who torments me. He is of a world beyond the
grave, and has the detached and prophetic tenderness of those who
will soon be no more. And all this has to be said with do, re, mi, fa,
sol, la, si, do!!! What a life!   [*Chausson: 87–8*]

Nevertheless towards the end of February he had finished the first act of *Pelléas* 'and also managed to pay the rent—which was less easy'. He then laid the opera temporarily aside, partly to resume work on the *Prélude à l'après-midi d'un faune* and the sketches for what would eventually become the orchestral *Nocturnes*, partly as result of a rupture in his relations with Gaby Dupont, with whom he had been living for the last three years. When he returned to it in May, he skipped the second act and started straight in on Act III, the crucial act in which the virgin love of Pelléas and Mélisande and the growing jealousy of Golaud become increasingly explicit. The opening scene, when Pelléas comes on Mélisande combing her hair at the window of the tower, contains some of the most erotic music in the opera, and its progress was watched impatiently by Pierre Louÿs, who wrote at the end of the month:

Louÿs   Dear friend, I am inviting some people *to hear Pelléas*. Don't forget. You will dine with the Natansons [of the *Revue blanche*] and [Paul] Robert. After dinner five or six friends are coming in—invited specially, I remind you again, for *Pelléas*.
   So be kind enough to bring with you:

   1. the first act,
   2. the scene by the well,
   3. a third scene, if it is done (the scene with Mélisande's hair even if it isn't).

   The piano has arrived.   [*Louÿs*: 32]

News of the piano must have been welcome as a change from the 'execrable' harmonium which was the only instrument normally available in Louÿs's apartment. Debussy never became the virtuoso pianist that his early promise had suggested, but the instrument always remained a deeply personal means of musical expression.

Léon-Paul Fargue   He would sit down silently . . . and start to improvise. Everyone who knew him will remember what that could be like. He would begin by stroking the keys, fingering them tentatively and moving his hands backwards and forwards, then draw out that velvet quality of tone, sometimes accompanying himself, his head lowered, in an attractive nasal voice like a sung whisper. He gave the impression of delivering the piano of its sound—cradling it, speaking to it gently, like a rider to his steed, a shepherd to his flock.   [*Fargue: x*]

Fargue, a poet and novelist, was one of the select circle of friends to whom Debussy would often play parts of *Pelléas* as its composition progressed; the minor composer Raymond Bonheur was another.

Raymond Bonheur   When I think of *Pelléas* I like to remember the different episodes not among the dusty sets of the Opéra-Comique but in the fascinating atmosphere of that apartment on the rue Gustave-Doré where I saw them being born and transformed one after another. It was usually on Saturday afternoons that I would climb up the four storeys, and it was rare that I didn't meet some friendly face when I got there; Satie, in any case, would never fail to heed the call and would come in from Arcueil, always on foot— and all the more punctually because on Saturdays he would have the use of the house piano until the evening. Debussy would begin by preparing tea with minute care, then, between a witticism and some newly hatched titbit of gossip, would sometimes let fall a brief but penetrating insight into his current artistic direction—but quite without insisting on it, because he had no taste for the solemn or the professorial— . . . unless he was particularly pleased with what he had been doing, in which case he might show us the pages he had just written, jumping from one act to another as the mood took him. . . . Everyone knows what an incomparable player he was of his own works, producing along with the illusion of an orchestra an extraordinary impression of life and movement. His hollow voice was all accent, all expression, and anybody who has not heard him in the terrible scene [of Golaud's jealousy] in the fourth act of *Pelléas* can have no conception of its tragic power. But it was when he played from a draft that was still only half finished, while he was still almost in the fever of improvisation, that he was truly extraordinary—'How I envy painters', he said 'who can catch their dreams in the freshness of a sketch'.   [*Bonheur: 6, 7*]

Not everybody appreciated what they were hearing. When Lerolle invited Vincent d'Indy and Debussy to bring their latest work to a little *réunion* of friends, Debussy claimed not to have brought *Pelléas* 'because it would make too much music', and the company were treated to the third act of d'Indy's *Fervaal* instead. At a quarter to midnight the party began to break up:

Lerolle   Benoît tried to drag off Poujaud, who wanted to stay, while Debussy picked at the piano with an air of thinking about something quite different. I could see that he was mad keen to play something. All right then, 'get on with it' [I said]. 'But I haven't anything to play'. A sudden suspicion crossed my mind; I told him I thought he hadn't been telling me the truth, and in fact I found *Pelléas* in his portfolio. So he started. We stood round the piano, while Benoît, in a fury, threw himself down on the sofa, and Debussy took off. D'Indy made faces with his moustache as he turned the pages, and Poujaud looked flabbergasted, while Benoît shifted restlessly with boredom, yawned out loud, wound up his watch noisily, turned over, didn't find the sofa big enough for his legs, and then at the very last note, before Debussy had mopped his brow or even taken his hands from the keyboard, went off without saying a word to anyone . . . and we heard the front door shut with a bang. . . . Then came comments on *Pelléas*, which I think had really astonished them. . . . And they all left at half past eleven [that would have been half past eleven the following morning of course], very cheerful and, I think, content.   [*Tienot: 86*]

Benoît was not the last to find Debussy's dramatic technique hard to take, and the subject was one to which the composer often returned.

Debussy   I have attempted to obey a law of beauty which seems to be strangely ignored when it comes to dramatic music: the characters in this opera try to express themselves like real people, not in an arbitrary language made up from antiquated traditions. This is the origin of the reproach that has been levelled at my so-called obstinate taste for monotonous declamation, which is seen as having no melody. . . .
          [*Debussy. 63*]
     Melody, if I may put it this way, is almost anti-lyrical; it is essentially suited to song, which presents a single mood. . . .   [*Id: 276*]
     It is completely illogical to suppose that a *fixed* melodic line can be

made to embrace the innumerable nuances of feeling that an [operatic] character passes through—that's not only an error of taste but an error of 'quantity'.

If symphonic development finds, on the whole, little place in *Pelléas*, this is a reaction against that disastrous neo-Wagnerian aesthetic which claims to render at one and the same time the feelings expressed by the character and the inner thoughts which prompt him to act. . . . In my opinion these are two contradictory operations from an operatic point of view which, being brought together, can only weaken one another. Perhaps it's better that music should try by simple means—a chord? the curve [of a phrase]?—to express successive changes in mood and atmosphere as they naturally occur, rather than make painful efforts to follow a prescribed symphonic development which is *always arbitrary*, and to which one will inevitably be tempted to sacrifice the development of feeling. . . . That is why there is no 'guiding thread' in *Pelléas*, and the characters do not have to suffer the slavery of the 'leitmotif'. . . . Notice that the motif which accompanies Mélisande never changes; it comes back in exactly the same form in the fifth act—because in reality Mélisande herself never changes, and dies without anybody—except old Arkel perhaps?—ever having understood her.

[*Nichols & Smith: 184–5*]

Again and again Debussy insisted that his aim was always to simplify. The vocal lines are almost never allowed to overlap each other—let alone indulge in any form of duet.

Debussy   My one engrossing ambition in music is to bring it as near as possible to a representation of life itself. . . . When two persons talk at the same time they cannot hear one another. Besides, it is not polite, and the one who interrupts should stop.   [*Daily Mail*]

Once he had completed the scene by the tower, probably by mid-July, Debussy went ahead fast with Act III, 'sheltered only by the dark foliage of semi-quavers amid which Pelléas and Mélisande move restlessly to and fro'. 'And a very accomplished pair of young people they always are,' he wrote to Louÿs; 'I have decided to do the scene in the vaults of the castle, in a manner that you will do me the favour of finding curious when you see it'. By the end of August, 'working like a cart-horse', he was able to tell Lerolle: [*Lesure, 1993: 103, 102*]

Debussy   The scene in the vaults is done, charged with an uncanny sense of terror and enough mystery to induce vertigo even in the most well-balanced soul. Also the scene when they climb up from the vaults, full of sunshine, but sunshine refreshed by our dear mother the sea. I hope it will make an attractive impression—anyhow, you'll see all this for yourself, I wouldn't influence you for anything in the world. I've also finished the scene with the little sheep [the scene for Yniold, Act IV, Scene 3], where I have tried to put across something of the compassion of a child for whom a sheep is simply a kind of toy that he can't touch, as well as the object of a pity that is no longer felt by people who are only interested in comfortable lives.

   And now I'm at the scene between the father and child, and I'm afraid—I have to find ways of saying things that are so profound, with such absolute accuracy! That 'petit père' there gives me nightmares.
[*Id: 104–5*]

Fear of this harrowing scene, in which Golaud forces his terrified little son to spy on the lovers, appears to have induced Debussy to make a detour from Act III and experiment first with the treatment of Yniold in Act IV. But there was no escaping the violence buried in the agonized depths of Golaud's soul; Debussy returned to face the nightmares, and by mid-September he had finished the act.

   Another pause during the next few months gave him time to complete the orchestration of the *Prélude à l'après-midi d'un faune* and work again on the *Nocturnes,* now recast as three movements for violin and orchestra. To the Belgian violinist Eugène Ysaÿe, for whom they were intended, he wrote: 'I am not abandoning *Pelléas* for this'. . .

Debussy   . . . though the further on I get the more I am beset by dark misgivings . . . And then this constant straining to find the expression for a dream, which can vanish into thin air at the touch of a mere nothing, and the deliberate suppression of all musical irrelevances, ends up making me feel like a paving stone that's had carriages running over it. [*Id: 106–7*]

But the success of *L'après-midi* at its first performance on 22 December (the reception was so enthusiastic it had to be repeated at once) seems to have triggered a new burst of activity.

Debussy   Pelléas and Mélisande are my only friends at the moment; perhaps we are beginning to know one another rather too well and only talk about things of which we already know the ending—and then finishing a work, isn't it a little like the death of somebody you love?   [*Id: 108*]

Early in 1895 he set to work on the two remaining scenes of Act IV, the brief dialogue in which the lovers arrange to meet by the well in the park, and the terrible scene in which Golaud gives way to gnawing jealousy and seizes Mélisande by the hair. 'I am working at things that will only be understood by the children of the twentieth century' he wrote to Louÿs:

Debussy   They are the only ones who will understand that the 'clothes don't make the musician'—they will tear the veils off the idols of music and find that underneath there was nothing but a wretched skeleton. . . .   [*Id: 109*]
   How much one must first find, and then suppress, to reach the naked flesh of emotion!   [*Ingelbrecht: 155*]

By April he was at the fifth act: 'I have suddenly come up against the death of Mélisande; it upsets me, and I work at it trembling . . .'. But he was not done even now: Act II still remained unwritten. 'I had always thought that the second act would be child's play, and it's sheer hell!' he wrote at the beginning of August, and to Lerolle . . .
                                                      [*Louÿs: 50: Lesure, 1993: 111*]

Debussy   . . . the scene between Golaud and Mélisande above all! Because it's there that the seeds of the catastrophe begin to stir, there that Mélisande begins to lie to Golaud and to reach some understanding of herself. . . . I think you'll like the scene in front of the cave; it's an attempt to capture what is mysterious in the night, where the silence is so profound that a blade of grass disturbed in its sleep makes a noise that is actually disturbing. And then there is the sea nearby, unfolding its sorrows to the moon, and Pelléas and Mélisande who are a little afraid to speak amidst so much mystery.

I won't tell you any more, in case it turns out like one of those descriptions of a distant country when you build yourself a whole fabric of dreams only to find them wiped away by the cruel sponge of reality. Now all my anxieties begin; how is the world going to treat these two poor little creatures? . . . In the end, any attempt to try and make your contemporaries recognise the sublime is a complete fool's game, except for yourself.   [*Lesure, 1993: 111–12*]

The draft score of *Pelléas* was finally completed by July 1895, though it was to be intermittently revised over the next six and a half years and the full orchestral score not actually written down until a few months before the first performance. All the same, now that a version of the whole opera was in existence, Debussy's thoughts turned inevitably to the prospect of performance. He received encouragement from Maeterlinck.

Maeterlinck   As for *Pelléas*, it goes without saying that it belongs to you entirely and that you are free to have it performed where and when you wish.   [*Ingelbrecht: 144*]

But the whole concept of *Pelléas* was so unusual and so contrary to current taste that the possibility of finding a theatre willing to take it on was slight, and from the start Debussy set himself against a concert performance, or any performance of the music in part. To Ysaÿe, who had written suggesting something of the kind, he replied:

Debussy   I must tell you, in all modesty, the reasons why I don't agree with you about a performance of extracts from *Pelléas*. To begin with, if this work has any merit it lies above all in the connection between the movement on the stage and the movement in the music. It is obvious, and undeniable, that in a concert performance this aspect would be lost, and you could hardly blame people for seeing nothing specially eloquent in the silences with which the piece is studded. What's more, the simplicity of the means employed only has any real point if it is related to what is happening on the stage; at a concert performance the audience would throw in my face the American wealth of Wagner, and I would look like some poor devil who couldn't afford to pay for—contra-bass tubas! In my opinion *Pelléas et Mélisande* must be given as they are; then it will be a matter of taking them or leaving them and, if we have to fight, we shall fight in a good cause.   [*Lesure, 1993: 123*]

Debussy was not a natural fighter. During the years that followed, he continued to play the opera to his friends, but he made little headway in more influential musical circles and the prospect of performance grew no nearer. He toyed with a libretto by Pierre Louÿs, made deeply erotic and profoundly original settings of his *Trois chansons de Bilitis* (which are vocally the nearest things to *Pelléas* that he ever wrote) and struggled to complete the *Nocturnes*. He gave piano lessons, but his financial position, always precarious, was at times desperate, and Gaby Dupont, who had attempted to kill herself in 1897, left him in the following year for a wealthier lover. It was probably the darkest period of his life. In April 1898 he wrote to Louÿs:

Debussy   I promise you I have need of your affection, I am so lonely and helpless. Nothing has changed in the blackness that is the background of my life, and I hardly know where I am heading if not towards suicide—a stupid ending to something which perhaps deserved better, and all this because I am tired to death of battling with imbecile impossibilities which are despicable in any case. You know me better than anybody, and you are the only one who has the right to tell me that I am not altogether an old fool.   [*Louÿs: 110–11*]

Louÿs   You haven't the shadow of an excuse for nightmares of this kind. . . . It's not by giving music lessons that you will be assured of a livelihood, it's by doing everything possible to get *Pelléas* performed. You think of practical negotiations as beneath you, but I think you could be mistaken. . . .   [*Lockspeiser, I: 166*]

If Louÿs could do little but encourage, there was another supporter whose position enabled him to do more. André Messager, a successful composer of light opera who had recently been appointed principal conductor of the Opéra-Comique, was an intelligent and sensitive musician. He had heard parts of *Pelléas* played by Debussy, and now he took the matter to his director, Albert Carré. His enthusiasm was persuasive, and in May 1898, Carré heard the score for the first time in the composer's apartment in the rue Gustave-Doré. He was evidently impressed, because he agreed in principle to produce the opera.

But at this stage Carré was only contemplating a few special performances, and he hesitated to proceed even that far with a work so unlikely to prove popular. For three years he did nothing—and Debussy did little to chase him, instead completing the *Nocturnes* and a few works for piano, and embarking on his ill-considered first marriage with the dressmaker's model Lily Texier. It was in their new apartment in the rue Cardinet that Messager set the ball rolling again with another play-through for Carré. This time Carré took the plunge; he agreed to risk a production at the Opéra-Comique, and on 5 May 1901 Debussy wrote to Louÿs:

Debussy   Since you are, none the less, my good old Pierre—I shouldn't like you to hear from a third party that *I have the written promise of M. Albert Carré that he will put on Pelléas et Mélisande* during the coming season.   [*Lesure, 1993: 167*]

When Maeterlinck heard the news, he at once proposed visiting Debussy, to discuss 'our *Pelléas*'. The opera being already completed on lines agreed with the poet, what he now hoped to discuss can only have been theatrical style and the casting of the principal roles. The latter was a delicate point, since Maeterlinck's mistress, Georgette Leblanc, was herself an operatic soprano who had achieved some success at the Opéra-Comique—most recently in Carré's production of *Carmen*, a role that hardly suggests any great suitability for Mélisande. She was there when Debussy first played Maeterlinck his score, at the end of May.

Leblanc   The position of the piano forced him to turn his back on us and permitted Maeterlinck to make desperate signs to me. Not understanding music in the least, the time seemed long to him. Several times he wanted to escape but I held him back. Resigned, he lit his pipe.

   Just before [Debussy] left we talked of the casting. I longed to play the role. Maeterlinck urged it. Debussy said he would be delighted. It was decided that I should begin to study Mélisande immediately. We arranged for the first rehearsal.   [*Leblanc: 169–70*]

But this was not the way in which either party later remembered the scene. When relations between the two men had deteriorated to the point where it was felt necessary to refer the case to the Society of Authors, Debussy's official deposition stated that he had simply said 'We shall see', Maeterlinck's that 'M. Debussy did not reject [my] demand, but was of the opinion that M. Carré must not be offended, and that it was better to wait'. The truth is that Georgette Leblanc was not really a very good singer, and certainly not suited to Debussy's conception of Mélisande; if Debussy was not aware of this when they first met, he had plenty of opportunity to find out during the four or five rehearsals she claimed to have had with him.

Carré was no doubt informed of Maeterlinck's demand, though for the time being he and Messager kept their own ideas about casting to themselves. But at some point during the early autumn of 1901, Debussy was asked to play his score through to a group of artists from the Opéra-Comique. Among them was a young Scots girl who had recently made a surprise début in Charpentier's *Louise*. Her name was Mary Garden.

Mary Garden   One afternoon we were all invited to M. Messager's home. We were there only a short while when the door opened and in came Debussy. We were all presented to him, and he spoke the usual words of greeting. Without another word, he sat at the piano and played and sang the whole thing from beginning to end.

[*Garden: 63*]

Messager   Debussy at the piano played his score and sang all the parts in that deep, hollow voice which often forced him to transpose the vocal line down an octave, but achieved an intensity of expression which gradually became irresistible. The impression the music created that day was, I think, unique. To begin with there was resistance and suspicion, but gradually the listeners grew more and more deeply engrossed; little by little the emotion mounted until the last notes of Mélisande's death were sounded amid silence and tears.   [*Messager, 1926: 110*]

According to Mary Garden, the first hearing of this music reduced her to tears, and she fled into the next room with Mme Messager.

Mary Garden   [We] returned to the drawing-room just as Debussy stopped. Before anyone could say or do anything he faced us all and said:
    '*Mesdames et messieurs*, that is my *Pelléas et Mélisande*. Everyone

must forget that he is a singer before he can sing my music. *Oubliez, je vous prie, que vous êtes chanteurs!'*

Then he murmured a quick *'Au revoir'* and, without another word, was gone.   [*Garden:* 63–4]

With the principal artists now 'eager to get to work', the details of casting provided few problems—except in the crucial case of Mélisande.

Debussy   It had always seemed to me that the character of Mélisande would be difficult to interpret on the stage. I had done my best to express in music her fragility and elusive charm, but there still remained her whole bearing and manner, her long silences where a single false gesture could ruin the effect or even make her incomprehensible. And above all Mélisande's voice, so tender in my secret dreams—how was that going to be realised?   [*Debussy:* 201]

He must by now have recognized that Georgette Leblanc's voice was never going to provide him with the sound of which he had dreamed, and when Carré and Messager revealed their own suggestion for the title role, the relatively untried Mary Garden, he was doubtful, but agreed to give her an audition.

Garden   [He] was already in the small rehearsal room when I arrived. Without any preliminary chatter, except a quick exchange of 'How do you do's?' we began. I opened my score, and Debussy sat down at the piano. We did the first act, Debussy singing the role of Golaud . . . and never saying a single word. When we came to Pelléas he sang that too, and all the other roles as well, except mine. Then we came to the scene of the Tower. I was singing my lines when, without a word, he got up abruptly and left the room. I stayed there a little while and waited, quite bewildered. I had a feeling I had offended him in some mysterious way and I began to prepare myself for the shock of not singing Mélisande.   [*Garden:* 67–8]

She need not have worried. Debussy had left her only to burst into Carré's office exclaiming, 'It's her—she is my Mélisande'.

Garden   I put on my hat and was about to leave the rehearsal room when a boy came in and said: 'Miss Garden, M. Carré would like to see you in the office'. When I walked in, there sat Debussy with M. Carré. Rising from his chair, he came right up to me and took both my hands in his.

'Where were you born?' he asked.

'Aberdeen, Scotland'.

'To think that you had to come from the cold far North to create my Mélisande . . .'

Then he turned to M. Carré, and I remember he put up his hands, and said: '*Je n'ai rien à lui dire*. I have nothing to tell her'.

He paused, as if embarrassed, and, still looking at M. Carré, added: 'What a strange person, this child.' With that, he fell silent, in that curious detached way of his, took his hat, and, mumbling a 'Good-bye', walked out of M. Carré's office. [*Id: 68*]

Meanwhile, Georgette Leblanc was continuing to work on the role and wrote to Debussy:

Leblanc   You simply can't imagine how passionately attached I am to your work; it is the realisation of all my dreams. . . . I have sung a few of Mélisande's phrases to Maurice; he understood them perfectly and said that he found the words 'prettier like that'. It's a triumph for your logic. I am just so astonished, so ravished to find at last a lyric drama that fully satisfies the demands of reason. [*Ingelbrecht: 147–8*]

But on 29 December the cast list for *Pelléas* was published in *Le Ménestrel*, with Mary Garden's name at its head.

Leblanc   My work with Debussy was progressing when one day Maeterlinck read in a paper that another artist had been engaged to create Mélisande and that she was rehearsing with the composer.

[*Leblanc: 173*]

Leblanc is not necessarily the most reliable witness in this matter, but she later admitted that 'while we worked our understanding was perfect, though when we stopped to rest we found it difficult to talk', and it does look as if Debussy—probably out of shyness—had allowed the situation with his leading ladies to get a bit out of hand.

At any rate, the news provoked a grotesque series of reactions from Maeterlinck.

Leblanc   Brandishing his cane, [he] announced to me that he was going to 'give Debussy a drubbing to teach him what was what'. . . . This threat of a beating terrified me and I clung to Maeterlinck who jumped briskly out of the window [it was, in fact, a ground-floor flat]. . . . I waited in agony, convinced of disaster, [and] watched the deserted street for Maeterlinck's return. Finally he appeared at the top of the hill, flourishing his cane to heaven with comic gestures. The story was pitiable. As soon as he entered the salon he had threatened Debussy who dropped into a chair while Madame Debussy distractedly ran toward her husband with a bottle of smelling salts. She had begged the poet to go away and, *ma foi!* there was nothing else to do.

    [Maeterlinck's attempt to laugh it off] scarcely reassured me. I thought that after he left Debussy would arise from his armchair in terrible wrath. Perhaps his seconds would call on us the next day.

[Id: 174–5]

Maeterlinck later corroborated this unlikely story as being '*à peu près exacte*'—though in fact, as things turned out, it was the poet and not the composer who actually threatened a duel. At this point Carré, who knew that Maeterlinck was a swordsman for whom Debussy would be no match, offered to take Debussy's place, and Maeterlinck at once set about rehearsing for this preposterous scene, stationing his friend the theatre director Aurélien Lugné-Poe against the garden wall, sword in hand, to represent the adversarial Carré. He even consulted a medium on the likely outcome, and a neighbour, Lucie Delarue-Mardrus, claimed to have seen him practicing with a revolver: 'one morning in his garden, as his black cat walked purring towards him, he took her as a moving target and killed her without hesitation'.   [*Delarue-Mardrus: 126*]

    'In the face of such blind delusion I am powerless,' wrote Maeterlinck's friend, the novelist Octave Mirabeau:

Mirabeau   I cannot appeal to his reason, for he is beyond reasoning with. And anything else that I might risk doing . . . would only excite still further a mood of exasperation which has reached such a pitch that this kindly and eminently reasonable man has fallen into a veritable raving fury. . . . I have never seen a man possessed to such a degree by the evil genius of a woman.   [*Peter: 177*]

Dissuaded from violent action, Maeterlinck still found pretexts to issue his veto on the production, but Debussy and Carré refused to back down, and Maeterlinck referred the matter to the Society of Authors. At the hearing on 14 February he refused arbitration and threatened to take the matter to court, but his legal position was weak and he was advised to withdraw his case—a victory that Debussy had in fact already hailed with premature delight.

Debussy   Maeterlinck is in the bag and Carré agrees with me that his case borders on the pathological. But there are still mental hospitals in France.   [*Lesure, 1993: 169*]

Meanwhile practical developments meant that Debussy could no longer put off the job of turning his original draft of the opera into a full orchestral score; a mention in a letter of 'this little neurasthenic who is so fragile that she can only bear violins if they are divided into 18 parts' suggests that he had begun on it as early as September, and later references to 'repairs to the inner workings of the *Pelléas et Mélisande* machine' imply that something more than simple transcription was involved.   [*Louÿs: 165, 169*]

In any case, the job was still not finished when preliminary rehearsals began on 13 January, and for the first few weeks Debussy worked on his score at night and coached its interpreters during the day. Messager remembered the piano rehearsals as taking place in an atmosphere of growing enthusiasm, with 'none of the artists betraying the least ill humour at the exacting demands of the composer', but as Mary Garden said, 'it was all so different from anything any of us had ever sung', and some of her colleagues found it difficult (and possibly humiliating) to follow Debussy's injunction to 'forget that they were singers'.

Debussy   The realisation of a work of art on the stage, no matter how beautiful, is always at variance with the inner vision from which . . . it had originally emerged. In the world of charmed illusion where you and your characters have lived for so long it would sometimes seem as if they were about to step out of the silent pages of the manuscript—

as if you could almost touch them. Is it surprising, then, that you are bewildered when you see them brought to life through the intervention of this or that chance performer? You feel almost frightened and hardly dare speak to them. . . .

[Yet the rehearsals for *Pelléas* provided] my most precious hours in the theatre, hours in which I experienced the wonderful devotion of great artists. And among them one individual stood out as curiously personal. I hardly had to tell her anything as little by little the character of Mélisande took shape, and I waited with a strange mixture of confidence and curiosity.

At last came the fifth act—the death of Mélisande—and I cannot describe the amazement I felt. Here was the gentle voice that I had heard in my secret imagination, the frail tenderness, the captivating artistry I had not dared to hope for. . . .   [*Debussy*: 200–1]

'You'd have to have ears plugged with lead to resist the charm of that voice', he said later; 'for myself, I can't conceive of a *timbre* more sweetly insinuating. It's almost like some sort of tyranny, it's so impossible to forget'.   [*Lesure, 1993: 175*]

Nevertheless the ingrained habits of traditional opera were hard to drop; according to Henri Büsser, the assistant conductor, Debussy was for ever appealing to the artists 'Piano, piano, not so loud, I beg you', and Büsser noted in his diary: 'At today's rehearsal Messager and Debussy are in a foul temper. They consider, and rightly, that Périer [Pelléas] and Dufranne [Golaud] are singing at the tops of their voices'.

[*Büsser: vii; Nichols: 79*]

He took the same line with the orchestra. The first read-through on 21 March brought an outburst of angry incomprehension from the players, and precipitated what Messager described as 'a series of sombre days and discouraging sessions'—made worse by the fact that the orchestral parts, which had been copied by a neighbour intending to help the composer, were full of mistakes; it took four sessions simply to correct them. Messager was furious and the situation became so difficult that at one point Debussy withdrew his score. During twenty-one rehearsals the players, too, began to understand the music, but by this time Debussy had a new headache. The backstage and wings at the Opéra-Comique were unable to cope with the scene changes that the opera required, and on 1 April, the day before the first full stage rehearsal, Messager and Carré, who was producing the opera, realised that they were going to need more music for the interludes between the scenes.

Debussy   Claude Debussy proposes and M. Messager disposes. . . . He arrived last night about ten o'clock and asked me for a linking passage of 75 bars for the second act of *Pelléas*—needless to say he has to have it at once, so that's put paid to the pleasant evening I had been looking forward to.   [*Lesure, 1993: 170*]

Messager   The composer had to go back to work once more, cursing and grumbling, and I was forced to call every day and tear out of his hands the sheets he had filled between one rehearsal and the next.
                                                              [*Messager, 1926: 111*]

In the end, Messager got only 52 bars for Act II, most of them in the interlude between the first two scenes. Nothing was needed in Act III (the wonderful transition from the vaults to the sunlit terrace of the castle being part of the original score), but Act I needed attention, and in Act IV, Debussy had to provide a hefty forty-eight bars to cover the change between the scene of Golaud's jealousy in the castle and the well in the park that is the setting for the emotional climax of the opera. Strange that music of such quality and integral significance should have been added as an afterthought to the score.

Under extreme pressure even the smallest practical details of the production began to worry the composer. He complained that the theatre was too dark, 'which creates real problems for the safety of the performance—it makes it very difficult for the orchestral players, and the singers find it impossible to see the conductor'. And there was too much darkness on the stage as well.

Debussy   . . . as for the fifth scene—Golaud in bed—surely it shouldn't be necessary to have a lamp lighted! Golaud's accident has just happened, so it must be about three o'clock in the afternoon. Besides, [darkness in this scene] spoils [the contrast with] the scene by the cave which comes immediately afterwards. In general, there are too many sombre episodes in this piece for us not to take advantage of what little light there is. . . . And then, doesn't it worry you that having Golaud in bed in his nightshirt might weaken the effect of the final scene [of the opera]? . . . He could be resting with his cloak spread over his legs. Besides, Mélisande sitting in an armchair looks a bit like someone visiting the sick.   [*Lesure, 1993: 170–1*]

On 13 April the Opéra-Comique announced the first performance of *Pelléas et Mélisande* for the 23rd. And on the morning of the 14th a letter appeared in *Le Figaro*.

Maeterlinck   Sir, the management of the Opéra-Comique announces the forthcoming performance of *Pelléas et Mélisande*. This performance will take place against my express wishes, for MM. Carré and Debussy have disregarded my most obvious rights. . . .

In fact M. Debussy, who was at first in agreement with me over the choice of the only artist whom I considered capable of creating the role of Mélisande in accordance with my wishes and intentions, eventually—in view of M. Carré's unjustifiable opposition to this choice—saw fit to deny me the right to any word in the casting, on the strength of an all too trusting letter I had written to him nearly six years ago. . . . I have thus been excluded from my work, which is being treated as conquered territory. Arbitrary and absurd cuts have been carried out which have made it incomprehensible; other passages which I wished to suppress or improve have been retained. . . . In a word, the *Pelléas* in question is something which has become alien and almost hostile to me and, deprived of all control over my work, I am reduced to wishing for its immediate and resounding failure.

Maurice Maeterlinck.   [*Peter: 175–6*]

Maeterlinck swore never to see the opera, and did not do so in Debussy's lifetime. But in 1920, two years after the composer's death, he heard it in New York and wrote to Mary Garden: 'Yesterday I violated my vow and I am a happy man. For the first time I have entirely understood my own play, and because of you'.   [*Lockspeiser, I: 202*]

Meanwhile the date of the first performance was twice postponed, but eventually, almost seven years after its first completion, the première of *Pelléas et Mélisande* was fixed for 30 April, 1902. The public dress rehearsal took place two days earlier.

Dress rehearsals in Paris were given before an invited audience of musicians and artists of established reputation, senior government officials and others who had a customary right to be present. It was not the ideal audience for such a controversial piece, and to make matters worse a parody programme book, ridiculing Debussy's intentions (and widely believed at the time to have been inspired by Maeterlinck himself), was on sale at the entrance; from the outset the audience was predisposed to mirth.

Messager   The first act, none the less, unfolded in an atmosphere of relative calm; the house was uneasy, manifestly hostile, but at least remained silent. It was at the second scene of Act 2 that the trouble really started.   [*Messager, 1926: 112*]

Mary Garden   Something frightful happened. People began to laugh. In moments of the greatest seriousness someone would scream hysterically. We hadn't the faintest idea what was going on, and we were all suddenly paralysed on the stage. Here was a drama of pure poetry and tragedy, and people were giggling and chuckling as if they were at the Folies Bergère.   [*Garden: 70–1*]

For an audience in such a mood, the traces of Aberdeen in Mary Garden's French accent were a gift, and her despairing cry of 'Oh! Oh! je ne suis pas heureuse!' set them off.

Messager   At Mélisande's cry . . . all those who had only been waiting for an opportunity to express their hostility pounced on the words to voice their dislike of the music, and [successive phrases] drew 'Oh! oh!'s of indignation and loud bursts of laughter.
                                                        [*Messager, 1926: 112*]

'Je n'ai pas de courage' was another target (particularly since 'curage', as Mary Garden pronounced it, means 'cleaning the drains'), and Yniold's constant repetitions of 'petit père' in the spying scene with Golaud were greeted with ever-greater merriment. Debussy took refuge in Carré's office, smoking cigarette after cigarette, and left his friends and colleagues to make what headway they could against the tide of enmity.

Messager   Feeling ran high in the foyers too, during the intervals. There the musicians, almost to a man, gave vent to lamentation: 'Where on earth will such tendencies lead us? This is the end of everything!' In spite of the efforts of a handful of supporters, opinion was virtually unanimous that a work of this kind could not possibly succeed.

Fortunately the singers on the stage, though severely shaken, kept their heads; so did the orchestra and all the other participants on this tempestuous occasion. In the end the perfection of the performance and the emotions engendered by the closing scenes of the opera impressed themselves even on the most vindictive members of the audience, and the performance closed at least in silence.   [*Id*: *112–3*]

Nevertheless the dress rehearsal brought other problems. The inexperience of the boy who had been chosen to sing the part of Yniold persuaded Carré to cut the scene with the sheep in Act IV as a precaution against further hilarity, and the Under-Secretary for Fine Arts was so shocked by references to the bed at the end of Act III that he wanted the whole of the last scene suppressed. This Debussy 'refused outright', though in return he had to agree to the removal of Golaud's anguished cry '*Et le lit? Sont ils près du lit?*'—an absurd and damaging cut that was ridiculously perpetuated in the published score.

The première itself, before a more conventional audience, passed off without major disruptions, though critical opinion was fiercely divided between those who understood what Debussy was doing and appreciated it, those who tried to understand but had reservations, and those who could only see Debussy's 'utter contempt for all the principles transmitted by the great masters of music'. There were a good many of the latter, among them the director of the Conservatoire, Théodore Dubois, who banned his students from attending performances—not that this appears to have made much difference.

Messager   It was certainly not a triumph, but no longer the disaster of two days earlier. . . . From the second performance onwards the audience remained calm and above all curious to hear this work that everybody was talking about. . . . The little group of admirers, Conservatoire pupils and students for the most part, grew day by day.
[*Id*: *113*]

But after only three performances Messager, who had stood by Debussy so staunchly throughout rehearsals, was obliged to relinquish the baton and leave for London, where he had been appointed director of the Royal Opera House in the previous year. Büsser, who succeeded him, showed little of Messager's sensitivity in his handling of the score, yet the public response grew rapidly warmer; the opera ran for fourteen performances—and all except two of them made a profit. Debussy wrote to Messager in London:

Debussy   They're actually turning people away—explain that if you can! . . . I forgot to tell you that we made 7,400 francs last Friday. And you can't imagine how I have risen in everyone's estimation! To have written *Pelléas*, that was just an interesting footnote, but to be making money—that's quite another matter.   [*Messager, 1938: 19, 21–2*]

As the opera became more and more widely accepted in the years that followed, Debussy was unable to leave his score alone, making every new production a pretext for revisiting the instrumentation and even details of the music. But he never again wrote anything like *Pelléas*—even *La chute de la maison Usher,* though he struggled with it for years, eluded him to the end. He had chanced to stumble, as a young man, on the perfect opportunity to realise a very specific and personal dream: substituting for the roar of romantic passion the intimate and sensuous voice of understatement, he created a world in which the intensity of love and agony, and the extremes of violence they can lead to, are distilled with devastating clarity and musical economy. Some, like Benoît, felt that he went too far—and some think so still. But 'nobody dares enough in music,' he said, and it is hard to think of any of his contemporaries, and few successors, who dared so much. Perhaps the composer with whom *Pelléas* has most in common is Monteverdi who, two and a half centuries earlier, had rejected the polyphonic complexities of the late Renaissance to present drama in its barest form—much as Debussy sieved the polyphonic richness of Richard Wagner in his search for 'the naked flesh of truth'.   [*Lesure, 1993: 105*]

Debussy   It is important to emphasise the simplicity in *Pelléas*—I spent [many] years removing anything *parasitic* that might have slid into it—I never at any time tried to use it to revolutionise anything whatever. . . . I have attempted to show that when people sing they can still be human and natural, without ever needing to look like idiots or automatons! . . .

I wanted for music that freedom of which she is perhaps more capable than any of the other arts. . . . I don't pretend to have discovered everything in *Pelléas*, but I have tried to beat a path that others can follow, and broaden it with discoveries of my own which will perhaps free dramatic music from the heavy yoke under which it has existed for so long.   [*Nichols & Smith: 185; Debussy: 62, 64*]

Richard Strauss (right) and Hugo von Hofmannsthal at one
of their rare meetings

Ariadne auf Naxos

Quite casually, in a letter from Hugo von Hofmannsthal to Richard Strauss about a totally different operatic project, squeezed between brackets into a subsidiary clause, comes the first mention of *Ariadne* . . .

Hofmannsthal . . . a thirty minute opera for small chamber orchestra which is as good as complete in my head; it is called *Ariadne auf Naxos* and is made up of a combination of heroic mythological figures in eighteenth century costume with hooped skirts and ostrich feathers and, interwoven in it, characters from the *commedia dell' arte*; harlequins and scaramouches representing the buffo element which is throughout interwoven with the heroic. . . .

[*Correspondence: 75–6*]

. . . and so back to more weighty plans in a characteristically endless sentence which reads as if he didn't want to hold up the flow of his imagination over so slight a matter. *Ariadne* was thus conceived, in the spring of 1911, as a kind of stopgap until the big work which Hofmannsthal was beginning to formulate should be ready for the composer.

For big works were undoubtedly what Strauss wanted. In November 1903, when he saw Hofmannsthal's adaptation of Sophocles' *Elektra* produced in Berlin by the talented young theatre director Max Reinhardt, he had been so deeply impressed that a couple of years later he returned to the play and made of it the most violent and radical music drama that he was ever to write. In the process he came to recognise in this distinguished poet and dramatist many of the qualities that he needed in a librettist. But what he clearly hoped for was more in the same vein: 'Have you got an entertaining Renaissance subject for me?' he wrote in one of his first letters to Hofmannsthal; 'A really wild Cesare Borgia or Savonarola would be the answer to my prayers!'

What Hofmannsthal gave him was *Der Rosenkavalier*—a big work, and a highly successful one, but no *Elektra*. Indeed, it made a curiously ambivalent start for a partnership that was to produce another four major operas over a period of eighteen years. But the two collaborators were men of widely differing character: one subtle, sophisticated, critical, acutely conscious of his position as a poet and the responsibilities that he felt went with it, a distinct touch of the prig; the other bluff, impulsive, a fluent and prolific creator with a strong theatrical sense but little time for the niceties of literary style or philosophical content. They rarely met, and their long correspondence is a fascinating mixture of respect and near misunderstanding, sometimes digging deep into emotional territory, yet retaining to the end a formality of address that preserved a safe personal distance between two conflicting personalities.

The work that Hofmannsthal was ruminating in the aftermath of *Rosenkavalier* was eventually to result in the biggest opera that Strauss ever wrote, and the toughest test of their entire relationship. But the libretto of *Die Frau ohne Schatten* was a long time in gestation, and Strauss, who hated being without work, was getting restive. Hence the idea of *Ariadne*. But how was such a slight entertainment to fill an evening in the opera house? For some time Hofmannsthal had been toying with the possibility of 'a little Molière piece', something perhaps for Reinhardt (whose production of *Rosenkavalier* had won golden opinions) to work his magic on; it was an idea which had always intrigued Strauss but had never actually taken shape, and now, after a meeting with the impatient composer, Hofmannsthal took it up again.

Hofmannsthal   15 May 1911. My dear Dr Strauss . . . I have the Molière. I had never thought of anything except his less well-known plays, but in Paris suddenly it came to me how splendidly *Le Bourgeois Gentilhomme* would lend itself to the insertion of our operatic *divertissement*. There are five acts, which I shall easily concentrate into two. I shall leave out the Turkish ceremony (being in *lingua franca* it is untranslatable and no German audience can enjoy the fun which the French get out of this barbaric pidgin-French), and, together with the Turkish ceremony, there will disappear as a matter of course the whole subsidiary plot and the figures of the daughter, Cleante,

Covielle—more than one third of the whole comedy. The divertissement *Ariadne auf Naxos* itself is to be performed after the dinner,
in the presence of Jourdain, the Count and the dubious Marquise,
and will be punctuated now and then by brief remarks from these
spectators. It concludes the whole work. . . . The short dances in the
play will be preserved (not all of them, but certainly the tailors' dance
and the brief scene of the musicians). During the dinner I should like
instrumental music: no singing, since the opera is just about to begin.

I suggest you get hold of the old Bierling translation at once. . . .
Perhaps this will give you some ideas for the dinner music, and for
the small ballets which must be very brief. . . . I dislike writing into
the blue, so please let me have a line on a postcard as soon as this
letter reaches you. I shall then send you the *Ariadne* sketch at once.
The full libretto . . . I can promise you (in so far as one can promise
anything at all) for the beginning of July, perhaps even the end of
June. That will give you work for July/August.   [*Id:* 79–80]

The idea was an unusual one—a straight performance of the Molière
play with incidental music, concluding with a little Hofmannsthal opera;
'it can, I believe, turn into something most charming', he wrote, 'a new
genre which to all appearances reaches back to a much earlier one . . .'—
and Strauss found it immediately attractive.   [*Id:* 76]

Strauss 20 May 1911. Dear Poet—Have read *Gentilhomme*: the first
half is very nice, especially the first scene: Composer and Dancing
Master—perhaps you will accentuate it a little with topical points.
One might cock a pretty snook here at the critics. The second half
is thin, and in my opinion you would have to add a good deal here to
round off the action more and to point it towards a climax. It seems
to me that the piece lacks a proper denouement. . . .

For the dances of the Dancing Master, tailors and scullions one
could write some pleasant salon music. I shall enjoy the thing very
much and I am sure that I can bring off something striking.

[*Id:* 80–81]

Hofmannsthal Here, for your information, is the rough sketch of the
two-act adaptation, without any cuts as yet. The play, as you quite
rightly say, possesses no real point and this is exactly what serves our

purpose—the insertion of our divertissement—so well. One could hardly tack an opera on to a play which culminates in an effective and pointed curtain. I have already discussed the conclusion with Reinhardt, and the whole thing will be excellently filled out on the stage, with a lot of amusing ceremonial and so on.   [*Id: 81*]

Having nothing else to do, Strauss rushed headlong into the composition of the incidental music for the play, without waiting for details of the opera which was to follow it. This he anyhow still regarded as a twenty-minute piece that could be polished off in six weeks—and Hofmannsthal, too, appears not to have taken it over-seriously at first.

Hofmannsthal   Dear Doctor Strauss—please read through the enclosed [scenario for the opera] and tell me how it appeals to you. This is how I imagine it: not as a slavish imitation, but as a spirited paraphrase of the old heroic style, interspersed with buffo ingredients. I imagine the character of Ariadne gently outlined but altogether *real,* as real as the Marschallin. There is ample opportunity here for set numbers: duets, trios, quintets, sextets. It would be good if you were to indicate to me points where you mean to place definite *numbers,* and where you intend merely to suggest them as you did repeatedly in *Rosenkavalier.* This slight scaffolding for your music will have served its purpose if it gives you the opportunity to express yourself on a deliberately reduced scale, half playfully and yet *from the heart.*   [*Id: 80*]

Strauss   *Ariadne* may turn out very pretty. However, as the dramatic framework is rather thin everything will depend on the poetic execution. But with you one doesn't have to worry about flowing verse. So get your Pegasus saddled.   [*Id: 81*]

Hofmannsthal   You call the scenario a little thin—that is quite true. Perhaps a still better way of putting it would be: a little rectilinear, possibly a little too rectilinear. There is no turning, no proper dramatic twist. When I think of heroic opera, whose spirit we mean to invoke, when I think of Gluck, of *Titus,* or *Idomeneo* this kind of thin, rectilinear quality does not seem to me a fault. Besides, the intermingling with the other, the buffo element, possesses great attractions and disposes of monotony. . . .   [*Id: 84*]

I am marshalling all my strength for this slight but by no means easy piece of work. I am thinking of nothing else and have abandoned all correspondence even, so rest assured I am doing what I can. . . . We do, after all, mean to make something really good of whatever we undertake, don't we, even if it is only an interim work—this duty we owe above all *to ourselves*.   [*Id:* 88, 84]

Strauss How is the transition effected from play to opera: change of scene on the open stage? Or does the curtain fall? Can an overture of some length be played before the opera? Or would it be better to have just a few introductory bars . . . ?   [*Id:* 89]

Hofmannsthal The transition to the actual opera takes place on the open stage. I shall lead up to it by a short scene in prose in which Dancing Master and Composer . . . talk about the public, critics, etc. During this conversation the stage is being set for the opera. . . . The lights are being lit, the musicians are tuning their instruments, Jourdain and his guests appear and take their seats in the fauteuils—and at this point, I must say, a little overture seems to me stylistically indispensable; a little symphony of the old kind would, I feel, be charming.   [*Id:* 90]

As soon as he received the draft libretto from Hofmannsthal, Strauss jotted down on it a number of musical notes: they are brief—a single chord beside Ariadne's opening words; the same chord expanded to a two bar phrase against Harlequin's 'Wie jung und schön' (with the notes C sharp, G, F, and B flat written over the words); a series of keys and time changes for Ariadne's first two arias. For Zerbinetta's great scene he indicates keys, mood and places for coloratura, writes out three bars of chromatic harmony at 'Eine kurze Nacht, ein hastiger Tag', and notes the exact vocal phrase for 'Prinzessin, hören Sie mich an'.

But Strauss's annotations are as nothing compared to the torrent of musical suggestions and advice with which Hofmannsthal annotated the margins of his text. On the very first page, for example, at the end of the trio for Naiade, Dryade and Echo, Strauss found himself confronted with:

Hofmannsthal The last three lines to be repeated ad lib—an elusive, continuously flowing vocal line, expressing the smiling indifference

of nature towards human suffering. Something of the fluttering of
leaves and the undulating of waves already suggested in the overture.

[*Libretto*]

Ariadne's 'Ach!' is 'half-way between an outcry and a sigh', Echo's response
'identical but soulless'. The opening phrase of Ariadne's first aria, 'Ein
Schönes war, hiess Theseus-Ariadne', is to be . . .

Hofmannsthal   . . . a glowing, beautiful singing phrase, with the second line perhaps repeated once, or even twice—such repetitions
are enchanting, and in fact one often repeats one's thoughts in this
way. . . . [Then] A new thought goes through her poor disordered
head . . . a sudden, nervous idea which the music can practically
ignore and treat in purely melodramatic terms. . . . [And in the last
section] Now she has the thread again, now the rest flows along in a
visionary state, tenderly, like a song.   [*Id*]

There are stage descriptions for the harlequinade, and the beginning
of Zerbinetta's big solo has a rather self-conscious note:

Hofmannsthal   Recitative and Aria (Cavatina and Rondeau). The words
for the recitative are deliberately written in a pompous, somewhat
theatrical style, completely different from the soulful, natural tone of
Ariadne.   [*Id*]

The two sections of the aria are specifically marked 'Andante' and
'Allegro', and there is a *cri de coeur* at the beginning of the rondeau:
'Please, in setting the text, don't overlook the little variants'. And another
cri, even more significant, follows when the aria ends and Harlekin takes
over the dialogue: 'Prose melodrama, with very light accompanying
chords'.

This sort of musical prompting from a librettist is very rare, if not
unique in operatic history. But the whole scheme, with its subtle mixture
of styles, its delicately balanced artificiality and what Hofmannsthal at
any rate saw as profound symbolical undertones, was one very much after
his heart, and Hofmannsthal, who never for a moment forgot his role as
the cultural arbiter of the collaboration, was clearly worried that Strauss
might not appreciate the finer points of his text. Nor was he entirely

wrong: to the composer of *Salome, Elektra,* and *Der Rosenkavalier* all this was new territory, and in the early stages Strauss's attitude remained tepid.

Strauss   If, after Reinhardt, . . . [other] playhouses are to take up the piece with any success or profit there must be some star singing parts in it, for the plot as such holds no interest and interesting costumes won't turn the scale either. Personally, I am not particularly excited by the whole thing myself: that was why I asked you to spur your Pegasus a bit, so that the ring of the verses should stimulate me a little. You probably know my predilection for hymns in Schiller's manner and flourishes à la Rückert. Things like that excite me to formal orgies, and these must do the trick where the action itself leaves me cold. Soaring oratory can drug me sufficiently to keep on writing music through a passage of no interest. The interplay of forms: the formal garden must come into its own here.   [*Correspondence: 85*]

Hofmannsthal   28 May 1911. My dear Doctor. We have always understood each other well, but on this occasion I feel we are in the best way not to understand one another. . . . During the past few days (before your letter arrived, the effect of which would have been to put me off rather than to encourage me) I have got through the hardest and most attractive part of the work; namely, to settle the psychological motives of the action, to establish, in my own mind, the relations between the various characters and between the different parts of the whole thing—in short, to sketch a detailed outline of the underlying motives which the poet must have before him (rather as you must have to picture a symphony) if he is to be attracted, roused and held by the work. The essence lies in this tracery of ideas, and all the rest (what you so strikingly call the formal garden) is mere trimming, just as in *Rosenkavalier* the period flavour, the ceremonial, dialect and so on lie merely at the fringe of the essential meaning. . . .

But if my libretto does not attract you in this way, then by all means leave it alone; there will be no hard feelings. . . . I am flattered that you should promise yourself so much from my poetic diction, but we must not expect too much from the diction *alone*. A framework which failed to satisfy your imagination, if it were to fail in that, could never be made to appeal to you, and to inspire you, by diction only. . . . What matters is the central idea of the piece, and though two men like us who know their job should not despise the flourishes, they can never be a substitute for the main thing.

[*Id*: 85–6, 84, 86–7]

Even when, by the middle of July, Strauss had the finished libretto of the opera complete before him, he was not exactly enthusiastic.

Strauss   The whole of *Ariadne* is now safely in my hands and I like it well enough: I think there'll be some good use for everything. Only I should have preferred the dialogue between Ariadne and Bacchus to be rather more significant, with livelier emotional *crescendo*. This bit must soar higher, like the end of *Elektra*, sunnier, more Dionysian: harness your Pegasus for a little longer. . . . I need something more soaring: 'Freude schöner Götterfunke'.   [*Id*: 92]

Hofmannsthal   My dear Doctor Strauss, I must confess I was somewhat piqued by your scant and cool reception of the finished manuscript, compared with the warm welcome you gave to every single act of *Rosenkavalier*—which stands out in my memory as one of the most significant pleasures connected with that work. I believe that in *Ariadne* I have produced something at least equally good, equally original and novel, and . . . I cannot help asking myself whether any praise in all the world could make up to me for the absence of yours.

You may, of course, have written your letter or read the manuscript when you were somewhat out of sorts, as happens so easily to creative artists, and so I am not without hope that closer acquaintance with my libretto will bring home to you its positive qualities. . . .

Let me try and explain in a few sentences the underlying idea or meaning of this little poetic work. What it is about is one of the straightforward and stupendous problems of life: fidelity; whether to hold fast to that which is lost, to cling to it even unto death—or to live, to live on, to get over it, to transform oneself, to sacrifice the integrity of the soul and yet in this transmutation to preserve one's essence, to remain a human being and not to sink to the level of the beast, which is without recollection. . . . We have the group of heroes, demi-gods, gods—Ariadne, Bacchus (Theseus)—facing the human, the merely human group consisting of the frivolous Zerbinetta and her companions, all of them base figures in life's masquerade. Zerbinetta is in her element drifting out of the arms of one man into the arms of another; Ariadne could be the wife or mistress of one man only, just as she can be only *one* man's widow, can be forsaken only by *one* man. One thing, however, is still left even for her: the miracle, the God. To him she gives herself, for she believes him to be Death: he is both Death and Life at once; he it is who reveals to her the immeasurable depths in her own nature, who makes of her an enchantress, the sorceress who herself transforms the poor little Ariadne; he it is who conjures up for her in this world another world beyond, who preserves her for us and at the same time transforms her.

But what to divine souls is a real miracle, is to the earth-bound nature of Zerbinetta just an everyday love-affair. She sees in Ariadne's experience the only thing she *can* see: the exchange of an old lover for a new one. And so these two spiritual worlds are in the end ironically brought together in the only way in which they can be brought together: in non-comprehension. . . .

It would be a very great joy to me if, by an early reply to this personal, friendly letter, you were to restore to me that sense of fine and intimate contact between us which I so much enjoyed during our earlier collaboration, and which has by now become indispensable to me.   [*Id*: 93–5]

Strauss   19 July 1911. Dear Herr von Hofmannsthal. I am sincerely sorry that in my dry way I failed to pay you the tribute you had hoped for and which your work certainly deserves. But I confess frankly that my first impression was one of disappointment. Perhaps I had expected too much. . . . The piece did not fully convince me until after I had read your letter, which is so beautiful and explains the meaning of the action so wonderfully that a superficial musician like myself could not, of course, have tumbled to it. But isn't this a little dangerous? And isn't some of the interpretation still lacking in the action itself?

. . . An author reads into his play things which the sober spectator doesn't see, and the fact that even I, the most willing of readers, have failed to grasp such important points must surely give you pause. . . . Surely, the symbolism must leap out alive from the action, instead of being dug out of it by subsequent laborious interpretation? Besides,

I'm only human: I may be wrong, and am indeed out of sorts; I've been here alone without another soul for the past four weeks, I haven't touched a cigarette for a month—let the devil be cheerful in such circumstances! Be patient therefore: maybe my incomprehension will spur you on after all—and don't take it as anything else. After all we want to bring out the very best in each other. [*Id:* 95–6]

Hofmannsthal   23 July 1911. Nothing you might have said could have appealed to me more than that we must try to bring out the very best in each other. . . .

To your kind letter, let me first of all reply this: there exists a certain productivity not only of creation, but also of reception. One day I may take up my Goethe or Shakespeare and find that they produce in my imagination a heightened response; another day the essence may be missing, the contact between mind and mind. . . . Now in so delicate a matter as the production of a poetic text intended for music I must be able to count on this kind of productive receptivity on your part. During the past few weeks you have lacked it. . . . I knew of it, or felt it, when I sent you the *Ariadne* sheets. . . .

For God's sake please work little or not at all while you feel run down. It would be too absurd for me to write something expressly for you, just because you are in the unhappy position of having nothing to do, and you were then to make yourself ill over the work. What does it matter when this thing gets done? . . .

Let me say something about the point which agitates you at the moment, about your own original non-understanding, about the probable incomprehension of the public, the certain incomprehension of the critics. The pure poetic content of a work of art, the real meaning it contains is never understood at first. What is understood is only that which needs no understanding, the obvious, plain anecdote: *Tosca, Madam Butterfly* and such like. Anything more subtle, anything that really matters, remains unrecognised, *invariably*. . . . Understanding emanates from a very few people who are in close touch with the world of poetry, and it takes decades to spread.

But it is equally true that the poet's text must possess another attraction, through which it can reach even the non-comprehending majority. . . . In the case of *Ariadne,* the attractive style of this supporting opera, the bizarre mixture of heroic with buffo elements, the gracefully rhymed verses, the set numbers, the playful, puppet-show look of the whole piece, all this gives the audience for the time being something to grab and suck like a child. . . . As for the symbolic aspect, the juxtaposition of the woman who loves only once and the woman who gives herself to many, this is placed so very much in the centre of the action, and is treated as so simple and so clear-cut an antithesis—heightened perhaps still further by an equally clear cut musical contrast—that we may hope at least to avoid utter incomprehension by the audience.   [*Id:* 97–98]

It was the formal aspect of the opera that had first attracted Strauss's interest—in particular the stylistic possibilities of the more obviously separable 'numbers' in Hofmannsthal's libretto.

Strauss   The form of coloratura variations sprang to my mind unwittingly as I read your draft of Zerbinetta's first aria. . . . Great coloratura aria: *andante* then rondo—theme with variations and all coloratura tricks (if possible with flute *obbligato*) when she speaks of her unfaithful lover (*andante*)—and then tries to console Ariadne . . . A *pièce de résistance.*   [*Id:* 87, 82]

Hofmannsthal later paid tribute to the success with which Strauss handled the music for the harlequinaders—though he never for a moment allowed his own credentials to be in doubt.

Hofmannsthal   In every task before us the final criterion can only be sensitivity in the matter of style, and of this I must consider myself guardian and keeper for the two of us. . . . The conception of *Ariadne* actually made it necessary for you to put *some* of your music into period costume, to treat it as a quotation, and you solved this with wonderful tact.   [*Id:* 150, 149]

In an interview Strauss himself commented:

Strauss   *Ariadne* is the trickiest of my works, and though I need an orchestra of only thirty-five players all told they must be of the very best because there are no *ripieno* [i.e. full orchestra] players—at least in the strings. Each player has his own part. So in this score the orchestra becomes practically chamber music. . . . It was also clear that music would be needed earlier, at various points in the Molière comedy, so I have written a little overture to each act of the play, and also a number of songs, a serenade, a pastoral duet and an extensive *scène de ballet*. The opera itself, on which I worked for a full year, ended up longer than had been intended. Originally it was calculated to run for twenty minutes, but as it turned out a whole hour was added and the work is now exactly the same length as my *Salome*.

[*Karpath*]

Strauss's natural tendency to musical expansion brought with it other problems too; in his *Recollections* he remembered the difficulties he had experienced in relating this world of stylised charm with the romantic, idealistic heroism of Bacchus and Ariadne.

Strauss   [The composition of] the opera, went very well up to the appearance of Bacchus, when I began to fear that the small 'chamber orchestra' would be inadequate for my dionysiac urges. I informed Hofmannsthal of my fears and asked him whether I could not here change over to 'full' orchestra, if necessary behind the stage. Admittedly, a stupid idea. Hofmannsthal implored me to give it up.

[*Strauss, 1953: 161–2*]

Hofmannsthal   This lyric tenor will have to be interpreted in the most delicate manner, almost boyish. This Bacchus is but lately fledged, and is shy. . . . Innocent, young and unaware of his own divinity he travels where the wind takes him, from island to island. His first affair was typical, with a woman of easy virtue you may say, or you may call her Circe. To his youth and innocence with its infinite potentialities the shock has been tremendous: were he Harlekin, this would be merely the beginning of one long round of love affairs. But he is Bacchus; confronted with the enormity of erotic experi- ence all is laid bare to him in a flash—the assimilation with the animal, the transformation, his own divinity. So he escapes from Circe's embraces still unchanged, but not without a wound, a long- ing, not without knowledge. The impact on him now of this meeting with a being whom he can love, who is mistaken about him but is enabled by this very mistake to give herself to him, . . . who entrusts

herself to him completely, exactly as one entrusts oneself to Death—
this impact I need not expound further to an artist such as you. . . .

[*Correspondence: 87, 95*]

All the same, in the draft libretto he had felt it necessary to include
a warning note against Bacchus's first entry:

Hofmannsthal   The musician will not fail to appreciate the sensitive
mood of this song, the mysterious, almost frightening effect of the
first sexual adventure on his young soul. . . . [And later] . . . Diffi-
dently, in deep confusion after the adventure with Circe.   [*Libretto*]

As he wrote elsewhere:

Hofmannsthal   Up to [the Bacchus scene] the acting, the stage upon
the stage, the hooped skirts, the wax candles . . . are a chief ingredient. As soon as Bacchus appears we are at once in the regions of great
poetry, of sublime music. . . . Nothing must remain of the play within
the play; Jourdain, his guests, his lackeys, his house, all this must be
forgotten and the spectator remember it as little as the sleeper in a
deep dream knows of his bed. The small stage expands into the infinite; night, and the twinkling of the stars, must be round Bacchus
and Ariadne. . . .   [*Correspondence: 116; Script*]

22 October 1911. Dear Doctor Strauss. After all those letters we
exchanged in July, we both laid off for a while: what a pleasant surprise it was, therefore, suddenly to come across the most unexpected
news in the *Münchner Neueste Nachrichten* that you have actually
finished! But surely not the scoring yet? This presumably means that
I must make haste over the gay short transition scene?

[*Correspondence: 103*]

The spoken transition scene between the play and the opera had
always been an essential component of Hofmannsthal's plan.

Hofmannsthal   I have another vehicle to bring home to people the
central idea of the opera; I mean the prose scene which is to pre-
cede it. . . . Composer and Dancing Master are on the stage. The
Composer, we are told, is to conduct a short heroic opera: *Ariadne*

auf Naxos. . . . After the opera, a light-hearted afterpiece is planned for the Italian Comedians. That is how the programme reads. And now Jourdain suddenly sends his footman with the message that he wishes the two pieces to be performed *simultaneously*, that he has no desire to see Ariadne on a deserted island; the island is on the contrary to be peopled by the Italian players who are to entertain Ariadne with their capers. In short Jourdain asks them to arrange one show out of the two operas. Consternation. The Composer is furious, the Dancing Master tries to soothe him. Finally they summon the clever soubrette (Zerbinetta); they tell her the plot of the heroic opera, explain to her the character of Ariadne, and set her the task of working herself and her companions as best she may into this opera as an intermezzo, without causing undue disturbance. Zerbinetta at once grasps the salient point: to her way of thinking a character like Ariadne must be either a hypocrite or a fool, and she promises to intervene in the action to the best of her ability, but with discretion. This offers us the opportunity of stating quite plainly, under cover of a joke, the symbolic meaning of the antithesis between the two women. Does this appeal to you?   [*Id:* 99]

Strauss   In your letter you moot the brilliant idea of preparing the ground for *Ariadne* by a big scene which would explain and motivate the whole action. That's excellent. . . . The Composer and the Dancing Master are anyway two Molière figures which could be enormously expanded. . . . Give your sense of humour its head, drop in a few malicious remarks about the 'composer'—that sort of thing always amuses the audience and every piece of self-persiflage rakes the wind out of the critics' sails. . . . Zerbinetta might have an affair with the Composer, so long as he is not too close a portrait of me.
                                                        [*Id:* 100–1]

Anything less like Richard Strauss than the Composer, as Hofmannsthal eventually portrayed him, would be hard to imagine. For the time being, however, the transition scene offered Hofmannsthal the opportunity to fill out this character, whom he at first regarded as 'smug and bourgeois as Molière made him', and to tighten up the tenuous and risky connection between the two disparate parts of the entertainment.

Strauss meanwhile, now that he was more or less done with the composition of the opera proper, took up again the incidental music for the play—which, as he said, 'like almost everything I dashed off, as it were, "with my left hand", turned out a great success'. Though it has no part (except for a few thematic references) in the later, purely operatic version of *Ariadne*, Strauss's affection for this music was such that Hofmannsthal subsequently created a separate function for it in a new adaptation of the Molière play (minus the opera)—from which comes the *Bourgeois Gentilhomme* Suite that is familiar to concert audiences today. For the time being, however, these brilliant and apt little pieces were very much a part of the Molière-Hofmannsthal-Strauss synthesis that made up the original *Ariadne*.

The conditions under which this complex project would eventually be put on the stage had preoccupied Hofmannsthal from the start, and now sudden last-minute attempts by Strauss to find a suitable theatre for the première were to cause his librettist much anguish—particularly when the crucial participation of Max Reinhardt seemed to be endangered.

Hofmannsthal   As you know I am not obstreperous, but wild horses will not get me to carry out this adaptation of Molière and the intro-ductory scene, unless Reinhardt is to produce it. . . . A world pre-mière at some Court theatre or other would mean a complete flop, or a dreary *succès d'estime*; with Reinhardt it can and will be a brilliant first night. . . . This 'opera', with its subtle stylistic make-up, . . . framed as it is by the Molière piece, . . . is one of my most personal works, and one I cherish most highly. It is conceived as a whole com-posed of several parts and can only exist, or come into being, where a theatrical genius of a superior order knows how to weld the parts together. . . .

The 'little bit of Molière' is just as difficult as Mozart. . . . [It] fills three-fifths of the whole evening, and on it I am risking my skin—since this dovetailing of the two works which I have devised will prove an amusing conceit only if the overall intention comes out; otherwise it is rubbish.   [*Id: 105–7, 112*]

Perhaps since you live, move and have your being more in the musical than the visual side of *Ariadne* you do not yet quite realise the difficulties and secrets which—not to speak of the evening's entertainment as a whole—are involved even in *Ariadne* alone, points where only a producer of genius can bring to life what we have

created. . . . It will be lost, meaningless, a tattered rag in incompe-
tent hands. . . . *Love* is what it needs, enthusiasm, improvisation; it
needs a theatre conscious of its ability to achieve something which
is today altogether out of the ordinary; it needs a real man at the
conductor's desk whose heart and soul is in it—not that appalling
atmosphere of the commonplace, the drab routine, the conductor
with the cold heart, the opera singers who get through their music
somehow. Everyone concerned must stake his life, the impossible
must become possible. . . .

I know exactly what I have in mind, but only Reinhardt can make
it reality.   [*Id: 116, 109–10, 116*]

Strauss   Of course Reinhardt must be in with us . . . I have written
off to Stuttgart and offered them the world première, provided they
agree to the cast chosen by yourself, Reinhardt and me. Reinhardt
as the producer, any stage designer of your choice, etc., in fact everything the heart desires. I have today received the enclosed reply, . . .
[and] I believe we couldn't ask for anything better. . . . The piece will
have been staged twice in an exemplary production and that's the
main thing.   [*Id: 113, 115*]

Strauss, who himself conducted at Stuttgart, began rehearsing the
orchestra as long as four months before the première. He called his score
'a real masterpiece of a score', and wrote to his wife in the highest spirits.

Strauss   Everything splendid. Here my wish is a command: no bow-
ing and scraping, no battling with nincompoops to put across my
simplest artistic ideas. . . . The music sounds magnificent, and
more beautiful than anything I have ever done. . . . [And later] The
work, I'm certain, will make an *enormous impression*. The Molière
is indescribably funny, and hugely effective on the stage. I laughed
till I cried. You can come without any anxiety: you'll be delighted.
                                                   [*Strauss, 1912*]

But it didn't live up to his expectations, even though Reinhardt
(whose prompt book is still in existence) clearly approached his task with
immense care. Of the première, on 25 October 1912, Strauss wrote in his
Recollections:

Strauss Two things had been left out of account. Firstly, that the audience was looking forward to the Strauss opera so much that it did not show sufficient interest in the splendid Molière, played admirably by Reinhardt's actors, . . . and secondly that after the Molière the amiable King Karl of Württemberg, with the best of intentions, held a reception lasting three quarters of an hour which meant that *Ariadne*, which lasts an hour and a half, began about two and a half hours after the beginning of the play—so that the audience was somewhat tired and ill-tempered.   [*Strauss, 1953: 163*]

In fact the music, both then and at the performances immediately following, was enthusiastically received; of the Molière, on the other hand, critics spoke with impatience, indeed disdain; there was talk of yawns. Of Hofmannsthal's transition scene they had heard practically nothing: it was heavily cut, and what Strauss had described as 'inspired' and 'the core of the whole evening's performance' fell victim largely to the good intentions of the King.

Strauss The charming idea—to begin in the most sober of comic prose and proceed, via ballet and *commedia dell'arte*, to the heights of the purest symphonic music . . . had proved a practical failure; frankly, because the play-going public has no wish to listen to opera and vice versa. The proper cultural soil for this pretty hybrid was lacking.
                              [*Id: 161, 163*]

After the first performance, things went from bad to worse. Seven months later Strauss wrote:

Strauss [In Munich] I heard a performance of *Ariadne* the day before yesterday: the opera performed very well, but the comedy so unspeakably lousy you'd hardly credit it. Of all the Molière performances which I have so far seen it was by far the most awful. All parts either entirely miscast or badly cast, with crazy cuts in the text, and without a glimmer of humour.   [*Correspondence: 165*]

Strauss proposed that Hofmannsthal should attempt to mend matters by substantial cuts. But Hofmannsthal was already hatching a far more radical remedy—nothing less than the complete removal of the

Molière comedy and the substitution of an independent, wholly musical, pedestal for *Ariadne*.

Hofmannsthal   What is the use of tinkering, of cutting this scene or that, or patching it up? . . . The only real remedy has been on my desk for the past week. . . . I have rewritten the [transition scene] in the dressing-room with great zest and vigour: the Composer now occupies the very centre of the scene; he is, symbolically, a figure half tragic, half comic; the whole antithesis of the action is now firmly focused on him; everything has been extended and enriched, there are slight, witty occasions for arias. . . . Get down to it at once; set it in secco recitative, put in a few highlights and have it performed from the manuscript in August after three rehearsals—it will be an enchanting surprise for everybody.

   I am satisfied with the whole thing as it has now turned out, . . . all this I believe is poetic and has substance, it can last—whereas that improvised misalliance with the prose comedy cannot persist in the long run and in a way ought not to, because it is too much like a centaur or the Siamese twins. . . . Please take to it kindly.

[*Id: 168–9,170*]

It must have been a difficult decision for Hofmannsthal, after the care and enthusiasm he had put into the original design. His proposal was an honest and thoughtful attempt to preserve the best of his and Strauss's work, yet it was received by the composer with little enthusiasm.

Strauss   Dear Herr von Hofmannsthal. Many thanks for your letters. . . . To be quite frank, the scene just received from you I have so far not found to my liking at all. Indeed, it contains certain things that are downright distasteful to me—the Composer, for instance: to set him actually to music will be rather tedious. . . . Besides, I now cling so obstinately to our original work, and still regard it as so successful in structure and conception, that this new version will always look to me like a torso . . . , no more than a makeshift. I should therefore be grateful if you wouldn't mention this second version in public yet.

[*Id: 171–2*]

So there matters rested for nearly three years. But early in 1916, after composer and librettist had together seen a performance in Berlin, Strauss at last agreed to adopt Hofmannsthal's remedy and drop the Molière comedy. The opera *Ariadne* itself was to remain more or less unchanged, but the new prologue, in contrast to the earlier transition scene, was now to be set to music. Yet, though the play was removed, most of the characters in the Vorspiel were still Molière-inspired, with the Composer, above all, dominating Hofmannsthal's conception.

Hofmannsthal   Everything is intended for secco recitative: only round the figure of the Composer is there a glimmer of something more— music. For this I have provided the following *points d'appui*: first the genesis of the tune ('O, Du Venussohn') from the *Bourgeois*—this twice; then at the end of the conversation with Zerbinetta, rising emotionally to something more than mere *parlando*; perhaps the thing might lead up to a tiny duet or something of the kind. . . . And finally the lyrical climax . . . I mean the Composer's outburst: 'Musik ist heilige Kunst'—a kind of little Prize Song. . . . Here the words ought to inspire you to find a new, beautiful melody, solemn and ebullient.

　　I am satisfied with the figure of the Composer as it now stands, tragic and comic at the same time, like the musician's lot in the world; the two fundamental *Ariadne* motifs, anchored or rooted as they are in the heart of the musician.　　　　　　[*Id: 169–70*]

Strauss's latter-day interpretation of Hofmannsthal's demand for 'secco recitative' may not have been precisely what Hofmannsthal had in mind. The score he eventually wrote is intricate and subtle. But it sets the ideal pace for a scene that is basically conversational, and yet allows room for sentimental expansion and even for the passionate fervour of the Composer's final—and profoundly Straussian—apostrophe to the art of music. His first reactions to the new plan, however, did not meet with approval.

Strauss   The part of the Composer (since tenors are so terrible) I shall give to Mlle Artôt. Only you'll have to consider now how we might further furnish the part for her with, say, a little vocal number; or perhaps you could write an additional pretty little solo scene for the Composer at the end [of the opera]: wistfully poetical—possibly making him burst out in despair after *Ariadne*: 'What have you done to my work', and then the Major-domo could appear and pay the poor devil his salary, or the Count might appear and pay him some compliments, announce the acceptance of the opera by the Imperial Opera House . . . or any other amusing idea that comes to your mind. . . .

Please let me have this soon: because I can only win Mlle Artôt for our piece if I can offer her a kind of small star part.   [*Id: 241*]

Hofmannsthal   For the past two days I have been thinking over, backwards and forwards, your letter with its astonishing proposal for the end, but I have failed to come round to it; on the contrary. I fear your opportunism in theatrical matters has in this case thoroughly led you up the garden path. In the first place the idea of giving the part of the young Composer to a female performer goes altogether against the grain. To prettify this particular character, which is to have an aura of 'spirituality' and 'greatness' about it, and so turn him into a travesty of himself which inevitably smacks of operetta, this strikes me as, forgive my plain speaking, odious. . . . Oh Lord, if only I were able to bring home to you completely the essence, the spiritual meaning of these characters. I am not, on the other hand, quite so opinionated as not to understand what you want to avoid: the frightful tenor! Yes, I can understand that. . . .

And finally, whether man or woman, this idea for the end is truly appalling; if you will forgive me, my dear Dr. Strauss, this letter was not written in one of your happiest moments. Consider the lofty atmosphere which we have striven so hard to create, rising ever higher from the beginning of the Vorspiel . . . , reaching in the [final] duet almost mystical heights. And now, where the essential coda ought to be over in a trice, . . . now some rubbish of this kind is to spread itself once more (the emphasis is on *spread*): the Major-domo, the fee, the Count and God knows what else! And all this merely to make the part an inch longer! . . . Please send me a few words by express, telling me that you understand me; I feel quite faint in mind and body to see us quite so far apart for once!   [*Id: 241–2*]

Poor Strauss, one cannot help feeling sorry for him. But for once he was not to be cowed.

Strauss   Dear Herr von Hofmannsthal,
    Why do you always get so bitterly angry if for once we don't under-

stand each other straight away? You almost act as if I had never understood you! . . . My suggestions concerning the end of *Ariadne* were, as you know, only quite unconsidered suggestions which you could have thrown into your wastepaper basket without another thought: their only purpose was to induce you to consider seriously the closing words of the Composer—and how was I to know that you might not think of something particularly brilliant for the ending if I told you that Artôt was to do it? Well then, you do whatever you like about the ending, only do it soon, please! But as for Artôt—as a young Mozart, say, at the Court of Versailles, or among the Philistines of the Munich Court. . . . I am not going to budge on this point, for artistic as well as for practical reasons. . . . So we stick to Artôt, and it's got to be a delightful part! That's final!   [*Id:* 243]

Two or three weeks later both men had regained their composure. In the body of the opera Strauss made a few modifications; he took the opportunity to shorten Zerbinetta's big aria and simplify some of its more fantastically difficult *coloratura* (a fact which may be greeted with disbelief by singers of the revised version), and he removed entirely an intervention by Zerbinetta at the moment of Bacchus's imminent arrival—a scene by which Hofmannsthal had originally set great store, though he agreed readily enough to its removal when Strauss argued that it held up the action at a crucial point (which it does). Since M. Jourdain and his guests make no personal appearance in the new Vorspiel, their appearance as spectators during the opera itself was cut, but the problem created by their absence in the closing scene continued to make last-minute difficulties. The original ending had allowed Zerbinetta and her companions to make a final appearance that deftly deflated the high romanticism of the Bacchus-Ariadne duet, and permitted M. Jourdain to close the proceedings with a few words that return the listener to the artificial framework which had, after all, been the *raison d'être* of the entire work.

On reflection, the idea of replacing Jourdain with some sort of fleeting reappearance by the Composer seems to have struck Hofmannsthal as not so appalling after all. But the devil was in the detail.

Hofmannsthal   It is quite extraordinarily difficult for me to put into the mouth of the Composer the final words which belong to the very fringe of the framework. Coming from Jourdain, . . . that *Monsieur tout-le-monde* who hasn't an idea of what he has been up to and what he has set afoot, the words were organic. But coming from the Composer! For him to complain where the opera has after all succeeded in forging harmony out of the two components, that would be absurd; for him to rejoice would be more absurd still. There is a risk that this will make nonsense of the whole thing. A curse on all revision!   [*Id*: 245]

In the end, they agreed to drop both M. Jourdain and the Composer altogether, and close the opera with a short but powerful orchestral peroration following directly on the Bacchus-Ariadne duet. Though this provided an effective curtain (which suited Strauss), it also involved the removal of the harlequinade; this Hofmannsthal only accepted after extracting from Strauss an agreement to include a brief 'last word' from Zerbinetta: 'if need be let her only begin to sing, sing the first line—then let the orchestra drown her. . . . I am satisfied with her symbolic, mocking presence and exit'. There is a touch of resignation, but also of relief, in his tone.   [*Id*: 247]

The first performance of the revised *Ariadne* took place in Vienna on 4 October 1916. The reception was satisfactory but not enthusiastic, and remained much the same in subsequent performances. Nevertheless the later version rapidly established itself as the definitive form of the work. There are still those who hanker for performances of the original version, and occasionally get one, but problems of staging and expense militate against it, and for many the new Vorspiel remains, perhaps, the most wholly satisfying work of art that Strauss and Hofmannsthal produced together. So at least Hofmannsthal seems to have thought.

Hofmannsthal   The music for the Vorspiel is as enchanting in recollection as anything could be; like fireworks in a beautiful park, one enchanted, all too fleeting summer night.   [*Id*: 256]

'Looking at the whole thing', he later wrote, 'I still draw lasting pleasure from the thought that I forced upon you so unusual and important a work'. Hofmannsthal was never in doubt about the value of his own role in the partnership, but in this case at least his pleasure in Strauss's music was profound and genuine.

Hofmannsthal   Of all our joint works this is the one I never cease to love best. Here alone you have gone wholly with me and—what is more mysterious—wholly even with yourself. Here for once you freed yourself entirely from all thought of effect; even what is most tender and most personal did not appear too simple, too humble for you here. You have lent your ear to the most intimate inspiration and have given great beauty; of all our works, this is the one which, believe me, *possesses the strongest guarantee that it will endure.*   [*Id:* 299]

Giacomo Puccini in the garden of his villa at Viareggio, 1923

Turandot

'I TOLD YOU, *I want to make people weep*', wrote Puccini to Luigi Illica in the autumn of 1912, 'that's all there is to it. But do you think it is easy?'

Puccini   It is horribly difficult, my dear Illica. . . . Love and grief are as old as the world, and we know well the changing favours of both—especially those of us who have passed the half century. So we have to find a story that grips us with its poetry, its love and its grief, and inspires us to the point where we can make an opera of it. But I repeat to you. . . . I feel shaken in my faith and it begins to desert me!

[*Carteggi*: 404–5]

It was the power to make people weep that had clinched the popular success of Puccini's earlier operas, and it was Illica, the librettist with Giuseppe Giacosa of *Bohème*, *Tosca* and *Madame Butterfly*, who had provided Puccini with material to achieve that end. But the death of Giacosa in 1906 had robbed the collaboration of its guiding spirit and, left to himself, Illica's struggles to provide the composer with another libretto had again and again come to nothing. The list of authors whose works Puccini considered seriously, read hopefully or summarily turned down in the years following *Madame Butterfly* range from Shakespeare to Pierre Louÿs via Hugo, Cellini, Wilde, Balzac, Gorky, Kipling, Mérimée, and Tolstoy; there was an on-and-off attempt to dramatise the last days of Marie Antoinette which occupied the long-suffering Illica for at least five years, and even a projected collaboration with the swashbuckling poet Gabriele d'Annunzio which at one point seemed on the verge of success—'so that from the finest possible verses should blossom forth the most beautiful possible music'—, though after two precious offerings had been rejected out of hand d'Annunzio gave Puccini up in a huff.

D'Annunzio   My contacts with the Maestro from Lucca have been ster-
ile. He is overwhelmed by the power of Poetry. . . . He went so far as
to confess to me that he needs 'a small, light thing, to be put to music
in a few months, between one trip and another'. And for this he came
to the poet of *Francesca da Rimini*!

New paragraph: The disillusionment has been very sad. Not art but commerce. Ah
me!   [*Marek:* 215]

Leaving aside wounded pride, it is true that the Maestro from Lucca
had no great use for beautiful poetry in itself, although he had as good
a nose for the right treatment of a subject as he had for the subject in
the first place. And the problem was compounded by Puccini's mid-life
preoccupation with the development of his musical and dramatic style.
Making people weep was all very well, and still desirable, but at another
level he was no longer satisfied with the emotional limitations of his earlier works. 'I see darkness ahead of me!' he wrote a year after the *prima*
of *Butterfly*, 'shall I ever find anything? . . .'

Puccini   . . . I must! Never before now have I felt time flying by so
quickly, and never before have I been in such a frenzy to get on. But
on, not back! With a work that is modern in construction, and *from
the heart.* . . .   [*Epistolario:* 157]

And two years later:

Puccini   Enough now of *Bohème*, *Butter* and co [*sic*]—even I am
fed up with them!—but I am worried, really worried. . . . All the
world expects this opera from me, and it's certainly high time. . . .
                                                    [*Carteggi:* 340]

When at last it came, the subject was something of a surprise—a
lurid drama of the gold rush in California. With its tough, gun-toting heroine and big choral scenes for the roughneck miners, *La fanciulla del West*
extended the range of Puccini's style and in that sense certainly marked an
advance on Bohème, Butter & co; the tremendous success of the première
in New York (conducted by Toscanini with Caruso in the tenor lead) confirmed the composer's international reputation, and the performances that
followed made him a rich man. But in the end, *Fanciulla* never received
the critical recognition that its power and originality deserved. And Puc-

cini had been left exhausted, not only by the protracted labour on the opera itself, but by the domestic tragedy that interrupted its composition.

In the late summer of 1908 Puccini's wife Elvira, a tempestuous and difficult woman, began to suspect that he was having an affair with Doria Manfredi, a twenty-one-year-old girl from a local family in service with the Puccinis. The girl clearly adored Puccini; the evidence that he treated her with much more than fatherly affection is flimsy, but his reputation as a womaniser was against him and Elvira's inflamed imagination ran riot; she turned upon Doria, sacked her, and spread accusations that were slanderous and totally untrue. She claimed to have caught the two of them *in flagrante*, threatened the poor girl with physical violence, and hounded her with such vitriolic malice that she eventually drove Doria to take her own life. Puccini was devastated. A post-mortem cleared him from Elvira's worst allegations, and the Manfredi family brought a legal action against Elvira, which he settled out of court. After a separation of seven months he and Elvira reached a reconciliation that held their marriage together until the end of Puccini's life, but the affair had left an indelible mark upon him: 'it's a continual torment', he wrote to Sybil Seligman two months later; 'the fate of that poor child was too cruel. . . . I can't get her out of my mind'. And he never did.   [*Seligman: 174*]

If Elvira was all too frequently a negative influence in Puccini's life, Sybil Seligman, the English society hostess with whom, after a brief, preliminary fling, he settled into a close but platonic intimacy, was an indefatigable supporter, providing him with an ever-ready shoulder on which to lean when the world plunged him into one of his recurrent fits of melancholy. She also supplied him with a stream of ideas for possible operatic subjects—though in this she had no more success than anyone else. Thanking her for one such in 1911, he wrote:

Puccini   . . . *tout court* I must tell you that I don't care about it very much. . . . The plot is not an interesting one to put to music—there is no fluttering of the spirit behind the words, that something which evokes music, the divine art which begins, or ought to begin, where the words cease. . . .   [*Id: 206*]

It was this indispensable 'something' which had again and again proved the stumbling block for librettists and would-be librettists. In the far off days of *La Bohème*, Illica had written to Puccini's publisher and protector Giulio Ricordi:

Illica   Puccini has told a friend in confidence that he can do without my librettos . . . and that in any case *nobody* is able to understand him, because he is always dreaming of something . . . something . . . something . . . that . . . !

You will understand that this *something*, communicated in this way, is not easy to pin down. So, faced with this impenetrable darkness, I have to grope around here, there and everywhere in an attempt to identify the something that is the something that Puccini is dreaming of, only to meet in the end with the same [broad Tuscan] 'Don' like it'. . . .

Contrary to what Puccini thinks, I regard a libretto as a collaboration. And for this reason Puccini should explain himself well and clearly, because as it is I don't know where to turn in order to find the thing which is the thing that Puccini calls something but which we still don't know what is.   [*Carteggi:* 78–9]

It is remarkable that Illica remained loyal to Puccini as long as he did; in the two years since *Fanciulla* he had continued doggedly to suggest and work on new projects, but by 1912 their long relationship was at last petering out. Nevertheless more and more subjects poured in, were pored over, and sooner or later rejected—*Lorna Doone, Rip van Winkle, Trilby, Les trois mousquetaires*—and there was even a last attempt to collaborate with d'Annunzio, though it met with no more success than its predecessors.

Puccini   D'Annunzio had given birth to a small, shapeless monstrosity, unable to walk or live! I am as usual in mid-ocean without any hope of ever reaching harbour! I am in despair!   [*Seligman:* 226–7]

In this difficult situation Ricordi, who was now Puccini's regular publisher, felt that some new and perhaps younger blood might be helpful, and drew the composer's attention to a protégé of his, the author and playwright Giuseppe Adami. Adami, who was twenty years younger than Puccini and nervous of meeting him, was summoned to discuss the maestro's latest project for a libretto. Puccini, characteristically, came straight to the point with a question about some small dramatic detail that was preoccupying him.

Adami   The question was fired point blank . . . and my courage left me then and there. I seemed to be undergoing interrogation by some surly, impenetrable examiner, and I would have given my life to guess the right answer and make a good impression. . . . And of course I was wrong. . . . Dear great Puccini, so different from what he seemed to be, that morning long ago, hidden behind a rough, probing, almost brutal manner, cold and diffident to the point of raising a lump in my throat so that I could have wept. . . .

The meeting . . . took place in April 1912, at Ricordi's in Milan, in that audition room graced by the two portraits which Verdi and Boito had presented to the Prince of Publishers on the first night of *Falstaff*. . . . The purpose was twofold: to give Puccini a libretto . . . , and me the chance of working with the Maestro. This was the more difficult task, since there was nothing in my brief and humble past which could inspire the confidence of the creator of *Bohème*, other than the intuitive faith of Giulio Ricordi in my future. . . .

[Nevertheless], after that first meeting, the possibility became almost a certainty. 'Yes', said Ricordi, 'Puccini was very much attracted by the plot. He went off very happy . . . and I hope, I hope very much. But start work. Start work at once. Don't let him cool down . . .'. [*Adami:* 61–6]

Alas, he cooled down—as he had done many times before and was to do again. 'I believe that the opera libretto is an extinct plant on this earth', he wrote to Illica in January 1913.

Puccini I look round and I am convinced. . . . Strauss (like others) found one good subject and then choked on the ones that followed. . . . Debussy? Pelléas—and silence. I could mention others in our own country. . . . My dear Illica, it is really more difficult to find a good subject than to discover the pole—and even that seems to be a disappointment. . . . [*Carteggi:* 408]

As Illica's star waned, Adami gradually became an indispensable assistant, and in the end it was he who enabled Puccini to break this new and painful silence. *La rondine*, intended for Vienna but owing to wartime conditions produced in Monte Carlo in 1917, was a sortie into the field of operetta which Puccini never repeated; it may not be the high point of his output, but it proved Adami's sympathetic qualities as a collaborator, and it was Adami again who provided the libretto which marked the more significant turning point at this stage of Puccini's career, the one-act melodrama *Il tabarro*. When, with the addition of two further one-act operas,

the completed *Trittico* came to performance in December 1918, the evening was stolen by the one comedy among the three, *Gianni Schicchi*,
but in fact each of these short, brilliant pieces marked an unquestionable
advance in the subtlety and control of Puccini's musical style. None of
them, however, could be described as the large-scale work the composer
was dreaming of and this, for lack of a subject, seemed as far off as ever.

Faced with what looked like deadlock, the composer decided to call
in another collaborator, since Adami alone seemed unable to do the trick.
Puccini, as a quintessential Tuscan, was an enthusiastic—not to say
obsessive—*cacciatore*, for ever buying new and larger guns with which to
decimate the population of wild duck that gathered around his home on
the Lake of Massaciuccoli, and in September 1919, hearing that Adami's
friend the distinguished scholar and dramatic critic Renato Simoni was
in the vicinity of Lucca, and knowing him to be an enthusiastic shot, he
sent him a note:

Puccini   Dear Simoni—you promised that you would come to Torre
del Lago one day; let me know when, and we'll go out on the lake
in search of rare birds. With this unrelenting sun, the game is a bit
behindhand this year—but it doesn't matter: we can talk and enjoy
the marsh air. . . .   [*Id: 489*]

Adami   During those days the idea of a collaboration was born. 'When
you get back to Milan', said Puccini, 'why not go and talk things over
with Adami. He's always looking for a libretto for me, but never finds
one.'

To begin with, Simoni hesitated. He was afraid of intruding
between myself and the Maestro. But his scruples vanished when
he realised, after our first meeting, just how much I welcomed his
assistance. I said to him: 'Either with you, or I won't take it on'.

Finding a subject for Puccini—no, it wasn't an easy task. . . .
[*Adami: 195–6*]

Puccini however, reinvigorated by the idea of a new collaboration, at
once started to urge his librettists on with enthusiastic advice.

Puccini   Dear Adami—well, have you and Simoni gone into battle?
Courage, and wring your hearts and brains to create for me something that will make the world weep. They say that emotionalism is

a sign of weakness. If that's the case, I like to be weak! To the so-called *strong* I leave the triumphs that fade: for us those that endure!

[*Epistolario: 255–6*]

Adami   In our first enthusiasm and our hurry to satisfy Puccini, we right away worked out a plot—shall we say—à la Dickens. It was called *Fanny*. . . .   [*Adami: 196*]

But early in March 1920, Puccini made a flying visit to Milan, heard the scenario of *Fanny* (which was in fact an adaptation of *Oliver Twist*) and turned it down flat. He was bitterly disappointed, as much for the lost labour of his librettists as for himself. They did their best to reassure him—and had lunch with him before he left Milan.

Adami   During that lunch, Puccini expounded more clearly his hopes and aspirations. One phrase he drove home again and again: 'to try unknown paths'. He felt that the traditional melodrama was on its death bed. He dreamed of something new that would carry him with a great surge out of the old-fashioned formula. He felt already the musical evolution in himself that could lead to a new style. . . . And it was then that Simoni, with convincing warmth, put forward the idea of the mythical, the unreal humanity of the fable. 'And Gozzi? If we went back again to Gozzi?'   [*Id: 197–8*]

Next to his more sophisticated rival Goldoni, Carlo Gozzi was the outstanding playwright of eighteenth-century Venice. His ten *fiabe*, dramatisations of popular legends and fairy tales, deliberately retained those elements of the traditional *commedia dell'arte* which Goldoni discarded, and met with great popular success. The plots were mainly taken from *The Thousand and One Nights*, though the story of Turandot, the cold, beautiful princess who defends her integrity against the male sex by all means in her power, until she is released by a suitor whose love proves stronger than her will, has its origin in Persian legend. Transferred to China, and coupled with the challenge of the riddles—the device by which Turandot disposes of unsuccessful candidates for her hand and consigns them to the executioner—it had already attracted the attention of a number of composers though not as yet with any notable success.

What appealed to Puccini at first sight were the immense dramatic and emotional possibilities of the heroine's ultimate surrender, and for this it mattered little that, in the train on the way home from Milan, he first read the play not in Gozzi's original version, but in an adaptation by Schiller, retranslated into Italian by Verdi's friend Andrea Maffei. On 18 March he wrote to Simoni:

Puccini   I have read *Turandot* and I don't think we ought to let this subject go. Yesterday I talked to a foreign woman who told me about a production of this work in Germany, done by Max Reinhardt in a most curious and original way. She will write for photographs of the *mise en scène*, so that we can see what it's all about. But for my part I should advise sticking to this subject. Simplify it by reducing the number of acts and rework it to make it quicker, more economical; above all build up the amorous passion of Turandot herself, for so long suffocated beneath the ashes of her great pride. . . . A *Turandot* seen through the contemporary mind—yours, Adami's and mine.   [*Carteggi:* 490]

And to Adami:

Puccini   I am sending you back the volume of Schiller, and we will discuss everything by letter. For now it's a question of adapting, stylising, animating, stuffing out and yet reducing the subject. As it is it won't do. But worked on, chewed over, it could really turn out to be something . . . *astonishing*. . . .

   Gozzi's *Turandot* as a basis, but out of it must rise another figure— I mean—I can't explain! But from our imaginations (and we shall need them!) must come so much that is beautiful, attractive, enjoyable, that our story will become the whole blossoming of a conquest. Don't overdo the Venetian harlequinaders—these ought to be clowns and philosophers who now and then throw out a joke or comment (carefully chosen—and the moment for it too), but they mustn't become petulant or boring. . . .   [*Epistolario:* 257, 258]

It sounds very much as if the 'something' that had so tantalized Illica was once again making an appearance. Nevertheless the two librettists set to work at once—but they were hard-pressed with other literary pre-occupations, and Puccini's impatience was irrepressible.

Puccini   I put my hands on the piano and I am covered in dust! My desk is a sea of letters—but of music not a trace. Music? . . . How can I write music if I have no libretto? I have the great weakness of being able to compose only when my insatiable puppets move about on the stage. If I were a symphonist I might cheat my time and my public. But me? I was born many years ago . . . and the Good Lord touched me with his little finger and said, 'write for the theatre—mind now, only for the theatre', and I have obeyed the supreme command. Had he marked me out for some other trade, well, perhaps I shouldn't be in the plight I am now, with nothing to write. Oh you, who say you are working but all the time are occupied with something entirely different—films, plays, poetry, articles—and never think, as you should, of a man with earth under his feet who feels the ground slipping, every hour, every day, like a landslide that is sweeping him away! I get the nicest, most encouraging letters, but oh, oh, wouldn't it be better if I got an act of this counterfeit Princess?   [*Id:* 259–60]

By 15 May, Puccini at last had a full scenario for Act I in his hands.

Puccini   *Turandot!* First act—excellent! . . . The three harlequinaders have turned out well. I'm not quite sure about the close, but I may be wrong. Altogether this act is good and well laid out. What about the second? And shall we need a third—or will the action be exhausted in the second? Courage—and keep at it with skill and imagination. . . .   [*Id:* 260–1]

It is typical of Puccini's dramatic flair that he foresaw so early what was going to be the essential problem of the libretto, the difficulty of spreading the action over three acts; it is also ironic, when two months later he had the full scenario of the opera in his hands, that he immediately put his finger on the point which was to cause him such anguish in the coming years.

Puccini   Packet received. At first sight it looks good . . . apart from a few comments on the second and third acts—in the third I had imagined a different denouement—I thought Turandot's moment of conversion would be more striking, and I should have liked her to burst out with her love *coram populo*—shamelessly, violently, excessively, like a bomb exploding. We must meet as soon as possible. The great canvas is there, the basis of an original, perhaps unique work. But it needs adjustments, which we will find when we talk about it. . . .   [*Id:* 261]

It seems curious that neither of the librettists realised, at this stage, the crucial difficulty presented by the structure of the original play.

Gozzi's fable is laid out in five acts. Rather surprisingly, for those who know the opera, the nucleus of the dramatic action, right up to the asking of the riddles, is concentrated entirely into the first two. The next two are taken up by various attempts to discover the names of Calaf and his father—allowing Gozzi the opportunity to entertain his Venetian audience with a variety of intrigues and temptations in which the popular figures of the harlequinade are much involved—and in a short final act Turandot announces both names, offers Calaf his freedom and, when he threatens to kill himself, eventually confesses her love.

It was on this structure that Adami and Simoni had based their original scenario, but by running Gozzi's first two acts into one, they produced a dense concentration of action in the opening scene that left dangerously little dramatic substance for the remainder of the opera. Nevertheless, Puccini was full of enthusiasm and wrote to Simoni ten days later:

Puccini   Tomorrow I go to Bagni di Lucca. Will you come, with Adami? Our princess (on whom my mind is more and more firmly fixed) will be happy to see us united to vivisect her soul. I shall be staying at the Hotel Victoria and I shall wait for a telegram there to tell me you are coming. . . . I think our meetings will be delightfully fruitful, because there really is material, and of the first order, in this *Turandot*.

I am already beginning to improvise in the evenings, and I search for chords and phrases as 'Chinese' as I can. So I wait for you, in glorious anticipation.   [*Carteggi*: 492–3]

Any search for 'Chinese' effects in music is always likely to start with the five note (or pentatonic) scale, which is the foundation of much Eastern music and one example of which is represented by the black notes on the piano keyboard. Though we have no means of knowing what form Puccini's improvisation took in the early stages of *Turandot*, we do know that he habitually worked at the piano, and it is perhaps worth remarking that, in Act II of the opera, the great theme in which Turandot expresses her resolution to defend her chastity falls entirely on the black notes, and that Liù's first aria in Act I is a black-note tune throughout.

But that was in the future; meanwhile he seized every opportunity to absorb everything he could of Chinese culture.

Adami   There lived at Bagni di Lucca a close friend of Puccini's, Baron Fassini, who had worked for many years at an Italian consulate in China, and had decorated his villa in perfect Chinese style. There we were received, amidst dragons and incense, silks and lanterns, to the strains of nothing less than the authentic Imperial Hymn played on a valuable musical-box in the Baron's possession. This hymn, almost as we then heard it, was later transformed into the solemn finale to Act II of the opera. And then from the depths of the musical box came yet another characteristic Chinese tune which was to give the Maestro an idea for the music of the three harlequinaders. Puccini was delighted with this discovery. . . .   [*Adami:* 200]

Baron Fassini's musical box actually provided Puccini with three tunes, the third being the one associated with the princess which is first heard as the haunting children's chorus in Act I. But in the end, the Fassini musical box was as near as Puccini ever came to hearing Chinese music played on genuine Chinese instruments. For the rest he was dependent on books, and as with *Madame Butterfly* sixteen years earlier, he searched for oriental material to incorporate in his score, even enlisting the help of the British Museum.

Puccini   I've filled several sheets of music paper with notes and the beginnings of ideas, chords, possible progressions. I've written for books. One has arrived, which I'm sending you; but which I *want back*, because there is some music at the end which might come in useful. . . . So don't go to sleep, my dear poets; I'm tired of doing nothing.   [*Epistolario:* 262]

With Puccini life was always subject to unpredictable swings of emotion, and his impatience, as usual, was beginning to get the better of him. A visit to Vienna in November to see the revised version of *La rondine* failed to provide the hoped-for distraction, and by the time of his return his mood had darkened.

Puccini   One can't work like this. When the first fever diminishes it ends by disappearing altogether, and without fever there's no creativity, because art that is truly felt is a kind of illness, an exceptional state of mind, an over-excitement of every fibre, of every atom of one's being—and one could follow it *ad aeternum*.

I am going to the Maremma towards the end of the month, to sink myself still further in brutishness. Will you join me there . . . ? It depends on you, and on the work you have done. And Simoni . . . , will he be back again at full blast? Because a libretto for me is not something you can fool with. It's not just a question of finishing it. It's a question of giving enduring life to something that must be alive before it's born, and so on and so on, right up to the masterpiece. . . .

[Id: 263–4]

In October of the preceding year Puccini had bought a shooting lodge on a lonely stretch of coast in southern Tuscany; it was here that he elected to spend Christmas, 1920, and it was to this somewhat forbidding retreat that Adami (but not Simoni) at last brought the completed first act of the libretto. He read it to the composer.

Adami   When we began our work Simoni and I—especially Simoni—had taken immense trouble to create for our distinguished composer a setting of exquisite exoticism. Simoni knew China from personal experience and had studied its literature. . . . Obsessed, therefore, by a desire to flaunt the rich colouring of its customs and manners, we had decided to open the first act under the walls of Peking, with a great, busy crowd scene; groups and characters, men and women, gentlemen and beggars, episodes and details were mixed together there, as they waited for the Mandarin to appear, high on the bastion, and deliver his tragic proclamation. This opening scene extended to a good eighteen pages of verses which were, in our view, most beautiful and original. Then the action developed, amply, solemnly, relentlessly, up to . . . the asking of the three riddles and their miraculous solution . . . in fact an endless, an interminable act which, set to music, would have taken on gargantuan proportions. . . .

Puccini was appalled. My reading had lasted about an hour. He said: 'But this is not an act; this is a lecture! Do you think I can set a lecture to music?'

I didn't breathe. I looked at him in horror. . . . The Maestro could no longer feel (and he was right) the proportions which, in the scenario, had been clearly outlined and balanced with such care. During the writing, China had got the upper hand, had inundated, submerged and drowned us. And in the first angry flush of disappointment he told me, without ceremony, that there was nothing more to be done and that he gave up the project. [*Adami*: 200–2]

In an immediate letter to Simoni, Puccini expressed himself more tactfully.

Puccini Dear Renato—Adami has brought me the first act. On the whole I liked it, but to be honest I must tell you that it absolutely needs shortening in many places. . . . In the scenario I felt that it all moved faster. . . . I must say that I was expecting scenic proportions that were more concise and—let me say it—less literary, however skilful and ingenious the verses may be. . . . So, we shall have to prune and prune, and speed up the individual scenes. As a general plan, it works. [*Carteggi*: 499]

Adami, meanwhile, would not admit defeat.

Adami After having telegraphed to Simoni the news of the disastrous reading, and had his authorisation in reply, I felt calmer, and stayed up till late at night studying the situation.

Next morning the sun was shining. . . . Even Puccini felt new hope in the air. He was quieter, gentler . . . and no longer got angry when I showed him the manuscript. It was a cemetery. How many of those verses had been consigned to oblivion? To start with, just to start with, nineteen whole pages. All the long opening of the act, all that commotion under the walls of Peking, all gone. No longer was the Mandarin awaited. He was there already, high on the bastion, under the golden umbrella. And the crowd, prostrate and immobile, hung upon his lips 'People of Peking, the law is this . . .'. [*Adami*: 202–3]

It must have been a painful decision, but the result was the draft of an opening scene that was both potent and concise. All the same, Puccini was aware that much remained to be done; in early January he went to Milan and began a series of daily conferences with his two librettists, and by the end of the month could report that they were 'really on the right road'.

Puccini *Turandot* is shaping into something fantastically beautiful. Adami and Simoni are doing extremely well. It will be a splendid libretto, full of colour, surprises and feeling, and above all highly original. . . .   [*Carteggi:* 502]

He told Sybil that he hoped to start work 'soon', but it was not until March that he felt sufficiently optimistic to leave Milan. As soon as he was home in Torre del Lago, he settled down seriously to the composition of Act I.   [*Seligman:* 324]

In spite of the cuts and revisions, the first act of *Turandot* remained essentially a big crowd scene with lyrical interludes, with the people of Peking taking a true part in the action. From the outset the range and power of the music, as well as the continual onward drive, make it clear that Puccini was really attempting something new.

Puccini   I am working, and I think well. I have just finished the tremendous hymn to the Executioner, and I am starting on the [Invocation to the] Moon and the Funeral March [for the Prince of Persia]—I've already got plenty of material for these two episodes, so they won't take long. The opera is assuming sumptuous proportions.

[*Carteggi:* 506]

'Sumptuous proportions' were something that no Puccini opera had ever assumed before; the choral and ensemble writing that had been such a striking departure in *La fanciulla del West* is now handled with complete mastery, the exotic atmosphere maintained without any sacrifice of Italian lyricism. But whereas in *Madame Butterfly* the plot had been modern, depending on a conflict between the cultures of East and West, in *Turandot* the action was consistently oriental, the atmosphere consistently legendary, and the musical texture well suited to the inclusion of any Chinese material that he was able to find. In the end, this was more or less limited to the tunes from Baron Fassini's musical box and, eager to establish an authentic flavour, he seems to have included all three of these in the original first act, transcribing the melodies with scrupulous accuracy in their original keys, and providing them with imaginative harmonic settings to typically Puccinian effect.

There remained the problem of the three masks from the harlequinade. In Gozzi's fable these characters from the world of the *commedia dell'arte* had provided comic relief in the traditional Italian manner, and when he first read *Turandot*, Puccini had been uncertain whether it would be possible to work such down-to-earth Venetian figures into the oriental surroundings that he was now trying to establish. In fact a footnote in the Maffei translation of the play reads, 'if it is intended to put *Turandot* onto the [modern] stage, it would be advisable to provide the Masks with different names, their original ones being unacceptable'—though whether the choice of Ping, Pang and Pong as alternatives to Tartaglia, Pantalone and Truffaldino was an altogether happy one perhaps remains open to question. In any case, when Adami suggested dropping them altogether, Puccini had at first been inclined to agree.

Puccini: As soon as I got your express letter today, I telegraphed my immediate approval . . . . But I don't want this first impulse of mine to weigh too heavily on you. Maybe by preserving them, with discretion, the masks might contribute a homely element, a touch of ourselves, of sincerity, in all this Chinese mannerism. The sharp observations of Pantalone and company would bring us back to the reality of our own lives. In fact, do a bit of what Shakespeare often does when he sets up three or four extraneous figures who drink and swear and speak ill of the King . . . . But they could also spoil things, these masks. Perhaps you'll find some way of enriching them and having a bit of fun with the Chinese element?   [*Epistolario:* 258–9]

In the end, the masks became Chinese and, as ministers at the court of the Emperor Altoum, play an ambivalent role, sometimes buffo, sometimes nostalgic, that provides the *scherzo* element in Puccini's great dramatic canvas. But if, in Calaf and Turandot, Puccini had the very prototype of the recklessly heroic and the icily impregnable, and in the masks a contrasting thread of comedy, there was still something missing—the romantic victim who had always been the main source of Puccini's emotional and musical inspiration.

He appears to have felt the need early; he probably introduced the idea at that first discussion of the scenario at Bagni di Lucca, because only a few days later he had written to Simoni: 'Have you thought seriously about the new insertion of the *piccola donna*?'. Though she is not mentioned by name this must surely be the origin of Liù, the little slave girl from the palace of Calaf's father, who loves and adores the young prince and in the end lays down her life in order to safeguard her hero's secret. She is not to be found in Gozzi, and it seems likely that she was

Puccini's own invention; he was certainly very fond of her, and to the soprano Gilda dalla Rizza, who had recently won golden opinions as Angelica and Lauretta in *Il trittico*, he wrote in May 1920:

Puccini   Liù, it seems to me, is becoming something delicious. . . . I think that [she] will be a role for you, but don't think it's a secondary one—far from it. . . .   [*Carteggi*: 505]

All the same, it was Turandot who necessarily took first place in the development of the drama, and in his own personal preoccupations. In Act I her first brief appearance is a silent one, so that her return for the scene of the riddles at the end of the original first act was Puccini's first musical attempt on the person of his frigid heroine. But the density of the action left little room for lyrical expansion; it depended mainly on impact and suspense, and there was not much to get hold of. 'I am at the enigmas and can't get started', he wrote to Adami in June, and to Simoni: 'the first two enigmas are too wordy; I want them more concise—like this they don't seem right.'   [*Id*: 509]

Gozzi's own stage direction required Turandot to deliver her questions *con tuono accademico,* and the music Puccini eventually produced for this scene is tense and concentrated, but strangely dry and bare; he missed the warmth of human feeling.

Puccini   The first act is almost done. The last part has been driving me mad, or anyhow causing me a lot of trouble. I beg you for lyricism and emotion in the third: choruses, colours, emperors, executioners etc.,—all very fine and good. But it is only when the human soul speaks through a single mouth that the emotions come across with direct and natural force. . . .   [*Id*: 508]

By August, Act I was complete, at least in sketch form.

Adami   I got back from Torre del Lago last night. The great news is that *Turandot* is developing marvellously. I heard and reheard the first act and have carried away a tremendous impression of it. Richness of colour, breadth of human feeling and exoticism of a very individual kind—all is there. Clear oases of melody punctuate the onrush of the drama like deep breaths of pure air. Only Puccini could have done something so original, so vast and so striking.

The second act, which I took with me and read to him, pleased him very much—and he has settled down to work at once.   [*Id:* 513]

Since the riddles were already disposed of in the first act, and Turandot's confession of her love had to be reserved for the last, the whole of the second act was to be devoted to the intrigues and devices by which the princess tries to get Calaf to reveal his name. From scattered comments in letters it can be gathered that the temptation of Calaf by women, riches and finally the offer of escape was to be placed in a spectacular setting, with a banquet, dancers, and a scene involving the ghosts of Calaf's unfortunate predecessors. Puccini, whose dramatic instinct was certainly the strongest of the three collaborators, gradually began to realise that something was wrong. 'To hang about after the riddles doesn't seem to me a good idea,' he wrote to Adami, 'for me that *dilutes* the action.' And in September he wrote to Simoni with a new and drastic solution: [*Epistolario:* 269]

Puccini   That second act! I can't see a way out—perhaps I'm torturing myself because I've got an idea fixed in my head: *Turandot* ought to be in two acts. What do you say? Doesn't it seem too much to you, this watering down [of the action] after the enigmas, before arriving at the final scene? Reduce some incidents, cut out others, and get on to the final explosion of love. . . . I don't know how to suggest the right structure, but I feel that two more acts are too much. *Turandot* in two great acts! And why not?   [*Carteggi:* 514–5]

And in spite of his protested incompetence, he provided Simoni with a rough structure of what he had in mind.

Puccini   I have sent Renato a plan for the second act. Entry of Turandot, nervous after the riddles. Short scene, ending with the threat: 'None shall sleep in Peking'. Tenor aria. Then no banquet, but instead scene in which the 3 masks dominate the action. Offerings of money, wine, women begging and imploring Calaf to speak. He: 'No, I should lose Turandot'. Agitated proposals for escape. He: 'No, I should lose Turandot'. Then threat to his life with daggers. Appeal by dignitaries, quick, brief conference, and assault. Enter Turandot; general flight. Duet, shorter—then torture, this shorter too, and so on, up to 'I have lost her'. Turandot leaves with burning face and beating heart. Liù stays to speak to Turandot. Darkness—change of scene. . . .   [*Epistolario:* 269–70]

Much of this sounds very much like the opening of the third act as it stands today, but it wasn't to reach that position for some time yet, and for the time being the two-act solution continued to obsess Puccini.

Puccini   I am still for a magnificent and varied 2nd and final act. . . . As we have it, it absolutely can't work, believe me, like this it's wrong. There's no excitement, no speed of action. I realise the subject doesn't offer a lot—but for that very reason it's important to be less wordy and make sure that successive incidents are clear, striking to the eyes more than to the ears, and varied, constantly changing. . . .
[*Id:* 270]

By now Adami and Simoni had been struggling to keep pace with Puccini's demands for the best part of eighteen months; they both had careers of their own to follow, and they found this apparent rejection of all their best efforts difficult to take. But Puccini was adamant.

Puccini   We absolutely must meet to discuss that blessed/cursed second act. If not we shall never get anything done, and we shall end with a total shipwreck. . . . Try and find a free week to come to Torre del Lago with Adami.
[*Carteggi:* 515]

And to Adami: 'Am I finished? . . .'

Puccini   . . . am I completely written off? . . . I haven't been well, and not getting letters from you makes me more miserable still. And Simoni has buried me altogether! I see clouds gathering over *Turandot*. . . . Is it perhaps because I've gone back to the idea of two acts that you have relapsed into silence? . . . This is not the way that I should be treated. You have so often expressed your faith in me and accepted me as a good judge of human actions in the theatre, and you should listen to me now and not hide your heads under your wings. . . . I say and I repeat that the second act, as it stands, is a big mistake. . . .
     Leave Gozzi alone for a bit and use your own logic and fantasy. Perhaps find some new more daring way? Who knows? But by myself I can't do it.
[*Epistolario:* 273, 274]

To Sybil he unburdened himself with even more than his usual desperation. '*Turandot* will end by going to the wall, because the libretto of the second act is no good'. And a few days later, more ominously still:

[*Seligman:* 336]

Puccini   *Turandot* has sunk into oblivion. I'm still waiting for my poets, but they don't stir—I'm looking for another libretto. . . .   [*Id:* 337]

At one point shipwreck seemed imminent, but sometime in December 1921 the three men met, buried their differences and found the basis for a solution. Puccini's two-act plan was rejected in favour of the original three; the crucial point, Puccini's insistence that Turandot's defeat in the riddles must be followed as soon as possible by her conversion through the power of love, was finally accepted, and the decision made to transfer the riddle scene from its original place at the end of the first act to a similar position at the end of the second. As a result, the whole action had to be refashioned, with a new second act using music already written for the first but with significant additions. It meant a lot more work, but Puccini was optimistic: 'I feel now how much you are in agreement,' he wrote on 21 December, 'indeed that all three of us etc., etc.—*excellent!*', and from his new villa at Viareggio he wrote on Boxing Day: [*Epistolario:* 276]

Puccini   Yesterday, after so long, I played over the first act of *Turandot* again, and I enjoyed myself. . . . If we could just find a way to bring down the curtain after the masks have finished their pleading! . . . The two, the father and the slave girl, must finish their piece, along with the three masks, and end up, after the panegyrics of Calaf . . . , with the beating of the great gong. Anyway, I am preaching to the converted. . . .   [*Carteggi:* 517]

Strange that no one had realised before that the three strokes on the gong would make the perfect climax for Act I. But the changes needed for the new version of Act II were not to be done in a hurry—in fact, they were not completed until the following autumn—and Puccini, as usual when he thought he saw light at the end of the tunnel, was impatient to get on. Only three days into the New Year he was already nagging Simoni:

Puccini   How much time wasted! I have been expecting from you, or from Adami, the trio from the Act I finale—the bit broken off from the old, big act. . . . When will this work of ours come to an end? Either when I'm old and decrepit, or in the other world! . . . I am in a

reproachful mood (I think with justice), as well as being quite ready
to go to that place to which you may well want to send me. But I'm
also ready to embrace you both, if you've got something done. . . .
[*Id: 518*]

The trio 'broken off' from Act I was to become a spacious intermezzo
opening the new Act II, in which Ping, Pang and Pong reflect sadly on the
present state of China and long for the peace of their own homes in the
country. In contrast to the passionate turmoil of the first act, the sprightly
bitonal opening has a distinct flavour of Stravinsky, which becomes even
more marked in the thudding, dissonant march, with its sharp little trumpet calls, that leads into the Imperial Hymn. Puccini was always anxious
not to be written off as old-fashioned; he had listened attentively to much
contemporary music, and claimed that his scores of 'Debussy, Strauss and
others' were worn with study. Certainly his admiration for the former and
grudging interest in the latter—especially *Salome*, which he never missed
an opportunity of seeing—left their mark on his work, and although *Turandot* was never going to be 'modern' in the sense of an opera like *Wozzeck*
(which was being completed at exactly this moment) or even *Elektra* (written more than a decade earlier), he was skilful in adapting contemporary
techniques to reinforce the atmosphere and impact of his score. His feelings about Stravinsky had always been ambivalent; after attending the
original production of *Le Sacre du printemps* in Paris in 1913, he called the
music 'sheer cacophony, . . . as a whole, the stuff of madness', but he liked
Stravinsky personally, admitted that the music was 'curious, and not without a certain talent', and clearly retained something of its acerbic magic in
his composing ear. In any case, when he finally received the text for the
intermezzo at the beginning of March, he seemed cheerful and optimistic
and was already looking forward to getting text for the third act as well.
[*Carner: 185; Epistolario: 239*]

Nevertheless the sense of creative insecurity was never far from the
surface: 'I think that if Stravinsky pleases, Puccini is on the decline,' he
wrote in a moment of depression, and only two months later, to Simoni:
[*Sotheby*]

Puccini   Tell me the truth—you don't have faith in me any more! . . . I
torture myself with fear that you have lost confidence in me: perhaps
you think that my work is pointless. And it could be true. The public
that goes to hear new music nowadays has something wrong with its

palate; it likes, or endures, music that is illogical, lacking any sense. Nobody writes melody any more, or when they do it's commonplace. There is a belief that symphonic development is the thing, whereas I believe it is the end of opera in the theatre. Italians used to sing, but no more. . . . [*Carteggi:* 524]

But the mood passed, as it usually did, with a shrug of the shoulders:

Puccini   *Turandot* is a subject which should be treated in a morbid manner. . . . I instead remain normal with modern intentions, but my music is straightforward and the language is clear, perhaps too clear for this troubled world. . . .

And yet—the royalties do not diminish. Which means that the world still enjoys my sunset. . . . [*Sotheby*]

At the end of June, Puccini reported to his publishers that Simoni and Adami had sent him the finished libretto of *Turandot*, and that he was well and working 'with pleasure and with faith'. But there was still at least one major gap that needed attention. A little over a month later Adami reported:

Adami   Giacomo is in a good mood—rare piece of luck!—and is working. . . . He is now profoundly convinced by everything and told me yesterday that he feels himself capable of doing extraordinary things in the third act. . . . I am preparing for him the big piece for Turandot in the second. . . . [*Carteggi:* 526]

The climax of Act II, the scene of the riddles, was of course already composed for its original place in the first act, and Puccini had only to retouch it for its new position—where he now had the space to introduce his icy heroine with an expansive introductory aria. But with the riddles he had been able to hide behind the cold, callous mask of Turandot's public manner; in the great scene which was now being planned it was a question of an aria that would justify and motivate her fierce clinging to virginity, and he was soon losing confidence again.

Puccini   *Turandot* is sleeping. There's got to be a big aria in the second act, but it has to be grafted on . . . and ideas found for it; and then I have all the third act to do. [*Id:* 530]

In spite of his 'complete satisfaction' with the libretto only three months earlier, he was once more dissatisfied with the third act. He even toyed with a return to the two-act plan. Nothing seemed to go well; the intermezzo for the masks, which had begun so optimistically, had run into trouble, he was making no headway with Turandot's aria, and time was passing.

Puccini   I can't get on with the opening scene of the second act—no matter how many times I've tried. . . . Can I be satiated with China after having done one act and most of the second? The truth is that I just can't get anything good to take root. I'm old too. No doubt about that. If only I'd had a little subject, the sort of thing I was always looking for . . . , I should have had it staged by now. But this Chinese world! I shall decide something definite when I come to Milan. Perhaps I'll give the money back to Ricordi and cancel the contract. . . . [*Epistolario*: 283–4]

He begged Adami for another libretto altogether, 'a small, sweet thing, something simple', and when at last, in early March, he received the latest modifications—

Puccini   No! No! No! *Turandot* no! I've got part of the third act. It won't do. Perhaps, or even without perhaps, it's me that won't do any more. But like this the third act won't do either.   [*Id:* 284]

All the same, work on the second act was at last nearing completion.

Puccini   The ensemble for the masks is going ahead well. . . . Turandot's aria is practically done, but what a job it has been! It needs a few word changes. I think that coming from up there, from the top of the great staircase, it ought not to make too bad an impression.
                                                                              [*Id:* 286]

At the end of nearly six months' struggle the final version of *In questa reggia* gave Turandot the entry aria she deserved. 'Let's hope that the melody which you rightly demand of me will come fresh and piercing to the soul', he had written to Adami, 'for without this there is no music', and the result justified his hope; the theme that he found for Turandot's defiant words: 'No man shall ever have me'—*Mai nessun m'avrà*—is not only compelling in its sheer musical sweep and power, but endows Turandot once and for all with the hidden passion which will enable her to contradict the terrible pride that it seems to express. [*Id:* 279]

With the second act finished, Puccini was able to tackle the beginning of the third—the easy part—and by the end of June reported that the offstage voices had turned out well and that the big aria for Calaf, which had apparently been brewing in his mind for some time, was now 'finally in place'. Though it may be difficult, nowadays, to hear *Nessun dorma* with fresh ears, in its right place in the third act of *Turandot* it remains a stroke of lyrical genius, the last and not the least of Puccini's great tenor arias. With it, and with *In questa reggia*, Puccini had set his sights high.

But he had always realised that for the culmination of his opera he must reach higher still. [*Id:* 288]

Puccini The coming of love must be a shining meteor amidst the clamour of the people, who absorb its influence with ecstacy, their taut nerves vibrating like the plangent strings of a violoncello. . . . Calaf must kiss Turandot, I think, and thus demonstrate his love to this frigid woman. After he has kissed her for several long seconds, he says: "Now nothing matters, even death", and he whispers his name to her lips. . . .

For me the duet is the key—but it must contain in itself some great, daring, unexpected element and not just leave things as they were before. . . . [*Id:* 266, 272, 273–4]

Turandot's surrender to the power of love was for Puccini the entire reason and justification for the whole of the rest of the work. But as the climactic moment approached, he realised more and more clearly the difficulty of the task he had set himself. 'This infamous *Turandot* terrifies me', he wrote to Sybil: 'I shan't finish it, or if I do it will be a fiasco'. But it wasn't just the opera, it was Turandot herself who terrified him; she presented a challenge, both musical and emotional, of a kind that he had never faced before, and in his uncertainty he clung to a hope that the words would provide him with the inspiration he needed. And he turned back to Liù for a dramatic ingredient that he was better able to understand.

Puccini In the grand duet, as the icy demeanour of Turandot gradually melts, the scene, which might even be in an enclosed space, is transformed little by little into a large *ambiente* . . . where the crowd, the emperor, the court and all the apparatus of ceremonial are ready to welcome Turandot's cry of love. I believe that Liù should be sacrificed to some kind of grief but I think this mustn't be developed—that is, if she isn't made to die under torture. And why not? This death could have an influence on the softening of the princess. . . .   [*Id: 282*]

Even as he suggested this idea, Puccini seems to have sensed the problem that it would create—the danger that Liù's sacrifice, if too much developed, would monopolise the emotional impact of the final scene and detract from, even risk invalidating, the final apotheosis of love. Whatever form the duet between Turandot and Calaf eventually took, it was going to be heroic rather than sentimental, while in Liù, Puccini had a heroine of a kind with whom he had always been in sympathy. 'I am tossed on a sea of uncertainty,' he told Adami, 'this whole subject has caused me great agony of spirit'.   [*Id: 282*]

And in the end, of course, he could not resist the opportunity to make people weep once more. The episode of Liù's death has been regarded by some critics with almost moral distaste, a gratuitous symptom of the less attractive aspects of Puccini's character. But the real significance of this scene lies not in the suffering to which an innocent girl is subjected, but in the demonstration of selfless love to which it gives rise. There is heroism in her adoration of Calaf and poignancy in her suicide, and though her torture does not in the end move Turandot, her resulting sacrifice moves us—as it clearly moved Puccini. Perhaps there was still a lingering memory of the cruel fate of Doria, 'that poor child' whom the composer could never get out of his mind; in any case he had no difficulty in finding music for Liù, and by November 1923 her last aria was already formed in his head. He wrote to Adami:

Puccini   . . . I still have no verses for Liù's death. The music is all there, it's a question now of writing words for what is already composed. It's only a bare outline, to develop the whole of this sad little episode properly, the words are necessary. . . . They are lines of seven syllables. . . . Would you like me to scribble something in rough form? All right, I'll try.

      Tu che di gel sei cinta . . .   [*Id: 289*]

. . . and he wrote the words of the aria exactly as they appear in the final score. It is curiously fitting that, for his farewell to a type of heroine that he had made particularly his own, he should have written both the words and the music himself.

With Liù's death, Puccini had reached the point of no return. Nothing was now left between him and the fateful duet: 'The duet! The duet! Everything that is beautiful, vivid, incisive, must be there!', and in his desperation to find his way in this uncharted territory he had the text for the final scene rewritten four, five, six times. But his librettists continued to prevaricate and on December 22nd he turned again to Simoni: [*Id:* 276]

Puccini   You've forgotten me. . . . My mind will not be at ease until the duet is done. Do me a favour and get down to this last job for me. . . . Sneak a few hours from your many occupations. . . .   [*Carteggi:* 545]

He begged for help from his publisher and from Adami but, beyond a promise in the New Year that he would have everything 'in two or three days', he received nothing from Simoni. Until at last, on 14 February:

Puccini   I've got the text from Simoni, but we're not there yet. . . .
    [*Id:* 547]

It must have been a big disappointment, but he insisted that the material was good, and if Adami could make up his mind to come to Viareggio for two or three days, everything could be arranged—'I need it urgently now, because the second act is finished, orchestration and all'. A month later Adami made up his mind, and Puccini reported to Sybil that the duet 'has finally come out very well indeed'. Yet it still needed Simoni's last attentions, 'to strengthen the imagery a bit more and give it a few little "Chinese" touches'.   [*Id:* 548, 550; *Seligman:* 354]

But Simoni's contribution, when it eventually arrived at the end of May, seems to have been an extraordinary step backwards.

Puccini   Caro Adamino, Simoni has sent me the duet in prose. There are embellishments and ideas which are a little different but which seem to me good. Now it has to be put into verse. The action remains as it was . . . so it's a question of translating everything into metre, and trying to keep the rhythm of the existing version, . . . because you know that the music is already there—it's not written out yet, but the *theme* is the one that you both know. . . .   [*Epistolario:* 295–6]

Ever since the beginning of work on the final scene Puccini had been noting and developing ideas for each of its successive forms, either in rough sketches or simply in his head. As a result, the librettists were more and more tied to shapes and rhythms created by previous versions of the text. But it was now the end of May. Time was passing. And besides, Puccini was not physically well. For some time he had been complaining to Sybil of 'a sore throat and an obstinate cough', and by the summer it had got painful enough to demand medical investigation. 'I've been through horrible crises', he wrote at the beginning of September:

Puccini   . . . that throat of mine that has been tormenting me since March looked as if it might be something serious. I'm feeling better now and I have the reassurance of knowing that it is rheumatic in origin, and that with a cure I shall recover fully. . . . Now I shall pick up the work that has been interrupted for six months. And I hope soon to get to the end of this blessed princess!   [*Id:* 297]

With the worry about his health at least temporarily on hold, his musical imagination was fired once more. He seems to have been thinking of his last great creative effort in positively Wagnerian terms—attached to a sketched melody for Turandot's final revelation that she knows Calaf's name are the enigmatic words *poi Tristano*—'then *Tristan*'.

Puccini   It's got to be a grand duet. These two beings, almost from another world, are transformed into humans by way of love, and this love in the end must engulf the whole stage in a great orchestral peroration.   [*Id:* 301]

At last, on 8 October, he was able to report that he had received the final verses from Simoni. 'They are really beautiful', he wrote enthusiastically to Adami, 'and complete and justify the duet . . .'
But his physical condition showed no signs of improving, and only two weeks later he wrote again with more ominous news:

Puccini   This trouble in my throat is giving me no rest. . . . I am going to Brussels to see a famous specialist. . . . Like this I can't go on. And there's *Turandot*. Simoni's verses are good . . . they are what is needed, and what I have dreamed of. . . . We'll see—when I get back from Brussels and start work again. . . .   [*Id:* 300–1]

Puccini never started work again. The sore throat had turned out to be an inoperable cancer—a fact that was kept from the composer himself until the last moment—and the only remaining hope of a cure seemed to be the new radium treatment being pioneered in Brussels. Though agonisingly painful, the treatment was successful, but Puccini's heart was unable to take the strain and on 29 November he died.

The first performance of *Turandot* took place under Toscanini at La Scala, Milan, on 25 April 1926. As the body of Liù was carried from the stage by the mourning people of Peking, the music faded into silence, and after a brief pause Toscanini turned to the audience and said: "At this point, Giacomo Puccini laid down his pen". The curtain was slowly lowered. On the following night the opera was given with the final scenes completed by Franco Alfano—though his original score was later heavily cut at Toscanini's insistence, and it is in this shorter second version that the conclusion of the opera has been normally heard ever since. (A more recent attempt at completion by Luciano Berio has not yet found general acceptance.)

Alfano did a competent and conscientious job, using some (though not all) of the sketches left by Puccini, many of which dated back up to two years. But inevitably the ultimate achievement of Puccini's ambition to make *Turandot* his crowning masterpiece depended upon what he would have done had he lived to complete the opera himself, and the material Alfano inherited bears no sign of the level of inspiration that the final scenes demanded; the icy princess remains untransformed, the splendid promise of *In questa reggia* unfulfilled. As it stands, the score is certainly the richest, most powerful and accomplished of any that Puccini wrote—a last, worthy expression of the great Italian lyric tradition. And with Liù, at least, he had been at home. But the crisis of the opera took him to a place where, emotionally, he had never been before, and the question must remain: would he have continued to be defeated by the struggle to find expression for 'something' that this time lay beyond his experience? 'This infamous Turandot terrifies me', he had written to Sybil, and in spite of the magnificent music he gave his two protagonists, in the end it is Liù who has our sympathy—Liù, not Turandot, who makes us weep.

Alban Berg in 1930

Wozzeck

On 22 MAY 1911, at Grinzing cemetery in Vienna, Alban Berg and his teacher Arnold Schoenberg watched as the body of Gustav Mahler was lowered into the grave.

For Schoenberg it was not only a tribute of respect and admiration to the last true representative of the great Austro-German symphonic tradition, but also a gesture of gratitude to the powerful director of the Vienna Opera whose support and encouragement had earned his young colleague's undying loyalty. For Berg, who was too young to have known Mahler personally, it was something more intimate; from his earliest years he had felt for Mahler's music a passionate attachment, almost a form of spiritual affinity, that affected the whole development of his musical personality and was to stay with him for the rest of his life. But by the time of Mahler's death Schoenberg's latest compositions were already challenging virtually every established principle of the art of music, and it was between these two widely differing poles, the last fling of the great romantic tradition and the uncompromising statement of a new and radical idiom, that Berg's work as a composer was always to be balanced.

Berg was nineteen when he began to study with Schoenberg—'a very tall youngster, and extremely timid', Schoenberg later remembered—and in fact he was not physically strong, with a heart problem and recurrent attacks of asthma that were to plague him all his life. His background was comfortably middle-class; he came from a family with a talent for music, where an elder brother and younger sister provided domestic performances for the songs that he poured out from the age of fifteen onwards, and it was a selection of these, secretly shown to him by Alban's brother, that first aroused Schoenberg's interest.

Schoenberg From his very earliest work, however clumsy, one could see two things: first, that music was to him a language and that he did really express himself in that language; and secondly, an abundant warmth of feeling. . . . He was diligent, enthusiastic, and did everything to the best of his ability. Whether I recognised originality in him at that stage I can't be sure. He had, of course, like all these gifted young people in Vienna at that time, soaked himself with music and lived in music. He visited every opera and concert, played duets on the piano at home, soon read scores and was enthusiastic, uncritical, but open to everything beautiful, whether old or new, in music, literature, painting, sculpture, theatre or opera.   [*Reich, 1963: 27*]

Schoenberg's character could hardly have been more different from that of his pupil. A man of unshakeable moral rectitude and enormous energy, driven by an obsessive belief in the value of what he was doing, he was fierce, arrogant, and quick to take offence. There was understandable bitterness too: his stature as a composer was never recognised by his Viennese colleagues, and he suffered both in Austria and in Germany from virulent anti-Semitism. But he was a charismatic and inspiring teacher. 'Schoenberg had the gift of assembling pupils and admirers around him,' wrote Mahler's widow, Alma. 'He had real power of leadership and possessed great intellectual fascination. But the master had the lion's paw, and they followed him demurely'. And indeed they did. 'You'd never believe how infatuated they all are!' commented Berg's wife, Helene, to a friend: [*Mahler, 1960: 77*]

[Helene Berg]   'Whenever they were discussing something and Schoenberg got up and wandered around the room, one of them always ran around after him with an ash tray'—'Even Alban?' I asked.—'Him? He was the worst!'   [*Pople: 14*]

It was perhaps inevitable that Berg, whose own father had died when he was only fifteen years old, should have seen his teacher as a father figure, and Schoenberg responded by interesting himself in every aspect of Berg's life and character. From the start he seems to have had his doubts about his young pupil's middle-class background, and perhaps to have seen his easy receptiveness for 'everything that is beautiful, whether old or new' as a potential limitation. Nevertheless it was to have a profound effect on Berg's work as a composer; the lyrical quality at the heart of his musical personality, however radical and dissonant the idiom in which it was expressed, was something that existed in him from the beginning.

Schoenberg   In the condition in which he first came to me, Berg's imagination apparently refused to undertake the composition of anything
other than *Lieder*. Even the piano accompaniments to his songs had
something of the vocal style. To write an instrumental movement, or
to invent an instrumental theme, was absolutely impossible to him.
You can hardly imagine the pains I have had to take to overcome this
deficiency in his talent.   [*Schoenberg, 1958: 17*]

But while he worked with his pupil on the traditional disciplines of
harmony, counterpoint, form and instrumentation, Schoenberg came to
recognise another of the characteristics which was to be a hallmark of
Berg's mature work—his extraordinary facility in handling the intricacies
of his musical material.

Schoenberg   I found that I could work with him on counterpoint in
a way that was quite unusual with my pupils—and I should like to
single out a five part double fugue for string quintet which was a
richly overflowing work of art. But I already saw, then, what I could
make him capable of: when the fugue was finished I told him to add
a piano accompaniment in the style of a *continuo*, which he not only
did brilliantly but cleverly brought into his solution a whole lot more
little devilries as well. . . .   [*Reich, 1963: 27*]

It was when Schoenberg moved on to 'free composition' that difficulties began to appear.

Schoenberg   Composition lessons went well up to and including his
piano sonata. Then problems arose which neither of us were able to
understand at the time. Today I can see that Alban, who occupied
himself most intensively with the music of the time, with Mahler,
Strauss and perhaps even Debussy (of whom I knew nothing), and no
doubt with my own music, naturally had an ardent desire to compose
no longer in the classical forms and their accompanying harmonic
and melodic structures, but, in accordance with the development of
his personality, in a contemporary manner. . . .   [*Id: 27–8*]

It was precisely during the period of his work with Berg that Schoenberg was developing, in his own music, the method of composition that
later became known as 'atonal'. It was a method that had arisen, as he

was always keen to point out, from historical necessity, and in particular from developments in the realm of harmony. Throughout the nineteenth century the treatment of this aspect of music had become more and more complex, until the rich and satisfying sounds to which audiences had become accustomed in the later works of Wagner and Richard Strauss were blurring the harmonic borderlines and undermining the distinctions that had traditionally governed the relationship of one harmony to another. The idea of a tonal centre—the sense of a recognisable key as the basis of any piece of music—was gradually becoming lost; the familiar concepts of dissonance and consonance, of tension and release, had less and less meaning, and the whole fabric of musical logic was under threat. From about 1907 onwards Schoenberg, accepting the reality of this situation, began substituting for the old structural principles a system in which the twelve semitones of the octave were treated as exact equals, with no recognised centre of gravity at all. It represented a complete break with the basic principles which had governed the development of music over the centuries, and it was in adapting this new world of harmonic uncertainty and structural ambivalence to the promptings of a late romantic sensibility that Berg was to find his own individual voice.

His first attempts did not altogether meet with Schoenberg's approval. To begin with, they were extremely short, allowing no space for the thematic development which Schoenberg had always regarded as a weakness in Berg's technical equipment. True, the outsize orchestra used in the *Five Altenberg Songs* gave him the opportunity to experiment with new and useful instrumental sonorities, but when in 1912 he began work on a 'large, one movement symphony', apparently with the intention of dedicating it to the master he venerated, it too came under heavy criticism. To judge from the one identifiable fragment that has survived—a few bars of deeply emotional *adagio* which were to reappear in the great threnody that closed the tragic history of Wozzeck nearly ten years later—the memory of Mahler still lingered, and there may have been charges of intellectual laziness. But Berg's personal life was passing through a romantic phase; in May 1911 he had married Helene Nahowski, and the very evident domestic bliss that followed certainly coincided with a significant lack of creative output—only two works in a little over two years. In any case, whatever the reasons, Schoenberg clearly did not like the direction in which Berg's music, and perhaps his life, were developing, particularly as the older man had now left Vienna and could no longer exert the influence of his physical presence. There was an unhappy meeting between master and pupil in Berlin in the summer of 1913.

Berg   You will surely understand, dear Herr Schoenberg, that into the most beautiful memories of untroubled enjoyment there intrude memories of that last afternoon with its depressing home-truths. But I must <u>thank you</u> for your censure as for everything else I have received from you, knowing as I do that it is meant well—and for <u>my own good</u>. Nor do I need to tell you, dear Herr Schoenberg, that my deep pain is assurance that I will take your censure to heart. . . . I hope I can soon prove to you in deed what I have scarcely been able to express here in words. . . .   [*Brand: 180*]

The work that eventually received the promised dedication, the *Three Orchestral Pieces*, Op. 6, in fact marked a turning point in Berg's development. For the first time they provided proof of the ability to organise emotional material in an intellectual, almost mathematical framework, which was to become an essential feature of his style. For Schoenberg this had always been one of the outstanding difficulties with a musical language that abandoned the framework provided by the accepted norms of key, tonality and harmonic progression.

Schoenberg   Fulfilment of these functions—comparable to the effect of punctuation in the construction of sentences, of subdivision into paragraphs and of fusion into chapters—could scarcely be assured with chords whose constructive values had not as yet been explored. Hence it seemed at first impossible to compose pieces of complicated organisation or of great length. . . . The foremost characteristics of these pieces *in statu nascendi* were their extreme expressiveness and their extraordinary brevity. At the time, neither I nor my pupils were conscious of the reasons for these features. Later I realised that our sense of form was right when it forced us to counterbalance extreme emotionality with extraordinary shortness. . . . [Subsequently] I discovered how to construct larger forms by following a text or a poem. . . .   [*Schoenberg, 1951: 105–6*]

'Extreme emotionality' (Schoenberg's English) was certainly a characteristic of the vocal works that Schoenberg composed at this period. *Pierrot*

Lunaire, a setting of twenty-one poems by Albert Giraud for speaker and chamber ensemble, has achieved notoriety for its use of *Sprechstimme*, a form of vocal enunciation midway between speech and song, and although it has always been difficult to achieve a completely satisfying realisation of a vocal technique that is by its nature pulled constantly in two opposing directions, there has never been any doubt about the brilliant effectiveness of its use to underline the parodistic, sometimes nightmarish satire of Giraud's verse. This was not lost on Berg when he came to deal with parody, satire and nightmare of his own. But emotionality and brevity were driven to the ultimate extreme in Schoenberg's first attempt at opera, the monodrama *Erwartung*, where the single character, a woman, is supported by an enormous orchestra that weaves its atonal, themeless, dreamlike web of sound to a pitch of Expressionist intensity that has never been equalled in a work for the stage. It lasts for only half an hour—it is difficult to imagine it lasting longer—though even so it had to wait fifteen years before anyone was brave enough to perform it. But for Berg it was an instant revelation. Getting to know *Erwartung*, he wrote, 'is among my most treasured memories . . .'

Berg   . . . slowly practicing the piano reduction at home and being allowed to play from it at every lesson, and your then telling me so much about it that in the end the results [even] at the piano were halfway decent. So it is that I live more in my memories than in the present, am more with you than with myself, and perhaps that's what enables me to bear these excruciating times. . . .   [*Brand*: 211]

It was just three months before the outbreak of the First World War that Berg's own ambition to write an opera found its catalyst.

Georg Büchner's dramatic fragment, *Woyzeck*, a social drama written in the 1830s, was one of the first works for the theatre to deal exclusively with the poorest members of society. The plot was taken from the real-life case history of Johann Christian Woyzeck, a simple soldier and barber who suffered hallucinations and killed his mistress for being unfaithful. From this bare material Büchner began to construct a play filled with deep sympathy for its subject and dominated by the sense that human beings are passive objects, the victims of an absurd social system which condemns them to an unjust destiny. It was left unfinished in a fragmentary condition at the author's death, and remained unknown and unperformed for the best part of forty years until a workable performing version was put together from disordered fragments by the novelist Karl Emil Franzos—though so faded was the manuscript and so 'microscopically small' Büchner's handwriting that Franzos actually misread the name of the chief character, with the result that, when his edition was published in 1879, it bore the now familiar title *Wozzeck*. In this form the uncompromising rigour of Büchner's message secured the play recognition as a masterpiece among the more progressive literary circles, who saw in it a precursor of the emerging Expressionist movement and, after a further revision by Paul Landau, it finally reached performance in Munich in November 1913. The poet Rainer Maria Rilke, who saw it not long after the first performance, wrote to Marie von Thurn und Taxis:

Rilke   It is a monstrous thing, written more than eighty years ago, . . . nothing but the fate of a common soldier who stabs his faithless mistress, but presenting with immense power how even in the lowliest creature . . . there is all the greatness of existence, and how he cannot prevent the walls of his dull mind from being torn open to the awe-inspiring and the infinite; a spectacle without equal, the way in which this misused and maltreated human being in his stable-jacket stands in the universe, *malgré lui*, in endless relation to the stars. This is theatre, this is what theatre should be.   [*Rilke, I*: 426–7]

Berg was at the first Viennese performance at the Residenzbühne on 5 May 1914, and the effect that it had on him was remembered many years later by the nineteen-year-old Paul Elbogen.

Elbogen   We young people knew the play very well from Franzos's publication. A German actor, Albert Steinrück, rude and rather brutal, played Wozzeck. I sat in the gallery of the little Kammerspiele. Four rows behind me sat Alban Berg, whom I greeted as I came in because I had known him very well for years. They played the drama for three hours without the smallest interruption in complete darkness. Indescribably excited and enthusiastic I stood up amidst wild applause, met Alban Berg a few steps behind me. He was deathly pale and perspiring profusely. 'What do you say?' he gasped, beside himself. 'Isn't it fantastic, incredible?' Then, already taking his leave, 'Someone must set it to music'.   [*Jarman, 1989: 1*]

Within weeks he had begun to do so himself.

With its stark, varied action divided into abrupt episodes, and its taut, powerfully expressive language, *Woyzeck* was in many ways a good starting point for an opera. What appealed to Berg above all was the sense of compassion for the disinherited creature, harassed and half-crazed in his confusion, and it is probable that the negative, passive attitude to life may have struck a kindred chord in the brittle, slightly morbid side of his essentially gentle nature. But there were other aspects of the play to attract a composer: the military background with band music and the macho figure of the Drum Major, the scenes of common life in the taverns, the element of the grotesque, especially in the figures of the Doctor and the Captain who torture and taunt poor Woyzeck, the opportunities for lyrical music in the songs of Marie and Andres—in fact, it was the street scene with the Captain and the Doctor in Act II that attracted his very first sketches, closely followed by fragments of Marie's lullaby in Act I, Scene 3, and Andres' song in Scene 2. But these were immediate, tentative ideas, without as yet much context, and from July he turned instead to the serious arrangement of his libretto.

Berg   When I decided to write an opera I had nothing in mind—apart from the wish to write good music and translate [into this music] the spiritual content and poetic language of Büchner's immortal drama— except to give to the theatre what is of the theatre. That meant to shape the music so that it remained fully conscious of its duty to serve the drama, indeed so that it provided and expressed whatever the drama required for realisation on the stage. This demanded from the composer the solution of all the essential problems of an ideal producer. On the other hand, the justification of the work as a musical entity must not suffer; nothing must interfere with the music's autonomy.   [*Reich*, 1963: 60]

Not everyone, however, was so optimistic.

Schoenberg   I was greatly surprised when this soft-hearted, timid young man had the courage to engage in a venture which seemed to invite misfortune: to compose *Wozzeck*, a drama of such extraordinary tragic [*sic*], that seemed forbidding to music. And even more: it contained scenes of everyday life which were contrary to the concept of the opera which still lived on stylized costumes and conventional characters. [*Redlich, London:* 245–6]

In fact, for most of the period of *Wozzeck*'s composition Schoenberg's attitude to his pupil's ambitious plan was anything but encouraging. His objection to the scenes of everyday life is consistent with the puritanical streak in his character, which saw opera as a noble, idealised art form that should not be degraded by trivialities. But it was precisely this closeness to the grim details of day-to-day existence that excited Berg's sympathy, as his friend and fellow pupil, Erwin Stein, realised.

Stein   The everyday tragedy of simple folk moved Berg deeply; this was the sort of story which he in the greatness of his heart desired to surround with music's compassion. For seven years he was occupied with the planning and the composition of the opera, a long period if compared with his short life—he died when he was only fifty. Perhaps it is the prolonged maturing which gives to the whole work its quality of unusual richness and which helped the music to crystallize into a so well-defined form. It was world events that caused the delay. Berg had to become a soldier himself and he was as little martial as his hero Wozzeck. [*Stein: 103*]

Though he was at first turned down as unsuitable for military service, Berg was passed as fit in June 1915, but active training lasted little more than a month before he succumbed to asthma attacks and breathing problems and had to be transferred to a military hospital. Nevertheless life in the barrack room had not been without its value. 'While his mind was with the story and the characters of his opera,' wrote Erwin Stein, 'he could see around him, like ghosts, similar characters and similar scenes'. The Doctor and the Captain probably owe all too much to their real-life prototypes, and there were unexpected surprises, too. 'Have you ever heard a lot of people snoring at the same time?' he wrote to his pupil Gottfried Kassowitz:

Berg   . . . this polyphonic breathing, gasping and groaning is the most peculiar chorus I have ever heard. It is like some primeval music that wells up from the abysses of the soul. . . . [*Reich, 1963: 41*]

It was a memory that was to return vividly when he came to write the chorus of snoring soldiers in the guardroom scene in Act II.

For the time being, however, any serious musical work on the opera was out of the question. On his discharge from hospital he was transferred to guard duty in Vienna, but even this proved too strenuous, and in May 1916 he was drafted to a desk job in the Ministry of War—which seemed in the end an almost more senseless form of imprisonment. 'It's months now since I did any work on *Wozzeck*', he wrote to Helene, 'everything is suffocated, buried. And this may go on—yes, will go on—for years'. To make matters worse his relationship with Schoenberg, always crucial to his state of mind, was going through a difficult phase, and at one point he even seems to have considered dropping *Wozzeck* altogether and looking to Strindberg or Goethe for an alternative subject. But by the summer of 1917 the air between them had cleared, and from his first short leave in the long-missed solitude of the country, he reported to his intransigent mentor: [*Berg, 1965: 313*]

Berg   I've been here for ten days now. During the first week I was still suffering terribly from the effects of years of confinement: asthma attacks of such severity that on one occasion I really thought I would not survive the night. But now it's much better and, as happens every summer I spend here, the desire to work is—at last—beginning to stir again, and I'm working again on the composition of Büchner's drama *Wozzeck*. . . . Of course there is no chance of drafting out a larger section: in another week I lose my freedom again and the servitude in Vienna resumes. . . .   [*Brand: 266*]

Nevertheless, Berg managed to complete his libretto during the war years, changing few of Büchner's actual words but condensing the sprawling structure of the original play.

Berg   For my libretto it was necessary to make a selection from Büchner's twenty-six loosely arranged, sometimes fragmentary scenes: repetitions that did not lend themselves to musical variation had to be avoided, the scenes had to be contracted, linked and grouped into acts. Whether I liked it or not, this task was already more a musical than a literary one, and its solution depended not on the laws of dramatic but of musical structure.   [*Reich, 1963: 60*]

In fact, his office job in Vienna, soul-destroying as it was, gradually allowed him more time to get back to the music—though its effect on his health continued to be a problem. A year later he was again on leave in the country.

Berg　I have to avoid long hikes—which I used to take daily in peacetime—and constant shortness of breath even disturbs me while composing. After several unsuccessful attempts to write piano or chamber music I finally returned to my old plan of composing *Wozzeck* and immediately found it quicker and easier to get back to work on that. And after years of not working, that may be the main thing.　　　　　　　　　　　　　　　　　　　　　　　　[*Brand:* 269]

To his friend and fellow pupil Anton Webern, the composer who more than anyone else followed Schoenberg's ideas to their logical conclusion, he wrote at about the same time:

Berg　Whether I am content with what I have done so far I can hardly say. While writing, I feel such warmth all the time, and it all flows more easily than I would have thought after so long an interval. What moves me so deeply is not only the fate of this poor creature, exploited and tortured by the whole world, but the incredible emotional content, the mood, of each individual scene.　　　　[*Reich,* 1963: 42–3]

Nevertheless in attempting the construction of a full-length opera in the new atonal idiom, Berg still faced the same problem of structural coherence that had given his teacher pause . . .

Berg　. . . how could I achieve, without the proven means of tonality, and without recourse to the formal structures that are based on it, the same degree of coherence, the same compelling musical unity? And, what is more, coherence not only in the smaller forms—the individual scenes with their exits and entries— . . . but also, and this was the more difficult part, a sense of unity in the larger forms of each successive act and indeed in the coherent architectural structure of the work as a whole.

The text and dramatic action by themselves could not guarantee this coherence—least of all in a work like Büchner's *Woyzeck,* which is well known to consist of many . . . loosely connected, fragmentary scenes. And even if it were possible to devise a three act plan in which Exposition, Development and Catastrophe were clearly separated into three sections of five scenes each, and thus ensure the unity of the *action*, the dramatic coherence of the work, this would in no way guarantee its *musical* unity and coherence as well.

[*Redlich, Vienna:* 312]

Berg's solution to this problem was entirely original and was later to attract much controversial publicity. The music for each act, and for the individual scenes within each act, is organised in accordance with the principles of an accepted musical form: the first act, in which Wozzeck appears in successive scenes with each of the other characters in the opera, is a set of five 'character pieces'; the second and most substantial act, in which the drama develops, is a symphony in five movements; the third act, in which tension is screwed up to the final climax, is a series of five inventions on single musical ideas—the last being preceded by a long orchestral interlude described as an 'invention on a key'. These forms are blatantly manipulated to conform to the action of the scenes, and may not be easily recognised by the listener—though it would be hard to miss the dramatic confrontation between the Drum Major and Marie implied in the 'Military march and lullaby' in the third scene of Act I, or the claustrophobic use of the constantly repeating form of the 'Passacaglia' to drive home the Doctor's repeated obsessions in the scene that follows. But if, as is very likely, these formal structures mostly pass the listener by, they are very definitely there in the score, and for the composer they were of critical importance in providing him with the inner framework essential to any coherent work of art.

Berg's was in any case a mind that relished structural subtleties: the thematic material in *Wozzeck* is treated to all kinds of intellectual devices—imitations, inversions, palindromes, cryptograms—private musical, even numerical, puzzles which are intricately woven into the texture of the score and contribute to the sense of constant thematic activity with which the music teems. Yet the extraordinary complexity of these structural techniques developed alongside the instinctive dramatic and lyrical gift which represented the other side of Berg's musical character. And the memories of his wartime experiences were never far away. To Helene he wrote towards the end of that last leave in the summer of 1918:

Berg   . . . I went up the mountain by myself, extremely slowly, resting
often in accordance with instructions, and as I plodded on, suddenly—
though I didn't have the least intention of thinking about work—I
happened on the musical expression for an entrance of Wozzeck's that
I had been trying to find for ages. There is something of me in his
make-up, because during these war years, I have been dependent in
just the same way on people that I find hateful, a prisoner, tied down,
sick, resigned—yes, humiliated. If it weren't for this military service I
should still be as healthy as I used to be. . . .   [*Berg, 1965: 376*]

All the same, a couple of weeks later he told Webern that he had finished composing the second scene of Act II (the Captain and the Doctor
in the street), and that he hoped to get Act I, Scene 4 (Wozzeck and the
Doctor) finished before his leave was over.

But back in Vienna composition progressed slowly. The Society for Private Musical Performances which Schoenberg set up in November 1918
with himself as president and three of his pupils as performance directors, involved Berg in a frenzy of administrative activity that his work on
Wozzeck could ill afford. His release in the same month from the shackles
of military service, though welcome in itself, meant that he had to find
some means of earning a living; the private income of the Berg family,
already diminishing, would soon be further reduced by the disastrous
depreciation of the Austrian currency after the war, and Berg began giving
lessons in composition and publishing polemical articles for the avant-garde
press. And the care of Berghof, the Berg country home in Carinthia, was
soon making another heavy claim on the composer's time. In the reduced
circumstances in which Berg's mother now found herself, the family had
no alternative but to dispose of the estate—either by leasing it or by an
outright sale. In either case it was necessary for the house to be maintained
in a saleable condition and, though deeply reluctant to leave Vienna (and
Helene), Berg felt it his duty to oversee the process until, in May 1920, the
house was finally sold to an Italian industrialist—who turned it into a factory for shoe-trees.

Nevertheless the first scene of Act I was finished by the early summer
of 1919, and at the end of July he reported to Webern from the country:

Berg   I'm not as far forward with *Wozzeck* as I hoped to be. But Act I
is quite finished (five scenes) and one big scene of Act II. Scarcely

any is scored yet. But it's a big thing. Up till now about 900 bars are
composed.   [*Jarman, 1979: 8*]

'Perhaps I'll manage to finish the 2nd act here', he wrote to Schoenberg
on the same day.

Berg   My health has improved substantially. . . . Contributing factors, in
addition to good food, are my daily swims in the lake, rain or shine,
and long walks. And in general not having to worry about life for
the immediate future. . . . The balance of my daily routine includes:
country activities like fishing, driving the coach, riding, boating,
repairs to the house and farm, reading the paper. . . . [*Brand: 274–5*]

By the end of July the following year the overall plan of the last
two acts had finally been fixed, and a month later only the scene in the
inn was needed to complete Act II. The inn scene is the longest in the
opera, the most crowded and varied, and the most visually theatrical.
Soldiers, girls and apprentices (one of them conspicuously drunk) dance
to the waltzes of a band on the stage; there are cheeky references to *Don
Giovanni* and *Der Rosenkavalier* and a rousing male-voice hunting chorus. Formally the scene provides the *scherzo* of the symphony on which
the overall structure of Act II is based, and the complex confusion of pub
life which it encapsulates within this structural unity was not achieved
easily. 'I think all the time of the music still to be written for the most
difficult scene of all, the scene in the inn, but it still won't quite come
. . .' he wrote to Helene early in June 1921, and a couple of days later:
                                                            [*Berg, 1965: 456*]

Berg   My head is constantly filled with *Wozzeck* (except when it's with
you . . .). The inn scene is coming along very slowly, but it *is* coming.
If I can manage to get it down as I have it in my head, then the hardest part is done and the rest will be child's play.   [*Id: 458*]

The details of the stage band preoccupied him.

Berg   By tram along the Neubaugasse to a big accordion maker. In *Wozzeck* there's going to be a sort of local scratch band which should be
great fun. Consisting of a fiddle (a high-tuned violin), dulcet wood-

wind (a clarinet), accordion, guitar and bass tuba. So to see how far I can go with modern ideas on an accordion, I must get to know all the possibilities. . . .   [*Id: 461*]

But once he had got it down 'as I have it in my head', the floodgates were open to the last act.

Berg   I have been so deep in work on *Wozzeck* that I couldn't get round to writing letters. . . . Things are going well for the first time here. The second act is finished. Only a quarter of the third. I'll take it up again tomorrow. . . .   [*Jarman, 1979: 8*]

As he approached the climax of his opera, the music seems to have come with greater facility, and the musical form of the last act, the succession of six 'inventions', is in some ways the most intimately blended with the dramatic action. The five scenes are short, intense, and each concerned with the development of a single idea, both in the drama and in the music: the single note (B natural), which dominates the musical texture of Scene 2 with ever-increasing persistence as Wozzeck prepares to kill his mistress, and finally explodes in a unison crescendo for full orchestra that is one of the most shattering dramatic effects in all opera, gives way with merciless abruptness to a jaunty polka, strummed on an out-of-tune piano, which provides the obsessive rhythm that continuously belies Wozzeck's frenzied attempts to conceal his guilt as he dances and flirts with Margret. When he rushes from the tavern to search in the pond for the knife that could betray him, it is the ever-changing permutations of a single six-note chord which gather in intensity as he loses his reason and finally engulf him altogether; the moon turns blood red, frogs are heard croaking, and the Captain and the Doctor, passing the pond and mistaking the sound for that of a drowning man, hurry quickly away.

It is at this point that Berg changes his dramatic stance. Instead of standing apart as a sometimes caustic, sometimes sympathetic, sometimes simply bemused commentator on the action, for the first and only time he allows us to feel the full intensity of his compassion for Wozzeck. The orchestral threnody that follows, by far the longest of the interludes that separate the scenes of the opera, is described as an invention on a key, and certainly it is the one section of the score that both opens and closes in a well-defined tonality—in this case D minor. But the origin of its opening theme goes deep into Berg's personal history: after first appearing in an early, unfinished piano sonata, it formed an important element in the symphony intended for dedication to Schoenberg, and when the symphony was abandoned, he appears to have considered turning it into a little piano piece for Helene—though 'I just can't get it right' he wrote; 'perhaps the idea itself is for once not quite original—somehow derivative in feeling and tone, though I can't think of any model for it. . .'. What is curious is that he didn't recognise himself that the model was, and had always been, Mahler. In any case, the theme clearly had some special significance for Helene for it was at her insistence that it was eventually included at the climactic point of *Wozzeck*—where it dictated the strongly Mahlerian tone of the breathtaking orchestral peroration that follows. 'The interlude at the end I owe to you, and to you only', he wrote to Helene, 'it was *you* who *composed* it, I just wrote it down'. But the true debt was to the great romantic symphonist whom he could never get entirely out of his mind. And in the end the origin of the final interlude of *Wozzeck* is unimportant; wherever it came from, it provides an unforgettably powerful expression of Berg's feelings for his simple, persecuted hero, and throws into stark and pitiless contrast the chilling reality of the brief final scene.   [*Berg, 1965: 253, 487*]

By the middle of October 1921 the short score was finished, and by April of the following year Berg had completed the orchestration. 'The last days in Vienna were pretty exhausting', he wrote to Schoenberg, 'but at least *Wozzeck* is <u>entirely</u> finished. 2 identical, beautifully bound scores now exist'. 'The [piano] reduction is largely finished too', he added—though for the composer himself this seems to have been of limited value.
                [*Brand: 314*]

Berg   I am very nervous about playing *Wozzeck* for people. 1. I play too poorly. 2. I feel self-conscious about doing it in any case. It only makes sense when one can do it convincingly, indeed with the intention of convincing others of its "beauty". Doing this for my <u>own</u> work would embarrass me to such an extent that I would do it even worse than I would anyway because of my awkwardness at the keyboard.   [*Id: 319*]

'Alban was no pianist', observed Alma Mahler, 'for the master frowned on "playing the piano to make composition easy for yourself"', and when

Berg visited Frankfurt and Darmstadt in December 1921, it had been his friend the American pianist Edward Steuermann who had played the score to the operatic authorities—though with no positive result. All the same, it was clearly essential to get the piano reduction published as soon as possible, though not easy to find a publisher willing to take on such a controversial work. A first attempt to raise the money for private publication fell through, and Berg turned for help to one of his oldest and most loyal supporters. [*Mahler, 1959: 168*]

Alma Mahler   Now that the opera was finished, Alban and Helene Berg came to me, showed me the score, and asked me to accept the dedication of the work. They were in trouble: a friend [of Berg's sister] who had lent them money to have the score printed was pressing for repayment. The matter weighed heavily on the Bergs, and having taken up collections in the past for Schoenberg and others, I went on another begging tour. . . . [*Id: 168*]

The irrepressible Frau Mahler proved impossible to resist, and the completed vocal score was published in the following year. But when Berg sent copies to various opera houses in the German-speaking world, the reaction was no more encouraging. Sales were minimal—even at the 'low price' of 150,000 kronen. Of greater value were the one or two articles which appeared in the more forward-looking musical periodicals, but in general there was a broadly accepted belief that *Wozzeck* was impossibly complicated, relentlessly dissonant and virtually unsingable. Nor did Schoenberg, in spite of professing that 'it would be very interesting to see an opera of yours', offer much encouragement. Berg, who found it difficult to leave his score alone, was still tinkering with the instrumentation when the two men met in April 1923.

Berg   Schoenberg was again insufferable, criticizing everything about me: that I'm still always working on *Wozzeck*—'it's very Karl-Krausish [pernickety], all this endless correcting'—, that I smoke, *that I shouldn't imagine I shall have a success with Wozzeck* because it's too difficult, and worst of all that I still haven't begun work on the Chamber Concerto. . . . [*Berg, 1965: 505*]

However, in August news arrived that the conductor Erich Kleiber, who was due to become director of the Berlin State Opera later in the year, had been shown a copy of the vocal score, liked what he had seen, and was interested in mounting a production in Berlin.

Berg   Kleiber is coming to Vienna and asked Hertzka [now Berg's publisher] to tell me to play *Wozzeck* for him. . . . I have asked Dr Bachrich to assist me. So we are practicing the piano score, partly together, partly alone.   [*Brand:* 330]

Nevertheless it was Bachrich, a competent pianist, who effectively played the score—Berg's contribution being to add details when the music became too complex for a single pair of hands. And the joint execution had the desired effect, because after hearing only two scenes Kleiber's mind was already made up. 'It's settled!' he said, 'I am going to do the opera in Berlin, even if it costs me my job!'   [*Carner:* 57]

Before the Berlin performance could be set up, however, another conductor, Hermann Scherchen, suggested to Berg that he should make a suite of extracts from the opera for concert performance in order to raise interest in the music before the coming operatic production. The extracts were carefully chosen to present the more readily approachable aspects of the score: the interlude and third scene of Act I, including the orchestral reminiscence of Andres's song, the passing military band, and Marie's lullaby; the first scene of Act III, with Marie's reading from the Bible; and a conflation of the two scenes at the pond, leading to the final orchestral interlude and the last scene of the opera. The first performance of *Three Fragments from Wozzeck* was conducted by Scherchen at the Frankfurt International Musical Festival in June 1924. The success was immediate; it gave Berg the first real triumph of his career as a composer, which was repeated when the *Fragments* were given again under Zemlinsky in Prague a year later.

The preparation of the first performance of the opera in 1925 was a more arduous undertaking; it was rumoured to have involved 137 rehearsals, of which Kleiber probably directed 34 for the orchestra alone, and 14 for the full ensemble. Berg arrived in Berlin on 13 November.

Berg   Under the megalomaniac impression that *Wozzeck* is something really great, and that therefore the performance is bound to be something equally great, I presented myself for the first rehearsal with Kleiber, Schützendorf [Wozzeck], Witting (Andres), Marie and child.

I would not have believed it possible to find such understanding, as a musician and dramatist, as I find in Kleiber, qualities that naturally get communicated to the singers who are almost without exception first-class. The stage sets (on paper at least) are magnificent, and it is Kleiber, too, who really leads the production—and how! Hörth [the resident producer] is pretty well out of it. Greatest possible enthusiasm by everybody concerned. I can happily leave everything in Kleiber's hands. . . .

This morning . . . I was with him till 2 o'clock: fabulous lunch, a bit of rest in the hotel, now briefly writing this note in a café, then to a second rehearsal: doctor, apprentices, and Wozzeck-Marie once again. Then with Kleiber to a big party tonight.

Tomorrow rehearsal with piano . . . Leave early Sunday morning. . . .

[*Berg, 1965: 542–3*]

His first visit lasted only two days, but he was back again on 30 November and the following morning went straight to a full orchestral rehearsal of the second half of the opera. His excitement in his letter to Helene is palpable: 'Imagine in an hour's time I shall hear my orchestra! If only you were here!'. But by the evening his mood had changed.

Berg Be glad that you weren't at the first rehearsal! Along with the joy of at last hearing the whole work in the orchestra went the anguish that I suffered from the things that are still not right. If I didn't know that one must not judge after a rehearsal like this, I should be, if not actually depressed, at least very uneasy. But from everyone's assurances, and above all from the colossal eagerness of all concerned to get it right, I'm sure it will still turn out as I imagined it. And much of it does sound wonderful. . . . The orchestra itself is fabulous. But will Kleiber be able to carry out all my intentions, given that he is having no more rehearsals with the orchestra alone, but from now on always with the singers on the stage? There are really not many more orchestral rehearsals. . . .   [*Id: 545*]

The complexity of the orchestral writing in *Wozzeck* was undoubtedly a challenge for the instrumentalists of the Berlin State Opera, particularly since, although the orchestra used is a very large one, much of the scoring has a delicate, almost chamber-music quality that is merciless to inaccurate playing. But if the score was a problem for the orchestra, the unprecedented mixture of vocal styles in an unfamiliar atonal idiom was an equally tough assignment for the singers. Berg always insisted that, apart from the few spoken passages, the bulk of his opera could, and should, be sung using the traditional operatic *bel canto* that had originated in Italy. 'It has often been said that this is not a *bel canto* opera', he wrote later, 'but people often do not realise how much of what is genuinely conceived as vocal can be expressed in the '*bel cantare*' style . . .'. And in this context he saw the much discussed *Sprechstimme* as a valuable middle course between the sung and the spoken word.

Berg   There is hardly any [sung] recitative in my opera, but I think that I have made full amends for this deficiency by employing, for the first time in opera and uniquely at such length, the so-called 'rhythmic declamation' that Schoenberg introduced . . . in his *Pierrot* melodramas, and giving it so substantial a role. It has shewn that this melodically, rhythmically and dynamically fixed use of the speaking voice—which fully preserves, remember, the formal possibilities of absolute music in a way that recitative, for instance, has failed to do—not only offers one of the best means of ensuring that the words are understood (as the words really must be in opera, now and then), but also enriches operatic music with a valuable means of expression, from the tonelessly whispered word to the virtual *bel parlare* of broad-ranging speech melodies, that is derived from the purest musical sources. . . .   [*Redlich, Vienna: 317*]

All the same, for artists used to singing Wagner and Puccini, it must have been a difficult concept to grasp, and they appear to have tackled it with considerable success, even if problems of ensemble and staging still remained to be overcome.

Berg   Tomorrow (Wednesday), Thursday and Friday, I am having stage rehearsals with Hörth, and I shall use the afternoon sessions to go over the last details with the singers. Above all, the music of the inn scene, which is still quite impossible and really worries me a lot. . . .
                                        [*Berg, 1965: 545*]

However, the stage rehearsal next morning restored his confidence: 'impression, despite interruptions and repeating things, *terrific*, unbearably powerful'.

Berg   All the singers wonderful. Schützendorf quite overwhelming. The Captain—no exceptional voice, but characterization a joy. The Doctor—not a very intelligent singer, but a marvellous voice, and well able to cope with his 'unsingable' part. . . . So if Kleiber can only manage to draw out that last bit from the orchestra—as he will—we shall get a performance which really makes the effect that it should. Today I once more believe that it is going to become something tremendous, something unheard of till now. Director Hörth is gushingly friendly; the explanation, as he tells me again and again—he is quite simply shattered by my work.

    This afternoon a very important rehearsal with guitarists, accordion and clarinet, so I hope that now the stage band will be good too.
[*Id:* 547–8]

Although the scene in the tavern garden in the last act was now going well, the difficult, big inn scene in Act II, in spite of intensive rehearsing, continued to give trouble. 'The staging is fine and full of brilliant details . . .'

Berg   . . . but I'm afraid the musical side gets lost with all the production and acting. Added to which, the stage band is still not good—my biggest problem child. (Despite lots of extra rehearsals).   [*Id:* 550]

The arrival of new blood in the form of 'a magnificent accordion player, an American virtuoso,' a couple of days later seemed to have resolved the problem of the band at least . . .

Berg   . . . but the orchestral rehearsal with full action on the stage was still a real muddle. How everything—orchestra, stage management, will fit smoothly together in a week's time I really don't know, and can only console myself with the thought that Kleiber never produces an unfinished article. Above all in this case, where he himself stands or falls by the outcome of the first night. So he knows, and knows perfectly well, that it must and will be finished—and finished *in time.* . . .   [*Id:* 551–2]

For Berg, too, time was a concern, and his determination to involve himself in every aspect of the performance, combined with the social demands made upon him in Berlin, must have taxed his precarious physical stamina. But his letters to Helene were reassuring.

Berg I am quite well, in spite of working 16 hours a day, in spite of
irregular (but sufficient) intakes of food, in spite of two daily hikes
through deep snow and not enough sleep. Today, for example, I was
away before 9 o'clock and already working on the score in the underground; 10 to 11 stage band, 11 to 2 second act, 2 to 3 production
meeting, 3 to 5 eating and talking shop with Schmied [a pupil], 5 to 8
with Kleiber, going over all the tempi again with the score. With him
on foot to the Kroll opera, where we listened to a guest singer, 9.30
to 12.30 with Kleiber and Arravantinos (the stage designer—a *real*
artist) at a restaurant. Home by underground, and through the snow,
with 5 kilos of score under my arm, where I am now lying in bed at
1.30 a.m., finishing this last letter. . . .   [*Id:* 553]

The tensions surrounding the preparation of the opera were not all
musically inspired. The polemical press campaign against this 'unperformable' work, which had been under way for some time, was complicated
and fuelled during the last three weeks of rehearsal by developments in
the administration of Berlin's opera houses. Max von Schillings, who had
been Intendant of the State Opera for the past six years, had been dismissed from his post on 26 November, and in the resulting media furore
Kleiber, who owed his position to Schillings and was to some extent his
protégé, found his position becoming increasingly insecure. The success
of *Wozzeck* was therefore at least as important to Kleiber as it was to
Berg, and the possibility, at one point very real, that the production of
this controversial work might be cancelled altogether did little for the
nerves of either conductor or composer.

Musically, however, the performance was coming together, and though
the Inn Scene remained a problem, there were moments of great happiness. Berg was particularly pleased with Marie, for whose touching
role he had written some of his most tender music—'how fine the jewel
scene sounds, my favourite scene!' he wrote—and also with the Doctor
—'very good, flowing *bel canto*, just as I wanted it. Everything singable'.
In spite of the many stylistic hurdles, the essentially lyrical quality of
Berg's music was gradually being appreciated by its interpreters. But he
was aware, all the same, of the difficulties that the score would present to listeners unfamiliar with the idiom. To friends who were coming from Prague for the première, he sent a significant word of advice:
                                                                       [*Id:* 551]

Berg   Tell them the dress rehearsal is on Saturday morning at 11.00, so that if possible they should leave on Friday night at the latest. To hear it only once is not enough. It's terribly hard to understand.   [*Id:* 553]

The first performance of *Wozzeck*, which took place as scheduled on 14 December 1925, was a sensation, and a predictably turbulent one. Much of the antagonism was motivated by the internal politics of the Berlin theatres and directed at Kleiber, but the intellectual and cultural elite of Berlin were there in force, and the strength of feeling both for and against this 'unperformable' opera was evident from the start. Among the supporters of the composer was Hans Heinsheimer, a representative of Berg's Viennese publishers.

Heinsheimer   *Wozzeck* was my first unforgettable encounter with a great, contemporary operatic work. Today [1953] it has its place beside *Pelléas et Mélisande*—not as a 'popular' opera, but recognised throughout the world as a work of powerful, incontestable greatness. But at the première there were bouts of fisticuffs, battles of words between the stalls and the occupants of the boxes, derisive laughter, hisses and loud whistling, and for a time it seemed as if the opponents of the work might overwhelm the few but eventually victorious supporters of the composer. . . .   [*Reich, 1959:* 28]

Schoenberg, who was recovering from an operation for acute appendicitis, could not be there but sent good wishes in a cautious telegram. He eventually saw the fourth performance on 7 January, and recorded his reactions in a characteristic letter to Berg.

Schoenberg   Dear friend, we saw *Wozzeck* the day after we arrived It made a very good impression on me. Can't say, of course, that I know the work well yet. But . . . with repeated hearings (they say it's becoming a hit; been in the papers so often!) I'll certainly be able to get an overview. Unfortunately the performance isn't particularly good. . . . I'm not sure whether after one hearing I'm justified in saying that there are some things I don't find good, things that I'd like to discuss with you in detail. . . . But on the whole it's very impressive and there's no doubt I *can* be proud of such a student.
[*Brand:* 342]

It is not the most effusive of congratulatory notes, and is there perhaps a whiff of reproof in the idea that any serious pupil could have achieved 'a hit'? But a hit, if a controversial one, *Wozzeck* undoubtedly was, helped rather than hindered by the continuing polemics in the press.

Heinsheimer   The violent differences of opinion continued unabated in the newspapers during the next days and weeks. High praise and humble recognition of the greatness of the work and the significance of its creator on the one hand; venomous, almost hysterical condemnation on the other. . . . In the words of a Berlin critic one could read:

'When I left the Staatsoper last night I was no longer sure whether I was coming out of a public art institute or a public lunatic asylum. . . . In Berg's music there is not a trace of melody, only bits and scraps, whines and belches. . . . A whole zoological garden is being got up. . . . I consider Alban Berg a musical confidence trickster and a common nuisance as a composer. Indeed one must go further: unprecedented events demand unprecedented methods. One must seriously ask oneself whether, and how far, the pursuit of music may be considered a criminal occupation, for here it is a question of a capital crime in the musical sphere. . . . Only one hope remains: that the public, in an overwhelming majority, will not be prepared to enter the Augean stable of Berg's art'.   [*Reich, 1959*: 28–9]

Nevertheless the positive reaction of the public at large ensured a success which was confirmed at the 11 performances that followed—and was to be repeated at more than 160 more until Berg's music was officially proscribed by the Nazis as 'cultural bolshevism' nine years later. But how much of the reaction, whether for or against, really had anything to do with the quality of Berg's music?

Heinsheimer   Did we, who applauded and screamed so bravely until the lights went out and the iron curtain came down—did we really understand the new, great and revolutionary aspect of the work? A few perhaps, but most of us not. What was it, then, that moved us so deeply? There is an internal ear, an invisible receiver which, though it does not take in all the refinements of compositional technique, is magically touched by beauty, power and strength, and it is this ear that is able to distinguish the resounding tread of the giant from the busy scampering of the dwarf. [*Id: 28*]

Heinsheimer was right. Although *Wozzeck* is a technically and aurally complicated opera, its fundamental purpose is simple and never in doubt—to express the reaction of a sensitive, deeply compassionate middle-class individual to the horrors of a class system which denied hope to the weak, the vulnerable and the outcasts of society. Inevitably the complexity of the music used to convey this message was disconcerting to early audiences, and as well as the usual invective about dissonance and unperformability, the use of abstract musical forms to provide musical structure became a prime target for criticism. It was a subject that had already attracted much controversial attention even before the first performance, and it has continued to provide material for musicological discussion ever since. But Berg's own attitude was relaxed.

Berg In one sense the use of these forms in the opera, particularly to such an extent, was unusual, even new . . . , but I must reject the claim that I am a reformer of opera through such innovations . . . and I would like to suggest something which I do consider my particular accomplishment.

No matter how much any specific individual may be aware of the musical forms contained in the framework of this opera, of the precision and logic with which everything is worked out and the skill that is manifested in every detail, there is no one in the audience, from the moment the curtain parts until it closes for the last time, who pays any attention to the various fugues, inventions, suites, sonata movements, variations, and passacaglias—no one who heeds anything but the social implications of this opera, which by far transcend the personal destiny of Wozzeck. This I believe to be my achievement. [*Berg, 1927: 23–4*]

It is Berg's deep and genuine concern for the inherent meaning of his opera, rather than the technical means by which it is achieved, that makes *Wozzeck* one of the most powerfully moving experiences in the operatic repertory. The glimpses of lyrical sympathy that break through the satire, irony and prevailing dissonance, and the overwhelmingly powerful expression of human feeling with which the opera ends, may owe something to Berg's inheritance from an earlier age, but in the end *Wozzeck* is, of all operas, the one that crucially turned the corner from the nineteenth to the twentieth centuries, leaving for future generations what is probably the toughest, most unflinching delineation of the human condition ever put on the operatic stage.

Brief Plot Outlines

L'INCORONAZIONE DI POPPEA

Nero, infatuated with Ottone's wife Poppea, is determined to divorce his own wife Ottavia and make Poppea his empress; his tutor and mentor, the philosopher Seneca, opposes him, and Nero, prompted by Poppea, orders Seneca to take his own life. He then celebrates Seneca's death in a drinking session with his boon companion Luciano. Ottone, rejected by Poppea, has now transferred his affections to Poppea's erstwhile friend Drusilla. He is commanded by Ottavia to kill Poppea, and to gain the necessary access he disguises himself in Drusilla's clothes; after his half-hearted attempt has been foiled by the intervention of Cupid, it is Drusilla who is accused of attempted murder. Ottone confesses to the crime and Nero, in a rare moment of compassion, commutes his instant death penalty to banishment for both. He then officially repudiates Ottavia, announces his marriage to Poppea, and has her crowned empress.

Important subsidiary roles are played by Poppea's old nurse Arnalta, Ottavia's nurse, and Ottavia's page (Valletto). The opera is preceded by a prologue for Fortune, Virtue, and Love—who reappears as Cupid at various points during the opera to emphasise his superiority to his rivals.

ALCESTE

The inhabitants of Thessaly are anxious for news of Admetus, their much-loved king, who is on the point of death. The queen, Alceste, after addressing her people, leads a ritual sacrifice in the temple of Apollo, but the oracle decrees that Admetus must die unless someone else can be found to die in his place. Alceste offers herself to the gods as the victim. She wins their permission to return to the world to take leave of her husband and children, but Admetus, miraculously restored to life, cannot understand why she does not share his happiness, and is horrified when she reveals the truth. In spite of his protestations that he cannot live without her, she bids her children farewell and follows the infernal deities to her death. Admetus threatens to kill himself, but Apollo suddenly appears, revokes his decree, and restores Alceste to life and to her husband.

The later (French) version introduces Hercules in the last act. To repay an old debt of hospitality to Admetus, he undertakes to rescue Alceste, battles single-handed with the infernal deities and brings her back from the underworld with the final approval of Apollo.

IDOMENEO

The Trojan War has ended, and the Cretan king, Idomeneo, has sent prisoners back to Crete, among them Priam's daughter, the princess Ilia. Idomeneo's son, Idamante, and Ilia have fallen in love, though he has not declared himself, and she conceals her feelings out of loyalty to her deceased father. But this does not protect her from the jealousy of the Greek princess Electra, who is also in love with Idamante.

Idomeneo, returning home with his army, is shipwrecked in a storm off the coast of Crete, and vows to Neptune that, if his life is saved, he will sacrifice the first living thing he meets after reaching dry land. This turns out to be his own son. In an attempt to evade the consequences of his vow he plans to send Idamante away to Argos with Electra, but Neptune raises another storm and a dreadful monster appears which ravages the island. The people insist on knowing who has offended the gods and Idomeneo admits his guilt, but not the full implications of his vow.

Idamante and Ilia confess their love, and are surprised by Electra, in a paroxysm of jealousy, and Idomeneo, who is still obsessed by the idea of banishing his son from Crete. Idamante, devastated by his father's apparent rejection, leaves to seek his death, but the people of Crete are still adamant and Idomeneo is forced to reveal the whole truth. Meanwhile, Idamante has fought and killed the monster and, at last understanding Idomeneo's predicament, offers himself to his father as the sacrificial victim. But as Ilia rushes forward to stay Idomeneo's hand, the voice of Neptune is heard: Idamante is to be spared, Idomeneo must abdicate, and Idamante succeed to the throne of Crete with Ilia as his queen.

Le nozze di Figaro

Figaro, Count Almaviva's personal servant, is to marry the Countess's maid, Susanna. But Susanna is being pursued by the Count, intent on obtaining his *droit de seigneur* before the marriage, and Figaro is being held to a contract to marry Marcellina, housekeeper to the local doctor, Bartolo, if he fails to pay back money he has borrowed. The interventions of the young page Cherubino and the music master, Don Basilio, further muddy the waters, and the frivolous behaviour of Cherubino, who is in love with the Countess, so enrages the Count that he packs him off to join the army.

The Countess plans to get even with her philandering husband. Susanna will write him a note arranging an assignation, but her place will be taken by Cherubino in woman's clothes. While the page is being dressed for the part, the Count is heard arriving; Cherubino is quickly hidden in a locked closet, and while the Count goes to fetch tools to break down the door, Susanna takes the place of Cherubino who jumps out of a nearby window. The Count is forced to apologise and the situation is further complicated by the arrival, first of Figaro, then of the gardener whose plants have been crushed by Cherubino in his fall, and finally by Bartolo and Marcellina in pursuance of their claim on Figaro.

The discovery, resulting from an attempt by Figaro to prove his own parentage, that he is in fact the son of Marcellina and Bartolo by an old liaison, resolves the situation, and Figaro and Susanna are married. But the Countess continues her plan to fool the Count, this time taking up the assignation herself in Susanna's clothes. In the darkness of the palace garden at night the ensuing confusion is compounded by the arrival of Figaro, not forewarned of the plot and in jealous mode, but the situation is eventually sorted out and the Count magnanimously forgiven by his long-suffering wife.

FIDELIO

In a prison near Seville, Florestan, a Spanish nobleman, is being secretly held as a political prisoner. His wife Leonore hopes to rescue him and, disguised as a young man calling himself Fidelio, has secured a job as assistant to Rocco, the jailer. Unfortunately, Rocco's daughter, Marzelline, has fallen in love with him/her, and Rocco encourages them to marry—to the distress of Marzelline's lover, Jaquino.

Pizarro, the prison governor, is warned that the minister, Don Fernando, intends to inspect the prison and, afraid of being caught illegally detaining a political rival, determines to kill Florestan and destroy the evidence. Leonore persuades Rocco to allow the prisoners out for a brief moment of sunlight, and has time to see that Florestan is not among them before Pizarro angrily orders them back to their cells.

Rocco, a reluctant accomplice to murder, descends with Fidelio to the dungeon where Florestan lies chained and starved, and prepares to dig his grave. Florestan and Leonore recognise one another, and when Pizarro enters, Leonore draws a pistol and holds the governor at bay. After a moment of stunned deadlock, sounds of martial music from the courtyard above announce the arrival of Don Fernando; in the ceremonial presence of the minister, Don Pizarro is arrested, the prisoners are released and, after Leonore has freed Florestan from his shackles, husband and wife are reunited amid the jubilation of the attendant crowd.

IL BARBIERE DI SIVIGLIA

Count Almaviva is in love with Rosina, the ward of Doctor Bartolo, an old curmudgeon who intends to marry her himself. Adopting the guise of Lindoro, a poor student, Almaviva is serenading Rosina under her window when Figaro, the barber and self-styled factotum of Seville, turns up and offers to help him gain access to Bartolo's house. They concoct a plan, and the Count, disguised as a drunken soldier, presents himself at Bartolo's door with an official billeting order. Bartolo and his friend, the music master Don Basilio, try to get rid of him but without success, and he manages to slip a note to Rosina before the growing tumult in the house attracts the attention of the police force. Almaviva extricates himself by secretly revealing his identity to the officer in charge: there is a moment of stunned astonishment, and the act ends in general confusion.

The Count returns to Bartolo's house, now disguised as Don Alonso and claiming to be a substitute for Don Basilio, who is ill and cannot give Rosina her music lesson. As the lesson proceeds, Figaro arrives to shave Doctor Bartolo, from whom he filches the key to a window which will enable Rosina and her lover to elope. Don Basilio unexpectedly appears, not at all ill, but the sight of the money which the Count produces from his pocket soon persuades him that he is ill after all; nevertheless Bartolo, his suspicions aroused, decides to call a notary in order to get on with his own marriage to Rosina as quickly as possible—warning her as he goes out against the wiles of Lindoro. As a result, Lindoro, when he reappears, gets a frosty reception, but he now reveals his true identity and declares his love to satisfying effect; the discovery that the ladder by which the pair had intended to escape has been removed seems a fatal blow, but when the notary arrives, he is quickly duped into substituting Almaviva for Bartolo in the projected marriage ceremony, and Don Basilio is pressed into service as witness by financial arguments that he can hardly refuse. Bartolo's fury on his return is tempered by Almaviva's waiving of the customary guardian's dowry, and eventually gives way to a resigned acceptance of the *fait accompli*.

LES TROYENS

The first two acts take place in Troy, where the Greek army has suddenly disappeared, leaving only a wooden horse on the plain outside the city. Cassandra, daughter of King Priam, foresees the doom of Troy but is unable to convince anyone, least of all her lover Coroebus. Andromache, Hector's widow, brings her son Astyanax to receive Priam's blessing, but the proceedings are interrupted by the sudden appearance of Aeneas with news that the high priest Laocöon has been devoured by a sea serpent after throwing a spear at the wooden horse. In spite of Cassandra's warnings, the horse is dragged into the city amid celebrations.

At night Aeneas is visited by the ghost of Hector, who tells him that Troy has fallen and that he must flee to establish a new city in Italy. While Troy is sacked by the Greek soldiery, Cassandra, determined not to submit to the invaders, assembles a group of Trojan women in the

Temple of Vesta; inciting them to mass suicide, she stabs herself, and as the Greek soldiers rush into the temple, the assembled women ecstatically follow her example.

The action moves to Carthage, where Dido is addressing her people; in private with her sister, Anna, she affirms her fidelity to her dead husband, Sychaeus, but Anna insists that she will love again. News arrives that a foreign fleet has been blown onto the Carthaginian coast. Dido offers them sanctuary, and is greeting their leaders (among them Aeneas in disguise) when Narbal, her chief minister, brings news that Carthage is being attacked by the Numidian king, Iarbas. Aeneas throws off his disguise and offers to help Dido repel the attack; leaving his son Ascanius in her care, he sets off to do battle.

Dido is now in love with Aeneas; caught in a storm while out hunting, they take shelter in a cave and consummate their passion, then return to Dido's palace to luxuriate in their new-found happiness. But Mercury descends and recalls Aeneas to his duty. As the Trojans make ready for departure, Aeneas wrestles with his despair, but he is deterred from returning to Dido by the appearance of the ghosts of Trojan heroes. Dido, in a fury, accuses him of betrayal, and calls upon the gods for vengeance; she orders a funeral pyre to be built and in a solemn ceremony mounts it and kills herself—seeing as she dies a vision of the future glory of Rome.

Tristan und Isolde

Tristan, the nephew of King Marke of Cornwall, has been sent to Ireland to bring back Isolde as a bride for his uncle. On the ship back to Cornwall, Isolde describes to her maid Brangäne how, some time ago, she had been sought out by an unknown knight who had been wounded in a fight, and had tended him with her magic arts until, suddenly realising that the man she was nursing was the slayer of Morold, her betrothed, she had raised a sword to kill him. But something in his eyes had prevented her from striking, and now she feels that death for both of them is the only honourable course left to her. She tells Brangäne to prepare a poisoned cup, but Brangäne substitutes a love potion, and both Tristan and Isolde drink it.

At King Marke's castle in Cornwall, Isolde and Tristan arrange to meet while Marke is out hunting with Tristan's friend, the courtier Melot. Brangäne, suspecting that Melot has set a trap for the lovers, urges caution, but they ignore her warning and abandon themselves to passion. They are interrupted by the sudden arrival of Tristan's loyal henchman Kurwenal, who warns them of King Marke's imminent approach. But when he discovers the lovers, Marke is too deeply distressed by their betrayal to take any action, and when Tristan and Isolde once more swear their undying love for one another, it is Melot who attacks Tristan with a sword.

Brought back to his castle in Brittany by Kurwenal, the wounded Tristan wakes from a deep coma. As they await the expected arrival of Isolde's ship, he gives way to a frenzy of despair; he curses the fatal elixir of love and when the ship arrives leaps to his feet, tears off his bandages and falls dying in Isolde's arms. A second ship brings Marke, who has been told by Brangäne the truth about the love potion and has come to forgive Tristan, and Melot, who is attacked and killed in a fit of fury by Kurwenal. Kurwenal, too, is wounded and, falling, dies at Tristan's feet, but Isolde, in an ecstasy of love, can only see Tristan transfigured in death, and at last, sinking onto his lifeless body, finds death herself in Brangäne's arms.

CARMEN

In a square in front of the cigarette factory in Seville, Micaela is looking for her childhood friend Don José, now a corporal in the army. As he appears, the girls come out of the factory for their daily break, among them the gypsy Carmen, who is besieged by a mob of passionate admirers. But José is not interested and doesn't even pick up the flower that she tosses to him before going back to work. Micaela returns with a letter for José from his mother urging him to take Micaela for his wife. Suddenly the cigarette girls reappear, quarrelling furiously; Carmen has been fighting with one of her fellow workers, and José is sent into the factory to bring her out. When she refuses to answer Lieutenant Zuniga's questions, she is arrested and put in charge of Don José, but by now he has fallen for her charms and by a trick allows her to escape. He, too, is arrested.

At the tavern of Lillas Pastia, Carmen and her gypsy friends are carousing with Zuniga and other officers. They are joined by the toreador Escamillo and his entourage. Escamillo's advances to Carmen are rejected (though not unnoticed), and he invites the assembled company to his next bullfight. The tavern empties and José, freed that day from detention, arrives to find Carmen alone. She dances for him, but when distant bugles sound the retreat, he stops her and tells her that he must return to barracks. She turns on him in a fury and to his passionate declaration of love replies that if he really loved her he would desert and join her comrades in the mountains. When Zuniga returns to try his luck with Carmen, José attacks him in a fit of jealousy, then, having assaulted a superior officer, realises that in the end he has no alternative but to escape with Carmen to the hills.

At their mountain hideout the smugglers are planning the evening's operation. Two of the gypsy girls try their fortunes at cards, but when Carmen joins them the cards show death for her and for José. Micaela appears at the encampment but hides as Escamillo is heard arriving; as rivals for Carmen's love he and José fight, and when Escamillo slips, José is only restrained from killing him by Carmen's intervention. Micaela is discovered, and José is torn between Carmen and his own past but, hearing that his mother is dying, leaves precipitately with Micaela.

Outside the bull-ring in Seville, Carmen's companions await the arrival of Escamillo, who appears with Carmen on his arm. Being warned that José is in the crowd, she determines to face him and remains when Escamillo's cortège disappears into the ring. José pleads passionately with her, but Carmen is adamant that she no longer loves him and with bitter scorn tears his ring from her finger. As the crowd in the bull ring applaud the victorious Escamillo, José stabs her and, calling upon the police to arrest him, falls upon her dead body.

EUGENE ONEGIN

The Larin family are taking the air outside their home in the country. Olga, the younger daughter, chatters happily while her elder sister Tatyana dreams sentimentally of the novel she is reading. Lensky, a neighbour in love with Olga, calls to introduce his friend Eugene Onegin who is on a visit from St Petersburg. Tatyana sees in Onegin a romantic ideal of the man fate has chosen for her and, alone in her bedroom that night, writes him a letter declaring her love in a flood of adolescent emotion. A few days later Onegin calls upon her and coldly, though with great correctness, explains to her that he has no intention of marrying and condescendingly advises her to practise self-control.

When the Larins give a ball for Tatyana's name day, Onegin, who is thoroughly bored, amuses himself by dancing with Olga, to Lensky's growing annoyance. There is a brief interlude while Monsieur Triquet sings some couplets in honour of Tatyana, but when he has finished, Lensky picks a quarrel with Onegin and, to the consternation of the assembled company, challenges him to a duel. Next morning the duel takes place with due formality and Lensky is killed.

Some years later, in St Petersburg again after an extended trip abroad, Onegin attends a ball given by the elderly Prince Gremin. Recognising Tatyana among the guests, he discovers that she is now married to Gremin, who presents him to her. Onegin at once realises what he has lost and, begging for a private meeting, declares his love for Tatyana with hopeless passion. Though she cannot deny loving him in return, she determines to remain faithful to her husband and, after a final embrace, bids Onegin farewell for ever. He leaves in despair.

OTELLO

On the main square in front of the governor's castle the people of Cyprus watch as a storm batters the Venetian fleet returning from a victorious encounter with the Turks. Otello, the Venetian military governor of the island, lands to the acclamation of the waiting crowd, but their enthusiasm is not shared by Roderigo, who is unhappy because he is secretly in love with Otello's wife, Desdemona, or by Iago, Otello's ensign, who is bitter at having been passed over when Otello appointed Cassio as his lieutenant. Wine is produced and the two men get Cassio drunk; they provoke him to a duel and to Iago's delight Otello dismisses Cassio from his new office. Desdemona appears, awakened by the brawl, and she and Otello declare their love for one another.

Iago advises Cassio to ask Desdemona to intercede with Otello on his behalf and, when Otello observes them talking together, uses the opportunity to plant the seeds of jealousy in his master's mind. Desdemona asks Otello to pardon Cassio and, as she does so, lets her handkerchief (one that had been given to her by Otello) fall to the ground; it is retrieved by Desdemona's maid Emilia (who is also Iago's wife), but immediately seized from her by Iago, who feeds Otello's suspicions by describing how he has heard Cassio talking in his sleep of his love for Desdemona, then swears that he has seen Cassio with Desdemona's handkerchief in his hand. In a paroxysm of jealousy Otello joins Iago in an oath of vengeance.

While Otello awaits the arrival of ambassadors from Venice, Desdemona again raises the subject of Cassio; Otello asks to see the handkerchief and, when she is unable to produce it, accuses her of adultery. Urged by Iago to hide himself, he watches as Cassio actually shows Iago Desdemona's handkerchief, but from his concealment he is unable to hear Cassio's explanation—that he has found it by chance in his house, put there by an unknown hand. It is at this moment that the Venetian ambassadors are announced, but by now Otello's jealousy is beyond all control; after the opening formalities, in front of the full assembly of officials, he furiously insults his wife and flings her to the ground. Iago watches with ill-concealed contempt.

As Desdemona prepares for the night, she sings a melancholy song about unhappy love, then, wishing Emilia a sudden, passionate farewell, says her prayers and gets into bed. Otello enters. He warns Desdemona that he is going to kill her, and refuses to believe her protestations of innocence. As he is suffocating her, Emilia knocks at the door with news that Cassio has killed Roderigo (the opposite of Iago's intention)—then cries out in horror at what she sees. Others come running, including Cassio, Iago and the Venetian envoy; Iago's villainy and Cassio's innocence are exposed, and Otello, drawing a hidden dagger, stabs himself. With a last kiss he falls dead on Desdemona's lifeless body.

Pelléas et Mélisande

Prince Golaud, the elder grandson of Arkel, King of Allemonde, has lost his way in the forest while hunting. He comes upon a young girl sobbing by a pond; she is trying to recover a crown that has fallen into the water, but she is timid and refuses his help. She will not tell where she comes from, but says her name is Mélisande. Golaud persuades her to come home with him.

Six months later the news that Golaud has married Mélisande reaches his grandfather and mother, Geneviève, who prepare to welcome her to Allemonde. They persuade Golaud's half-brother, Pelléas, to defer a visit to a dying friend until after she arrives. Pelléas takes her to sit by a well in the park. She plays with her wedding ring, which falls into the water out of reach, and as it does so the castle clock strikes midday. At exactly the same moment Golaud, out hunting, is thrown by his horse.

While Mélisande is tending his wounds, Golaud notices that the ring is not on her finger; she tells him that it must have slipped off in a cave she visited to collect sea-shells, and though it is dark, he insists that she go back at once to find it. He tells her to take Pelléas with her.

The following evening, as Mélisande combs her hair at a tower window, Pelléas tells her that he must leave the next day and tries to reach her hand to kiss it. Her long hair falls down the side of the tower and Pelléas buries his head in it in erotic ecstacy, but as he does so Golaud appears. He dismisses them as children, but next day he takes Pelléas on an ominous visit to the dungeons under the castle, then warns him not to see too much of Mélisande, who needs quiet because she is expecting a baby. Later, sitting under the tower with Yniold, his little son by his first wife, he plies him with questions that become ever more agonised until, lifting Yniold up to spy through the window of Mélisande's bedchamber, he discovers that Pelléas is with her.

Pelléas arranges to meet Mélisande in the park on the evening before he leaves. While she is alone with Arkel, Golaud enters unexpectedly and, his jealousy bursting out, he seizes her by the hair and throws her to the ground. In the park she and Pelléas confess their love for one another, but it is too late; the gates of the castle are heard shutting them out and Golaud, emerging from the shadows, strikes down Pelléas with his sword. Though Mélisande is unhurt, the exertion precipitates the birth of her baby and she weakens. Golaud, torn between self-reproach and suspicion, is desperate to know whether she and Pelléas had actually become lovers, but she prevaricates and dies without giving him the answer that he craves.

Ariadne auf Naxos

In the original version the opera is given at the end of Molière's comedy *Le bourgeois gentilhomme* as an entertainment for M. Jourdain and his guests; the programme is to be in two parts, a short heroic opera, *Ariadne auf Naxos*, followed by a lighter masquerade by a troupe of Italian comedians. In a short scene (by Hofmannsthal) linking play and opera the two groups of performers are seen as already suspicious of one another, and just as the entertainment is about to begin, Jourdain's major-domo announces that, in order to allow time for a firework display at the end of the evening, his master wishes to have the two pieces performed simultaneously. The composer of the opera gives way to despair, but Zerbinetta, the leader of the Italian troupe, is given an outline of the action so that she and her comrades can improvise around it during the performance, and the opera is then presented in this form—interrupted by occasional comments from M. Jourdain and his guests.

In the revised version Molière's play is dispensed with entirely, and the essence of the linking scene is set to music in a prologue covering much the same ground, with roles for the music master, dancing master, wigmaker, and the prima donna and tenor who will sing Ariadne and Bacchus, but placing the young composer firmly as the central character and allowing him a brief, touching moment of emotional understanding with Zerbinetta.

Apart from a few cuts and changes of detail (including the removal of off-stage comments by the audience) the actual opera is the same in both versions. Ariadne, abandoned on the island of Naxos by her lover Theseus, lies asleep, watched over by three nymphs who describe her bitter tears. She awakens to memories of Theseus and, longing only to die, waits for Hermes, the messenger of death, to transport her to that blessed land where all is pure. The Italian comedians cannot understand the terminal grief of one so young and lovely; they attempt to cheer her with music and dancing, and Zerbinetta launches into a virtuoso exposition of the joys and inconstancies of love as she sees them. But neither this nor the renewed efforts of the comedians produce any effect on Ariadne.

Distant trumpet fanfares herald the approach of Bacchus, the young god newly escaped from the embraces of the magician Circe on her island. Ariadne at first believes him to be Theseus, then sees in him the longed-for god of death; he, innocent and inexperienced, sees her as the goddess of this island, perhaps another Circe. But gradually all misunderstandings become irrelevant as they fall ecstatically in love, and Zerbinetta, in a brief final appearance, points out that, in the end, every new god who comes along leaves you just as stunned as the one before.

TURANDOT

It has been decreed by the Emperor Altoum that Princess Turandot will only marry a prince of royal blood who can solve the three riddles that she will set for him. All who fail will pay with their heads.

Before the walls of the city the people of Peking await the execution of the latest unsuccessful candidate for Turandot's hand. Among the crowd the young Prince Calaf, travelling incognito, recognises his father Timur, the deposed King of Tartary, who has escaped from his native land attended by his faithful slave girl Liù. As they greet one another, Turandot appears on a balcony to give the signal of death, and Calaf, dazzled by her beauty, at once determines to solve the riddles himself. His father and Liù (who is herself secretly in love with Calaf) try desperately to dissuade him and are joined by the three ministers, Ping, Pang and Pong—but to no effect. He strikes the gong which announces his entry as a contestant.

The three ministers lament the condition into which China has fallen since the fatal decree and discuss the prospects of Turandot's latest victim; Ping dreams of the tranquillity of his house in the country and all three long for the day when Turandot restores peace to China by succumbing to the power of love. When Altoum arrives with his court, Calaf makes a formal request to try his fortune. The aged emperor, by now bitterly regretting his oath to his insatiable daughter, attempts to dissuade him, but Calaf insists, and Turandot, invoking in justification the murder of her ancestor Princess Louling by a male invader in this very palace, sets the three riddles. When Calaf successfully answers them all, she protests, but her father is adamant that she must abide by the decree. Calaf eventually resolves the situation by offering himself for execution if Turandot is able to discover his name by sunrise the following day.

On pain of death no one in Peking may sleep until the name of the unknown prince is discovered. Calaf is offered all sorts of temptations by Ping, Pang and Pong, but refuses to reveal his name; Timur and Liù are detected, and in Turandot's presence Liù is subjected to torture. Calaf attempts to protect her, but rather than give him away she takes her own life. In spite of Turandot's resistance, Calaf claims his reward and kisses her, and in the presence of the emperor and the people of Peking, Turandot at last announces that she knows the name of the unknown prince: it is Love.

WOZZECK

Wozzeck, a poor simple-minded soldier, is shaving the Captain, who criticizes him for being always in a hurry and philosophises crazily about time and eternity. He taunts Wozzeck and accuses him of having no moral sense because he has a child 'not blessed by the Church'. As Wozzeck chops sticks with his friend Andres in a field outside the town, he is alarmed by strange visions. Meanwhile, Marie, alone with Wozzeck's child, watches as a military band passes by; she exchanges flirtatious glances with the well-built Drum Major but is singing a lullaby to the baby when Wozzeck returns. He is still distraught, and when the Doctor, by whom he is paid as a subject of psychological experiment, questions him about his visions, he is so delighted by Wozzeck's answers that he gives him a bonus payment of a penny. But Marie is visited by the Drum Major and, unable to resist his robust attractions, takes him into her house.

Marie sits admiring the golden earrings given to her by the Drum Major. When Wozzeck enters, his suspicions are aroused, but he gives Marie the money from the Captain and the Doctor and leaves. The Doctor, meeting the Captain in the street, terrifies him with medical prognostications, and when Wozzeck passes by, the two men hint at Marie's infidelity. Wozzeck confronts Marie with the allegation and she denies it furiously. Yet when he goes to a tavern garden that evening, she is there, dancing with the Drum Major; an idiot smells blood and Wozzeck leaves precipitately with a red mist rising before his eyes. Back in barracks among his snoring comrades, he cannot sleep and talks to Andres of a flashing knife blade. The Drum Major enters, very drunk; he brags of his success with Marie and, when Wozzeck affects to take no notice, attacks him and beats him up.

In her room, alone with the child, Marie reads from the Bible and dwells on her sins. Later she and Wozzeck walk together through a forest in the dusk. They sit down beside a pool and Wozzeck draws a knife and stabs and kills her. He reappears at an inn, where he tries to get himself drunk, but one of the company sees blood on his hand, and he rushes back to the pool where he has left the knife that could betray him. He stumbles on Marie's corpse, then, finding the knife, tries to hide it deeper in the pool, wading in further and further until gradually he drowns. The Doctor and Captain, passing by, are disturbed by the sounds of drowning and hurry off. Outside Marie's house the child is hopping on his hobby horse; the other children, hearing that Marie is dead, rush off to see what's up, and after a moment's hestitation, he hops after them. . . .

List of Sources

Select bibliography including all sources quoted in the text. (Please note that dates of publication are those of the editions I used in preparing the text, and do not necessarily represent the most recent editions or reprints, which may have different pagination.) A number of reasonably accessible books in English are also suggested for further reading. These are indicated with an asterisk and are intended for the general reader who would like to know more about a composer's life or examine an individual opera in greater detail.

L'INCORONAZIONE DI POPPEA

Anonymous. Preface to libretto of *Le nozze d'Enea in Lavinia*. See Rosand, 1991.

*Arnold, Denis. *Monteverdi*. 3rd rev. ed. by Tim Carter. London: J. M. Dent, 1990.

Badoaro, Giacomo. See Rosand, 1991.

Bardi, Pietro De'. See Solerti, 1903.

Busenello, Giovanni Francesco. See Rosand, 1991.

Caccini, Giulio. See Solerti, 1903.

*Carter, Tim. *Monteverdi's Musical Theatre*. New Haven and London: Yale University Press, 2002.

Contarino, Luigi. *Il vago e dilettevole giardino ove si leggono gli infelici fini di molti huomini illustri*. Rev. ed. Venice: 1619.

Curtis, Alan, ed. *L'incoronazione di Poppea*. Vocal score. London: Novello, 1989.

Evelyn, John. *The Diary of John Evelyn*. Vol. 2. E. S. de Beer, ed. Oxford: Clarendon Press, 2000.

Fabbri, Paolo. *Monteverdi*. Turin: EDT/Musica, 1985.

*———. *Monteverdi*. Trans. Tim Carter. Cambridge: Cambridge University Press, 1994.

Da Gagliano, Marco. *See* Solerti, 1903.

Galilei, Vincenzo. *Dialogo della Musica Antica et Moderna*. Facsimile reprint of the 1581 edition with preface by Fabio Fano. Rome: Reale Accademia d'Italia, 1934.

Goretti, Antonio. *See* Fabbri, 1985.

Mangini, Nicola. *I teatri di Venezia*. Milan: Mursia, 1974.

Paoli, Domenico de', ed. *Claudio Monteverdi—Lettere, dediche e prefazioni*. Rome: De Santis, 1973.

Peri, Jacopo. *See* Solerti, 1903.

*Rosand, Ellen. *Opera in Seventeenth-Century Venice: The Creation of a Genre*. Berkeley: University of California Press, 1991.

Solerti, Angelo, ed. *Le origini del melodramma: Testimonianze dei contemporanei*. Turin: Fratelli Bocca, 1903.

Stevens, Denis, trans. *The Letters of Claudio Monteverdi*. Rev. ed. Oxford: Clarendon Press, 1995.

Strozzi, Giulio. *See* Rosand, 1991.

Tacitus, Cornelius. *The Annals of Imperial Rome*. Trans. Michael Grant. Rev. ed. London: Penguin Books, 1981.

*Whenham, John, and Richard Wistreich, eds. *The Cambridge Companion to Monteverdi*. Cambridge: Cambridge University Press, 2007.

ALCESTE

Algarotti, Francesco. *Saggio sopra l'opera in musica*. 1st ed., Venice: Giambatista Pasquali, 1755; 2nd ed., Leghorn: M. Coltellini, 1763.

Anderson, Emily, trans. and ed. *The Letters of Mozart and His Family*. 3rd ed. London: Macmillan, 1985.

*Burney, Charles. *Dr. Burney's Musical Tours in Europe*. Vol. 2, *An Eighteenth-Century Musical Tour in Central Europe and the Netherlands; being Dr. Charles Burney's Account of His Musical Experiences*. Percy A. Scholes, ed. London: Oxford University Press, 1959.

Calzabigi, Ranieri de'. 'Dissertazione'. In *Poesie del Signor Abate Pietro Metastasio*. Vol. 1. Paris: Vedova Quillau, 1755.

———. Letter in *Mercure de France* (August 1784).

Casanova, Jacques. *Histoire de ma vie*. Vol. 5. Francis Lacassin, ed. Paris: R. Laffont, 1993.

Corancez, Olivier de. 'Lettre sur le Chevalier Gluck'. *Journal de Paris*, no. 237 (24 August, 1788).

*Einstein, Alfred. *Gluck*. Trans. Eric Blom. London: Dent, 1936.

Fétis, F. J. *Biographie universelle des musiciens et bibliographie générale de la musique*. Bruxelles: Leroux, 1835–44. Vol. 3.

Fucilla, Joseph G. 'Nuove lettere inedite del Metastasio.' *Convivium*, no. 26 (1958): 586–93.

Gluck, Christoph Willibald. *Alceste*. Preface to the orchestral score. Vienna: Giovanni Tomaso de Trattnern, 1769.

———. *Paride ed Elena*. Dedicatory letter to the Duke of Braganza in the orchestral score. Vienna: Giovanni Tomaso de Trattnern, 1770.

———. Letter to *Mercure de France* (February 1773).

———. 'Corréspondance inédite de Gluck'. In *Revue musicale S.I.M.* (publiée par la Société internationale de musique), no. 10, part 6 (June 1914): 1–16.

Hammelmann, Hanns, and Michael Rose. 'New light on Calzabigi and Gluck'. *The Musical Times*, no. 110 (1969): 609–11.

*Howard, Patricia. *Gluck: An Eighteenth-Century Portrait in Letters and Documents*. Oxford: Clarendon Press, 1995.

Lappenberg, J. M., ed. *Briefe von und an Klopstock: Ein Beitrag zur Literaturgeschichte seiner Zeit*. Braunschweig: G. Westermann, 1867.

Mannlich, Johann Christian von. *Histoire de ma vie*. Excerpts, ed. Henriette Weiss von Trostprugg, 'Mémoires sur la musique à Paris à la fin du règne de Louis XV' in *La Revue Musicale* 15 (1934).

Metastasio, Pietro. *Tutte le opere di Pietro Metastasio*. Bruno Brunelli, ed. Milan: Mondadori, 1951–54. Vol. 3.

Mueller von Asow, Hedwig and E. H., eds. *The Collected Correspondence and Papers of Christoph Willibald Gluck*. Trans. Stewart Thomson. London: Barrie and Rockliff, 1962.

Nohl, Ludwig. *Musiker-Briefe: Eine Sammlung Briefe von C. W. von Gluck, Ph. E. Bach, Jos. Haydn, Carl Maria von Weber und Felix Mendelssohn-Bartholdy*. Leipzig: Duncker and Humblot, 1866.

Noverre, Jean-Georges. *Lettres sur la Danse, sur les Ballets et les Arts*. St. Petersburg: J. C. Schnoor, 1803–4. Vol. 2.

Prod'homme, J.-G. *Écrits de musiciens*. Paris: Mercure de France, 1912.

———. *Gluck*. Paris: Société d'Éditions Françaises et Internationales, 1948.

Ricci, Corrado. *I teatri di Bologna nei secoli xvii e xviii*. Bologna: Successori Monti, 1888.

Roullet, Marie François Louis Gand Leblanc, Bailli du. Letter in *Mercure de France* (October 1772).

IDOMENEO

Anderson, Emily, trans. and ed. *The Letters of Mozart and His Family*. 3rd ed. London: Macmillan, 1985.

Burney, Charles. *Dr. Burney's Musical Tours in Europe*. Vol. 2, *An Eighteenth-Century Musical Tour in Central Europe and the Netherlands; being Dr.*

Charles Burney's Account of His Musical Experiences. Percy A. Scholes, ed. London: Oxford University Press, 1959.

*Cairns, David. *Mozart and His Operas.* London: Allen Lane, 2006.

*Dent, Edward J. *Mozart's Operas: A Critical Study.* Rev. ed. London: Clarendon Press, 1991.

*Einstein, Alfred. *Mozart: His Character, His Work.* Trans. Arthur Mendel and Nathan Broder. London: Cassell, 1966.

*Heartz, Daniel. *Mozart's Operas.* Berkeley: University of California Press, 1990.

Novello, Vincent and Mary. *A Mozart Pilgrimage: Being the Travel Diaries of Vincent & Mary Novello in the Year 1829.* Nerina Medici and Rosemary Hughes, eds. London: Novello and Co., 1955.

*Rushton, Julian. *Mozart.* Oxford: Oxford University Press, 2006.

Varesco, Giambattista. 'Argomento'. In *Idomeneo: dramma per musica da rappresentarsi nel Teatro nuovo di Corte . . . nel Carnovale 1781.* Monaco: Francesco Giuseppe Thuille, 1781.

Le Nozze di Figaro

Attwood, Thomas. Unpublished memoir sold at Sotheby's, London, May 1981. *See* Landon, 1989.

Beaumarchais, Pierre-Augustin Caron de. *Le mariage de Figaro.* In *Théâtre de Beaumarchais.* René Pomeau, ed. Paris: Garnier-Flammarion, 1965.

*Cairns, David. *Mozart and His Operas.* London: Allen Lane, 2006.

Da Ponte, Lorenzo. *Le nozze di Figaro: Opera comica in quattro atti.* Vienna: 1786. Reprinted in *Tre libretti per Mozart.* Milan: Rizzoli, 1956.

———. *An Extract from the Life of Lorenzo Da Ponte with the History of Several Dramas Written by Him.* New York: Mondon and Berrard, 1819. *See* Della Chà, 1999.

———. *Memorie.* Giovanni Gambarin and Fausto Nicolini, eds. 2 vols. Bari: G. Laterza, 1918.

Della Chà, Lorenzo, ed. *Lorenzo Da Ponte: Estratto delle Memorie.* Milan: Il Polifilo, 1999. (Reprints original English text of 1819.)

*Dent, Edward J. *Mozart's Operas: A Critical Study.* Rev. ed. London: Clarendon Press, 1991.

Deutsch, Otto Erich. *Mozart: Die Dokumente seines Lebens.* Vol. 10/34 of *Neue Ausgabe sämtlicher Werke.* Kassel: Bärenreiter, 1961.

*Heartz, Daniel. *Mozart's Operas.* Berkeley: University of California Press, 1990.

*Hodges, Sheila. *Lorenzo Da Ponte: The Life and Times of Mozart's Librettist.* London: Granada, 1985.

Holmes, Edward. *The Life of Mozart.* Ernest Newman, ed. London: J. M. Dent, 1932.

Kelly, Michael. *Reminiscences of Michael Kelly, of the King's Theatre, and Theatre Royal Drury Lane, Including a Period of Nearly Half a Century . . .* 2 vols. London: H. Colburn, 1826.

*Landon, H. C. Robbins. *Mozart: The Golden Years.* London: Thames and Hudson, 1989.

Mozart, Wolfgang Amadeus. *Briefe und Aufzeichnungen: Gesamtausgabe.* W. A. Bauer and O. E. Deutsch, eds. Kassel: Bärenreiter, 1963. Vols. 3 and 4.

Niemetschek, Franz Xaver. *Lebenbeschreibung des K. K. Kapellmeisters Wolfgang Amadeus Mozart aus Originalquellen.* 2nd rev. ed. Prague: Herrlische Buchhandlung, 1808.

Payer von Thurn, Rudolf. *Joseph II als Theaterdirektor.* Vienna: L. Heidrich, 1920.

Pezzl, Johann. *Skizze von Wien.* In 6 parts (Heften). Vienna: 1786–90. Heft 3, 1787.

*Rushton, Julian. *Mozart.* Oxford: Oxford University Press, 2006.

*Steptoe, Andrew. *The Mozart–Da Ponte Operas: The Cultural and Musical Background to* Le Nozze Di Figaro, Don Giovanni, *and* Così Fan Tutte. Oxford: Clarendon Press, 1988.

Weigl, Joseph. *Selbstbiographie.* 1819. See Deutsch, 1961.

Zinzendorf, Count Johann Karl von. *Diaries* (ms). In the Haus-, Hof- und Staatsarchiv, Vienna. See Deutsch, 1961, and Landon, 1989.

FIDELIO

Albrecht, Theodore, trans and ed. *Letters to Beethoven and Other Correspondence.* 3 vols. Lincoln: University of Nebraska Press, 1996.

Allgemeine Musikalische Zeitung. Review of performance of *Fidelio,* 8 January 1806.

Brandenburg, Sieghard, ed. *Beethovens Briefwechsel: Gesamtausgabe.* 7 vols. Munich: G. Henle, 1996.

*Breuning, Gerhard von. *Aus dem Schwarzspanierhause: Erinnerungen an L. van Beethoven aus meiner Jugendzeit.* Trans. and ed. Maynard Solomon as *Memories of Beethoven: From the House of the Black-Robed Spaniards.* Cambridge: Cambridge University Press, 1992.

*Dean, Winton. 'Beethoven and Opera'. In *Essays on Opera.* Oxford: Clarendon Press, 1990, pp. 123–63.

Kerst, Friedrich. *Die Erinnerungen an Beethoven.* 2 vols. Stuttgart: J. Hoffmann, 1913.

Radant, Else, ed. 'Die Tagebücher von Joseph Carl Rosenbaum 1770–1829'. In *Das Haydn Jahrbuch*, Band V. Bryn Mawr, PA: Theodore Presser, 1968.

Röckel, Joseph August. *See* Thayer, 1964.

Rosenbaum, Joseph Carl. *See* Radant, 1968.

*Solomon, Maynard. *Beethoven*. London: Cassell, 1978.

*Sonneck, O. G., ed. *Beethoven: Impressions of Contemporaries*. New York: Dover Publications, 1967.

*Thayer, Alexander Wheelock. *The Life of Ludwig van Beethoven*. Rev. and ed. Elliot Forbes as *Thayer's Life of Beethoven*. 2 vols. Princeton: Princeton University Press, 1964. Quotes Röckel's letter to Thayer of 26 February 1861.

Treitschke, Georg Friedrich. 'Fidelio'. In *Orpheus. Musikalisches Taschenbuch für das Jahr 1841*. August Schmidt, ed. Vienna: F. Riedl, 1841, pp. 258–64.

Wegeler, Franz and Ferdinand Ries. *Biographische Notizen über Ludwig van Beethoven*. Trans. Frederick Noonan as *Remembering Beethoven*. London: André Deutsch, 1988.

*Wyn Jones, David. *The Life of Beethoven*. Cambridge: Cambridge University Press, 1998.

Zeitung für die elegante Welt. Letter from a correspondent. November/December 1805.

———. Reviews of performances of *Fidelio* (second version). 29 March and 10 April 1806.

Il Barbiere di Siviglia

Gossett, Philip. *The Operas of Rossini: Problems of Textual Criticism in Nineteenth-Century Opera*. (Ph.D. dissertation, Princeton University, 1970.)

Mazzatinti, G., F. Manis, and G. Manis, eds. *Lettere di G. Rossini*. Florence: G. Barbèra, 1902.

Michotte, Edmond. *Une soirée chez Rossini à Beau-Sejour (Passy) 1858*. Brussels: 1910. English trans. in Weinstock, 1968.

———. *La visite de R. Wagner à Rossini, Paris 1860*. Paris: Fischbacher, 1906. Original French text reprinted in Rognoni, 1968.

Morgan, Lady (Sydney). *Italy*. 3 vols. London: H. Colburn, 1821.

*Osborne, Richard. *Rossini: His Life and Works*. 2nd rev. ed. Oxford: Oxford University Press, 2007.

Pougin, Arthur. *Rossini: Notes, Impressions, Souvenirs, Commentaires*. Paris: A. Claudin, 1871.

Radiciotti, Giuseppe. *Gioacchino Rossini: Vita documentata, opere ed influenza su l'arte*. 3 vols. Tivoli: Arti grafiche Majella di A. Chicca, 1927–29.

Righetti-Giorgi, Geltrude. *Cenni di una donna già cantante sopra il maestro Rossini, in risposta a ciò che ne scrisse nella state dell'anno 1822 il giornalista inglese in Parigi e fu riportato in una gazzetta di Milano dello stesso anno.* Bologna: Sassi, 1823. Reprinted in full in Rognoni, 1968.

Rinaldi, Mario. *Due secoli di musica al Teatro Argentina.* 3 vols. Florence: L. S. Olschki, 1978.

Rognoni, Luigi. *Gioacchino Rossini.* Turin: ERI, 1968.

Rossini, Gioacchino. *Lettere e documenti.* Bruno Cagli and Sergio Ragni, eds. Vol. 1. Pesaro: Fondazione Rossini, 1992.

———. *Lettere e documenti.* Bruno Cagli and Sergio Ragni, eds. Vol 3a, 'Lettere ai genitori'. Pesaro: Fondazione Rossini, 2004.

Spohr, Louis. *Selbstbiographie.* 2 vols. Kassel: G. H. Wigand, 1860–61.

Stendhal (Henri Beyle). *Vie de Rossini.* Henry Prunières, ed. 2 vols. Paris: E. Champion, 1922.

*———. *Life of Rossini.* Trans. Richard N. Coe. London: Calder, 1956.

——— (pseudonym 'Alceste'). 'Rossini'. *The Paris Monthly Review*, January 1822. Italian trans., Milan, 1822.

The Times. Review of the first London performance of *Il Barbiere di Siviglia* on 10 March 1818.

*Weinstock, Herbert, trans. and ed. *Richard Wagner's Visit to Rossini . . . and an Evening at Rossini's in Beau-Sejour . . . by Edmond Michotte.* Chicago: University of Chicago Press, 1968.

Zanolini, Antonio. *Biografia di Gioachino Rossini.* Rev. ed. Bologna: Nicola Zanichelli, 1875.

Les Troyens

*Berlioz, Hector. *The Memoirs of Hector Berlioz.* David Cairns, trans. and ed. Rev. ed. London: Everyman, 2002.

Bernard, Daniel. 'Notice biographique'. In *Correspondance inédite de Hector Berlioz.* Paris: Calmann-Lévy, 1879.

*Bloom, Peter. *The Life of Berlioz.* Cambridge: Cambridge University Press, 1998.

*Cairns, David. *Berlioz.* 2 vols. London: Allen Lane, the Penguin Press, 1999.

Correspondance. Hector Berlioz. *Correspondance générale.* Hugh Macdonald and François Lesure, eds. Vols. 5 and 6. Paris: Flammarion, 1989 and 1995.

Mémoires. Hector Berlioz. *Mémoires.* Pierre Citron, ed. Paris: Flammarion, 1991.

Revue et gazette musicale de Paris. 28 janvier 1841.

*Rose, Michael. *Berlioz Remembered.* London: Faber and Faber, 2001.

Tristan und Isolde

Hornstein, Robert von. *Memoiren*. Munich: Süddeutsche Monatshefte GmbH, 1908.

Keller, Gottfried. *Gesammelte Briefe*. Carl Hebling, ed. Vol. 2. Bern: Benteli, 1951.

Lippert, Woldemar. *Richard Wagners Verbannung und Rückkehr 1849–1862*. Dresden: P. Aretz, 1927.

Liszt, Franz. *See* Wagner, *BWL*.

*Magee, Bryan. *Aspects of Wagner*. Rev. ed. Oxford: Oxford University Press, 1988.

*Newman, Ernest. *The Life of Richard Wagner*. 4 vols. New York: A. A. Knopf, 1933–46.

Sayn-Wittgenstein, Princess Marie von, Wagner's letters to. *See* Sternfeld, 1926; and Wagner, *FZ*, 1909.

*Spencer, Stewart. *Wagner Remembered*. London: Faber and Faber, 2000.

Sternfeld, Richard. 'Richard Wagner in seinen Briefen an "das Kind." ' *Die Musik* xix/I (October 1926).

Strobel, Otto. *Richard Wagner: Leben und Schaffen*. Bayreuth: Verlag der Festspielleitung, 1952.

*Tanner, Michael. *Wagner*. London: HarperCollins, 1996.

Wagner, Richard.

BC   *Letters of Richard Wagner: The Burrell Collection*. John N. Burk, ed. London: Gollancz, 1951.

BDW   *Bericht an den deutschen Wagner-Verein über die Umstände und Schicksale, welche die Ausführung des Bühnenfestspiels 'Der Ring des Nibelungen' begleiteten*. 1871. *See* Wagner, *GS*, vol. 2.

BHB   *Briefe an Hans von Bülow*. Jena: E. Diederichs, 1916.

BWL   *Briefwechsel zwischen Wagner und Liszt*. 2 vols. Erich Kloss, ed. 4th ed. Leipzig: Breitkopf & Härtel, 1919.

FZ   *Richard Wagner an Freunde und Zeitgenossen*. Erich Kloss, ed. Berlin: Schuster & Loeffler, 1909.

GS   *Richard Wagners Gesammelte Schriften*. 14 vols. Julius Kapp, ed. Leipzig: Hesse & Becker (Deutsche Klassiker-Bibliothek), 1914.

ML   *Mein Leben: Erste authentische Veröffentlichung*. Munich: List, 1963.

MMF   *Eine Mittheilung an meine Freunde*. 1851. *See* Wagner, *GS*, vol. 1.

MW   *Richard Wagner an Mathilde Wesendonk: Tagebuchblätter und Briefe, 1853–1871*. Wolfgang Golther, ed. Leipzig: Breitkopf & Härtel, 1922.

TV   *Tristan und Isolde—Vorspiel.* Paris: 1860. *See* Wagner, GS, vol. 9.

TVS   *Tristan und Isolde—Vorspiel und Schluss.* Vienna: 1863. *See* Wagner, GS, vol. 9.

ZM   *Zukunftsmusik.* 1861. *See* Wagner, GS, vol. 1.

Wille, Eliza, ed. *Fünfzehn Briefe von Richard Wagner, nebst Erinnerungen und Erläuterungen von Eliza Wille.* Berlin: 1894.

CARMEN

Berton, Pierre. *Souvenirs de la vie de théâtre.* Paris: P. Lafitte & cie, 1913.

Blaze de Bury, Henri. *Alexandre Dumas: sa Vie, son Temps, son Oeuvre.* Paris: Calmann Lévy, 1885.

Briggs, A. D. P. 'Did Carmen come from Russia?' In English National Opera programme for a production of *Carmen*. Autumn 1995–96.

*Curtiss, Mina. *Bizet and His World.* London: Secker & Warburg, 1959.

*Dean, Winton. *Georges Bizet: His Life and Work.* London: J. M. Dent, 1965.

*———. 'The True Carmen?' In *Essays on Opera*. Oxford: Clarendon Press, 1990, pp. 281–300.

Delmas, Marc. *Georges Bizet: 1838–1875.* Paris: P. Bossuet, 1930.

Galabert, Edmond, ed. *Georges Bizet. Lettres à un ami, 1865–1872.* Paris: Calmann Lévy, 1909.

Gallet, Louis. *Notes d'un librettiste: Musique Contemporaine.* Preface by Ludovic Halévy. Paris: Calmann Lévy, 1891.

Ganderax, Louis, ed. *Lettres de Georges Bizet: Impressions de Rome (1857–60), La Commune (1871).* Paris: Calmann Lévy, 1907.

Halévy, Daniel. 'Souvenirs de famille'. *Revue de Musicologie* xxii/68 (November 1938).

Halévy, Ludovic. 'La Millième Représentation de Carmen'. *Le Théâtre*, no. 1 (January 1905).

———. 'Les Carnets de Ludovic Halévy'. Daniel Halévy, ed. *Revue des Deux Mondes*, no. 43 (15 January–15 February 1937).

Henry, Stuart. *Paris Days and Evenings.* London: T. F. Unwin, 1896.

Imbert, Hugues. *Portraits et Études, Lettres inédites de Georges Bizet.* Paris: Fischbacher, 1894.

Malherbe, Henry. *Carmen.* Paris: Albin Michel, 1951.

Maréchal, Henri. *Paris: Souvenirs d'un musicien.* Paris: Hachette, 1907.

Mérimée, Prosper. *Lettres de Prosper Mérimée à la Comtesse de Montijo, publiées par les soins du Duc d'Albe.* 2 vols. Paris: 1930.

Mortier, Arnold. *Les Soirées Parisiennes par un Monsieur de l'Orchestre, 1874–83.* Paris: E. Dentu, Vol. 1, 1875; Vol. 2, 1876.

Pigot, Charles. *Georges Bizet et son Oeuvre.* Paris: Dentu, 1886.

Soubies, Albert, and Charles Malherbe. *Histoire de l'Opéra-Comique: La seconde Salle Favart, 1860–1887.* Paris: Flammarion, 1892–93. Vol. 2. (Quotes an article by Paul de Saint-Victor in *La Presse*, 1862.)

Vallas, Léon. 'Georges Bizet et Vincent d'Indy'. *Revue de Musicologie* xxii/68 (November 1938).

Wright, Leslie A., ed. *Georges Bizet: Letters in the Nydahl Collection.* Stockholm: Publications of the Royal Swedish Academy of Music, 1988.

EUGENE ONEGIN

Abraham, Gerald. '*Eugene Onegin* and Tchaikovsky's Marriage'. In *On Russian Music*. London: W. Reeves, 1939. (Includes partial translation of N. Kashkin, KIVC).

*Brown, David. *Tchaikovsky: A Biographical and Critical Study.* 4 vols. London: Gollancz, 1978–1991.

*———. *Tchaikovsky, The Man and His Music.* London: Faber and Faber, 2006.

Newmarch, Rosa, trans. and ed. *The Life and Letters of Peter Ilich Tchaikovsky by Modeste Tchaikovsky.* London: J. Lane, 1906.

*Poznansky, Alexander. *Tchaikovsky Through Others' Eyes.* Trans. Ralph C. Burr, Jr., and Robert Bird. Bloomington: Indiana University Press, 1999.

*Warrack, John. *Tchaikovsky.* London: Hamish Hamilton, 1973.

> KIVC N. Kashkin. 'Iz vospominany o P.I. Chaykovskom' (From my recollections of Tchaikovsky). In *Proshloiye russkoy muzyki* (Petrograd: 1920, partially trans. in Abraham, 1939).

> TPM P. I. Tchaikovsky. *Perepiska c N.F. von Meck* (Correspondence with N. F. von Meck). Vol. 1, 1876–1878. Moscow/Leningrad: 1934.

> TLP P. I. Tchaikovsky. *Polnoye sobraniye sochineniy: literaturnyye proizvedeniya I perepiska* (Complete collected edition: literary works and correspondence). 17 vols. 1953–81.

> TPR P. I. Tchaikovsky. *Pisma k rodnym* (Letters to his relatives). Moscow: 1940.

> TTP *P. I. Tchaikovsky: S. I. Taneyev. Pisma* (Letters to and from Taneyev). Moscow: 1951.

OTELLO

Abbiati, Franco. *Giuseppe Verdi*. 4 vols. Milan: Ricordi, 1959.

Adami, Giuseppe. *Giulio Ricordi e i suoi musicisti*. Milan: Fratelli Treves, 1933.

Alberti, Annibale, ed. *Verdi intimo: Carteggio di Giuseppe Verdi con il Conte Opprandino Arrivabene (1861–1886)*. Milan: A. Mondadori, 1931.

*Budden, Julian. *The Operas of Verdi*. 3 vols. London: Cassell, 1973–81.

Cesari, Gaetano, and Alessandro Luzio, eds. *I Copialettere di Giuseppe Verdi*. Milan: a cura della Commissione esecutiva per le onoranze a Giuseppe Verdi nel primo centenario della nascita, 1913.

Conati, Marcello, ed. *Interviste e incontri con Verdi*. Milan: Edizioni il Formichiere, 1980.

*———. *Interviews and Encounters with Verdi*. Trans. Richard Stokes. London: V. Gollancz, 1984.

De Rensis, Raffaello. *Franco Faccio e Verdi*. Milan: Fratelli Treves, 1934.

Luzio, Alessandro, ed. *Carteggi verdiani*. 4 vols. Rome: Vols. 1 and 2, Reale Accademia d'Italia, 1935; Vols. 3 and 4, Accademia Nazionale dei Lincei, 1947.

*Martin, George. *Verdi: His Music, Life and Times*. New York: Dodd, Mead & Co., 1963.

Medici, Mario, and Marcello Conati, eds. *Carteggi Verdi-Boito*. 2 vols. Parma: Istituto di studi verdiani, 1978.

Monaldi, Gino. *Cantanti celebri (1829–1929)*. Rome: Edizioni Tiber, 1929.

Morazzoni, Giuseppe, ed. *Verdi: Lettere inedite*. Milan: a cura della rivista *La Scala e il Museo teatrale* e della libreria editrice milanese, 1929.

*Phillips Matz, Mary Jane. *Verdi: A Biography*. Oxford: Oxford University Press, 1993.

Pascolato, Alessandro, ed. *Re Lear e Ballo in Maschera: Lettere di Giuseppe Verdi ad Antonio Somma*. Città di Castello: S. Lapi, 1902.

Prod'homme, J.-G., ed. 'Lettres inédites de G. Verdi à Léon Escudier'. *Rivista musicale italiano* XXXV (1928).

Roosevelt, Blanche. *Verdi, Milan and 'Othello'*. London: Ward and Downey, 1887.

*Rosselli, John. *The Life of Verdi*. Cambridge: Cambridge University Press, 2000.

*Walker, Frank. *The Man Verdi*. London: J. M. Dent, 1962.

PELLÉAS ET MÉLISANDE

Bonheur, Raymond. 'Souvenirs et impressions d'un compagnon de jeunesse'. *Revue musicale* 7, no. 7 (1 May 1926). (Numéro special, 'La jeunesse de Debussy'.)

Büsser, Henri. 'Souvenirs de jeunesse de Claude Debussy'. In *Claude Debussy: Catalogue de l'Exposition organisée du 2 au 17 mai au foyer de l'Opéra-Comique*. Paris: 1942.

Chausson, Ernest, ed. 'Correspondance inédite de Claude Debussy et Ernest Chausson'. *Revue musicale* 7, no. 2 (1 December 1925).

Daily Mail. Interview with Debussy. 28 May 1909. Quoted in Nichols and Smith, 1989, p. 42.

Debussy, Claude. *Monsieur Croche et autres écrits*. François Lesure, ed. Rev. ed. Paris: Gallimard, 1987. Contains reprints of:
  'Pourquoi j'ai écrit Pelléas' (written at the request of the manager of the Opéra-Comique, April 1902), pp. 62–4;
  'Mary Garden'. (*Musica*, January 1908), pp. 200–1;
  '*Pelléas et Mélisande*: Critique des critiques' (*Le Figaro*, 16 May 1902), pp. 276–7.

Delarue-Mardrus, Lucie. *Mes mémoires*. Paris: Gallimard, 1938.

*Dietschy, Marcel. *A Portrait of Claude Debussy*. William Ashbrook and Margaret G. Cobb, ed. and trans. Oxford: Clarendon Press, 1990.

Fargue, Léon-Paul. Letter to Auguste Martin. In *Claude Debussy. Catalogue de l'Exposition . . . au Foyer de l'Opéra-Comique*. Paris: 1942.

Garden, Mary, and Louis Biancolli. *Mary Garden's Story*. London: Michael Joseph, 1952.

Hoérée, Arthur, ed. 'Entretiens inédits d'Ernest Guiraud et de Claude Debussy: transcription littérale des notes au crayon du carnet de Maurice Emmanuel'. In *Inédits sur Claude Debussy*. Paris: Les Publications Techniques, 1942.

Ingelbrecht, Germaine, and D. E. Inglebrecht. *Claude Debussy*. Paris: Costard, 1953.

Leblanc, Georgette. *Souvenirs*. Trans. Janet Flanner. New York: E. P. Dutton & Co., 1932.

Lesure, François, ed. *Claude Debussy: Correspondance 1884–1918*. Paris: Hermann, 1993.

———. *Esquisses de Pelléas et Mélisande 1893–1895*. Geneva: Minkoff, 1977.

*Lockspeiser, Edward. *Debussy: His Life and Mind*. 2 vols. London: Cassell, 1966 (2nd ed.) and 1965.

Louÿs, Pierre. *Correspondance de Claude Debussy et Pierre Louÿs (1893–1904)*. Henri Borgeaud, ed. Paris: J. Corti, 1945.

Messager, André. 'Les premières représentations de Pelléas'. *Revue musicale* 7, no. 7 (1 May 1926).

Messager, Jean André. *L'enfance de Pelléas: Lettres de Claude Debussy à André Messager*. Paris: Dorbon-aîné, 1938.

*Nichols, Roger. *Debussy Remembered*. London: Faber and Faber, 1992.

———. The Life of Debussy. Cambridge: Cambridge University Press, 1998.

Nichols, Roger, and Richard Langham Smith. *Claude Debussy: Pelléas et Mélisande*. Cambridge: Cambridge University Press, 1989.

Peter, René. *Claude Debussy*. Rev. ed. Paris: Gallimard, 1944.

Script. *Birth of an Opera No 5* (BBC Third Programme, 1957). Details of original source not available.

Tienot, Yvonne, and O. d'Estrade-Guerra. *Debussy: L'homme, son oeuvre, son milieu*. Paris: Lemoine, 1962.

Vallas, Léon. *Claude Debussy et son temps*. Rev. ed. Paris: A. Michel, 1958.

ARIADNE AUF NAXOS

The Correspondence between Richard Strauss and Hugo von Hofmannsthal. Trans. Hanns Hammelmann and Ewald Osers. London: Collins, 1961.

Karpath, Ludwig. Interview with Richard Strauss. *Neues Wiener Tagblatt*. August 1912.

*Kennedy, Michael. *Richard Strauss: Man, Musician, Enigma*. Cambridge: Cambridge University Press, 2006.

Libretto of *Ariadne auf Naxos*. Ms annotations on a copy in the author's possession.

Script. *Birth of an Opera No 14* (BBC Third Programme, 1962). Details of original source not available.

Strauss, Richard. Extracts from two unpublished letters to his wife (1912). Reproduced by kind permission of Dr Christian Strauss.

———. Recollections and Reflections. Willi Schuh, ed. Trans. L. J. Lawrence. London: Boosey & Hawkes, 1953.

TURANDOT

Adami, Giuseppe. *Puccini*. 2nd ed. Milan: Fratelli Treves, 1935.

*Budden, Julian. *Puccini: His Life and Works*. Oxford: Oxford University Press, 2002.

*Carner, Mosco. *Puccini: A Critical Biography*. 3rd ed. London: Duckworth, 1992.

Carteggi Pucciniani. Eugenio Gara, ed. Milan: Ricordi, 1958.

Epistolario di Giacomo Puccini. Giuseppe Adami, ed. Milan: Mondadori, 1928.

Marek, George R. *Puccini*. London: Cassell, 1952.

*Phillips-Matz, Mary Jane. *Puccini: A Biography*. Boston: Northeastern University Press, 2002.

*Seligman, Vincent. *Puccini Among Friends*. London: Macmillan, 1938.

Sotheby & Co. *Catalogue of Printed Books, Music, Autograph Letters . . .* London: 15–17 December 1964. Lot 451.

Wozzeck

Berg, Alban. *Briefe an seine Frau*. Munich/Vienna: Langen, Müller, 1965.

———. Lecture on *Wozzeck*. 1929. Printed in the original German in Redlich, *Alban Berg . . .* , Vienna, 1957.

———. 'A Word About *Wozzeck*'. *Modern Music* 5, no. 1 (November/December 1927).

Brand, Juliane, Christopher Hailey, and Donald Harris, eds. *The Berg-Schoenberg Correspondence: Selected Letters*. Basingstoke: Macmillan, 1987.

*Carner, Mosco. *Alban Berg: The Man and His Work*. 2nd ed. London: Duckworth, 1983.

Elbogen, Paul. *San Francisco Chronicle*. 27 October 1981. *See* Jarman, 1989.

Jarman, Douglas. *The Music of Alban Berg*. London: Faber and Faber, 1979.

*———. *Alban Berg: Wozzeck*. Cambridge: Cambridge University Press, 1989.

Mahler-Werfel, Alma. *And the Bridge Is Love*. London: Hutchinson, 1959.

———. *Mein Leben*. Frankfurt: S. Fischer Verlag, 1960.

Pople, Anthony, ed. *The Cambridge Companion to Berg*. Cambridge: Cambridge University Press, 1997.

Redlich, H. F. *Alban Berg: Versuch einer Würdigung*. Vienna: Universal Edition, 1957. (English trans., abridged: *Alban Berg: The Man and His Music*. London: J. Calder, 1957.)

Reich, Willi. *Alban Berg: Leben und Werk*. Zurich: Atlantis Verlag, 1963.

*———. *The Life and Work of Alban Berg*. Trans. Cornelius Cardew. London: Thames and Hudson, 1965.

Reich, Willi, ed. *Alban Berg: Bildnis im Wort: Selbstzeugnisse und Aussagen der Freunde*. Zurich: Die Arche, 1959.

Rilke, Rainer Maria. *Briefwechsel mit Marie von Thurn und Taxis*. Ernst Zinn, ed. 2 vols. Zurich: Niehans- & Rokitansky-Verlag and Insel-Verlag, 1951.

Schoenberg, Arnold. *Style and Idea*. Dika Newlin, ed. London: Williams and Norgate, 1951.

———. *Ausgewählte Briefe*. Erwin Stein, ed. Mainz: B. Schott's Söhne, 1958.

Stein, Erwin. 'Wozzeck'. In *Orpheus in New Guises*. London: Rockliff, 1953.

*General background

Abbate, Carolyn, and Roger Parker. *A History of Opera*. New York and London: W. W. Norton & Company, 2012.

Bourne, Joyce. *Who's Who in Opera: A Guide to Opera Characters*. Oxford: Oxford University Press, 1998.

Boyden, Matthew. *The Rough Guide to Opera*. 3rd ed. London: Rough Guides, 2002.

Dent, Edward J. *Opera*. Rev. ed. Westport, CT: Greenwood Press, 1978.

Grout, Donald Jay, and H. W. Williams. *A Short History of Opera*. 4th ed. New York: Columbia University Press, 2003.

Holden, Amanda, ed. *The New Penguin Opera Guide*. London: Penguin, 2001.

Kerman, Joseph. *Opera as Drama*. 2nd rev. ed. Berkeley: University of California Press, 1988.

Kimbell, David R. B. *Italian Opera*. Cambridge: Cambridge University Press, 1991.

Kobbé, Gustav. *The New Kobbé's Opera Book*. The Earl of Harewood and Anthony Peattie, eds. London: G. P. Putnam's Sons, 2000.

Parker, Roger, ed. *The Oxford Illustrated History of Opera*. Oxford: Oxford University Press, 1994.

Pleasants, Henry. *The Great Singers: From Jenny Lind to Callas and Pavarotti*. New York: Simon and Schuster, 1981.

Sadie, Stanley, ed. *New Grove Handbooks in Music: History of Opera*. London: Macmillan, 1989.

Snowman, Daniel. *The Gilded Stage: A Social History of Opera*. London: Atlantic Books, 2009.

Credits

Text Credits

L'Incoronazione di Poppea: *The Annals of Imperial Rome*, by Tacitus, translated and with an introduction by Michael Grant (Penguin Classics, 1956; 6th rev. ed., 1989). Copyright © Michael Grant Publications Ltd, 1956, 1959, 1971, 1973, 1975, 1977, 1989. Reproduced by permission of Penguin Books Ltd.

Alceste: *Dr. Burney's Musical Tours in Europe*, Vol. II, edited by Percy A. Scholes (1959). 550 w. By permission of Oxford University Press.

Idomeneo: *The Letters of Mozart and his Family*, by Emily Anderson (The Macmillan Press Ltd, 1985), reproduced with permission of Palgrave Macmillan.

Fidelio: *Letters to Beethoven and Other Correspondence*, volumes by Theodore Albrecht (University of Nebraska Press, 1996).

Il Barbiere di Siviglia: From *Bizet and His World,* by Mina Curtiss, copyright © 1958 by Mina Curtiss. Used by permission of Alfred A. Knopf, a division of Random House, Inc.

Pelleas et Mélisande: From *Souvenirs: My Life with Maeterlinck,* by Georgette LeBlanc, translated by Janet Flanner, translation copyright 1932, renewed © 1959 by E. P. Dutton & Co. Used by permission of Dutton, a division of Penguin Group (USA) Inc.; Claude Debussy, Letter to Edwin Evans, April 18, 1909. Frederick R. Koch Collection, Beinecke Rare Book and Manuscript Library, Yale University.

Wozzeck: *The Berg-Schoenberg Correspondence*, edited by Juliane Brand, Christopher Hailey, and Donald Harris (1987), reproduced with permission of Palgrave Macmillan.

Photo Credits

Monteverdi: Anonymous engraving from the frontispiece of *Fiori poetici,* ed. G. B. Marinoni, Venice, 1644.

Gluck: From the collection of Michael D'Andrea, USA.

Mozart, *Idomoneo*: Staatsbibliothek zu Berlin—Preußischer Kulturbesitz Musikabteilung mit Mendelssohn-Archiv.

Index

Page numbers in *italics* refer to illustrations.